WAR OF WORDS

Washington Tackles the Yugoslav Conflict

Danielle S. Sremac

PRAEGER

Westport, Connecticut
London

Library of Congress Cataloging-in-Publication Data

Sremac, Danielle S., 1966–
    War of words : Washington tackles the Yugoslav conflict / Danielle
S. Sremac.
        p.   cm.
    Includes bibliographical references and index.
    ISBN 0–275–96609–7 (alk. paper)
    1. Yugoslav War, 1991–1995—Foreign public opinion, American.
2. Yugoslav War, 1991–1995—Propaganda.   3. Yugoslav War, 1991–1995—
Press coverage.   4. Public opinion—United States.   5. Propaganda,
American.   6. United States—Foreign relations—Former Yugoslav
republics.   7. Former Yugoslav republics—Foreign relations—United
States.   I. Title.   II. Title: Washington tackles the Yugoslav
conflict.
DR1313.7.P83S68   1999
949.703—dc21   99–14851

British Library Cataloguing in Publication Data is available.

Library of Congress Catalog Card Number: 99–14851
ISBN: 0–275–96609–7

First published in 1999

Praeger Publishers, 88 Post Road West, Westport, CT 06881
An imprint of Greenwood Publishing Group, Inc.
www.praeger.com

Printed in the United States of America

The paper used in this book complies with the
Permanent Paper Standard issued by the National
Information Standards Oragnization (Z39.48–1984).

10 9 8 7 6 5 4 3 2 1

To my brother, Milan,
my husband, Peter, and my parents,
for their inspiration and eternal support.

Contents

Preface

Life's events move faster than we can fully document them. There are no two exact accounts of human experience. Our memories and observations are shaped by the color of glass we look through, and there are countless shades of colors in the world. But there is one assumption which forms the basis of this book that is perhaps universal: the more shades of glass we look through, the better our understanding of the object we are observing. When we look through blue glass we may think the object is purple. When we look through yellow glass we may say the object is orange. But when combined, both observations tell us that the object is actually red.

The disintegration of Yugoslavia in 1991 and the violent civil war that broke out between the country's ethnic and religious groups—Serbs, Croats, Bosnian Muslims, and later with Kosovo Albanians—received unprecedented attention among Washington's foreign policy elites and opinionmakers. Having lived through this singular event, I too have looked at the Yugoslav conflict through my own "colored glass." But unlike most Washington-based observers, I formed my opinions from personal experiences and an intimate knowledge of the country itself. My link between two worlds—as an American of Serbian heritage—has helped me understand not only Washington's perceptions and actions during the Yugoslav conflict, but also historical and cultural factors, as well as realities of war taking place in the Yugoslav region that were misunderstood or overlooked.

I never imagined that Yugoslavia would be slashed up, dissected, and displayed on front pages of newspapers and on television screens, nor that the level of anti-Serb propaganda would become so intense as to be used to justify an 11-week-long U.S.-led NATO bombing campaign in 1999 that brought enormous death and destruction to Serbia. Throughout the 1990s, the U.S. media presented the American public with one vision of ethnic conflicts in Yugoslavia: a black and white, good guy versus bad guy story of war and misery. Washington's view of the war was often accompanied by misinformation, inaccurate labeling, and demonization of one warring party, distorting basic facts of what was happening in the region. It resulted in a misguided U.S. foreign policy in support of unrealistic solutions that persist in the region, even today. These views were first encouraged by Croatian and Bosnian Muslim governments, and later by supporters of an Albanian separatist movement in Kosovo, all of which established powerful and well-organized supporters, public relations firms, and lobbyists in Washington. The leadership of Serbia, on the other hand, underestimated the power of public relations. Serbian Americans tried to remedy the situation, but their efforts were inhibited by insufficient funds, inadequate organization, and lack of support from powerful individuals. As a result, Serbian-American perspectives were often absent from public forums. In an attempt to balance the way the American public was exposed to issues relating to the Yugoslav conflict, in September 1992 I became the director of the Serbian-American Affairs Office, as a leading voice in Washington for Serbian Americans.

As the media searched for a culprit in the Yugoslav civil war, I often found myself on the opposite end of the argument on television and radio debates. After the shows, I received telephone calls and letters from interested Americans who were confused and frustrated about the issue. Ironically, while the Yugoslav conflict aroused an abundance of intense debates among media pundits and political activists, the profusion of commentaries neglected to answer some basic questions about the Yugoslav war in the minds of average Americans. Who are the Bosnian Serbs, Croats, and Muslims? Why are they fighting? What is the cause of the war? What are U.S. interests in the region? Why are U.S. troops in Bosnia and Kosovo?

I believe public confusion continues to this day because of simplistic messages generated throughout conflicts in Croatia, Bosnia, and Kosovo. The Yugoslav conflict breathed life into former politicians and prosaic activists who were anxious to advance their opinions on national television but who did not have an adequate understanding of the Balkans. The media was intent on telling a story of human suffering through a saga of good and evil but was limited by the ultimate need to promote easily digestible, exciting accounts of foreign events. As a result, the public was not exposed to all the facts about what has happened in the Yugoslav region, and what is happening today. Why should the public care? Because media coverage of Yugoslav ethnic conflicts demonstrated how the public could be misinformed, even by Washington's best and brightest. In writing this book, I hope to encourage the public to become conscious of subtle or direct attempts by the media, government officials, or special interest groups to manipulate its sympathies in support of a particular view.

In covering events and facts in the following chapters, I have intentionally cited the very same media sources whose coverage of Yugoslav ethnic conflicts is critiqued. It is not the lack of such information, but rather the selective placement of these facts and biased method of conveying them, that ultimately obscured the reality of what was happening in the Balkans. Understandably, it has been very difficult to cover wars taking place in the Yugoslav region. It was dangerous, information was frequently unavailable, reporters did not understand the local language, and credibility of sources was difficult to assess. All of these problems were compounded by the need to write and produce a story quickly and with emotional appeal. But in a modern world, where Washington's views have been increasingly based on fly-by-night images of world events, sound bites, and emotional rhetoric, U.S. foreign policy has been adversely affected. This makes it all the more important for reporters and editors to explore all sides of a foreign issue and not fall prey to personal passions and manipulations by foreign groups vying for support from Washington.

On the whole, misrepresentation of Yugoslav ethnic clashes were the basis for Washington's irrational obsession to destroy the Serbs, and excessive reliance on use of force to impose unrealistic solutions that are likely to perpetuate further hostilities in the Balkans. The Serbs—targeted as the culprits of the war by Washington's policymakers and opinionmakers—need to be better understood before an equitable and lasting settlement can be made to benefit all ethnic groups in former Yugoslavia. I hope that this book will encourage steps in that direction.

Chapter 1

Washington's Mind-set Toward the Yugoslav Conflict

IMAGES MAKE A DIFFERENCE IN WASHINGTON

On the chilly winter morning of December 6, 1995, I hailed a taxi cab and headed for CNN's television studios near Capitol Hill in downtown Washington, D.C. I was invited to be a guest on CNN's *News Hour* to talk about the Dayton Peace Accords, which brought an end to the Yugoslav conflict among Bosnia's three warring parties—Serbs, Muslims, and Croats. U.S. troops were about to be sent to Bosnia, and the city of Sarajevo was to be handed over to Bosnian Muslim forces. However, more than 60,000 of the last remaining Serbs staunchly clung to Sarajevo's eastern section and refused to hand over control to the Muslims. One point I intended to make on CNN was that a compromise solution should be found. Allowing some type of self-government to Serbs in Sarajevo would prevent a mass exodus of Serbian civilians from the city.

I walked into CNN's eleventh floor studio ready to discuss how to resolve the difficult situation in Sarajevo and help explain Serbian perspectives which were often misunderstood. I sat across from CNN anchorman Reid Collins, who interviewed me on several other occasions on CNN where I discussed the ethnic conflict in former Yugoslavia. With cameras set for taping, microphones hooked on, earpieces in place, and volumes adjusted, we were ready to start. In no more than five minutes questions about the conflict were asked, answers were given, and our interview was done. I began to rise from my seat, hoping that the worldwide audience was able to somehow understand the complexities of the Bosnian conflict from a few snippets of information that were just provided on the show. As I was walking out, Reid Collins turned to me and said: "Your job isn't easy. The Serbs lost the public relations war in Washington. Not a lot of reporters in Washington remember what the Serbs were like when Yugoslavia was a whole country. If the Serbs had spent half their money on public relations instead of guns and tanks, they would have been much more effective."

Having been an active participant for a number of years in Washington's inside-the-beltway environment, I fully understood Collins's remark. Any foreign government that ignores the importance of public relations and lobbying in Washington soon feels the wrath of stinging editorials, slings and arrows of media pundits, and condemnations by State Department and White House officials. The existence of hundreds of public relations and lobbying firms, representing clients spending millions of dollars a year to make the right impression on the U.S. government, attests to the fact that a good image is important in Washington. Thousands of agents, lawyers, and foreign representatives go in and out of State Department and congressional offices, television studios, and newsrooms promoting the interests of their clients in a daily game of influence in Washington. Influence itself has become the main industry of Washington. By 1990, Washington had hundreds of professional public relations firms and over 15,000 representatives—including registered lobbyists, foreign agents, lawyers, public relations consultants, heads of political action committees (PACs), members of foreign policy institutes, or "think tanks," and members of other professionals in organizations—all working to convey the right message to Washington's policymakers.[1]

The phenomenon of how Washington develops and implements foreign policy has been part of America's democratic process for many years. Although advocacy occurs in public forums, the reasons why certain views are accepted while others are rejected by policymaking elites is often obscured to the public. U.S. policymakers do not perceive foreign events in a vacuum. Their opinions may not be based on objective, rational, comprehensive, case-by-case examination of facts, but rather on images and assumptions created by vocal individuals, lobbyists, and spin-doctors of public relations.

The disintegration of Yugoslavia in 1991 and the violent civil war that broke out between the country's ethnic and religious groups—the Serbs, Croats, and Bosnian Muslims—was the first major conflict in Europe since the end of World War II. More importantly, it was the first major ethnic crisis in the post–Cold War era. Attempts by the republics of Slovenia and Croatia and ethnic Muslims and Croats in Bosnia-Hercegovina to separate from Yugoslavia were resisted by the country's Serbs, particularly several million Serbs living in Bosnia and Croatia. A civil war ensued in Croatia in July 1991 between Croatian government forces and its local Serbian minority from the Krajina and Slavonia regions. By April 1992, the fighting spread to Bosnia-Hercegovina among the region's Muslim, Serb, and

Croat factions. Germany became the first country to recognize the Slovenian, Croatian, and Bosnian Muslim governments as new states, while other members states of the European Community, as well as the United States, willingly followed Germany's lead. In four years of war, the United States stood on the side of Bosnian Muslims and Croats in their fight against Bosnian Serbs, and similarly supported the Croatian government against ethnic "Krajina" Serbs. In November of 1995, following NATO air strikes on Bosnian Serb targets, the Yugoslav conflict was officially ended when the three warring sides signed the Dayton Peace Plan, whose terms were conceived and overseen by the United States. Since Dayton, the United States has taken on the role of Bosnia's peacemaker and policeman by continuing diplomatic and monitoring efforts aimed at maintaining a fragile peace between former warring parties. By February 1998, Serbia itself was at war when the Kosovo Liberation Army, an Albanian guerrilla group, launched an armed insurgency in Serbia's southern region of Kosovo. U.S. involvement in the Balkans reached another unprecedented step when U.S.-led NATO warplanes launched a bombing campaign over Yugoslavia—the first time in the organization's 50-year history that it attacked a sovereign nation.

The Yugoslav civil war caught global attention because of its importance to countries with political, cultural, and religious interests in the region: the United States, Western Europe, Eastern Europe, Russia, as well as the Islamic world—particularly Turkey. The conflict came at a remarkable time of geopolitical change. The breakup of the Soviet Union in 1990 allowed the United States to emerge as a triumphant leader of the post–Cold War world. As such, America was eager to demonstrate its leadership in European political and security matters. Washington aimed to demonstrate that a European crisis, such as the Yugoslav conflict, could not be handled without substantial U.S. involvement and U.S.-led NATO military action. Within this context, Yugoslavia's demise and ensuing civil war was the first post–Cold War challenge to America's foreign policymaking elites. Extraordinary interest was aroused among all sectors of the Washington establishment—governmental foreign policymaking agencies, foreign policy think tanks, congressional committees dealing with foreign affairs, and the U.S. media.

The American public was made aware of the Yugoslav war through emotional media coverage and impassioned rhetoric by U.S. government officials, political leaders, activists, journalists, and media pundits. As television screens captivated audiences with images of war, violence, and human suffering, Washington's foreign policymaking elites, activists, and newly minted "experts" jumped on the bandwagon to present their views on television, radio, and other public forums. Extraordinary attention to the Yugoslav conflict gave the impression that the war was being thoroughly investigated and all perspectives were being explored. This apparent wealth of information, however, did not guarantee that all the facts were understood or revealed. As ethnic turmoil intensified, the media presented neatly packaged sound bites describing the conflict. The outpouring of anti-Serb sentiment from Washington led one well-known Serbian poet, Matija Beckovic, to write: "Never before has there been so much talk about Serbs yet with so little knowledge about them."[2]

While activists and experts debated the pros and cons of U.S. action in the Yugoslav war, the American public was unaware of what lay behind the rhetoric—the "war of words" that was taking place in Washington. Surprisingly, this war had a more profound effect on the Yugoslav conflict than actions on the ground between the warring parties themselves. The "war of words" was a battle of influence of one perspective over another. Front lines were set up between those who pushed for active U.S. intervention in the Balkans and those who supported more restrained, conservative action. It pitted morality-based rhetoric and media-driven images against less-vocal, sober reasoning. It was guided by Washington's interventionists, spurred on by activists and special interest groups advancing the interests of some of Yugoslavia's warring factions.

The most effective time to convey a message in Washington about the Yugoslav crisis was while the issue was relatively unknown. It was precisely during this time that the Serbs were silent in Washington, while Croatian and Bosnian Muslim officials launched a full-scale public relations campaign that targeted U.S. foreign policymaking and media elites. In the early days of Yugoslavia's problems, Washington was a blank slate on which nearly any plausible story could be written. Information about the Yugoslav conflict provided by Muslim and Croat governments in the early days of war was welcomed by executive branch analysts and members of Congress facing the daily burden of sorting out complex international issues.

To most State Department analysts, congressional staffers, and journalists, Yugoslavia was a patchwork of different ethnic groups with complex histories and confusing borders. At a congressional hearing of the Senate Council on Foreign Relations in the Spring of 1992, two State Department analysts looked puzzled when asked what Yugoslavia's internal borders looked like before the Communist regime of Josip Broz Tito took over the country after World War II. The question was a good one. While listening to the hearings, I anxiously awaited the answer. I expected State Department representatives to pull out a map showing that ethnic Serbs inhabited areas of Yugoslavia's modern-day republics of Croatia and Bosnia-Hercegovina for centuries, and that Tito reorganized Yugoslavia's internal borders so that the Serbs were dispersed in several republics. This was key to understanding why a civil war would occur if the country broke up along internal borders that would leave millions of ethnic Serbs separated in several states dominated by increasingly hostile ethnic neighbors.

In responding to members of Congress, however, the leading State Department experts on the Balkans had no answer. After some hesitation, one State Department expert said to members of Congress: "I'll have to get back to you on that one."

At the time, a staff member of the Senate Council on Foreign Relations Committee present during the hearing, Peter Galbraith, told me he was interested in Yugoslavia's problems and asked me to send him the maps in question, which I did. One should never underestimate the importance of congressional staffers. Several years later, Galbraith became the U.S. ambassador to Croatia. Having become a key source of information and advice to the U.S. government, he had surprisingly little training, experience, or knowledge of the region. This characteristic was typical of many others dealing with the Balkans in Washington.

Lacking sufficient information on Yugoslavia's complexities, Washington presented a view on the subject that reflected assumptions generated by individuals who presented clear and concise answers. This made the establishment vulnerable to views of advocates and "missionaries" of the cause of certain Yugoslav warring parties. Croatian and Bosnian Muslim governments understood the implications of Washington's naivete regarding Yugoslav issues and quickly took advantage of the situation to present their own views to America's decision makers and the media. In 1991, as Yugoslavia was falling apart, the government of Croatia hired the public relations firm Ruder Finn, Inc. to lobby the U.S. government in support of Croatia's war aims against the Serbs. By 1992, the Bosnian Muslim leadership joined the Croats as the second Yugoslav client of Ruder Finn. Soon to follow, the same firm began representing the pro-separatist Albanian group struggling for Washington's recognition of their territorial aims in Serbia's southern province of Kosovo. At the same time as the public relations war was gearing up in Washington in the early 1990s, both the Serbian and the Bosnian Serb leadership virtually ignored the war of words taking place in Washington. The Serbs did not hire professional help and missed out on establishing contacts with U.S. policymakers and opinionmakers in Washington. As the Yugoslav conflict ultimately demonstrated, any foreign nation that underestimates Washington's role in international affairs pays a heavy price. Those who understand how Washington works, on the other hand, reap vast rewards. The Serbs wanted to keep Yugoslavia's ethnic problems an internal matter, while the region's Croats and Muslims internationalized the conflict and actively targeted Washington's elites for sympathy and support. The latter approach found fertile ground in Washington's post–Cold War environment whose ambitious government and media elites welcomed a new crusade in an era without the Soviet threat.

The U.S. media provided an effective vehicle, particularly for the Bosnian Muslim government, in communicating views on the Yugoslav conflict. Washington's political players seldom like to stand alone on any foreign policy issue. A context of legitimacy, therefore, had to be created for them by those who sought Washington's support. This legitimacy was most effectively created through the media. Once a view was implanted within Washington's popular rhetoric, it became difficult to challenge. During the Yugoslav conflict, Croatian and Bosnian Muslim lobbyists, foreign agents, and public relations professionals appreciated the power of images in Washington. They regularly contacted the media and participated on television and radio shows whose power of persuasion could stir public concern, influence policymakers' emotions, and move congressional legislators to favor Croat and Muslim interests against the Serbs.

In the end, the "war of words" was won by the Bosnian Muslim and Croatian governments, who fought their battle with vocal calls for the United States to intervene on their behalf in the Yugoslav conflict. Although Yugoslavia's Serbs in both Croatia and Bosnia-Hercegovina had the advantage of weapons, they did not fare well in the end. Bosnian Muslims, on the other hand, were less well armed in the beginning of the conflict but were able to use "words" as an effective weapon, which ultimately gained them Washington's support. For the greater part of the Yugoslav conflict, the government of Serbia, led by Slobodan Milosevic, did not recognize the importance of images and good public relations. It was not until the end of 1998 that Milosevic finally realized the problem, and observed: "I think the main problem in the United States is that we have very bad PR."[3] The realization, came too late however, to change the Serbs' image. As the Kosovo crisis developed in 1998, the same media biases and double standards demonstrated in Washington's policy throughout the Yugoslav conflict reemerged.

Washington's inside-the-beltway culture explains how inaccurate images were generated during the Yugoslav war. The 1990s was a time of the foreign lobbyist's rising influence on Washington. With the United States emerging after the Cold War as the sole superpower, foreign governments increasingly began to recognize that decisions made in Washington could bring war or peace and economic prosperity or destruction in faraway lands. Foreign governments sought to win favor among Washington elites with help from hired representatives who could persuade Washington to support U.S. military involvement, weapons sales, or international loans and grants.

Although the effects of foreign lobbying are difficult to measure, foreign influence has clearly left Washington with skewed impressions of certain foreign issues. Public relations efforts by the Kuwaiti government on the eve of the Persian Gulf War demonstrates this problem. In 1989, during the early stages of Iraq's occupation of Kuwait, a teary-eyed 15-year-old girl gave moving testimony to the House Committee of the Human Rights Caucus in which she stated that she witnessed Iraqi soldiers come into a hospital, take babies out of incubators, and drop them on the floor to die. At the time, Congressman John Porter said that he never heard anything so barbarous and sadistic in all his life. It was not until 1996 that the testimony was found to have been false. A multimillion dollar public relations firm Hill & Knowlton arranged the girl's participation at the congressional hearing. The witness was actually the daughter of a Kuwaiti ambassador.[4] The emotional story told by a credible witness had a powerful effect on members of Congress who at the time were considering whether the United States should fight a war against Iraq. The success of emotional stories with members of Congress would not stop with the "incubator" story. In the years to come, members of Congress would be bombarded with moving accounts of the Yugoslav war—through the media and personal contact with representatives of Bosnia's Muslim government. While the validity of many of these accounts could not be verified, and some were later proven false, the effects of the reports would yield tangible results for warring parties intent on winning Washington's favor.

Members of Congress have also responded to grass-roots special interest groups in the United States. In the Yugoslav case, the level of effectiveness of certain Yugoslav ethnic advocacy groups was determined by the level of funding, personal contacts, persuasive abilities, timing, and the degree of individuals' influence in generating opinions on U.S. policy matters. Ethnic lobbying in the United States continues to exemplify an important tenet of American democracy: those who are able to organize themselves into effective action groups are able to influence U.S. government decisions. Many ethnic-American special interest groups reflect the views of the governments in their native countries. In such a way, foreign governments can have an indirect influence over U.S. decisions. Special interest groups that are powerful, well-organized, and well-financed can guide congressional attention to one issue over another through a systematic, long-term plan to exert influence. Once a member is interested in the issue, he or she is encouraged to gather support among other members of Congress, to pressure the president, or to form coalitions to pass particular legislation.

In the 1990s Yugoslav conflict, one of the most powerful members of the Senate and a vocal advocate of U.S. intervention in Bosnia, former Senator Bob Dole, first got involved with Balkan issues when former congressman Joseph DioGuardi, of ethnic Albanian heritage, invited Dole to join him on a trip to Kosovo in 1989. From that time, Dole was sympathetic to pro-separatist claims by ethnic Albanian groups. Dole was also targeted by the Croatian government and Croatian-American groups, as well as Bosnian Muslim officials in seeking U.S. support for their cause.[5] Mira Barratta, a Croatian American, worked for many years as key adviser to Senator Dole on Balkan matters. Perhaps Barratta's Croatian background had something to do with Dole's unusual interest in the Yugoslav conflict and explains why he became a particularly powerful voice against the Serbs in the coming years—a fact that was never explored by media pundits on many television programs Dole participated on in the coming years. Dole's activism on Balkan issues extended beyond his congressional term when he became the chairman of the International Commission for Missing Persons in the Bosnian and Croatian Wars. This organization has supported the interests of the Bosnian Muslim and Croatian governments, and through it Dole continued his advocacy in 1998 in support of Albanians from Kosovo.

Another vocal interventionist during the Yugoslav war, Congressman Frank McCloskey, was targeted by the same groups. McCloskey became a vocal supporter of U.S. military intervention in the Balkans and a legal adviser to the Bosnian Muslim government. In the late 1990s, Congressman Eliot Engel was a strong advocate of Kosovo Albanian separatism, largely due to the congressman's friendship with local Albanian constituents in New York whose financial support helped his campaign.[6] The enormous media focus on the Yugoslav conflict, in combination with the fact that Bosnian Muslim, Croatian, and Albanian ethnic groups in the United States spearheaded well-organized campaigns to win over Washington's lawmakers and policymakers, gave them a tremendous advantage in influence over the less organized Serbian-American groups.

The complex influences on U.S. foreign policy and the nature of popular opinion in Washington during the 1990s explain how views of the Yugoslav conflict were formed and why flawed paradigms developed and persisted throughout the war. These kinds of flaws in U.S. decisions occurred in the Cold War years as well. Numerous scholarly studies showed how misperceptions within Washington's foreign policy establishment have caused political miscalculations time and again.[7] In recently published memoirs, former U.S. Secretary of Defense Robert McNamara wrote that all errors in Vietnam were committed by Spring of 1965. "After that," he said, "there seemed no way out."[8] He ascribed errors in Vietnam to policymakers' "profound ignorance of history, culture, and politics of the people in the area"—the kinds of mistakes that McNamara said the United States made in Bosnia during the 1990s. As in Vietnam, the U.S. foreign policymaking establishment formed its views of the Yugoslav conflict at an early stage and continued on this course throughout the war and beyond. Many early assumptions that shaped U.S. foreign policy toward the region failed to grasp Yugoslavia's historical, cultural, and political characteristics.

Instead of examining the true nature of the Yugoslav conflict—its historical realities, the national goals of the people, and the political beliefs of each ethnic group's leadership—Washington applied simplistic and sensationalized arguments to a complex ethnic dispute. Especially in the Bosnian conflict, the zero-sum views of good versus evil did little to facilitate a realistic solution to the region's problems. These misperceptions, and how they came about, form the main point of discussion in the following chapters. In essence, this book will attempt to answer the question: what shaped the U.S. foreign policymaking establishment's views and decisions during Yugoslav ethnic conflicts? The conclusion is that Washington's policies and perceptions were not based on urgent national interests of the United States. Nor were they knee-jerk reactions to events in former Yugoslavia that mandated moral leadership by America's foreign policymaking elites. *Instead, U.S. foreign policy toward the Yugoslav conflict in the post–Cold War 1990s was shaped by Washington's interventionist ideology, created in a media-driven environment that fostered a superficial understanding of the conflict.* The resulting U.S. foreign policy was an application of double standards to complex ethnic disputes that left an unstable, imposed solution in the Balkans.

SOURCES OF INTERVENTIONISM IN U.S. FOREIGN POLICY

Understanding how interventionist perspectives evolved in Washington is key to determining what guided U.S. foreign policy toward the Yugoslav conflict in the 1990s. America's modern-day activism in world affairs is a stark contrast to its isolationist beginnings. Having won independence and severed direct ties to Europe, 18th- and 19th-century America was more interested in expanding its vast western territories than meddling in European disputes. This attitude, however, changed in the early 1900s following World War I, when America emerged as a dominant economic power and international lender. In the 1920s and 1930s, American bankers and corporations saw new opportunities overseas and pushed for an expanded U.S. influence abroad to support their business interests. American industrialists created institutions, including the Council on Foreign Relations and the Carnegie Endowment for Peace, which brought together scholars, bankers, journalists, politicians, and government officials in a concerted effort to persuade Washington that taking an active role in restoring economic conditions in Europe was in the interests of U.S. bankers as well as the American public.

U.S. intervention in foreign affairs skyrocketed after World War II for more ideological reasons—to counter the threat of Communism. When the United States and Soviet Union emerged as global superpowers in the late 1940s, a bipolar world was created. Determined to halt the spread of Soviet expansionism, Washington pursued the policy of containment that became one of the guiding tenets of U.S. foreign policy in the Cold War years. As the fight against Communism became "institutionalized," a multitude of new government agencies and bureaucracies were created to implement America's world views. The National Security Act of 1947 gave life to an unprecedented growth of U.S. foreign policymaking agencies created to gather and analyze information needed in challenging the Soviets. These agencies became instruments of American global influence by overseeing covert activities, public diplomacy (or propaganda), and the distribution of foreign aid. By the 1950s, the United States was ready to put its foreign policymaking instruments to work on a global scale. Containing Communism was an integral part of all forthcoming U.S. foreign policy—the war in Korea, the policy of deterrence of the Soviets through massive retaliation, President Eisenhower's pledge that U.S. forces would remain in Europe through NATO as long as necessary, U.S. aid to Middle Eastern countries resisting Communist takeovers, the U.S.-supported invasion of Cuba at the Bay of Pigs, congressional approval of the Foreign Assistance Act to help foreign governments fight Communism, and the U.S. war against Communism in Vietnam—to name a few.

U.S. intervention in foreign matters subsided somewhat during the 1970s as the Nixon administration recognized constraints on America's ability to act as the world's policeman. U.S. military involvement in Vietnam came to a close, relations were improved with China, and two rounds of Strategic Arms Limitation (SALT) talks attempted to curb the nuclear arms race and thaw U.S.–Soviet relations. By the time of the Carter administration, Washington's mind-set was moving in a direction of "soft" interventionism—using human rights to exert influence in foreign affairs. The new foreign policy directive led to the creation of the State Department Human Rights Bureau in 1977. Under the Reagan administration, U.S. military capabilities and alliances were enhanced, while anti-Communist rhetoric was used to justify support for warring factions around the world. Radical Islamic *Mujaheddin* battling the Soviets in Afghanistan and the Contras fighting Nicaragua's Communist Sandinista regime were named "freedom-fighters"—in spite of congressional reports accusing both the Contras and Afghan *Mujaheddin* of human rights abuses. The U.S. media never seriously questioned the integrity of this policy.

HUMANITARIAN INTERVENTIONISM IN THE POST–COLD WAR ERA

The Yugoslav conflict coincided with yet another round of rising U.S. interventionism—this time, not to fight Communism but for humanitarian reasons. In the 1990s, Washington justified U.S. military actions from Bosnia to Somalia with the need to prevent humanitarian disasters. There was more to this policy, however, than was readily apparent. The popular 1990s concept of humanitarian intervention was used as a cover for an otherwise illegal act under international law, which, under United Nations Charter Article 2(4), states that all members shall refrain in their international relations from the threat or use of force against the territorial integrity or political independence of any state. Perhaps this is one reason why supporters of active U.S. global involvement have avoided defining U.S. military actions abroad as "interventions," even though the word's basic definition—"a policy or practice of intervening in the affairs of another sovereign state" or "to interfere, usually through use of force or threat of force, in the affairs of another nation"—clearly described U.S. action in Bosnia, Somalia, Serbia, and elsewhere.[9]

Although for decades nations have tried to apply exceptions to the international norm of nonintervention in the affairs of states—including humanitarian intervention, intervention to support self-determination, intervention on behalf of socialism, or intervention to preserve democracy—none of these was formally accepted.[10] In the post–Cold war era, however, the United States would not only launch an unprecedented number of foreign interventions, but would also expand the scope of U.S. interventionism to include hunting down leaders of "rogue regimes."[11] In Somalia, the Clinton administration pushed for changes in the original U.N. mandate to allow U.S. forces to go on a manhunt against General Mohammed Aidid, an enterprise that entangled American troops in dangerous search-and-seizure operations.[12] In Bosnia-Hercegovina, Stabilization Force (SFOR) troops acted primarily in response to enormous pressure from Washington in pursuing and capturing alleged war criminals. What set off this trend? Apart from the demise of the Soviet Union which gave the United States unrivaled powers in international affairs, Washington's pursuit of "humanitarian interventions" in the 1990s was also created by a phenomenon taking place closer to home.

The need for the Washington establishment to redefine itself was perhaps an unexpected precursor to post–Cold War U.S. policy. On the eve of the Yugoslav war, Washington's governmental and nongovernmental institutions that guided U.S. foreign policy through 45 years of Cold War were looking to redefine their roles in an era of budget-cutting. Lacking the Communist threat, the major impediment to U.S. interests abroad would no longer be a single monolithic Soviet menace but "rogue regimes"—to be coerced, constrained, and combatted throughout the world. The concept of a humanitarian intervention went hand in hand with the depiction of an "evil rogue regime" against whom Washington's pundits and policymakers could more easily motivate public support for U.S. military action.

In the case of Iraq's cross-border incursion into Kuwait, the "rogue regime" scenario was easily applied to Saddam Hussein. Extending this paradigm to other conflicts, however, was more difficult. During Somalia's civil war, the United States selected one of many warlords as the "rogue regime" to be hunted down but gave up after Somalia proved too complex and dangerous. In Yugoslavia, although Washington labeled the Serbian "rogue regime" as an "aggressor," the Europeans had a more realistic view. During a November 20, 1997 interview on PBS, when host Charlie

Rose asked former British Prime Minister John Major to explain the difference in building an allied coalition in Iraq compared to Bosnia, Major replied that in Iraq, there was a clear case of cross-border aggression by one country against another, whereas in Bosnia there was a civil war. Yet, for the better part of the Yugoslav conflict, Washington's policymakers and opinionmakers opposed this view. The popular perception of the Yugoslav war was a case of Serbian aggression—both in Croatia and Bosnia-Hercegovina. Washington believed in only one "rogue regime" per conflict. The civil war scenario, with no clear aggressor, did not provide the same simple, clean argument to rally support for U.S. intervention in the Balkans. Instead, Washington depicted the Yugoslav conflict as a case for countering rogue regimes, spreading democracy, promoting human rights, and pursuing moral imperatives.

Although Washington expounded the virtues of human rights to justify military actions from Yugoslavia to Iraq, double standards were evident in U.S. military relations with certain regimes. American special operations forces—part of a Joint Combined Exchange Training, or JCET, program, created in 1991 to establish military contacts with over 110 countries, including Bosnia—were found to have been training foreign militaries of governments that Congress and the State Department accused of gross human rights violations.[13] This included the militaries of Indonesia, Papua New Guinea, Rawandan Patriotic Army, and Turkey—whose U.S.-supplied equipment was documented to have been used to kill and expel Kurdish civilians in Turkey's southeastern regions.[14] U.S. military interventions on humanitarian grounds became even more hypocritical when use of force was justified by benevolent pretext. When the U.S. humanitarian mission in Somalia turned into U.S. entanglement in local factional fighting, members of Congress, including Senator John McCain of Arizona, protested. "We went to Somalia to keep people from starving to death. Now we are killing women and children because they are combatants."[15]

The same trend continued with U.S. intervention in the Yugoslav conflict. Throughout the 1990s, Washington's rhetoric stressed the need for humanitarian intervention in Bosnia to justify use of force. In reality, however, the attacks against Bosnian Serbs by U.S.-led NATO aircraft put the United States in a role of protector of one warring party in a civil war—the Bosnian Muslims. Washington's policy of "humanitarian intervention" in 1995 in Croatia resulted in U.S. aircraft helping Croatian forces attack minority Serbs and forcing another 250,000 Serbian civilians from the region. Intense U.S.-led NATO bombing raids over Serbia and Montenegro in 1999 resulted in the deaths of several thousand Serbian civilians and a devastation of Yugoslavia. The contradiction in U.S. policy formed because Washington's policymakers and opinionmakers refused to acknowledge that humanitarian interventions could not be accomplished without resolving the region's political and territorial contentions—factors that fueled every war in history. As Henry Kissinger commented on U.S. distribution of food in Somalia, "civil wars are about the distribution of power, physical and political. Intervention in civil conflict seems inherent in the U.S. role."[16] Kissinger's observation proved correct as humanitarian intervention mandated U.S. military actions from Somalia, to Haiti, to Bosnia.

Although Washington elites believed they were pursuing noble goals in Bosnia, they were actually applying misplaced moral paradigms to justify U.S. support of two warring parties in a three-sided civil conflict—a type of modern-day U.S. proxy war in the Balkans. Washington's government and media elites suffered from a lack of a healthy dose of reality. Again, the words of Henry Kissinger ring true: "Bosnia's civil war was triggered by the West's misconceived attempt to experiment with a multiethnic state among populations divided by religion and whose very reason for existence has been to prevent domination by the other ethnic groups."[17] Using moral reasons to justify use of force has led to the same problems in U.S. foreign policy characterized in previous years by one of America's foremost diplomats of the Cold War era, George Kennan. Kennan said that the most serious fault of U.S. foreign policy during the past 50 years was a "legalistic-moralistic approach to world affairs" that was intended to do away with war and violence, but in effect "[made] violence more enduring, more terrible, and more destructive to political stability than did the older motives of national interest."[18] The Yugoslav conflict is a modern example of the kind of U.S. policy behavior that Kennan warned about. U.S. humanitarian interventions will continue as long as the drive to arouse sympathy through televised pictures of starving people from northern Iraq to Somalia, to Bosnia is generated by the media. U.S. foreign policy based on media images has been reactionary and lacking in realistic guidelines— behavior that critics described as part of a "post–Cold War pattern that, without much thought, has put U.S. soldiers in harm's way more often than during even the worst years of the Soviet-American standoff."[19] This trend has put U.S. foreign policy on shaky grounds—most evidently in the Yugoslav conflict.

INTERVENTIONISTS AND ACTIVISTS FUEL WASHINGTON'S VIEW ON BOSNIA

U.S. foreign policy toward Yugoslav warring parties in the 1990s reflected the beliefs and interests of Washington's policymaking and opinionmaking insiders—from Cold war activists looking for a new cause for sabre rattling to members of the press anxious to publish award-winning stories. The Yugoslav war generated an astounding number of books, particularly on issues relating to Bosnia, some of which were written by individuals who had little, if any, prior experience with Balkan issues. Young hopefuls within the State Department, ambitious new members of Congress, aspiring journalists, and even retired U.S. government officials found Bosnia's sensationalist topics appealing. Their anti-Serb rhetoric brought them unprecedented media attention.

Between 1992 and 1993, the State Department was the scene of conflicting views between those who favored U.S. military actions against Serbs and those who felt that the conflict in Bosnia and Croatia should be handled through diplomacy, humanitarian assistance, and mediation between the warring parties. In 1993, several State Department officers resigned in protest of what they considered inadequate U.S. action. They immediately embraced the media as their weapon in pushing for a harder U.S. action against Serbs in Bosnia. In late 1992, when sensationalism was at its highest and television screens overflowed with accusations of rape and atrocities, these young State Department officers found fertile ground for anti-Serb rhetoric.

One of the first State Department officers to advocate U.S. military intervention against the Serbs was George Kenney. Kenney was unique, however, in that he was the only one to demonstrate a rare level of integrity when in later years he openly changed his views. He acknowledged that his original beliefs were formed by his sole experience on Yugoslav issues—a four-month assignment as the State Department's desk officer for Yugoslavia—and that he had no background in Balkan affairs—and had never been to Yugoslavia.[20] Kenney became a strong supporter of U.S. bombing of Bosnian Serbian areas and Serbia proper. When Kenney and I participated on the *Gill Gross Radio Hour* on April 30, 1993, his view of the Bosnian conflict was that "an evil regime in Belgrade [was] committing terrible acts of aggression against its neighbors" and that the United States must "use some kind of force to stop Serbian aggression and roll Serbs back and contain Serbia the same way we contained the Soviet Union"—a popular view frequently heard in Washington at the time. The State Department claimed that troops fighting in Bosnia were from Serbia proper and needed to be rolled back to Serbia—reminiscent of the Cold War era phrase to "roll back" the Soviets. This model, however, was inappropriately applied to the Yugoslav conflict. Regardless of any help Bosnian Serbs may have received from Serbia, the vast majority of soldiers fighting against Bosnian Muslim forces were Bosnian Serbs. It was unreasonable for U.S. troops to "roll back" Serbs who lived in Bosnia in the first place.

At the time of our radio debate, Kenney's passionate support for U.S. intervention made him an instant hit with Bosnian Muslim officials. "They put me on a pedestal," Kenney later recalled in a June 30, 1996 interview with the *Washington Post*. When Kenney was a vocal interventionist on U.S. policy in the Balkans, he was offered a position with the Carnegie

Endowment for International Peace whose president, Morton Abramowitz, also favored U.S. military intervention. After returning from two trips to Sarajevo, however, Kenney became a harsh critic of the Bosnian Muslim government which he described as "intolerant" and of Bosnian Muslim president Alija Izetbegovic whom he characterized as "incompetent, untrustworthy, and an unworthy ally."[21] Countering his former cry of genocide, Kenney now published articles arguing that the Bosnian Muslims were not even victims. He concluded that the Bosnian Muslim government claim of 250,000 people killed was never backed by evidence but rather was repeated by journalists without corroboration; that incidents of war crimes were roughly equal on all sides; and that there were between 25,000 to 60,000 military and civilian casualties among all three ethnic groups in Bosnia.[22] Articles published by Kenney in later years of war, however, were not given a fraction of the attention that his earlier anti-Serb pieces had garnered. Washington's interventionists and former admirers called Kenney a turncoat, and he lost his position with the Carnegie Endowment for International Peace.

While Kenney was able to go beyond the rhetoric and finger pointing, most of Washington's Bosnia pundits had no motivation to do the same. To many newly formed enthusiasts, Bosnia was not a call for objective research but a romantic, moral cause. It was their Spanish Civil War. It inspired Susan Sontag to direct *Waiting for Godot* in August 1993 in the middle of war in Sarajevo—an action intended to boost the spirit of Sarajevans, but which primarily got Sontag back in the media limelight. Her son, David Rieff, did fairly well for himself, too, by writing the book *Slaughterhouse*—a symbolic gesture of his personal solidarity with Bosnia's Muslims. In December 1994, Susan Sontag joined artists, writers, and actresses, including Vanessa Redgrave, in sponsoring a petition initiated by the Bosnian Muslim government to promote the idea of a "united" Sarajevo. In promoting the effort in a January 11, 1995, interview with PBS's Charlie Rose, Vanessa Redgrave spoke movingly of her personal commitment to the plight of Muslims in Sarajevo. She demonstrated no idea, however, of the political significance of the issue. How should Sarajevo be united? Should the Serbian part be handed over to the Muslim government, or should the Bosnian Serbs have jurisdiction over all of Sarajevo? Both proposals would have led to a united Sarajevo, but Redgrave was opting solely to support the Bosnian Muslim government position.

The "habit of absolute moral certainty in the face of daunting political complexities dies hard with these writers," wrote one observer about these Bosnia enthusiasts in the entertainment industry, "even in situations where they are clearly out of their depth."[23] The surge of actresses, writers, and even former wives of rock stars like Bianca Jagger taking up the Bosnian cause was bewildering. As the not-so-young flower-children and Bosnia activists poured into Sarajevo, their hunger to commit themselves to the cause went hand-in-hand with the media's desire to tell a story of good and evil. A normally reputable and serious news program, the *MacNeil-Lehrer Newshour*, went so far as to interview Bianca Jagger following her trip to Sarajevo. Her emotional portrayal of the war in Bosnia and her heart-wrenching accounts of Muslim victims brutalized by Serbs were very popular with the Bosnian Muslim government. Jagger has been a frequent guest of the government in Sarajevo, and her warm relations with Bosnian Muslim officials continue to this day. When I last saw her at a British embassy party in Sarajevo in the Summer of 1997, she was still making her rounds as a popular guest of the government.

POWER AND CONSTRAINTS OF NEWSMAKING

The way the media influenced new trends in U.S. foreign policy says a lot about the way Washington is likely to react to other conflicts. Coverage of the Yugoslav conflict demonstrated constraints on newsmaking that limit the media's ability to perceive and convey accurate information to policymakers and public alike. Although popular arguments point to the growth in media scrutiny in previous decades, greater media inquiry has not been evident on foreign policy matters. Whereas on domestic issues, correspondents and editors have greater access to diverse opinions and knowledge of familiar issues, in foreign affairs, the media tends to emulate government policies and attitudes. On only one issue during the entire Cold War period did the American press present serious challenges to the executive branch—Vietnam. Yet even in Vietnam, editorial boards of the major newspapers gave full support to U.S. intervention in 1965 and began to challenge Washington on Vietnam only following a significant outcry from freshman members of Congress and the public.[24] Throughout the Vietnam War, reporters received most of their information through daily briefings provided by U.S. government officials, and their movements were restricted.

Similarly, during the early days of the war in Bosnia, reporters' reliance on U.S. government views allowed the White House and State Department to set the agenda at press briefings, provide selective information, and influence public perceptions during a crisis. As on other foreign issues, in the case of the Yugoslav conflict, the White House frequently took steps to subvert the media's power. The media, which needs to maintain good relations with U.S. government officials on whom they rely for information, has often gone along with policymakers' views of foreign events. During the Bosnian war, the views of top-level U.S. foreign policymakers who supported an active U.S. military role in the Balkans—including U.S. Ambassador to the U.N. Madeleine Albright and U.S. Special Representative to Bosnia Richard Holbrooke—were frequently reiterated by the media, eager to maintain good relations with these important policymakers.

While priding themselves on investigative reporting, the U.S. media has more often supported U.S. government policy—particularly against foreign leaders that Washington opposes. In the case of Panamanian leader General Manuel Noriega, David Gergen observed that "U.S. officials spoon-fed stories about Noriega that portrayed him as a corrupt dictator who had gone mad."[25] With Libya in 1981, President Reagan authorized a secret disinformation campaign against Muammar Qaddafi and fed the media erroneous facts about the leader as part of the administration's fight against terrorism. Secretary of State George Shultz said at the time, "I don't have any problems with a little psychological warfare against Quadhafi. . . . The truth is so precious it must be attended by a bodyguard of lies."[26] In dealing with Iraq, General Colin Powell said that by demonizing Saddam Hussein, Washington was trying to gain public support for the massive U.S. military campaign in the Persian Gulf War.[27] Notwithstanding the possibility that Washington's views on certain foreign leaders may have been justified, excessive demonization of rogue regimes for the purpose of swaying public sentiment obscured reality. In the case of Yugoslavia, Washington was obsessed with Serbian President Milosevic, who was blamed for virtually all political, territorial, and ethnic problems during Yugoslavia's breakup—the war in Croatia, Bosnia-Hercegovina, and the war against a separatist Albanian faction in Serbia's southern province of Kosovo. Mirroring State Department views, the media published countless references to Milosevic as "hard-line," or "nationalist." The demonization of the Serbian leader obscured the real nature of contentions between Yugoslav ethnic groups that lay the foundations for war in the first place. This occurred not only because the media was limited by government views, but also because of the nature of the newsmaking business itself.

The need to produce exciting news stories quickly and inexpensively means that journalists' research is limited by deadlines and financial resources that may prevent adequate reporting of all sides of an issue. As John F. Kelly, editor of the *Washington Post*'s Weekend section, observed, a reporter is required to "gather, sort and present information at a time when we face a paradox: Our technology gives us ever increasing options, yet our culture gives us ever decreasing time and abilities to sort it out."[28] Lack of time in a world of complex information manifests itself in a phenomenon commonly referred to as "pack-journalism" in which opinions are accepted and repeated without adequate scrutiny. An obvious advantage of pack-journalism is safety in numbers—it is safer to repeat information already accepted in public than to present new, untested information. With most foreign correspondents based in Sarajevo's Muslim-held part of the city throughout the 1990s, it was not surprising that similar stories were coming out of Bosnia. The preponderance of news stories on

Bosnia did not mean the public was getting better, more closely scrutinized information, but merely more of the same information—however right or wrong it may have been.

Apart from limits in access to information and pack-journalism, one of the greatest constraints on newsmaking during the Yugoslav conflict was the growth of media sensationalism. It was the media that drove the interest in the war in Bosnia, not the American public. Traditionally, foreign affairs arouse far less interest among Americans than domestic issues. In the late 1980s, polls showed that Americans were not materially interested in monumental changes taking place throughout Eastern Europe. When *Time*, *Newsweek*, and *U.S. News & World Report* featured the dramatic 1985 summit meeting in Geneva between President Ronald Reagan and General Secretary Mikhail Gorbachev, it was the year's worst-selling cover for all three magazines.[29] When the Yugoslav conflict spread to Bosnia in 1992, however, the media found that shocking images of war demonstrated that foreign events could indeed provide powerful drama capable of fascinating the American audience. With attention-grabbing narratives and graphic demonstration of human suffering, the U.S. media was able to make Bosnia a "sellable" foreign news item. The drive for faster, attention-grabbing information launched the "sound-bite era." Newsmaking became simplistic and sensational—a characteristic especially evident in Bosnia. CNN's need to fill its 24-hour-a-day programming with "expert" talking heads went hand in hand with the career needs of Washington elites who were eager to present their views on television. One of Yugoslavia's warring factions, the Bosnian Muslim government, would make good use of these media trends.

MEDIA IN SARAJEVO: TRIUMPH OF IMAGES OVER REALITY

Writing a story was not good enough; it had be the "right" story. This was what *Europa Times* correspondent Jamie Owen realized after returning from Yugoslav regions to what he called a deep public misunderstanding of the crisis in the Balkans.[30] One of his editors told him that his story should be "more anti-Serbian." Another told him to write a story on war crimes with an angle emphasizing what the editor called the usual "Serbs are monsters" approach. Such views that emerged throughout the war in Bosnia made the media an important weapon for the Bosnian Muslim warring faction. Misguided views of the Yugoslav conflict in Washington demonstrated the changing nature of modern warfare in an information age in which images had become more important than reality. One example of this phenomenon was the ability of the Bosnian Muslim government to present itself as victim, while at the same time fighting a full-scale war against Bosnian Serbs whom they labeled as aggressors.

Perhaps one of the most effective messages put forth by the Bosnian Muslim government and quickly accepted by the U.S. press dealt with the "siege of Sarajevo." Media fascination with the image of Sarajevo under siege and the ensuing dramatization would arouse worldwide sympathy. The international press descended on Sarajevo and for almost four years covered intense fighting between the Bosnian Muslim-held center and Sarajevo's Serb-held, hilly suburbs. On almost a daily basis, news reports accused the Serbs of shelling civilians and bringing death and destruction to Sarajevo. The city was presented in ruins, and its people were said to be close to starvation. Often, however, this image was not put into context.

Although tragedies of war were not difficult to find on any side in Bosnia, the media notably ignored the existence of over 30,000 well-armed Bosnian Muslim soldiers in Sarajevo—based mostly on the front lines against the Serbs. These Muslim forces applied the same techniques of war against the Serbs as Bosnian Serbs did against them. The media focus, however, was exclusively on Sarajevo's Muslim civilians. Serbian civilians rarely caught the camera's eye. The view of Serbs presented to the American public was one of armed soldiers—a fitting image for the side depicted as an aggressor. The resulting image of Sarajevo was that of a city of innocent Muslim civilians incessantly pummeled by well-armed Serbs laying siege to the city from the surrounding hills.

The reality, however, was that civilians and soldiers were intermingled in Bosnia. Bosnian Serb soldiers stationed on the front lines around Sarajevo were mostly local residents, young Bosnian Serb volunteers and recruits, many of whose homes were in the city's suburbs. When I visited Serbian front lines in Sarajevo in the Spring of 1994, I talked with some of these young soldiers in Sarajevo's hillsides—only 40 yards from Muslim trenches. Most of them looked thin and complained about their meager food rations. One of the soldiers I met, Slavisa, described the reason why he chose to fight as a simple matter of life or death. "When I look in front of me," he said, "I see Muslim front lines—their soldiers are ready to shoot at me as soon as I let down my guard. When I look behind me, I see Serbian homes in the hillsides which depend on my ability to protect them. One of those houses is my home. It's as simple as that."

The words of a soldier, however, remained on the front lines of Sarajevo and far from Washington's ear. The situation in Sarajevo was perceived very differently by America's opinionmakers. On September 12, 1995, toward the end of the war in Bosnia, CNN's *Crossfire* host Michael Kinsley described the situation in the typical media jargon of the day: "NATO," he said, "will stop bombing any time the Bosnian Serbs lift the siege of Sarajevo which has been going on for 3 years now, killing hundreds of people, starving people, cutting off water, electricity, medical care, health, food, and killing innocent men and women." Ironically, when I appeared on a later *Crossfire* show in 1999, Kinsley said nothing about U.S. bombs that were killing civilians in Serbia and cutting off people's water, electricity, medical care, and food. At the time, however, I replied, "There is a great deal of misinformation about what is really happening in Sarajevo. It is a divided city, one side has Serbian areas where Muslim forces have shelled Serb civilians, and the other side. . . ." Kinsley interrupted, "Are you saying there is no siege of Sarajevo?" I was obviously treading on sacred ground. How could I have the impudence to dispute a claim that was the staple of CNN reporting? "No," I replied, "it is not a siege. It is a civil war between two sides where Bosnian Serbs live in certain districts in one part of Sarajevo and Bosnian Muslims live in the other. . . . Bosnian Muslim forces have been attacking Serbs from their positions in Sarajevo for many years—just yesterday they launched another attack—and this is what they will continue to do if Bosnian Serbs pull back their weapons as NATO demands."

Why was it so difficult for Kinsley to comprehend that both sides were shelling one another? Perhaps because the Bosnian Muslim government took great effort to convince Washington otherwise—an image that brought Washington in on the Muslim side and ultimately changed the course of the war. The U.S. media was an important ally that helped win support for U.S. military intervention on behalf of Bosnia's Muslims through NATO air strikes against the Serbs. A number of lesser publicized facts, however, flew in the face of Bosnian Muslim depictions of Sarajevo's civilians as victims of Serbian aggression. In August 1995, just a month before the *Crossfire* show, the *New York Times* printed an article revealing discoveries by French U.N. officers documenting Bosnian Muslim snipers in Sarajevo who were shooting at their own civilians—the kind of assault usually blamed on the Serbs.[31] Such articles were few and far between however.

Instead, Sarajevo was portrayed to the American public as a city on the brink of mass starvation. The media almost never mentioned that civilians experienced similar conditions on all sides of the war. Bosnian Serb civilians were sometimes even less fortunate than those in Sarajevo because they were often bypassed by U.N. food convoys. The plight of Sarajevo alone, however, became a political tool for the Bosnian Muslim government, which was willing to inflict short-term suffering on its own people to achieve long-term goals. In 1993, attempts by the International Relief Committee (IRC) to restore running water to over 60,000 homes in Sarajevo was obstructed by the Muslim government because, as one IRC official described it, "they don't want to diminish the suffering Muslim image. . . . The fact is that no one is starving in Sarajevo, or ever has been. One look at the quantity of goods on sale in the markets is enough to disprove the much-peddled image of a city totally besieged and isolated."[32]

During my own visits to Sarajevo, I saw damage to both the Muslim and Serbian parts of the city—sidewalks littered with shattered windows, metal, and stone debris from shelling, overturned cars, and buildings charred and riddled with bullets as soldiers hid within them for cover. By the end of the war, the Bosnian Muslim-held side of Sarajevo received moderate repairs and was once again a fully functioning city with designer outlet stores and bustling markets. Ironically, the most damaged part of the city was the former Serbian suburb of Grbavica whose ruined buildings and general state of neglect were a result of heavy shelling from Bosnian Muslim forces during the course of war.

On March 19, 1996, CNN cameras gave the public its first view of Grbavica when the area was transferred to Muslim control. While CNN cameras showed the suburb's destruction, reporter Jackie Shimansky commented that the damage was the result of some of the worst shelling over the past four years of war. But Shimansky neglected to explain that it was the Muslim side that did the shelling of Grbavica. With years of accusations against Serbs for shelling Sarajevo, viewers would not likely have understood that Muslim forces were responsible for damage to the Serb-held part of Sarajevo shown by CNN. The surrender of Grbavica to Bosnian Muslim forces was further downplayed by scenes of happy Bosnian Muslim civilians hugging and kissing as the camera focused on a little boy happily waving a Bosnian Muslim flag. The significance of the image of a destroyed Serb-populated part of Sarajevo was lost.

Since the early days of war, the Bosnian Serbs failed to promote their own plight in Sarajevo in suburbs like Grbavica and so failed to gain media sympathy and international support. The Bosnian Muslim government, on the other hand, made soliciting the foreign press into an art form. The locations to which the media was able to travel with greater ease while covering the Bosnian war certainly favored Bosnian Muslim government efforts to sway the foreign press. The vast majority of foreign correspondents were concentrated in Muslim-held parts of Sarajevo—the easiest location from which reporters could cover the Bosnian war. By flying into Italy, a reporter could get on one of many U.N. flights (for free) that regularly flew into Sarajevo and be there by nightfall. On arrival in Sarajevo, most reporters could stay in relative comfort at a hotel where they received regular meals—not a bad way to cover what was supposed to be a siege.

In contrast, arranging trips from Sarajevo to Bosnian Serb areas was nearly impossible, and frequently dangerous, as reporters crossing front-line areas were vulnerable to stray exchange of fire. The only other way to get to Bosnian Serb areas was through neighboring Serbia, a prospect that was just as discouraging for the press. International airlines were not permitted to travel to Serbia's capital, Belgrade, owing to a U.N. economic embargo imposed on Yugoslavia (Serbia and Montenegro). A trip to Bosnian Serb areas from Serbia required an all-day excursion by car or bus—too great an effort for correspondents who were not encouraged to report the Serbian side of the story in the first place. As a result, a very small percentage of news that came out of Bosnia included interviews with Serbian civilians and officials, photographs of Serbian refugees, wounded, and dead, or pictures of Serbian homes and churches destroyed by shelling. By contrast, American newspapers and news stories were overflowing with images of Sarajevo and emotional interviews with Bosnian Muslim civilians and government leaders.

Failing to draw the kind of media response that the Muslim government was able to accomplish, the Bosnian Serbs were often frustrated and contentious toward the media. Foreign correspondents, in turn, argued that they frequently were not allowed into Serbian areas. Although this was sometimes the case, Bosnian Serbs claimed that their media efforts often backfired on them. "When we invited them to film the burial of 23 Serbian civilians massacred by Muslim soldiers," Bosnian Serb leader Radovan Karadzic would later say: "the final news report said it was a burial of Muslims killed by Serbs. After that, we saw there was no point in dealing with the media." Frustrated with selective media coverage and unable to compete with the Bosnian Muslim government's influence over foreign reporters, the Bosnian Serb leadership began to treat foreign journalists as enemies. This, however, should not have prevented correspondents from reporting on war crimes against Serbs. Reporters did not need to get into Bosnian Serb areas to investigate these wrongdoings, since crimes against Bosnian Serb civilians were being committed in Muslim and Croat-held areas. Even in Sarajevo itself—the hub of the foreign presence in Bosnia—a report about atrocities committed during the war against the city's Serbian residents was published only after the conflict was over. It was not until November 12, 1997 that Chris Hedges of the *New York Times* reported on brutal killings of Sarajevo's Serbian civilians, many of them elderly and women, by the city's Muslim paramilitary police forces.[33] When asked during a National Public Radio interview whether correspondents reporting from Sarajevo knew about what was happening to Serbs at the time, Chris Hedges replied: "Yes, you did hear rumors, but Serbs who were in Sarajevo were especially afraid to speak."[34] Surely American and other correspondents could have found a way of investigating the murder of Serbs in Sarajevo without jeopardizing their sources. They certainly had no problem reporting on allegations of crimes against Muslims.

There was one important difference, however, in reporting on Serb victims in comparison to Muslim victims: a guest in someone's house never insults the host. All major media organizations were based in Muslim-held areas of Sarajevo. Journalists who exposed the Bosnian Muslim government's treatment of Serbs would certainly have a much more difficult time working from Sarajevo. They would be ostracized by Muslim officials, access to sources would become more difficult, and they would fall out of favor with a network of local activists and translators who enabled the foreign press easy access to numerous "witnesses" whose moving testimonies were an essential part of successful reporting. Instead of reporting on the Bosnian Serb victims of war, the U.S. media frequently conveyed quite the opposite view. They praised Sarajevo as a model city of multiethnic cooperation—an image the Bosnian Muslim government took great pains to portray. Yet, at the time, it was common practice in this city of "multiethnic" cooperation for Bosnian Muslim forces to force Serbs in the city to dig trenches on the front lines, where they were likely to be killed. Although some reporters were aware of this practice, such information was often not reported or was buried in backpage newspaper columns. Toward the end of a *Washington Post* article published on July 6, 1993 was a statement that "units within the Muslim-led government militia forces clashed in Sarajevo after military police arrested an officer who had been rounding up civilians and forcing them to dig trenches on the front lines."[35] The article failed to mention the nationality of the "civilians" who were rounded up. A casual reader would surely miss the connotation.

Another explanation of why certain facts of the Bosnian war were not reported was that reporters tended to accept most claims offered by the Bosnian Muslim government. This was made easier when reporters without substantive knowledge of the region or its language were sent off to Sarajevo to join the multitude of press competing to uncover the story of their career. Phil Davidson of the London newspaper, *The Independent*, said that in covering the Bosnian conflict, "journalists who really didn't know the full picture [were] painting a one-sided version . . . and exacerbated the situation by having their emotions run amuck."[36] The Bosnian Muslim government especially targeted reporters from the United States in an effort to engage U.S. military involvement in the Balkans. It was not too difficult to gain a friend in one CNN reporter—Christiane Amanpour. The Bosnian war was one of the high points of Amanpour's career. She covered the conflict from Sarajevo beginning in the early days of the war, and her reports were unabashedly anti-Serb, saturated with rhetoric that could have come directly from Bosnian Muslim government officials. In a December 1997 interview with PBS's Charlie Rose, Amanpour voiced her support for the Bosnian Muslim cause. Far from defending herself as an impartial reporter, she expressed her disdain for what she called reporting in an "objective and lifeless fashion" and prided herself for what she described as "the most emotional" reporting in the Yugoslav war.[37] Perhaps Amanpour's ethnic Iranian background points to reasons for her pro-Bosnian Muslim agenda.[38] She may have also been motivated by personal sympathies and acquaintances she developed during several years of working in Sarajevo and experiencing human suffering exclusively from one side of the war. Whatever her motivation, CNN's Christiane Amanpour did an enormous service to the Bosnian Muslim government. She was "idolized" in Sarajevo—a title she shared with other U.S. reporters who were later described by Bosnian Muslim prime minister, Haris Silajdzic, as his government's "artillery."[39]

In contrast, the Muslim-led government was not very friendly to any foreign diplomat, member of the media, or official from international organizations that was not ready to present an image of Sarajevo as a city in dire need of military intervention. When the head of U.N. peacekeeping forces in Bosnia, Major General Lewis MacKenzie, began criticizing the Muslim government for its war tactics in Sarajevo in the Fall of 1992, Muslim officials launched a smear campaign against him, accusing MacKenzie of raping and murdering Muslim women—allegedly supplied to him by Bosnian Serbs. While General MacKenzie felt strongly about maintaining a policy of U.N. neutrality in Bosnia, the Muslim government considered him an obstacle in their fight against the Serbs. Accusations against MacKenzie received widespread coverage in Muslim nations, as well as Germany and Croatia.[40] It was just one of a number of fabrications presented in their war of words that was ultimately aimed against the Serbs. MacKenzie was pulled out of Sarajevo ahead of schedule in June 1992.

Another such ploy was put into motion on March 30, 1993, as two captured Bosnian Serb soldiers, Borislav Herak and Sretko Damjanovic, were tried and convicted by a Bosnian Muslim-run military tribunal of "genocide" for the murder of unarmed civilians. Both men confessed to the murders. The Bosnian Muslim government featured this highly publicized case as a showpiece to foreign journalists and international organizations and as proof of what was called the Bosnian Serbs' systematic policy of ethnic cleansing and genocide. Trumpeting the Muslim government's claims, the *Washington Post* reported that the two Serbian solders were accused of killing "40 people, many of them young women who were first raped as part of the Serbs campaign of ethnic cleansing of the Muslim population from parts of Bosnia."[41] It was the kind of story that every reporter in Sarajevo wanted to cover. It was moving, it was dynamic, it had good guys and bad guys, it charged up emotions and feelings of revenge. There was only one problem: it was not true. Four years later, a March 31, 1997, *Washington Post* article reported that two of the alleged victims were found alive and well in the Sarajevo suburb of Vogosca.[42] Herak's original confessions were apparently extracted under torture by Bosnian Muslim police who brutally beat and injured both Damjanovic and Herak soon after they were arrested. Damjanovic maintained his innocence throughout the week-long trial and showed the court scars from knife wounds in both legs and a broken rib, all of which the court-appointed doctors confirmed were inflicted during detention. Although U.N. officials suspected irregularities at the time of the trial, the media chose to ignore information that would have cast doubt on the story's legitimacy. Four years later, revelations of errors in the original story received little attention from Washington's foreign policy elites. Damjanovic and Herak remained captive.

Media coverage of the Yugoslav war demonstrates that modern-day media perceives itself as more than mere conveyers of facts. It needs to tell a story—with good guys, bad guys, and a moral in the end. Carol Williams, who wrote many of the early articles on the Yugoslav conflict for the *Los Angeles Times*, stated that she abhorred the "he said, she said, all-sides-are-guilty" way of covering the war. Instead, Williams tried to present her personal agenda, characterizing the Yugoslav conflict as "an orchestrated, well-planned campaign of aggression."[43] Kate Adie of the British Broadcasting Corporation (BBC) explained that the media likes to tell a story of good and evil because, in her view, viewers like to identify with one side. "Where are the good guys? Who are the bad guys? When you're trying to report something like Yugoslavia where everybody's up to something, nobody's totally good, nobody's totally bad," she said, "then you lose out with viewers. It's not that viewers are simplistic—it's just that in understanding any complex problem, people wish to look for what is right and what is wrong, what is good and what is bad. And if it is not clear, people begin to lose either sympathy or interest."[44]

Sensationalism in media coverage of the Bosnian war—encouraged by a Bosnian Muslim government's desperate need for foreign intervention—ultimately influenced U.S. foreign policy. The same trend continued with the war in Serbia's southern province of Kosovo, where anti-Serb propaganda was encouraged by Albanian separatists who wanted U.S. military intervention against the Serbs. Washington's dependence on the media's on-the-spot reporting throughout several Yugoslav conflicts in the 1990s made it susceptible to conclusions drawn from insufficient or one-sided information. Hence, the public and government relied entirely on each reporter's integrity, knowledge, talents, objectivity, and willingness to seek the truth. As producers of meaning, journalists who covered the Yugoslav war were projecting personal hostilities and feelings of injustice on the public as part of what they considered their journalistic duty. This occurred whenever journalists attempted to supplant reality with personal emotions or objectives in covering a complex war about which many of them had limited knowledge. Relying on their emotions made the media vulnerable to manipulation by whichever side was more effective in gaining access and sympathy in the foreign press. In the Yugoslav case, it was clearly the Croats, Bosnian Muslims, and Kosovo Albanians—not the Serbs.

The media's emotional rendition of good versus evil, especially in Bosnia, made U.S. foreign policy react to sound bites rather than the reality of what was happening in the region. It also contributed to a lack of understanding of historical context and ethnic relations in the region, which formed the basis of Washington's early foreign policy mistakes in the Yugoslav conflict. The following chapter addresses common misconceptions about Yugoslavia's past harbored by U.S. foreign policy elites and the media alike and explains how these misconceptions arose.

NOTES

1. *Washington Representatives: 1995* (Washington, D.C.: Columbia Books, 1995), 3.
2. Matija Beckovic, "A Nation That Has Given Up on Itself," *Politika* (November 2, 1991).
3. Lally Weymouth, "I Can Only Be Proud of My Role," *Washington Post* (December 13, 1998): C4.
4. PBS's *Frontline*, January 9, 1996.
5. On Croatian and Bosnian Muslim government contacts with members of Congress, see U.S. Department of Justice, Foreign Agents Registration Section, *Registration Statement* (Washington, D.C., November 6, 1992), 2.
6. CNN's *Crossfire*, October 1, 1998.
7. See Alexander L. George, *Presidential Decisionmaking in Foreign Policy: The Effective Use of Information and Advice* (Boulder, Colo.: Westview Press, 1980), 17–24.
8. Paul Hendrickson, "Vietnam Spring," *Washington Post* (September 15, 1996): W10.
9. See "intervene" and "intervention" in *The American Heritage Dictionary, Second College Edition* (Boston: Houghton Mifflin, 1982).
10. Barry E. Carter and Phillip R. Trimble, *International Law* (Boston: Little, Brown, 1991), 1235–1237.
11. R. C. Longworth, "Lack of Guidelines Often Leads to Aimless Intervention by U.S.," *Houston Chronicle* (August 18, 1994): 22.
12. Richard A. Serrano, "Policy on Somalia, Haiti Angers Pentagon," *Houston Chronicle* (October 19, 1993): 10.
13. The JCET program was conducted pursuant to Section 2011 of Title 10, U.S. Code. See Dana Priest, "Free of Oversight, U.S. Military Trains Foreign Troops," *Washington Post* (July 15, 1998): A1, A22.
14. Lynne Duke, "Africans Use Training in Unexpected Ways," *Washington Post* (July 14, 1998): A1.
15. Peter Grier, "As Violence in Somalia Escalates, Senate Steps Up Troop Oversight," *Christian Science Monitor* (September 14, 1993): 6.
16. Henry Kissinger, "U.S. Intervention in Somalia Poses Risk," *Dallas Morning News* (December 13, 1992): 1J.
17. Henry Kissinger, "Limits to What the U.S. Can Do in Bosnia," *Washington Post* (September 22, 1997): A19.
18. George F. Kennan, *American Diplomacy* (Chicago: University of Chicago Press, 1951), 101.
19. Longworth, "Lack of Guidelines Often Leads to Aimless Intervention by U.S.," 22.
20. George Kenney, "Steering Clear of Balkan Shoals," *The Nation* (January 8, 1996): 21.
21. Mary Battiata, "War of the Worlds," *Washington Post Magazine* (June 30, 1996): 20.

22. Kenney, "Steering Clear of Balkan Shoals," 21.

23. Hilton Kramer, "In Sarajevo, False Echoes of Spain," *Wall Street Journal* (August 24, 1993): 14.

24. Noam Chomsky and Edward S. Herman, *Manufacturing Consent* (New York: Pantheon Books, 1988), 172.

25. David R. Gergen, "Diplomacy in a Television Age: The Dangers of a Tele-democracy," in Simon Serfaty (ed.), *The Media and Foreign Policy* (New York: St. Martin's Press, 1991), 59.

26. R. Gregory Nokes, "Libya: A Government Story," in Simon Serfaty (ed.), *The Media and Foreign Policy* (New York: St. Martin's Press, 1991), 37–40.

27. PBS's *Frontline*, January 9, 1996.

28. "Post Editor Gets Nieman Fellowship," *Washington Post* (May 13, 1998): A13.

29. Gergen, "Diplomacy in a Television Age," 53.

30. Jamie Owen, "Dubrovnik Is Not Destroyed," *Europa Times* (September 1994).

31. Mike O'Connor, "Investigation Concludes Bosnian Government Snipers Shot at Civilians," *New York Times* (August 1, 1995): 6.

32. Kenneth Roberts, "Glamour Without Responsibility," *The Spectator* (March 5, 1994): 13–14.

33. Chris Hedges, "Postscript to Sarajevo's Anguish: Muslims Killing of Serbs Detailed," *New York Times* (November 12, 1997): A1–A6.

34. National Public Radio's *Fresh Air*, November 12, 1997.

35. John Pomfret, "Bosnian Mourns 'Tragic Reality' of Partition," *Washington Post* (July 6, 1993): A11.

36. Roland Keating, "When Reporters Go over the Top," *The Guardian* (January 18, 1993).

37. Ibid.

38. Barbara Victor, "On the Front Lines for CNN," *Elle* (October 1992): 152.

39. Mary McGrory, "From Bosnia, with Gratitude," *Washington Post* (October 23, 1997): A2.

40. Mike Trickey, "War Propagandists for Hire: Croatia, Bosnia Use Western Public Relations Firms to Win Support," *The Spectator* (February 12, 1993): A11.

41. David B. Ottaway, "Bosnia Convicts 2 Serbs in War Crimes Trial," *Washington Post* (March 31, 1993): A21.

42. Jonathan C. Randal, "Serb Convicted of Murders Demanding Retrial After 2 'Victims' Found Alive," *Washington Post* (March 15, 1997): A17.

43. Sherry Ricchiardi, "Carnage in the Balkans," *Washington Journalism Review* (November 1992): 21–22.

44. Keating, "When Reporters Go over the Top."

Chapter 2

Prelude to War: A History of Ethnic Tension (up to 1990)

RELEVANCE OF HISTORY

At the onset of the Yugoslav crisis in 1991, most members of the media and Washington's foreign policymaking establishment possessed little knowledge of Balkan history and culture. In later years, some in Washington, like Susan L. Woodward of the Brookings Institution, recognized that "those making policy and shaping public opinion toward Yugoslavia misunderstood the nature and origins of the conflict from the beginning."[1] Ironically, it was these individuals, whose views were devoid of historical context, who ultimately became the most vocal activists in support of U.S. intervention in the Balkans. In a modern world, increasingly characterized by what Samuel P. Huntington described as "cultural identities," which are "shaping the pattern of cohesion, disintegration, and conflict in the post–Cold War world," the failure by Washington's policymakers and opinionmakers to put the Yugoslav conflict into historical context was remarkably short-sighted, though not surprising.[2] History has been unpopular among both U.S. policymakers and American journalists alike. The 1990s world of mass communications has been driven by the need to put international events into succinct sound bites, not long, drawn-out historical explanations. When American news correspondents asked questions about the 1990s Yugoslav conflict, a Serbian response invariably started with a look into the past: from the 1389 Battle of Kosovo, to World War I, World War II, and beyond. Pressed for time, reporters lost patience and sought individuals with simpler replies that clearly depicted victims and aggressors, good guys and bad guys. An effort to sidestep historical research among reporters covering the Yugoslav war was reflected in simplistic and sensational depictions of events taking place in the region.

Washington's unwillingness to account for other nations' histories may stem from lack of recent American experience with foreign invaders or significant internal strife. The day the Japanese bombed Pearl Harbor was a rare moment when the United States was attacked by an outside force. In Serbian history, however, Pearl Harbor happened repeatedly, to many generations. History has not merely been words on paper to the Serbs but a living thing, passed on from one generation to another—a guide for learning from the past in order to survive in the future. Serbian history constantly reminded new generations of their vulnerability to attack by neighboring ethnic groups. Knowledge of this reality built the Serbian psyche and permeated their culture to this day.

Serbian respect for their history and reverence for hundreds of thousands of Serbian victims in World War II was scorned by U.S. policymakers and the media. Jim Hoagland contemptuously described the Serbs as "a monolithic, irrational and loathsome tribe ruled by ancient hatreds and blood lusts."[3] Former U.S. ambassador to Yugoslavia Warren Zimmermann said the Serbs' "tragic defect is an obsession with their own history."[4] If the same statements were made regarding the Jewish people's commemoration of their Holocaust, there would be an outpouring of angry public response. Washington elites were applying double standards to which people's history they would accept. Unfortunately, their rejection of Serbian history negatively affected their ability to understand Yugoslav ethnic conflicts. During the Yugoslav war, Washington was more willing to accept Bosnian Muslims as jeans-wearing Westerners dancing to the tunes of a popular 1960s musical *Hair* than as one of three warring factions involved in a bloody ethnic conflict. Far from acknowledging historical realities, Washington elites believed the war was caused by a power-hungry Serbian leader, Slobodan Milosevic, who incited nationalism to fulfill his own political and territorial goals. This view was a gross simplification of the cause of Yugoslavia's problems. The 1990s Yugoslav conflict was an attempt by the country's ethnic groups to dominate one another in particular regions, a familiar theme of Yugoslav history. Elements of the same kind of rivalry and ethnic division caused problems in the Yugoslav region for hundreds of years and are still present today. These problems cannot be understood without historical context.

Yugoslav history is key to understanding the region's ethnic conflicts in part because Serbs, Croats, and Bosnian Muslims have all used past and recent history to justify their territorial and political objectives. The Serbs used older historic claims as centuries-old inhabitants of Krajina-Slavonia regions (modern-day Croatia), Bosnia, Hercegovina, and Kosovo in support of territorial claims. The Croats, on the other hand, diminished the Serbs' historic presence in regions they claimed for themselves, and they backed their arguments with recent history which designated these areas under Croatian control. Bosnia's Muslims also applied their own version of the history of Bosnia and Hercegovina to diminish Serbian claims and bolster their political and territorial goals.

More importantly, Croatian and Bosnian Muslim governments used historic revisionism to elicit Washington's support during the Yugoslav conflict. This historic revisionism was aimed at influencing how the U.S. media, foreign policy analysts, members of Congress, and academic community viewed events in former Yugoslavia. As the Yugoslav ethnic war was winding down, by 1998, yet another round of historic revisionism emerged with regard to Serbia's southern province of Kosovo, launched by supporters of Albanian separatism in Kosovo. Revisionist Yugoslav history has also became popular in a number of modern books published in the United States, which air the claims of Croatian, Albanian, and Bosnian Muslim scholars whose views of history are politically motivated. More realistic historical facts about Yugoslav regions can be found in older Western sources, written before the 1990s. These sources not only provide a realistic context of Yugoslav history, but also shed light on the importance of historic claims to territorial disputes in the 1990s Yugoslav war.

EARLY YUGOSLAV HISTORY

Yugoslavia's 20th-century existence as a nation was an attempt to unite Slavic ethnic groups that lived in the central Balkans for centuries. Ethnic and religious groups that comprised the modern-day republics of Serbia, Croatia, Slovenia, Macedonia, Montenegro, and Bosnia-Hercegovina descended from Slavic tribes that migrated into the Balkans between 600 to 650 A.D. and grouped themselves into three main divisions: Serbs, Croats, and Slovenes. The Serbs, the most numerous of the three, settled in regions of Serbia, northern Macedonia, Montenegro, and most of Bosnia, Hercegovina, and Dalmatia. The Croats settled in western areas of modern-day Croatia, as well as some areas of Bosnia, Hercegovina, and Dalmatia. The Slovenes settled in what was known in ancient times as Carniola and southern Carinthia.[5] The Bosnian region took its name from the river Bosanius where Serbian and Croatian tribes settled in the 7th century.

Serbs inhabited lands that were called the "gates" of the Balkans—territories vulnerable to attack from powers vying to control Balkan land routes. For this reason, British historian R.G.D. Laffan referred to the Serbs as the "guardians of the gates."[6] By the 11th and 12th centuries, three political centers formed within Serbian territory: (1) Raska, the birthplace of the Serbian state, included regions of modern-day Kosovo and the province of Novi Pazar that later became known as Sandjak; (2) Zeta on the coast of the Adriatic, known in modern times as Montenegro;

and (3) Bosnia and Hercegovina, roughly corresponding to the region's modern-day territories that were incorporated into the Serbian state prior to 12th century (see Appendix 2, map 1). From the 12th century, a powerful Serbian state gradually increased in size, until it reached its greatest extent in the reign of Czar Stephen Dusan in the mid-1300s (see Appendix 2, map 1). Dusan reigned over vast territories and was crowned "Emperor of Serbs, Greeks, Albanians, and Bulgarians" in 1346.[7] After Dusan's death in 1355, Zeta emerged as an independent Serbian principality. It became known as Montenegro in the 15th century and was ruled by Serbian Orthodox bishops until the mid-1800s.[8]

Lands ruled by Croatian kings and nobles were taken over in 1102 by Hungarian king Koloman who was crowned king of Croatia and Dalmatia. Croatian-populated lands were treated as vassal states and remained under Hungarian rule until the early 20th century.[9] This fact of history was frequently contradicted by Croatian government representatives and other revisionists during the 1990s, who claimed that Croatia was independent and even ruled over Bosnia-Hercegovina. Although some Croatian nobles did control parts of Bosnia—including the Croatian family, Subic, that united portions of modern-day Croatia, Slovenia, western Bosnia, and Dalmatia under their own rule for a short period in the early 14th century—Croatia's history was predominantly one of domination by Hungarian kings and later by the Austro-Hungarian empire.

A monumental event that launched centuries of division between southern Slavs was a break in 1054 from a dispute between the Christian churches of Rome and Constantinople on the issue of the Pope's supremacy. This led western Slavs, mainly Croats and Slovenes, to became Roman Catholic while the Serbs remained Christian Orthodox. Consequently, the Serbian Cyrillic alphabet was derived from Byzantine Eastern Orthodox script, while the Croats adopted the Latin alphabet from Rome—although the language spoken by Serbs and Croats remained essentially the same. Religion became the main distinguishing factor between Serbs and Croats. The regions of modern-day Bosnia and Hercegovina were divided primarily between Serbian Orthodox and Croatian Catholics.

In the 11th century, another form of Christianity, the Bogumil religion, began to spread from neighboring Bulgaria westward to Serbia. As the Serbian Orthodox Church took active measures to extinguish the new "heretical" religion, Bogumil Serbs left in great numbers for neighboring lands of Bosnia and Hercegovina.[10] Orthodox Serbs and Serbs of Bogumil religion jointly comprised the largest ethnic group in Bosnia and Hercegovina. The Serbs remained the largest ethnic group in Bosnia until the 1970s (see Appendix 1). This fact of Bosnia's ethnic makeup was often misrepresented during the 1990s war. Only a small number of journalists understood the historical and ethnic basis of Bosnia and Hercegovina, including *New York Times* columnist A. M. Rosenthal, who correctly described ethnic differences in Bosnia as one between "Serbian Christians" and "Serbian Muslims."[11]

Some of the first "Bans" or rulers of the Bosnian regions were of Bogumil religion and Serb ethnicity. One of the first Bans of the Bosnian regions, Kulin (1180–1204), stood out in Serbian lore as a ruler of prosperous times from which stemmed the saying "the days of Kulin are coming back." In the 14th century, Ban Kotromanic was of Bogumil religion, but his ethic Serbian background lay the basis for his alliance with neighboring Serbian king Dragutin and his marriage to Dragutin's daughter, Jelisaveta. In 1376, Kotromanic's son, Tvrtko, was even crowned "King of Serbia and Bosnia" at the Serbian Orthodox Christian monastery of Milisevo. Leadership of the Serbs passed from Serbian to Bosnian regions as Tvrtko became king, while neighboring Serbian leader, Lazar, accepted the more modest title of prince, or Knez. The close relationship between Serbs in Serbia, Bosnia, and Hercegovina continued as Tvrtko's successor, Stephen Vukcic, was later granted the title of "Duke of St. Sava," the Serbian patron saint. With the oncoming Ottoman Turk conquest, however, Serbs in Bosnia and Hercegovina would become almost permanently divided from other Serbian regions as the powerful Islamic force took over the Balkans.

THE TURKISH CONQUEST

The Turkish occupation of Yugoslav regions first began with Kosovo. Kosovo, described by Serbs as their "Jerusalem," stood at the heart of Serbian civilization beginning in the Middle Ages. In 1389, the Serbs united all their regional leaders, including King Tvrtko of Bosnia, to fight alongside Serbian prince Lazar in the epic "Battle of Kosovo" against the Ottoman Turk onslaught. The battle became a symbol of what historians called Serbia's historic role as defender of Europe and Christianity.[12] The battle would weaken the Serbs and open the way for Ottoman Turkish occupation of the Balkans for the next several hundred years. The occupation would cause waves of Serbian migrations from Kosovo to northern regions of Serbia's modern-day province of Vojvodina.[13]

In 1459, when the Turks captured the last Serbian stronghold in Smederevo, there was no one to protect Bosnia and Hercegovina from Turkish invasion. The last leader of the Bosnian region, Stephen Tomasevic, surrendered and was beheaded by the Turks in 1463. Serbs in neighboring Hercegovina, led by successors of Stephen Vukcic, were occupied by the Turks in 1482. Finally, the fall of the Serbian fortress of Belgrade in 1521 led to what one historian called "the gross darkness of Turkish rule over Serbian lands," which continued for 350 years (see Appendix 2, map 2).[14] With the Turkish occupation of Bosnia and Hercegovina, many of the Bogumils, whom historians described to have been of "Serbian race and

speech," converted to the Muslim faith and became one of the chief supporters of Turkish rule in the area.[15] These were the predecessors of the
Muslim population of modern-day Bosnia and Hercegovina. At the time
of Turkish conquest in the 15th century, the Turks viewed the Serbian
Orthodox Church as representing almost all Christians in Bosnia and Hercegovina. Catholicism declined and even disappeared in large areas of
Bosnia and Hercegovina and was restricted largely to barren regions of
the southwest. Many Catholics fled to Croatia, Slavonia, or Hungary, while
large settlements of Orthodox Serbs were expanded in northern Bosnia
up to the Kupa River. This relative distribution of Orthodox Serb and
Catholic Croat populations in the 15th century remained the same up to
the 20th century.[16]

The Bosnian Muslim government's claims in the 1990s that Bosnia-
Hercegovina enjoyed a peaceful, multiethnic coexistence for hundreds of
years were grossly untrue. The Turkish-imposed system during their occupation of the region was headed by a Muslim governor and supported
by a military caste of Bogumil nobles, called *begs*, that converted to Islam
and spoke their own Serbo-Croat language. Serbian converts to Islam for
all intents and purposes were considered to be Turkish.[17] The mostly Serb
Christian peasants, or *raja*, were defenseless against these Muslim nobles
who ironically belonged to the same race and spoke the same language as
the Serbian populace they oppressed. Serbs were obligated to till the soil
and pay taxes to their Muslim lords. Their sons were forcibly taken away
and recruited into the Turkish military corps of *Janizaries*, while many of
their daughters were forced into Turkish harems.[18]

During the 15th and 16th centuries, Turkish threats against Austria and
Hungary led to the organization of a Military Frontier in parts of modern-
day Serb-populated regions of Croatia (see Appendix 2, map 3). This region was largely vacant, as its inhabitants fled from Turkish attacks.[19] It
would become repopulated again only after large numbers of immigrant
Serbs willing to defend the buffer zone were welcomed by the Austrian
Emperor Leopold into these empty lands of eastern Croatia and Slavonia.
The Serbs were granted considerable privileges in return for becoming the
"guardians of the frontier" against the Turks.[20] This was the beginning of
generations of Orthodox Serbs in the Krajina, Slavonia, and Baranja
regions of modern-day Croatia, up until the 1990s Yugoslav war. This fact
of history was grossly revised in the 1990s by the Croatian government
and academicians who frequently portrayed the region as one where Croatian "kings" allegedly allowed Serbs to enter these regions. During my
appearance on a December 24, 1992 *CNN & Company* program, when I
tried to explain the Serbs' centuries-long claims to the Krajina-Slavonia
regions, a Croatian-American representative angrily responded that
"Serbs never controlled or owned the territories of these lands ever in
history . . . and any claim to the territory is completely false." A few years

later, during a *CNN Morning News* show on May 4, 1995, another representative from the National Federation of Croatian Americans attempted to diminish the Serbian presence in Krajina by saying that the region was populated by only "a percentage of Serbian population" and that the region was "historically Croatian land." This, however, was not true.

The Krajina-Slavonia Serbs became the vast majority of the population in the region in the 16th century. Hundreds of years of living and fighting to defend these lands against the Turks became the basis of Serbian claims in the 1990s for the right to self-determination of Krajina, which the government of Croatia sought to deny them. The Krajina Serbs' role as "guardians of the gate" of Europe continued into the 17th century. In 1690, when a joint Austrian-Serbian offensive failed to dislodge the Turks, in fear of Turkish reprisals, the Serbian patriarch Arsenije III led an exodus of 30,000 to 40,000 Serbs from areas of modern-day Kosovo, including Pec, Prizren, and northern Macedonia, across the Danube toward the northern Austrian military buffer zone of Vojvodina—Srem, Banat, and Batchka.[21] As the Serbs left, Albanian Muslims spread northward and eastward onto these Serbian lands in what was to become the start of demographic changes in Kosovo that affected relations between Serbs and Albanians well into the 20th century. In 1699, when the Turks ceded practically all of Croatia and Slavonia to the Hapsburg emperor, the Serbs found themselves split between Austrian and Turkish empires. The struggle for national liberation was about to begin.

LIBERATION FROM OTTOMAN TURKS AND AUSTRO-HUNGARY

The 18th-century Age of Enlightenment and national self-discovery fueled the Serbian dream to liberate their lands from the Turks. In 1774, the Turks agreed to give the Serbs provincial autonomy, but the Turkish *Janizaries* continued a campaign of slaughter and pillage throughout Serbian lands. In 1804, the Janizaries massacred 150 leading members of Serbian families and their leaders and put 72 heads on pikes in Belgrade as a warning to other "rebellious" Serbs.[22] A few years later, in 1807, a first major Serbian uprising, headed by the famous Serbian folk hero, Karadjordje, freed almost all of northern Serbia from Turkish control, and Karadjordje became the ruler of Serbia. Serbian Orthodox Bishop Danilo, the leader of neighboring Montenegro, declared himself prince, and his nephew, Nicholas, ultimately became the king of Montenegro.

Bosnia and Hercegovina were the greatest challenges to the Serbs' quest for national liberation. Although these territories were populated by ethnic Serbs, they were also inhabited by a large Muslim population that supported the Ottoman Turk occupation from which they derived vast privileges. By 1910, Bosnia and Hercegovina were populated by 825,418 Orthodox Serbs, 612,137 Bosnian Muslims (or Muslim Serbs), and 434,061 Roman Catholic Croats.[23] Another segment of the Serbian population was under the Austro-Hungarian empire in regions of Krajina-Slavonia in modern Croatia, and Vojvodina in northern Serbia. On the eve of the 20th century, however, only those Serbs living in Serbia could claim to be free and without foreign domination. In 1877, as Turkish power weakened and began to loosen its hold over the Balkans, Serbia and Russia declared war on the Turks in support of a Serbian rebellion for independence in Bosnia. Although the Turks were defeated, Serbia's King Milan agreed to discourage Serbian revolts in Bosnia, in exchange for control of Kosovo and Macedonia, which was reinstated as southern Serbia, and whose city of Skopje was the ancient capital of Serbian czar Dusan (see Appendix 2, map 4).

In 1868, the Austro-Hungarian monarchy granted provincial autonomy to the Croats and Serbs. Serbs made up two-fifths of the joint Serb-Croat population, with Croats living primarily in the western parts, while Serbs inhabited the eastern Slavonia regions. The Hungarian king, who valued the military services provided by Serbs of the Military Frontiers or Krajina regions to the south and east of Croatia, insisted on religious tolerance for Orthodox Serbs, independent Serbian schools, freedom for Serbs to use the Cyrillic alphabet, and Serbian newspapers, while Croat newspapers were regularly confiscated by Hungarian authorities.[24] In the late 19th century, however, Croats and Serbs began to form the idea of uniting all southern Slavs—the precursor to modern-day Yugoslavia. One supporter of southern Slav unity and a leading 19th-century figure in the Croatian cultural movement, Bishop Strossmayer, founded the south Slav (Yugoslav) Academy of Science and Art in Zagreb in 1867. Strossmayer's liberal Yugoslav views were opposed by the more extreme Croat nationalists who resented the Serbian population in the Croatia-Slavonia region. World War I would intervene to determine the fate of southern Slav integration.

CREATION OF YUGOSLAVIA AND THE TWO WORLD WARS

In an act of rebellion against Austro-Hungarian rule of Bosnia and Hercegovina, on June 28, 1914, a young Bosnian Serb national, named Gavrilo Princip, assassinated the heir of the Hapsburg monarchy, Archduke Francis Ferdinand, during his visit to Sarajevo. The event was a precursor to World War I, as Austria declared war on Serbia, which brought Russia and other European powers into the conflict. Serbia and Montenegro, as the only independent Serb-populated states on the eve of World War I, joined the allied war effort. The war took a devastating toll on the Serbs, resulting in the death of over one-third of their male population. To reward the

Serbs for fighting on behalf of the Allies, the great powers of Europe recognized the creation of the Kingdom of Serbs, Croats, and Slovenes in 1918 (see Appendix 2, map 4). It was the first independent state of southern Slavic peoples, ruled by a Serbian monarchy and parliament.

To avoid disputes between the Serbian majority and ethnic Croats, King Alexander changed the name of the country to the kingdom of Yugoslavia in 1929, meaning "southern Slavs." The country was reorganized into nine administrative internal provinces, or *banovinas*, that did not reflect national divisions (see Appendix 2, map 5). Alexander could not, however, overcome Croatian internal ethnic discontent. An anti-Yugoslav nationalist movement in Croatia was spurred on by an extreme right-wing group that sought independence by violent means. In 1934, they assassinated Yugoslavia's King Alexander during his visit to France, an incident also resulting in the deaths of several French officials. The assassination of the Serbian king brought King Peter to the throne while internal ethnic problems continued.

A growing fascist movement in Croatia, looking to outside help in achieving their territorial aims, found sympathy in Germany. While the Serb-led Yugoslav monarchy rejected an alliance with Hitler, leaders of Croatia's fascist movement backed Germany's drive toward European Nazi domination. Although history clearly showed that the Serbs opposed Hitler, some Croatian academics in the 1990s attempted to downplay Croatia's fascist alliance with Germany's Nazis by implying the Serbs followed the same course. For example, during a *CNN Morning News* show on May 4, 1995, when I explained that the Croatian fascist forces exterminated over 750,000 Serbs during World War II, a Croatian-American representative retorted that there existed "a similar Nazi puppet state in Serbia." These kinds of myths have only existed in Croatian revisionist history and in no other reputable source.

Far from cooperating with Germany, the Serbian people vehemently opposed Hitler. They took to the streets of Belgrade in protest of any concessions to Hitler, as demonstrators' slogans read "Better death than pact," a move which one historian called "a rare act of national heroism."[25] Yugoslavia's mostly Serbian army was crushed by Hitler's forces that attacked Yugoslavia on April 6, 1941. On that fatal day, Hitler's operation "Punishment" was put into effect against the Serbian capital Belgrade, as Goering's air force showered the city with bombs, burying 25,000 bodies beneath the ruins.[26] Serbs resisting the German invasion in the months to come were killed or sent to German prison camps where a large number of them perished—including my own grandfather. A continuing effort to oust the Germans was headed by Serbian general Draza Mihajlovic and his Chetnik forces who supported Yugoslavia's King Peter II, exiled in London. The Chetniks were said to have "performed acts of extreme heroism" against Hitler's Axis forces. American military historians noted that "what [Mihajlovic] and his warriors accomplished will go down as one of the most remarkable achievements in World War II."[27] The Chetniks were another group targeted for historical revisionism by Yugoslavia's Communists and by Croatian politicians in the 1990s. Mihajlovic was accused of collaborating with the Nazis—a remarkable piece of fiction, considering that he was awarded the Legion of Merit as Chief Commander by U.S. president Harry S. Truman on March 29, 1948 for his "instrumental [role] in obtaining a final Allied victory," and rescuing U.S. airmen and returning them to safety. In 1943, Winston Churchill convinced the Allied leaders to switch their support from the Serbian Chetniks to Communist Partisans headed by Josip Broz Tito who were believed to be making substantial gains over Hitler's forces in the region. The switch in Western support to Tito's Partisans lead to the execution of Mihajlovic by the Communists, in addition to tens of thousands of other Serbs who resisted the new regime.

Although the Serbs organized a military resistance to German occupation of Yugoslavia, Croatia's ruling fascist HDZ party welcomed Hitler's forces. The HDZ (the Croatian Democratic Union), under the notorious leadership of Ante Pavelic, was helped by German forces in taking over large territories, including all of Bosnia and Hercegovina, which they proclaimed as their own Independent State of Croatia. This included the mostly Serb-populated areas of Krajina, Baranja, Batchka, Bosnia, and Hercegovina. Croatia's HDZ party tried to rid themselves of Serbs living in Croatian-occupied territories in much the same way that Hitler dealt with the Jews. The solution, according to the HDZ, was to convert one-third of the Serbs to Catholicism, expel another third from Croatian occupied territories, and exterminate the rest. The grim task of exterminating Serbs was undertaken by Croatia's notorious Ustashi forces which developed a reputation for brutality that even German forces occupying Yugoslavia considered extreme.

A Croatian fascist government decree of September 25, 1941, established special extermination camps where vast numbers of mostly Serbian women, men, children, and elderly were subjected to some of the worst forms of torture and murder imaginable. The camp at Jasenovac, located in the southwestern region of Bosnia and Hercegovina, was one of the worst of its kind and became known as the "Auschwitz of the Balkans." Jewish groups estimated the death toll of Serbs and Jews at Jasenovac alone ranged between 200,000 and 600,000 between 1941 and 1945. By 1942, there were some 24,000 children in Jasenovac, of whom 12,000 were murdered.[28] The Ustashi established other special concentration camps for Serbian and Jewish children in towns including Labor, Jablanac, Mlaka, Brocice, Ustici, Stara Gradiska, Sisak, Jastrebarsko, and Gornja Rijeka where the butchery of infants and children took unimaginable form. Witnesses recount seeing an Ustasha soldier pick up a child by the legs and smash its head against a wall until it was dead, while other survivors saw Serbian and Jewish children burned alive in old brick ovens or killed by poison gas. Between 1941 and 1945, Ustashi murdered over 750,000 Serbs, 60,000 Jews, and 26,000 Gypsies in a systematic campaign focused primarily in areas of Bosnia, Hercegovina, and Krajina. In a region that comprised about 3.5 million Croats and 2 million Serbs before World War II, the genocide left less than half of the prewar number of Serbs in modern-day Croatia.[29] In Bosnia-Hercegovina, the Croatian Ustashi were also aided by Muslim forces who were allied with the Nazis and who themselves were responsible for wartime killings of Bosnia's Serbs. In the 1990s, the U.S. media and government rarely addressed the World War II massacres of Serbs as a major source of conflict and mistrust that Serbs felt against Croats and Bosnia's Muslims.

Serbian-Albanian relations were likewise seriously affected by World War II. Albania was another state neighboring Yugoslavia that was allied with Hitler. Italy's fascist forces moved in to help Albania occupy Serbia's southern province of Kosovo and create a "Greater Albania." Although Kosovo was populated by a Serbian majority prior to World War II, after the Albanian occupation of Kosovo from 1941 to 1945, up to 200,000 Kosovo Serbs were driven out, while Albanian families moved into Serbian homes and property.[30] The new demographic situation with Albanians becoming a large group in Kosovo remained in place after 1945, when Yugoslavia's borders were established under the Communist rule of Josip Broz Tito and a new era was launched.

"BROTHERHOOD AND UNITY" IN THE TITO ERA

Yugoslavia's reestablishment in 1945 under Tito's Communist regime was the start of a 35-year-long era that ended with Tito's death in 1980. The new regime attempted to forge a Yugoslav nation by uniting all ethnic groups within a single, functional state—no easy task considering that World War II was still fresh in the minds of ethnic Serbs. Tito set out to impose a vision of Yugoslav brotherhood and unity through a combination of coercion, indoctrination, suppression of nationalism, revision of historic fact, and political and territorial reorganization of Yugoslavia to weaken the country's largest and potentially most challenging ethnic group, the Serbs. The number of ways that Tito attempted to put Yugoslavia's Serbs at a disadvantage throughout the decades of his rule casts doubt on later claims by Croatian politicians that an alleged Serbian domination of Yugoslavia was the cause of Croatia's move toward independence in 1992. On the contrary, during the Tito era, Serbs were the greatest targets of Communist indoctrination and cultural denial.

Communist indoctrination was the glue that kept Tito-era Yugoslavia together. Yugoslavia's educational system, government-run media, and all public channels, especially in its capital and Serbia's largest city, Belgrade, stressed "brotherhood and unity" among ethnic groups. Serbian school children were expected to write essays and poems celebrating Tito's birthday every year. The most astonishing aspect of the practice of Tito-worship, most prevalent in Serbia, was the remarkable fact that no non-Serbian leader was ever more praised and admired by the Serbs than Tito. Tito was half-Croatian and half-Slovenian. Yet a large segment of the Serbian population believed that Tito's multiethnic background epitomized the new Yugoslav society where all nationalities were treated equally.

Tito attempted to eradicate nationalism because he knew that Yugoslavia could not be united if strong underlying ethnic tensions were allowed to flourish. Any ethnic splintering would cause the central Yugoslav Communist party to weaken and ultimately lose power. Nationalism among Serbs was perceived as particularly dangerous. As the largest ethnic group, the Serbs were in a position to mount the greatest challenge to Tito. The level of indoctrination was therefore especially strong within the Yugoslav Communist nucleus in Belgrade, where Tito initiated a process of "Yugoslavization" and "de-Serbianization." A city that was the seat of Serbian tradition and culture for centuries was now targeted to reflect Communist ideals. Belgrade's streets and monuments, formerly named after Serbian folk heroes and leaders, were renamed to honor non-Serbian Communist leaders. Properties and assets of Yugoslavia's Serbian monarchy were taken over by the Communist party. Paintings and art objects depicting events significant in Serbian history were stashed away or placed in the back halls of museums. Belgrade was losing its Serbian cultural identity. Far from allowing the Serbs to dominate Yugoslav government affairs, Tito was able to impose his own rule in Belgrade by manipulating the federal government's power structure. He filled top party ranks with Communists from other parts of Yugoslavia who were to keep a check on Serbia, while surrounding himself with Serbian Communist supporters who were frequently willing to sacrifice their ethnic group's national interests.

Historic revisionism was another form of indoctrination initiated under Tito. Modern-day myths about Yugoslav history stemmed from Communist indoctrination designed to suppress nationalism. History taught in Yugoslav schools focused on some World War II events while completely ignoring others. The Communist version of events during World War II was that Yugoslavia's Partisans were the sole liberators against Nazi occupation. They lumped both Serbian Chetnik forces and Croatian Ustashi into the same bag as "enemies of the people." No genocide against the Serbs was ever acknowledged. Instead, the Tito regime dedicated World War II monuments simply to "Yugoslav victims." By eliminating the past, Titoist revisionist history sought to avert Serbian ill feelings against the

Croats. Ultimately, however, as the 1990s Yugoslav civil war demonstrated, historical revisionism compounded the problem rather than solved it. A quiet denial of Ustashi World War II war crimes prohibited the Serbs from undergoing a healing process with their Croat neighbors, allowed the rise of new-age Croatian political enthusiasts nostalgic for Croatia's World War II "glories," and led to an armed Serbian rebellion in the Krajina and Slavonia regions of Croatia.

TITO'S ETHNIC MANIPULATION: DIVISION OF SERBS

The method by which interrepublic territories were organized in Tito-era Yugoslavia had a significant impact on the 1990s civil war. With the creation of Yugoslavia's six republics, the Serbian population was deliberately dispersed into several regions—Serbia, Montenegro, Bosnia-Hercegovina, Croatia, and later into Kosovo and Vojvodina, made autonomous from Serbia in 1974 (see Appendix 2, map 6). These divisions were at the disadvantage of the Serbs in every instance. As scholars later observed, borders "in Yugoslavia and the Soviet Union were often drawn specifically to divide ethnic and national groups, weaken them and set them against each other, rather than against the imperial power. These borders were accepted grudgingly as long as there was no prospect of overturning them. The end of the Cold War made them vulnerable."[31] The Serbs were tentatively willing to accept internal administrative divisions of Serbs within several republics as long as Yugoslavia was a single nation. By the 1990s, however, they were openly opposed to Croatian, Slovenian, and Bosnian Muslim attempts to split Yugoslavia along internal republic borders. The Serbs realized that Tito's creation of republic borders was to their detriment. The international community would ultimately accept internal divisions created by Yugoslavia's Communist regime in recognizing Croatia and Bosnia-Hercegovina as new nations.

Tito's division of Serbs went hand in hand with historic revisionism and ethnic manipulation. The Republic of Montenegro was a target of intense propaganda by the Tito regime, which artificially labeled Montenegrans as a separate ethnic group from the Serbs. Montenegro, meaning "Black Mountain," never referred to an ethnic group, but rather to the region. Montenegro had produced a history of Serbian epic legends, Serbian Orthodox rulers, and military leaders, and was inhabited by ethnic Serbs for centuries. In fact, both Serbia's leader Slobodan Milosevic and Bosnian Serb leader Radovan Karadzic were from Montenegro. It is difficult to imagine how the idea that Montenegrans are different from Serbs could ever have been accepted. Historic revisionism, however, made anything possible. Non-Serbs in the Yugoslav government as well as Serbian Communist party members from Montenegro had an interest in pursuing the myth in order to gain political benefits and power in the Yugoslav system.

Going beyond mere historical revisionism, Tito's territorial manipulations denied the Serbs power over Serb-populated areas of modern-day Croatia. What was previously known as the Croatia-Slavonia region, a centuries-old distribution of Croats in the west and Serbs in the east, and even recognized under the Austro-Hungarian empire, was merged and simply renamed the Republic of Croatia under Tito. The Serb-populated areas of Krajina, Slavonia, and Baranja where Serbs had lived since the 16th century and where they made up an ethnic majority, were not granted the status of independent republics or autonomous regions. Tito also enlarged Croatia by merging Dalmatia into the republic. Interestingly, the Tito regime never promoted the idea that Dalmatians were different from Croatians, even though historically, Dalmatia was inhabited by a large number of Serbs and Italian ethnic groups since the 14th century, when the region's cities were centers for a flourishing school of Serbian literature. At the time, the semi-independent city-state of Ragusa (modern-day Dubrovnik) was a major trade center and contributed to the economic strength and growth of the Serbian Empire.[32] Although a large number of Serbs inhabited Dalmatia, the region would never again be under Serbian control.

Tito's main task at hand was to divide and conquer the Serbs both politically and territorially in order to hold onto his power. In creating Yugoslavia's Republic of Bosnia-Hercegovina, he again denied Bosnian Serbs any territorial claims to a region in which he sought to curb Serbian influence. Serbs in Bosnia and Hercegovina—after trying to rid themselves of the Ottoman Turks since the 14th century, battling against Austro-Hungarian control of the region in the 19th and early 20th centuries, and struggling against German occupation and large-scale organized massacres by Croatian Ustashi aided by Bosnia's Muslims—now believed that they finally could live at peace in Bosnia-Hercegovina as part of a larger Yugoslavia. As the population of Muslims grew and the Serb presence decreased in Bosnia-Hercegovina, however, and as Bosnia's Muslims increasingly dominated local politics, Bosnian Serbs came to realize they had no land to call their own. Muslim attempts in 1992 to split the republic from Yugoslavia and dominate the region with their greater numbers would lay the basis for the 1990s war.

Macedonia was another republic created by the Tito regime whose territories throughout Yugoslav history neither were independent nor represented a separate ethnic group. The region changed hands between Serbs, Bulgarians, and later the Turkish empire. Its Christian Orthodox inhabitants were primarily ethnic Serbs, Bulgarians, and Greeks. The medieval Serbian empire left the greatest number of cultural monuments in the Macedonian region, including monasteries, fortresses, and ancient scripts. The Macedonian city of Skopje was the ancient Serbian capital during the reign of Czar Dusan. Tito, however, wanted to eliminate any possible Serbian claim or influence over Macedonian lands. Although the region was known as southern Serbia when Yugoslavia was created after World War I, Tito renamed the republic Macedonia, a name dating back to pre-Slavic settlement in the 7th century. To further promote the process of "de-Serbianization," Macedonians were encouraged to develop their own local dialect which differed from Serbian, and all Serbian Orthodox churches in Macedonia were separated from Serbia.[33]

Perhaps one of the most significant examples of Tito's ethnic manipulations was the political and territorial weakening of Serbs in Kosovo, their ancient cultural heartland. After tens of thousands of Kosovo Serbs were driven out during World War II and Albanian families moved in to take over Serbian homes and property, Tito intensified the problem by refusing to allow Serbs to return and reclaim their homes. Tito's reasons were primarily political. He hoped his pro-Albanian policies in Kosovo would appeal to the neighboring government of Enver Hoxha whom he was trying to befriend as part of a plan to form an alliance between Yugoslavia and Albania.[34] If Tito had allowed the Serbs to return to Kosovo, tens of thousands of Albanians would have to be sent back to impoverished Albania, a move that would have angered Hoxha and foiled the proposed alliance. By allowing these Albanians to stay in Kosovo, Tito brought about significant demographic changes. By 1946, Albanians comprised about 50 percent of the population of Kosovo, by 1961 they accounted for 67.2 percent, and by 1971, 73.7 percent of the population, while the number of Serbs continued to drop.[35]

By the 1970s, Tito began to appeal to Kosovo's growing Albanian population for internal political support. As one historian writes, "Tito went out of his way to help and develop the backward region of Kosovo, and came to be seen by Albanians there as an ally against the Serbs. Towards the end of the 1960s, the bulk of the federal budget for underdeveloped regions was transferred from Bosnia-Hercegovina and Macedonia to Kosovo, so that during the 1970s federal aid provided almost three-quarters of Kosovo's budget and investment."[36] In 1974, in a continuing effort to decentralize Serbian power, Tito split Serbia's northern and southern provinces into autonomous regions of Vojvodina and Kosovo. The move gave enormous political powers to Yugoslavia's Albanian minority in Kosovo. Albanians filled the ranks of Kosovo's newly created independent supreme court, while Kosovo's main university soon overflowed with books and professors from Albania, whose government never gave up its World War II aims to include Kosovo within a "Greater Albania." With promises of a better life in Kosovo, a surge of northern Albanians left their impoverished towns and crossed over high mountain ranges into Yugoslavia's southern region—a border far more difficult to control than the U.S.-Mexican border. Between 1961 and 1981, an estimated 150,000 to 200,000 Albanians were said to have illegally crossed into Kosovo.[37] Much of the unrest in the 1990s would stem from nationalist Albanian newcomers to Kosovo who ultimately launched a war to wrest the region away from Serbia.

RISING NATIONALISM IN POST-TITO YUGOSLAVIA

The death of Tito in 1980 brought a new era to Yugoslavia. The weak foundations on which Yugoslavia was created began to crumble. The country not only lost a leader who had kept a grip on the Serbs, but a skillful politician who was able to convince ethnic groups to sacrifice their own national identities for the good of the state as a whole. Although it was frequently argued in the 1990s that Serbian nationalism caused Yugoslavia' demise, nationalism always existed among all Yugoslav ethnic groups. One of its first overt manifestations came in the mid-1970s, when a powerful Croatian nationalist movement "Maspok" called for Croatia's separation from Yugoslavia. Although Tito halted the movement's political growth by ousting Maspok's Croatian supporters from government ranks, the Croatian population increasingly felt growing resentment toward the Serbs. As segments of the Croatian population began emphasizing their ethnic identity, so too did the Serbs and other ethnic groups.

Unlike in Croatia, a national revival was not fully felt in Serbia until after Tito's death in 1980. In 1986, with Tito gone, a group of intellectuals and writers prepared a memorandum published by the Serbian Academy of Arts and Sciences in Belgrade that called for a Serbian nationalist awakening. To the Serbs, the late 1980s seemed a time when they could finally express their cultural identity without risking reprisals from the Communist regime. Serbs living abroad were allowed to contribute funds to rebuild the St. Sava Shrine in Belgrade, while Serbian intellectuals, writers, and poets were allowed greater freedom of expression and an unprecedented ability to travel abroad. Even the son of the exiled Serbian monarch and heir to the throne, Prince Alexander, was free to visit Yugoslavia for the first time since his birth in London, England. The Serbian national revival was not viewed so benignly by some in Washington.

In the 1990s, Washington's Balkans experts and media pundits tended to blame the Serbian nationalist movement for the Yugoslav war, particularly in Bosnia. Washington failed to appreciate that other Yugoslav groups, including Albanians from Kosovo and Bosnian Muslims, had a far stronger nationalist movement than the Serbs. A significantly more powerful Islamic movement in Bosnia, for example, began decades before the Serbian nationalist movement. It would later become the basis of the Bosnian war, but it was little known to policymakers and opinionmakers in Washington during the 1990s. The Islamic revival began in the 1960s in Bosnia-Hercegovina when Yugoslavia's close association with the nonaligned nations movement promoted greater access to the local Muslim population. Tito granted various Arab groups free access to Yugoslavia from countries in the Middle East, which considered the Muslim population in Bosnia-Hercegovina ripe for Islamic influence and expansion. During the 1970s, Islamic groups were even allowed to recruit volunteers from Bosnia to join the Palestine Liberation Organization (PLO) and other organizations.[38] In the 1980s, there was a marked increase in the number of mosques throughout Bosnia-Hercegovina funded by these Middle Eastern countries.

Bosnia's growing Islamic movement gave prominence to Bosnian Muslim scholars and political activists who strictly followed Islamic doctrine. One of these individuals, Alija Izetbegovic, later became the leader of the Bosnian Muslim government. A congressional study in 1992 described Izetbegovic as "a fundamentalist Muslim and a member of the Fida'iyan-e Islam organization, who is committed to the establishment of Islamic rule wherever Muslims live," and who was close to the Iranian leadership of Ayatollah Khomeyni since the 1960s.[39] This fact made Washington's support for Izetbegovic all the more surprising. The U.S. media never publicized the more radical aspects of Izetbegovic's beliefs and friendships but instead attempted to portray the wartime Bosnian Muslim leadership as moderate. Izetbegovic's expressed beliefs, however, were far from moderate. In his book, *Islamic Declaration*, written in the 1970s, Izetbegovic said "Islam should be established in all areas of individuals' personal lives, in family and in society, by renewal of the Islamic religious thought and creating a uniform Muslim community from Morocco to Indonesia" and that "the Islamic movement should and must start taking over power as soon as it is morally and numerically strong enough to overthrow the existing non-Islamic government, as well as build a new Islamic government."[40] Words that would disturb Bosnia's Serbs, however, were ignored by Washington. Religious and ethnic feelings that increasingly polarized Yugoslav ethnic groups in the 1980s would never be fully understood by Washington's policymakers and opinionmakers who ascribed blame for the 1990s conflict solely to Serbian nationalism.

KOSOVO: A SIGN OF THINGS TO COME

By the late 1980s, Yugoslavia was undergoing serious economic difficulty—stagnant industrial production, rising unemployment, and skyrocketing inflation that rose as high as 2,000 percent in 1990. Without Tito's grip on Yugoslavia, a combination of rising ethnic nationalism and economic deterioration created an atmosphere of general dissatisfaction among all Yugoslav groups. These tensions would come to a boil in the late 1980s in Serbia's southern province of Kosovo, foreshadowing ethnic problems yet to come.

Notwithstanding significant governmental control and political and cul-

tural autonomy granted to Kosovo's Albanians by the 1974 Yugoslav constitution, an Albanian nationalist movement rose in the 1980s, encouraged
by neighboring Albania. As ideas of separating Kosovo from Serbia and
Yugoslavia grew, so did incidents of harassment and intimidation of Kosovo's Serbs as an increasing number of them began to leave the region.
The number of Serbs fell by 30,000 by 1981, with Albanians comprising
over 77 percent while Serbs made up about 15 percent of the region's
population.[41]

Although Kosovo's ethnic Albanian leaders contended that the Serbs
left solely for economic reasons, evidence clearly points to other causes
for the Serbian exodus. In 1982, the Serbian Orthodox Church in Kosovo
and Serbian civic groups documented numerous complaints of harassment,
intimidation, vandalism, destruction of Serbian monuments and churches,
and attacks on Serbian priests, nuns, and civilians by groups of nationalist
Albanians.[42] Although the exact number of cases of abuse against the
Serbs has varied, historians acknowledge that "proof exists that many
Serbs and Montenegrans who decided to leave Kosovo had experienced
intimidation, pressure, violence, and other severe abuses of their human
rights because of their ethnicity."[43] Some Albanians found guilty of attacking Serbs or damaging their property were given lenient sentences by
Albanian-dominated local courts. One such individual, Fljorim Hiseni,
who raped and beat a Serbian girl on May 26, 1988, was sentenced to only
30 days in jail by an Albanian judge.[44] With such incidents increasing
throughout the 1980s, between 1981 and 1988 another 30,000 Serbs were
estimated to have left Kosovo as the number of Serbs in the region fell
to little over 10 percent of the population by 1991.

Western human rights organizations appeared to be oblivious to what
was happening to the Serbs. In annual human rights reports by Amnesty
International, while cases of the Yugoslav government's imprisonment of
Albanian separatists were cited, cases of violence and intimidation against
the Serbs were completely ignored. Why did the West overlook Serbian
grievances in Kosovo? Because, as one historian observed, while hundreds
of thousands of Albanians who migrated from Kosovo were "good lin-
guists, persuasive talkers, and always ready to tell sympathetic journalists
an account of their suffering under the Serbian regime . . . foreign observers failed to notice that, although the Serbs were supposed to be the op-
pressors, they themselves were departing from Kosovo, complaining about
the destruction of property, the desecration of graves and many assaults
and rapes."[45] The plight of Serbs was noted almost solely by Serbian
priests and civic groups who complained that the Yugoslav government
was doing nothing to stop the desecration of ancient Serbian churches in
Kosovo and attacks on Serbs by Albanian separatists. In April 1987 over
60,000 Serbs from Kosovo rallied in the streets of Belgrade and presented
a signed a petition calling on the Yugoslav government to stop what they

called a "genocide of Serbs in Kosovo."[46] The Serbian public called for drastic measures to help Kosovo's Serbs. The energized mood coincided with the anniversary of a historic event in Serbian history that was about to spark a national reawakening.

1989 COMMEMORATION OF THE BATTLE OF KOSOVO

In spite of centuries of Turkish assaults on Serbs in Kosovo, the region remained the cradle of Serbian culture. To this day, over 75 percent of all Serbian cultural monuments are in Kosovo, including the historic 12th-century monastery of Studenica, the 13th-century monastery of Gracanica, and the 14th-century monastery of Samodrezi where Serbian Knez Lazar blessed his army prior to the famous battle against the Turks in 1389. In recognition of its historic significance, on June 28, 1989, the day known as Vidovdan (St. Vitus Day), almost 1 million Serbs gathered in Kosovo to commemorate six centuries since the Battle of Kosovo. The occasion was a time to recognize the past heroism and sacrifices of the Christian Orthodox Serbs who defended their lands against Ottoman Turk invasion. In an all too familiar repetition of history, in 1989 the Serbs believed they were facing a similar challenge in Kosovo, this time from ethnic Albanians. In his Vidovdan speech, Serbian President Slobodan Milosevic appealed to Serbian nationalism and sent a message of his intent to resist Albanian separatism.

Although Milosevic promised to protect Kosovo's Serbs, an observer at the time, the well-known author, Aleksa Djilas, noted that "Milosevic welcomed the Serbs' increased sense of insecurity for his own political gain."[47] With democratic opposition gaining popularity among the Serbian public, Kosovo certainly gave Slobodan Milosevic and his Socialist party an opportunity to extend their hold on power. Yet, in later years, those in Washington who criticized Milosevic's 1989 speech for rousing Serbian nationalism failed to distinguish between Milosevic's political interests and the genuine interests of the Serbian people. Regardless of politics, the Serbs had undeniable national interests in Kosovo—interests that Milosevic was willing to address. For this reason, Milosevic was embraced by Serbs, especially those from Kosovo, Krajina, and Bosnia-Hercegovina, where fears of their ethnic neighbors were the strongest. Even anti-Communist members of the Serbian intelligentsia and opposition leaders agreed that Serbia should reinstate control over Kosovo.

Milosevic's speech at Kosovo struck the right chord with the Serbian public who believed in the need to protect the rights of Serbs in Kosovo. Milosevic acted quickly on his promise. In 1989, the Serbian leadership and parliament revoked the autonomous status of Kosovo and Vojvodina. While Yugoslavia's Serbian population overwhelmingly approved the move, it greatly strained internal Yugoslav ethnic relations. On the one hand, Serbs saw Albanian separatism in Kosovo as a threat to Serbian culture and national interests; on the other hand, Croats and Slovenes saw it as a potential means for Serbia to expand its power. Far from being sympathetic to the Serbs, Croatia and Slovenia increasingly sided with ethnic Albanian separatists. The Serbian public was now convinced that Slovenia and Croatia were conspiring against them, thereby strengthening Milosevic's image as a strong leader and protector of Serbs.

As Serbia reinstated jurisdiction over Kosovo and intensified its police to counter a growing Albanian insurgency movement, pro-separatist Albanian groups in Kosovo became increasingly violent and influential with the local Albanian population. On July 2, 1990, the self-proclaimed parliament of Kosovo Albanians declared the province independent and under their control. Serbia responded by suspending the province's government and imposing direct federal control. Ethnic discontent would simmer in Kosovo and come to the forefront again in 1998, culminating into an international crisis in 1999. In the meantime, the Kosovo confrontation would move to the front lines of Washington.

TAKING THE KOSOVO BATTLE TO WASHINGTON

As Kosovo brewed with ethnic strife in the late 1980s, Washington became a political battle zone, and words became weapons. Leaders and supporters of the Kosovo Albanian separatist movement launched a public relations campaign among Washington's policymakers and opinionmakers to gain sympathy and political support for an independent Kosovo. Albanian activists talked of ultimately appending Kosovo in creating a "Greater Albania." The tight-knit community of 300,000 to 500,000 Albanians living in the United States strongly supported the movement. Their strategy in separating Kosovo from Serbia was twofold.

First, Albanians in the United States would purchase and supply covert arms to Albanians in Kosovo. These weapons were frequently confiscated by Yugoslav police who often discovered the illegal shipments concealed in Albanian homes in Kosovo. Fundraisers for weapons purchases would take place in Western countries, such as the United States, in support of a growing Albanian guerrilla group, later named the Kosovo Liberation Army (KLA). Although these fundraisers were originally kept secret, by 1998 Albanians in the United States were openly soliciting money for weapons to the KLA in the Albanian-American newspaper *Illyria*.[48]

The second and most important goal of Albanian supporters of an independent Kosovo in the United States was to gain favor among influential political leaders in Washington. A network of Albanian businessmen in the United States helped finance an Albanian lobby that focused on gaining congressional friends. A large concentration of wealthy Albanian constituents in New York explains why much of the congressional support for the Albanian cause throughout the 1990s came from this state. The original push on Congress came from former Democratic congressman from New York, Joseph DioGuardi, whose father was from Albania.[49] DioGuardi actively organized congressional hearings that featured emotional testimonies of Albanians from Kosovo against the Serbs and in support of Albanian claims for Kosovo's independence. In 1989, Dio-Guardi persuaded Senator Bob Dole to travel with him to Kosovo. Once in Kosovo, DioGuardi's connections with local Albanian activists provided Dole with a one-sided view of the region's problems. Nevertheless, Senator Dole's impressions of Kosovo would make a lasting impact on him in the years to come. The Dole–DioGuardi "fact-finding mission" to Kosovo provided an early example of how members of Congress could enter and leave a foreign country without gaining substantive, even-handed knowledge about the region.

The selective presentation of views to Washington's policymakers on what was happening in Yugoslavia was a trend that continued for two years and was carried over in the forthcoming conflicts in Croatia and Bosnia-Hercegovina. Without a substantive understanding of the intricacies of Yugoslavia's history and ethnic relations, Washington was not prepared to handle the oncoming Yugoslav turmoil. Certain Yugoslav groups would take advantage of Washington's naivete and befriend America's policymaking and opinionmaking elites in the hope of winning U.S. military support for their centuries-long territorial contentions in the Balkans.

NOTES

1. Susan L. Woodward, *Balkan Tragedy* (Washington, D.C.: The Brookings Institution, 1995), 3.

2. Samuel P. Huntington, *The Clash of Civilizations and the Remaking of World Order* (New York: Simon and Schuster, 1996), 20.

3. Jim Hoagland, "Nationalism: Not Necessarily a Negative," *Washington Post* (January 2, 1997): A17.

4. Warren Zimmermann, "The Last Ambassador: A Memoir on the Collapse of Yugoslavia," *Foreign Affairs* 74 (March 1995): 3.

5. Nevill Forbes and Arnold J. Toynbee, *The Balkans: A History of Bulgaria, Serbia, Greece, Rumania, Turkey* (Oxford: Oxford University Press, 1915), 79.

6. R. G. D. Laffan, *The Serbs: The Guardians of the Gate* (New York: Dorset Press, 1989), 3.

7. See Forbes and Toynbee, *The Balkans*, 87, 89; and Stephen Clissold, *A Short History of Yugoslavia: From Early Times to 1966* (London: Cambridge University Press, 1966), 98.

8. Clissold, *A Short History of Yugoslavia*, 73.

9. Forbes and Toynbee, *The Balkans*, 87.

10. Ibid., 88–89. See also *Larousse General Encyclopedia: Geography, History, Industry, and Technology*, Vol. III (Belgrade, Yugoslavia: Vuk Karadzic, 1967), 365 (translated from Serbo-Croatian by the author).

11. A. M. Rosenthal, "Why Only Bosnia?" *New York Times* (May 30, 1995): A17.

12. Raju G. C. Thomas and H. Richard Friedman (eds.), *The South Slav Conflict: History, Religion, Ethnicity, and Nationalism* (New York: Garland Publishing, 1996), 342.

13. Tens of thousands of Serbs were forced to flee from southern regions toward Zeta (modern-day Montenegro), while over 200,000 other Serbs fled to the Hungarian region of Vojvodina's three districts of Baranja, Backa, and Banat. See Clissold, *A Short History of Yugoslavia*, 74, 103.

14. Laffan, *The Serbs*, 22.

15. Ferdinand Schevill, *The Balkan Peninsula: From the Earliest Times to the Present Day* (New York: Harcourt, Brace, 1933), 164.

16. Clissold, *A Short History of Yugoslavia*, 63, 65.

17. Forbes and Toynbee, *The Balkans*, 107.

18. Clissold, *A Short History of Yugoslavia*, 64, 67, and Laffan, *The Serbs*, 22.

19. Clissold, *A Short History of Yugoslavia*, 30.

20. Ibid., 29, 30, 103, and Laffan, *The Serbs*, 27.

21. For statistics see Clissold, *A Short History of Yugoslavia*, 109 as well as Vladimir Grecic, *Serbian Exodus: Then and Now* (Belgrade, Yugoslavia: Institute for International Politics and Business, 1990), 27.

22. Laffan, *The Serbs*, 31, 33.

23. Clissold, *A Short History of Yugoslavia*, 71.

24. Ibid., 37, 40.

25. David Martin, *The Web of Disinformation: Churchill's Yugoslav Blunder* (Orlando, Fla.: Harcourt, Brace, Jovanovich, 1990), 20.

26. Edmond Paris, *Genocide in Satellite Croatia: 1941–1945* (Chicago: American Institute for Balkan Affairs, 1961), 132–33. See also Guy Dinmore, "Dinko Sakic: History's Shadow," *Financial Times*, London (July 7, 1998): 48.

27. Francis Trevelyan Miller, with a board of historical and military authorities, *History of World War II*, Armed Services Memorial Edition (Iowa Falls, Iowa: Riverside Book and Bible House, 1945), 280.

28. Paris, *Genocide in Satellite Croatia*, 3.

29. Ibid., 9, 283.

30. Thomas and Friedman, *The South Slav Conflict*, 342; see also Alex N. Dragnich and Slavko Todorovich, *The Saga of Kosovo: Focus on Serbian-Albanian Relations* (New York: Columbia University Press, 1984), 138.

31. Michael Mandelbaum, "The Global Politics of U.S. Intervention," *Newsday* (June 5, 1994): A37.

32. Forbes, and Toynbee, *The Balkans*, 90–91.

33. See Janice Broun, "Is Macedonia Next? The Chaos Moves South," *Commonweal* (August 14, 1992): 8.

34. Richard West, *Tito and the Rise and Fall of Yugoslavia* (New York: Carroll and Graf, 1994), 223.

35. Miranda Vickers, *Between Serb and Albanian: A History of Kosovo* (New York: Columbia University Press, 1998), 171.

36. West, *Tito and the Rise and Fall of Yugoslavia*, 342.

37. Dragnich and Todorovich, *The Saga of Kosovo*, 158, 164, 169.

38. "Iran's European Springboard?" Task Force on Terrorism & Unconventional Warfare, House Republican Research Committee, U.S. House of Representatives, Washington, D.C. (September 3, 1992), 3.

39. Ibid., 2.

40. Alija Izetbegovic, *Islamic Declaration* (Sarajevo: Mala Muslimanska Biblioteka, 1990), 3, 43 (translated from Serbo-Croatian by the author).

41. West, *Tito and the Rise and Fall of Yugoslavia*, 342. See also *Yugoslav Annual Statistics: 1990* (Belgrade, Yugoslavia: Savezni Zavod za Statistiku, 1990), 446.

42. Noel Malcolm, *Kosovo: A Short History* (New York: New York University Press, 1998), 331.

43. Vickers, *Between Serb and Albanian*, 220.

44. Tomislav Kresovic, Jelena Obradovic, Miodrag Danic, and Gorica Dokic, *Kosovo Dossier: Through Terrorism to Independence* (Belgrade, Yugoslavia: Bina Press, 1998), 24.

45. West, *Tito and the Rise and Fall of Yugoslavia*, 343.

46. Ibid.

47. Aleksa Djilas, "Profile of Slobodan Milosevic," *Foreign Affairs* 72, no. 3 (Summer 1993): 84.

48. Stacy Sullivan, "Albanian Americans Funding Rebels' Cause," *Washington Post* (May 26, 1998): A12.

49. Jonathan S. Landay, "Should Iran Help Fund War in Muslim Kosovo?" *Christian Science Monitor* (April 15, 1998): 9.

Chapter 3

Yugoslav Ethnic Strife Emerges Amid Post–Cold War Changes (1990 to 1992)

POST–COLD WAR INFLUENCES ON THE EVE OF THE YUGOSLAV CONFLICT

The Yugoslav conflict erupted on the eve of political and economic changes at the end of the Cold War that redefined America's role in world affairs and brought new perceptions of friends, enemies, territorial rights, and international law to Washington. With the disintegration of the Soviet Union and the Eastern Bloc, the balance of power shifted to the West. Devoid of the Soviet challenge, the U.S.-led NATO alliance redefined its objectives and was able to exert influence further eastward in Europe than ever before. This new geopolitical situation in Europe, combined with other factors—including Germany's ascent in 1990 as the most dominant economic and political power in European affairs and the changing nature of U.S. alliances with Islamic countries—defined U.S. actions in the Balkans during the Yugoslav conflict.

In 1989, when Gorbachev pledged that the Soviet Union would not interfere in Eastern Europe and that it would withdraw Soviet troops from the region, the Cold War came to an end. Monumental changes took place as the Soviets signed a landmark friendship treaty with West Germany, a 10-year trade agreement with the European Community, and an agreement to eliminate thousands of nuclear weapons. When Communist governments throughout Central and Eastern Europe began to fall, the destruction of the Cold War balance that existed in Europe since World War II brought in a new and unstable era. With the crumbling of the Soviet empire, an era of ethnic problems began. The new order was characterized not by the triumph of Western-styled democratic and multiethnic cultures, but by increasing national, cultural, and religious rivalries. The "Cold War division of humanity [was] over," Samuel P. Huntington observed, and "the more fundamental divisions of humanity in terms of ethnicity, religion, and civilizations remain and spawn new conflicts."[1]

It was feared that some of the potentially most dangerous ethnic clashes would occur in former Soviet states, with one of the first being a territorial dispute over Nagorno-Karabakh between Christian Armenians and Muslim Azerbajzanis. The fighting threatened to drag Turkey into the conflict on the side of the Azerbajzanis and posed a grave threat to peace and stability in Europe. Unexpectedly perhaps, it was not the fighting in former Soviet states but the oncoming conflict in Yugoslavia that would command international attention. The danger posed by ethnic divisions in former Soviet states, however, would influence the way the United States would view the Yugoslav breakup, insisting on new borders to reflect Yugoslav republics rather than ethnic distribution. The Soviet breakup would also give Germany and the United States greater say over events in Yugoslavia. When Yugoslavia began breaking up, Russia would be too weak from its own political, social, and economic problems to contribute political weight on behalf of its traditional allies, the Serbs.

Changes taking place in the geopolitical balance of European powers also influenced U.S. foreign policy on the Yugoslav conflict. In the Cold War years, the United States and Germany were bound by a common adversary, the Soviet Union. A special U.S.–German relationship was nurtured for decades characterized by German dependency on American military might, with American soldiers and NATO forces safeguarding Germany's border between East and West. The Soviet breakup in 1989, however, changed Germany's position in Europe and its relationship with the United States. Russian nuclear and conventional capabilities no longer posed the kind of threat to Germany that necessitated the U.S. military presence of Cold War years. The once-divided Germany now came together to form a single, powerful state, ready to lead the new post–Cold War European Union. Yugoslavia was to become the first test case for German political power. It was in pursuit of its new political influence that Germany ultimately became the first country to recognize Croatia in late 1991 and played a significant part in urging the United States to follow suit.

Changes in the NATO alliance in the post–Cold War era would play an important role in U.S. policy, especially in Bosnia. NATO was originally created in 1949 for the purpose of collective self-defense against Soviet expansionism. It was also an instrument of U.S. foreign policy that preserved American influence and presence in Europe. With the Soviet demise, however, NATO's 50-year role as guardian of Western Europe lost its *raison d'être*. NATO needed to redefine itself in order to survive. Observers such as the director of the Royal Institute of International

Affairs in London, Sir James Eberle, acknowledged that "unless [NATO] makes itself useful, it will wither and die."[2] NATO chose to adapt. The Persian Gulf crisis triggered by Iraq's invasion of Kuwait demonstrated to America's European allies that their security interests required U.S. protection well beyond the East–West arena. The Europeans, far more dependent on Persian Gulf oil than the United States, were reminded that a reliable flow of oil from the Gulf required joint political and military action that only U.S. leadership could provide. European needs for U.S. protection in the Middle East would open the way for an expanded U.S. military role on European matters as well—one that Washington felt could not be attained without a strong, U.S.-led NATO.

In anticipation of growing ethnic discord in Europe and the former Soviet Union, NATO's July 1990 London Declaration announced the organization's new commitment to counter "aggressions." While the traditional meaning of the term *aggression* under international law referred to a violation of a country's sovereign borders, NATO seemed ready to adopt a more flexible term. NATO's newly redefined commitment to fight against what it defined as "aggressions" brought the United States closer to becoming Europe's policeman. This evolving U.S. role was welcomed by Washington's interventionists who believed in active U.S. involvement in global affairs. The alternatives, for example, that the Conference on Security and Cooperation in Europe (CSCE) or the United Nations would take on NATO's new military role in Europe, challenged the existence of NATO, and hence, America's ability to lead. NATO would have to prove it was more effective in handling any crisis. Bosnia would become the greatest argument in favor of NATO military strength. In the coming years of war, the professed need to maintain a united multiethnic Bosnia, even if in word alone, justified a strong U.S. military presence in Europe that extended toward the eve of the 21st century. The goal of expanding America's presence in Europe supported by Washington's interventionists helped explain why U.S. foreign policy ultimately took on a military rather than a diplomatic role in the Yugoslav conflict.

Another important post–Cold War development that would influence how Washington viewed the Yugoslav conflict in years to come was the rising threat to U.S. interests in the Middle East, including terrorism and the disruption of the oil flow to world markets by anti-American regimes, demonstrated by Iraq's invasion of Kuwait. Washington recognized that by forging alliances with Muslim countries friendly to the United States, it could make valuable friends to counter such rogue regimes. It was for this reason that President Bush spent months actively lobbying Islamic countries in support of American use of force in the Persian Gulf. Turkey and Saudi Arabia would play a key role in providing military access necessary for U.S. attacks on Iraqi forces in January of 1991. Friendships established by Washington led the way for the creation of U.S. military bases in Saudi Arabia and profitable sales of U.S.-made weapons to the Saudis. In the six years following the Persian Gulf war, the United States led the world in arms sales, due largely to American success in winning contracts from countries in the Middle East.[3] The strengthening of America's alliances with Turkey and Saudi Arabia made Washington more amenable to the view of these two countries when the issue of Bosnia arose during the Yugoslav war.

SETTING THE STAGE: THE 1990 YUGOSLAV ELECTIONS

Against the backdrop of the crisis in the Persian Gulf and new geopolitical changes, by 1990 Yugoslavia was a tinderbox waiting to explode. The elections that were about to take place to determine the new leaders and parties in each of Yugoslavia's six republics marked the beginning of the most contentious period preceding Yugoslavia's civil war. Washington anticipated that Yugoslav elections would result in the fall of the country's Communist system, much as had happened throughout Eastern and Central Europe. As one of the more liberal Communist systems, it seemed likely that Yugoslavia would easily move toward a democratic, free-market economy. As Washington eagerly awaited newly fashioned converts from Communism, Yugoslavia's Slovenian and Croatian leaders sought to fit the part. Washington's aversion to Communism was understood by Croatian and Slovenian political leaders who courted Western nations with pro-democratic rhetoric. For many years, Slovenia's leading candidate, Milan Kucan, was a major force in Slovenia's Communist party. In the 1990 elections, however, he spoke of free-market reform and labeled himself a supporter of democracy—a move that made him popular in the West. The transformation of Croatia's candidate, Franjo Tudjman, was even more remarkable. Tudjman, a leading Communist general and Tito's former right-hand man, jumped on the bandwagon in 1990 and renounced his Communist past. By doing so, he gained friends, particularly in Germany and the United States, where he presented his government as "pro-Western" while labeling Serbia as "pro-Communist."

Although all Yugoslav republic-level candidates supported their own national interests, there was at least one major difference among them: Slovenian and Croatian candidates renounced their Communist past while the Serbian candidate, Slobodan Milosevic, did not. Milosevic was quickly denounced by Washington elites. Although U.S. diplomats in Yugoslavia and their counterparts in Washington viewed the 1990 Yugoslav elections through a prism of Communist versus non-Communist, to Yugoslavia's ethnic groups the elections were simply a struggle of national interests. In May 1990, the victory of Franjo Tudjman's Croatian Democratic Union

(HDZ) party in Croatia, with the same name as the Croatian party allied with Hitler, brought a new, right-wing agenda in favor of separating the republic from Yugoslavia. Slovenia's newly elected leader, Milan Kucan, proclaimed a similar aim. Kucan's nationalist rhetoric was followed by calls for Slovenia's progressive economy to abandon the burdens of Yugoslavia's nonproductive regions. In Serbia, although the population was anxious to remove Communists from power, the public appeared willing to ignore Milosevic's Communist ideology in exchange for his promise to protect Serbs in Kosovo.

The 1990 elections were particularly significant in the Republic of Bosnia-Hercegovina. Although the local government was envisioned as a system of power-sharing among Muslims, Serbs, and Croats, the 1990 elections demonstrated growing polarization among the three ethnic groups. The republic's main political parties were supported almost exclusively on an ethnic basis. Bosnia's Democratic Action party (SDA) was supported primarily by Muslims and was headed by Alija Izetbegovic, whose Islamic views were opposed by most Bosnian Serbs and Croats. Similarly, the Bosnian Croat HDZ party was a mirror image of the HDZ in Croatia. The June 1990 creation of the Serbian Democratic Party (SDS) in Sarajevo reflected a growing nationalist movement among Serbs in Bosnia that was partially a reaction to Bosnia's Islamic movement.

Within an ethnically competitive atmosphere, the first democratic, multiparty elections in Bosnia-Hercegovina took place on November 18, 1990. The resulting governing body was unlike that of any other Yugoslav republic. To provide a balance of power between Muslims, Serbs, and Croats, Bosnia would be governed by a seven-member presidency, two members representing each ethnic group and one representing other "Yugoslavs." Each voter in Bosnia-Hercegovina was allowed to choose two candidates from a list of names. The vast majority of voters chose candidates who represented their own ethnic group. At this time, Bosnia-Hercegovina was comprised of 43.7 percent Muslims, 31.3 percent Serbs, and 17.3 percent Croats. Concurrently, the Bosnian Muslim party (SAD) won 86 seats (or 42.6 percent), the Serbian Democratic party (SDS) won 72 seats (or 35.7 percent), while the Croatian Democratic Union (HDZ) won 44 seats (or 21.7 percent). As such, Bosnia's elected parliament roughly reflected the republic's ethnic makeup. The seven-member multiethnic presidency was chaired by a Muslim, Alija Izetbegovic, representing the largest ethnic group.

With new local governments in each of Yugoslavia's republics, there did not appear to be any outward reason why Yugoslavia should break up. Voters had participated in their first democratic elections—a step that theoretically should have led to greater confidence in the country's future. Nationalism, however, was gaining ground in all Yugoslav republics.

WASHINGTON IGNORES THE CROATIAN CRACKDOWN ON SERBS

Throughout 1990, as ethnic intolerance grew in the Yugoslav republic of Croatia between Serbs and Croats, the United States and Europe appeared preoccupied with other post–Cold War matters—the transformation of Cold War bureaucracies, disarmament, global economic integration, Iraq's invasion of Kuwait in August 1990, and unification of Germany in October 1990. It was precisely during this time, however, that ethnic tensions between Croats and Serbs were insufficiently monitored and poorly understood by the Washington establishment. Although an ethnic war was not likely to occur in Slovenia, which had a relatively homogeneous ethnic makeup and no territorial disputes, Croatia's attempts toward independence would be resisted by 600,000 Serbs, 12 percent of Croatia's population, who had a historic claim to Krajina-Slavonia regions, and constituted a majority of the population in those areas. This fact, combined with the election of Croatian leader Franjo Tudjman and the HDZ whose anti-Serb policies riled the Serbs, lay the groundwork for ethnic strife.

With the election of the HDZ party, Serbs in Croatia complained of systematic discrimination and harassment. Tension mounted in August 1990 when the Serbian minority in Croatia announced it would hold a referendum to decide whether to declare political autonomy from the republic. Croatian authorities pledged to prevent the referendum, arguing the vote would be illegal, since it would deny Croats living in the Serbian region the right to participate in an autonomous government. Yet the real cause of Croatia's concern was the knowledge that the Serbs, as a majority in the Krajina and Slavonia regions, would win the vote. Notably, while denying Krajina Serbs the right to vote without including the rest of Croatia, the Croatian government was perfectly content in later months to vote on the independence of Croatia without including all Yugoslav voters on the matter—in which case, the Serbian majority would have likely prevailed. This inconsistency was one that the West was willing to accept in Croatia and other regions of Yugoslavia.

On August 18, 1990, Croatian police in armored vehicles headed toward Serb-populated areas in an effort to stop Krajina Serbs from voting. Serbian villagers immediately blocked the roads into southwestern Croatia and prevented Croat police from halting the referendum. As clashes occurred between Serb villagers and Croat police, the Yugoslav National Army (JNA) moved into Knin, intercepted three Croatian helicopters, and forced them to return to their bases. On August 20, 1990, Krajina Serbs proceeded with the vote for autonomy. Problems in Croatia were just the beginning. A November 1990 U.S. intelligence report predicted that Yugoslavia would disintegrate by 1991.

In spite of warnings of an impending crisis in Yugoslavia, Washington's top policymakers made little effort to understand the situation. As the government of Croatia took increasingly hostile steps against its Serbian minority, Washington's policymakers as well as the U.S. media were silent. One of Croatia's moves that should have sounded an alarm in Washington was its December 22, 1990, adoption of a new constitution whose preamble declared Croatia to be solely "the nation state of the Croatian people."[4] It effectively revoked the political equality of the republic's Serbs and Croats and proclaimed the official language to be "Croatian," not "Serbo-Croatian," although the two were essentially the same. The official alphabet, formerly both in Latin Croatian script and Cyrillic Serbian script, now became only Latin—a reminder to local Serbs of a World War II fascist-era decree in Croatia forbidding the use of Cyrillic script in public and private life.[5] The new constitution reflected growing anti-Serbian policies in Croatia.

Ethnic Serbs were increasingly purged from Croatia's government and state-controlled media. No ethnic Serb held a senior rank in Croatia's government agencies. Serbian homes on the Adriatic coast were vandalized or outright confiscated. Anti-Serb rhetoric was regularly heard on television and radio by nationalist HDZ members, fanning fear among local Serbs who were reminded of HDZ massacres of Serbs in World War II. Historic revisionism was introduced in Croatia as Serbian writers and references to Serbian or Yugoslav history were removed from Croatian school books. Even names became a target. The Yugoslav Academy of Arts and Sciences in Croatia, created in 1866, was renamed the Croatian Academy of Arts and Sciences. A village existing under the name of *Srpska Kapela* (Serbian Chapel) since 1891 was renamed *Nova Kapela* (New Chapel) in August 1990.

For the Serbs, one of the most alarming characteristics of the Tudjman regime was the increasing number of policies and statements that rekindled the nightmare of Croatia's fascist past. In his early days in power, Tudjman openly exhibited disdain for Serbs by boasting that his wife was neither a Serb nor a Jew, and he also denied atrocities committed by Croatia's fascist Ustashi forces during World War II.[6] His attitude reflected trends in Croatia, described by the Simon Wiesenthal Center as a "society in denial."[7] Tudjman's anti-Semitic statements followed the kind of reasoning he expressed in his book, *The Wastelands of Historical Reality*, where he accused the Jews of purposely inflating the numbers of victims of the Holocaust and charged the Jews, rather than Croats, for running Jasenovac concentration camp. Jewish leaders were surprised that rather than distancing himself from Croatia's fascist past, Tudjman chose to seek inspiration from Croatia's brief period of independence during its World War II Ustasha regime.[8]

Tudjman reintroduced a number of Nazi-era symbols of Croatia's fascist past—embracing the checkered Croatian flag used by Croatian fascist forces, reintroducing the *kuna*, the former Ustasha currency, and giving amnesty to former Ustashi members living in exile. Within this atmosphere in Croatia, Jewish and Serbian cemeteries were desecrated.[9] In one of his first post-election trips abroad, Tudjman visited the president of Austria, Kurt Waldheim, with whom the United States had broken off relations because of Waldheim's participation in the Nazi extermination of Serbs and Jews in Bosnia-Hercegovina during World War II. Openly alluding to its fascist past, Croatia renamed some of its streets and squares, once named after Serbs or Yugoslav resistance fighters, to honor Croats who fought on behalf of the Ustashi and committed war crimes in World War II. As anti-Serb feeling and nationalism became more prevalent and open within Croatia's population, acts including the destruction of monuments to victims of World War II became commonplace.

Washington's elites and the U.S. media turned a blind eye to Croatia's discriminatory policies against the Serbs and to its growing neo-fascism. It was not until May of 1993 that a dozen members of Congress sent a formal letter to President Bill Clinton raising concerns about Tudjman's "authoritarian tendencies" and his efforts "to eliminate all independent print media . . . [and] intolerance toward different opinions and political opponents [who] died under mysterious circumstances."[10] Like many revelations about the Yugoslav war, however, this letter was written when Washington's views on who was right and who was wrong in the Balkans was already set and unlikely to change. The letter never made it into the news.

More surprising, perhaps, than Washington's disregard for Croatia's right-wing regime and intolerance toward Serbs was that the Serbs themselves drew no attention to the problem. Serbian authorities in Belgrade believed the problems between Serbs and Croats to be an internal, Yugoslav matter that required no outside interference. Unlike the government of Croatia, which made great efforts to convey its views to the foreign press, Belgrade made no serious attempt to appeal to Western governments and media. Similarly, while well-funded Croatian-American, Bosnian-Muslim, and Albanian groups established a strong presence in Washington, no significant, politically minded Serbian-American grassroots organization existed. It was not until September of 1992 that the Serbian American Affairs Office was formed in Washington, to provide information to the American public. By then, all the sound bites that were the staple of Washington's Bosnia rhetoric were entrenched among policymakers and the media alike.

ON THE EVE OF WAR: HISTORIC REVISIONISM BY THE U.S. PRESS

Between 1990 and 1991, the U.S. media could have helped policymakers by putting the growing Yugoslav crisis into context by examining the historic causes of ethnic discord. Articles that looked at Yugoslav history during this time, however, mirrored Croatian historical revisionism typified by Franjo Tudjman's diminution of the number of Serbs and Jews killed by Ustashi in World War II—as articulated in his book, *The Wastelands of Historical Reality*. The trend first became noticeable in Washington through commentaries by *Washington Post* correspondent Blaine Harden. In a June 8, 1991 article, Harden obscured Croatia's World War II crimes against Serbs and minimized Serbian deaths by stating that the "Serbs and Croats fought and killed each other by the hundreds of thousands during World War II." Such a description would be unthinkable if applied to the Holocaust—this would be tantamount to saying that Germans and Jews fought and killed each other during World War II. Again, in a June 11, 1991 article, Harden acknowledged "bloody massacres of Serbs by Croats during the war," but he quickly qualified the claim with the phrase "and [massacres] of Croats by Serbs afterward." Although revenge killings against Croats did occur, they were mostly against Croatian Ustashi soldiers, and the number paled in comparison to Serbian civilian deaths. More importantly, there were no *mass* killings of Croats by Serbs after World War II. In contrast, Serbs were massacred in over 30 camps, some of which were specifically designed for children, in which civilians, including 750,000 Serbs, 60,000 Jews, and 26,000 Gypsies were slaughtered. There were no similar camps where Croats were killed.

Once more, on June 23, 1991, Harden wrote a historical analysis demonstrating his tendency to downplay or draw attention from the mass extermination of Serbs during World War II: "of the 1.7 million Yugoslavs killed between 1941 and 1945," he stated, "an estimated 1 million died in ethnic fighting, much of it Croat against Serb." Here, Harden gives the impression that Serbs and Croats suffered equally by lumping together all deaths as Yugoslav. Finally, in an August 23, 1991, article, Harden again obscured Serbian deaths by stating that in World War II, Bosnia "was the site of ethnic massacres that killed hundreds of thousands" and that "it has been estimated that 60 percent of the 1 million Yugoslavs killed in fratricidal fighting during the war fell in this republic." The tendency among reporters not to distinguish Serbian victims, so as not to arouse sympathy, continued with the oncoming war in Bosnia-Hercegovina where reporters cited total numbers of "Bosnian refugees" or "Bosnians killed" in an effort to diminish the fact that many of these were Serbs. These historical revisions continued without substantial challenge from *Washington Post* editors.

The trend in understating Serbian deaths in World War II was evident among other reporters as well. On September 9, 1991, *Washington Post* reporter, Laura Silber, wrote that the Nazi-created fascist state of Croatia caused the deaths of only "tens of thousands of Serbs, Jews and Gypsies."[11] A July 24, 1991, *San Diego Tribune* reported that Serbs were slaughtered by Croatia's fascists "by the thousands," while other newspapers used the phrase "several thousand" to describe the largest mass extermination of Serbs in Yugoslav history. More recently, on March 10, 1996, the *Washington Post* stated that only 80,000, mostly Serbs and Jews, were killed in Jasenovac—a number frequently cited by Croatian sources. An April 15, 1998, *Los Angeles Times* article observed that "tens of thousands of prisoners were killed" in Jasenovac, conforming to the erroneously low numbers proclaimed by Tudjman. The media's revisionist tendencies were in clear disregard of the truth about the past and present government of Croatia. In response to Serbian accusations that the Tudjman government would repeat the genocidal excesses committed against Serbs in World War II, in a June 23, 1991, article, Harden dismissed the idea as "absurd"—a view articulated by other journalists as well. Serbian fears would be borne out in 1995, when virtually all Serbs were forcibly expelled from Croatia. By that time, no one in the media would step forward to say they were wrong.

CONFLICT OF INTERESTS: SERBS, CROATS, AND SLOVENES

It was clear that Slovenia and Croatia aimed to secede from Yugoslavia by force. Serbia, on the other hand, wanted Yugoslavia to remain intact within its internationally recognized borders. The Serbs had the most to lose from a Yugoslav breakup that would leave a total of up to 2 million Serbs split in Croatia and Bosnia-Hercegovina outside Serbia's protection. In a united Yugoslavia, Serbs were the largest ethnic group, whereas in the republics of Croatia and Bosnia–Hercegovina they constituted a minority. The Slovenes would have sole power in an independent Slovenia, the Croats would be an overwhelming majority in an independent Croatia, while the Muslims, though not a majority, would constitute the largest ethnic group in Bosnia-Hercegovina. The national interests of Yugoslav ethnic groups were clearly on a collision course.

Slovenia and Croatia initiated the breakup by trying to reorganize Yugoslavia into a loose confederation of republics—a move that would weaken the country's central government. Serbia and Montenegro wanted a continuation of a united Yugoslav federation. As early as June 1990, Milosevic warned that any moves by Slovenia and Croatia to divide the country would require a redrawing of borders so that the Serb-populated areas of Croatia and Bosnia-Hercegovina would remain in Yugoslavia. Undaunted by prospects of war, Slovenia held a referendum in December 1990 and voted for separation. Bosnia's Muslims appeared to be headed in the same direction. Two months after Bosnia's first multiparty elections, leading Muslim intellectuals held a press conference on January 7, 1991, during which they pledged to create an independent and sovereign Bosnia-Hercegovina. Significantly, the conference was held on the day of the Serbian Orthodox Christmas—timing that Serbs interpreted as a deliberate slap in the face. It was reminiscent of acts committed by World War II Ustashi fascists and their Muslim collaborators against Bosnian Serbs during Orthodox holidays. If Serbian "paranoia" was to be blamed for the oncoming ethnic Bosnian conflict, as was claimed in later years, leading Bosnian Muslim politicians and intellectuals certainly fanned Serbian fears.

As the likelihood of ethnic clashes appeared to be growing in Yugoslavia, Serbia's president Milosevic urged the increasingly disunited Yugoslav federal army to maintain the country's territorial integrity and act against Slovenian and Croatian separation. When Milosevic and senior Serbian generals of the Yugoslav National Army (JNA) asked the Yugoslav presidency to impose martial law, Slovenian and Croatian members opposed the move. The question now became, whose orders would the JNA obey? The answer came on March 19, 1991 when the army declared it would stay out of politics. The JNA's refusal to impose martial law and preserve Yugoslavia's borders was the beginning of the country's dismemberment. By now, Slovenia and Croatia were openly arming themselves. In March 1991, Slovenia's president Milan Kucan flew to Germany to seek loans from Chancellor Helmut Kohl, while Croatia began borrowing heavily from German banks. The Bosnian Muslim leader, Alija Izetbegovic, also set to work on procuring foreign aid for his own military forces. For instance, in his Spring 1991 trip to Libya, he secured a $50 million loan from Colonel Muammar Qaddafi.[12] As Slovenians, Croats, and Bosnian Muslims prepared for the coming conflict, Yugoslavia's federal government was leaderless and powerless to stop the country's breakup. Under Yugoslavia's system of a rotating presidency, Stipe Mesic, a Croat, was supposed to become the new Yugoslav president on May 15, 1991. Serbia and Montenegro blocked his appointment, knowing he would take steps to dismantle Yugoslavia.

On May 5, 1991, when clashes in Serb-populated towns and villages in Croatia left 12 police and 3 Serbs dead, the first refugees of the Yugoslav conflict left Croatia as more than 200 Serbian women and children fled to Serbia. In the coastal towns of Split and Sibenik, hotbeds of Croatian nationalism, Serbian-owned shops and homes were firebombed.[13] As violence escalated between the Krajina Serbs and Croatian paramilitary police, rather than toughening his position Milosevic suddenly backed down. In a June 1991 agreement, Milosevic accepted Slovenian and Croatian demands to allow Mesic to serve as head of state and transform Yugoslavia into a loose alliance of sovereign states. It was the start of what was to become the Serbian leader's unusual combination of nationalist rhetoric and tough policy, followed by concessions to his ethnic adversaries—a pattern that would continue in the years to come. After Serbia grudgingly

accepted Croatian and Slovenian demands, Yugoslavia fell apart the following month.

MEDIA COVERAGE OF DECLARATIONS OF INDEPENDENCE

Although official U.S. policy was to withhold recognition of Slovenia
and Croatia, the U.S. media was beginning to form its own policy in favor
of the two republics' independence. When Slovenia and Croatia formally
declared independence from Yugoslavia on June 25, 1991, media bias was
evident as the event was reported differently than the April 1991 declaration of independence by Krajina Serbs, only two months earlier. Most
major U.S. newspapers, including the *Washington Post, New York Times,
Chicago Tribune, Los Angeles Times*, and *Orange County Register*, to
name a few, used the words "rebel Serbs," "rebellious Serbs," or "Serb
rebels" to describe the creation of the Republic of Serbian Krajina (RSK).
In contrast, none of these newspapers used the word "rebel" to describe
declarations of independence by Slovenia and Croatia whose actions
clearly demonstrated "rebellious" behavior against a sovereign, internationally recognized state of Yugoslavia. To the contrary, *Los Angeles
Times* headlines read: "Croatia and Slovenia Declare Freedom from Yugoslavia." Major newspapers used phrases such as "Croatia and Slovenia
declared independence" or "proclaimed themselves independent and sovereign." Only the *San Francisco Chronicle* described Slovenia and Croatia
as Yugoslavia's "two rebel republics."[14]

At the time, the most influential newspapers on foreign affairs, the
Washington Post and *New York Times*, gave their support to the Slovenes
and Croats. On the day that Croatia and Slovenia declared independence,
the *New York Times* published an opinion column by Peter Millonig, a
registered foreign agent for the Republic of Slovenia, that praised Slovenia's decision to throw off Serbian "exploitation."[15] The *Washington Post*,
which had previously described Krajina Serbs as "rebel ethnic Serbs" that
proclaimed the "so-called Serbian Autonomous Region of Krajina," described the actions of Slovenia and Croatia in much more benign terms:
merely stating the two republics "formally declared themselves to be sovereign and independent."[16] Instead of labeling Croatian and Slovenian
governments as "rebels," the *Washington Post*'s approving tone legitimized the action by depicting Slovenia and Croatia as the "two richest
and most Westernized of Yugoslavia's republics" and echoing Croatian
and Slovenian propaganda by justifying their secession due to "fear by
Croatia and Slovenia that Serbia was dominating the federation and bleeding resources away from the more prosperous republics." Actions by Croatia and Slovenia were further legitimized through claims that "nationalist
passions in the federation peaked first in Serbia in 1988" and that "Serbia

emerged from the 1990 elections with the last hard-line communist government in Eastern Europe" and "a staunch opponent of country-wide free-market reforms that the governments of Croatia and Slovenia both have endorsed."[17] With these statements, the *Washington Post* sent a clear message to its readers as to who was right and who was wrong. It was clear that the war of words would be a difficult struggle for the Serbs.

THE DISINTEGRATION OF YUGOSLAVIA: SLOVENIA IS FIRST TO SPLIT AWAY

Early on, the United States was in favor of preserving Yugoslavia's sovereignty. During a June 1990 visit to Yugoslavia, U.S. Secretary of State James Baker advised against the country's breakup and urged Slovene President Milan Kucan to take no action without a negotiated agreement. Former U.S. ambassador to Yugoslavia Warren Zimmermann would later admit that "contrary to the general view, it was the Slovenes who started the war" since their independence declarations had "not been preceded by even the most token effort to negotiate," and by doing so, Slovenia "condemned the rest of Yugoslavia to war."[18]

After declaring independence, Slovenia abruptly closed off its borders and took over custom posts to Italy and Austria, thereby blocking Yugoslavia's economic gateway to the West and denying the country substantial financial revenue. Although both Slovenia and Croatia had declared independence, the Yugoslav army was reluctant to go into Croatia with full force—an act that would have likely resulted in large-scale fighting. In Serb-populated parts of Croatia where sporadic fighting was taking place, the JNA was trying to keep the peace but was accused of assisting the Serbs. By taking strong measures in Slovenia, however, the JNA believed that Croatia would be persuaded to drop its moves toward separation.

On June 27, 1991, JNA tanks, helicopters, and combat troops moved in to prevent Slovenia from breaking away. What followed, however, was the Yugoslav army's failure to implement clear military goals in Slovenia, which had the effect of encouraging, rather than discouraging, secession by other republics. When the Slovenes retaliated with powerful force, Yugoslav army generals were stunned. They did not plan for all-out war but merely to intimidate Slovenia into backing down. Slovenia's surprisingly forceful response called for stronger use of force by the JNA to keep Yugoslavia united—an unlikely scenario, considering that a leading Yugoslav military commander at the time was a Slovene. Lack of resolve by the Yugoslav army leadership rendered the operation ineffective.

When Yugoslav army troops overtook border posts around Slovenia, Slovenian troops barricaded themselves within the main city of Ljubljana and blocked major roads with hundreds of buses, gasoline tankers, and dump trucks. By now, most ethnic Slovenians had deserted the Yugoslav army and joined the ranks of their own local militia. The remaining Yugoslav army personnel stationed in Slovenian military bases were mostly 18- to 20-year-old Serbs, serving their compulsory two-year army terms. These recruits unexpectedly found themselves caught up in clashes with the Slovenes. The breakup of Yugoslavia was met with a feeling of disbelief. The level of confusion among young Serbs stationed in JNA barracks in Slovenia was so profound that one young Serb wounded by Slovenian fire was helped to the road by his army friend who asked for assistance from passing Slovenian motorists, oblivious to the fact that they were now supposedly enemies.

Slovenia's confrontation with the JNA ended quickly. In the end, Slovene fighters destroyed or seized 15 Yugoslav army tanks, took hostage hundreds of JNA soldiers, and shot down six JNA helicopters. Thirty-nine federal Yugoslav army soldiers, mostly Serbs, were killed in six days of fighting in Slovenia, while the Slovenes had fewer casualties.[19] After European representatives helped arrange a cease-fire between Slovenian and Yugoslav army troops, on July 18, 1991, the Yugoslav presidency announced that JNA troops were to be completely pulled out of Slovenia.

The Slovenian conflict was a fiasco. The JNA's half-hearted attempt to prevent Slovenian secession led to losses that could have otherwise been avoided if the JNA had done one of two things: (1) take all military measures to disarm Slovenian troops and preserve Yugoslav sovereignty, or (2) immediately dismantle JNA troops stationed in Slovenia and allow the republic to separate without force. Instead, the JNA's muddled approach was not only ineffective in curbing Slovenia's secession but a public relations failure as well. While the Yugoslav army avoided the international press, Slovenia welcomed foreign journalists to whom they presented an image of a tiny republic struggling for independence against the mighty Yugoslav Goliath. U.S. diplomats described Slovene actions during these weeks as "the most brilliant public relations coup in the history of Yugoslavia."[20]

CROATIA FOLLOWS SLOVENIA: CLASHES WITH SERBS

Serbs throughout Yugoslavia were shocked by Slovenia's unceremonious departure. They knew what Slovenia's actions foreshadowed. An invariable rule in the Balkans says that one group's triumph is another group's demise. Slovenia's demonstration that the Yugoslav army lacked motivation and guidance to enforce Yugoslavia's borders would encourage Croats to take the same forceful steps in separating from Yugoslavia. With few ethnic Serbs living in the republic and no historical Serbian claims to the region, Slovenia was able to separate from Yugoslavia relatively unblemished. Any moves to separate Croatia from Yugoslavia, however, would be a different matter, as Serbs in the Krajina-Slavonia region were ready to resist it.

During the 1990s, Washington's interventionists would become vocal supporters of U.S. intervention in the Balkans to protect the rights of ethnic groups, punish crimes, and right other wrongs, arguing that unless the United States stepped in to solve Yugoslav ethnic problems, America's image and credibility as a world leader would suffer, as would NATO's. Yet in 1991, these same Washington human rights interventionists completely ignored Croatia's treatment of Serbs—and America's image did not suffer for it. Numerous acts of violence were committed against Serbs in Croatia while Washington remained silent. A Serbian judge and community leader from Vukovar described to me in later years what life was like for the Serbs in Croatia during April and May of 1991. He recalled that there was at least one incident per day of a Serbian home being riddled with bullets or a drive-by shooting of Serbs. Serbs were frequently fired from work and replaced with Croats. In early May 1991, Radio Vukovar, an ethnically mixed radio station, was forcefully taken over by Croat police, and the station's Serbian personnel were replaced by Croatian employees. On May 1, 1991, in one of the first examples of an ethnic-related shooting in Croatia, a Croat killed a Serb for carrying the Yugoslav flag during a parade. The Croatian HDZ police were apparently targeting Serbs who supported or participated in political activities in Croatia.

The Serbian judge from Vukovar was arrested by Croatian police in May 1991 and subjected to interrogation and threats against his family, after which he decided to leave his home town. Before he left, he recalled that an increasing number of Serbs in Vukovar were killed. In mid-May 1991, a 25-year-old Serb, Miodrag Nadj, a member of the Serbian Democratic party, was killed in the outskirts of Vukovar in a drive-by shooting. On June 26 Jovan Jakoljevic was shot by an unidentified group of masked men who barged into his house. Others experienced Savo Damljanovic's fate: he left for his job at a hospital during the night shift and never returned. Mladen Mrkic, a Serbian farmer, also disappeared in the same period after going to work on his field. Another Serb, Vlado Skeledzija, was taken away from his house by Croat police and was never seen again.

What signified the Tudjman government's hostile intentions was the creation of a purely ethnic Croatian police force. All members of the police in Croatia were required to sign a statement taking an oath to protect the sovereignty and independence of the Republic of Croatia—even though it was still part of Yugoslavia and no country had yet recognized it. When the vast majority of Serbs serving in local Croatian police forces refused to sign the document, they were fired. A primarily Croatian police force remained. Disunity on security matters at Yugoslavia's federal level meant that there was no effective authority to enforce the country's laws. As police ranks in Croatia became a Croatian national force, random searches were initiated against Serbian homes and an increasing number of Serbs were arrested under the pretext that they were involved in activities against the Croatian republic. Emboldened by Croatian public support and growing intolerance toward the Serbs, the Tudjman government appeared to be doing everything in its power to intensify rather than diffuse tensions.

Croatia was clearly preparing for war. By mid-July 1991, Croatia's National Guard had already built up to about 35,000 men. Western observers suspected that Croatia's National Guard was about to launch a preemptive attack against Serb-populated villages.[21] Croatia's Defense Ministry spokesman Antun Abramovic acknowledged what he called "Croatia's success in smuggling weapons into the republic."[22] Croatia was quickly able to buy vast quantities of arms, including mortars, heavy machine guns, and armored cars bought from Western countries with money from Croats living abroad and loans from Germany. The Croatian government was also actively recruiting ethnic Croats from foreign countries to fight against the Serbs. Croatian volunteers arrived from Canada, the United States, Argentina, and Australia.[23] In mid-August, the U.S. Customs Service arrested four Croatians belonging to a radical, Chicago-based Croatian group, OTPOR, which illegally attempted to buy $12 million worth of U.S.-made weapons, including 100 Stinger antiaircraft missiles. Krajina Serbs were acutely aware of the impending threat of Croatia's National Guard and its 300,000-strong People's Defense forces. Serbs in Croatia's Krajina and Slavonia regions turned to Serbia for help. Small arms and other weapons were taken from local JNA depots in an effort to prevent the possibility of attack.

Serbia was determined not to repeat the JNA fiasco in Slovenia. Believing that non-Serbian elements of the army were obstacles to securing federal control over Yugoslavia's borders, former Slovenian and Croatian JNA members were now replaced by Serbian officers. General Blagoje Adzic was appointed as head of the Yugoslav army. The former Slovene commander of the 5th Yugoslav army regiment responsible for the territories of Croatia and Slovenia was replaced by a Serb general, Zivota Avramovic.[24] A mostly-Serb force was created to ensure that the JNA would be able to react swiftly to impending Croatian attacks against its Serbian population. The mood of the international community, however, was changing. Krajina Serb calls for self-determination and JNA claims to having the right to preserve Yugoslavia's unity and sovereignty would be undermined by Western views of self-determination that would enflame the Yugoslav conflict even more.

CHANGING VIEWS OF "SELF-DETERMINATION"

Some of the worst fighting between Serbs and Croats began in the week of July 25, 1991, in the town of Glina. European diplomats from Great

Britain and France suggested that a redrawing of borders in Serbia, Croatia, and Bosnia-Hercegovina was an immediate way of avoiding future bloodshed.[25] This was also what the Serbs were calling for. A redrawing of borders did not occur however, as Germany stood staunchly behind Croatian government claims, while Washington increasingly favored German over British and French perspectives on the matter. Profound changes would arise in how the United States and Western Europe were about to recognize emerging states in the post–Cold War era. Under international law, what would have been a clear case of a sovereign state exerting its authority over an internal dispute, the Yugoslav army's actions in Slovenia and Croatia were increasingly criticized in Western capitals. Although Washington initially supported Yugoslav sovereignty, in the months to come, with Russia's inability to support its traditional Serbian allies and without an effective public relations campaign to sway the West, Serbian attempts to keep Yugoslavia united gave way to separatism.

Politics, rather than traditional international law, would determine which Yugoslav ethnic group was allowed the right of self-determination. Washington viewed the Yugoslav breakup with one eye on the former Soviet states. U.S. policymakers did not want Yugoslavia to set a precedent for a Soviet breakup along ethnic lines—a move that would spark violent conflicts in a region filled with nuclear weapons. At the start of the post–Cold War period, out of an estimated 125 possible ethnic or minority disputes on Soviet territory, 25 of them were potentially violent. With Armenia and Azerbaijan already at war, similar ethnic disputes on former Soviet soil could destabilize Europe and jeopardize U.S. interests in the region. Extending the problem on a global scale, with over 3,500 groups around the world describing themselves as a separate national entity, and with only about 180 of them recognized as nation-states, the potential for ethnic conflict in the post–Cold War era was likely to become a significant threat to global stability. The United States, as a leader and protector of Europe, would need to set an example in Yugoslavia. No matter how Serbs were treated in Croatia, Washington would ultimately tolerate only a limited breakup. The same principle would be applied in Bosnia-Hercegovina.

The Serbs would be the clear losers in this scenario. Yugoslavia's division along the borders of internal republics would split the Serbian people into three different countries—Yugoslavia, which included Serbia and Montenegro, Croatia, and Bosnia. It would place over 600,000 Krajina Serbs under a hostile Croatian government and close to 2 million Bosnian Serbs under the control of a Muslim-dominated leadership in Bosnia-Hercegovina.

GERMANY AND THE VATICAN STAND BY CROATIA

To gain support for Croatia's independence, the Tudjman government solicited help from old religious and political allies for support. The Croats were in a far better position than the Serbs in seeking allies to back their cause. The Serbs looked to their traditional allies, the Russians, who were not in a powerful position to influence Western policy. Russia's military structures were weak, and its economy was increasingly dependent on U.S. economic aid and German investments. On the other hand, Germany, which viewed Croatia to be within its traditional zone of influence, had a significant say in post–Cold War EC policy. Samuel P. Huntington attributes the German and Vatican's unusual display of diplomatic muscle and support on behalf of Croatia as part of a larger, global trend based on religious alliances. This explains why Western Christian civilizations rallied behind the "coreligionists" of Croatia's Catholic regime early in the conflict, and why Europe and the United States would eventually follow the German lead.[26]

As Croatia sought to internationalize the Yugoslav problem, global trends were moving in their favor. Germany was eager to demonstrate its political prowess in Europe—a trend that suited Croatian aims. Increasing German support for Croatia and German influence over EC policy made the Serbs skeptical of the EC's neutral role as an arbiter in the crisis. Many EC actions seemed to confirm the Serbs' suspicions. In early August 1991, when Western European-brokered talks on defusing the Yugoslav crisis were about to begin, Croatian special forces launched a secret and brutal raid on Knin, headquarters of the Krajina Serb government. During the raid, Croatian commandos killed 60 Serbian resistance fighters. The next day, EC's representative, Dutch foreign minister Hans van den Broek, requested a meeting of Yugoslav contending parties. No reprimands were issued against the Croatian attack. Milosevic was furious and refused to attend EC negotiations. Far from sympathizing with the Serbs, however, the Dutch foreign minister blamed Milosevic for scuttling the talks. The next day, Germany's foreign minister, Hans-Dietrich Genscher, threatened Serbia with economic sanctions. Again, no reprimand was issued against Croatia for its role in the dispute. Germany's close ally, Austria, put additional pressure on Serbia by announcing it was considering recognizing Croatia.

The Vatican was also making its views clear on the issue. In an August 17, 1991 Mass in the Hungarian city of Pecs, less than 20 miles from Croatia, Pope John Paul II stated that Croatian actions to break away from Yugoslavia were "legitimate aspirations."[27] The Pope's comments were eagerly welcomed by Cardinal Franjo Kuharac of Zagreb and thousands of Croatians who cheered and waved Croatian national flags throughout the Pope's speech. Although support from Croatia's traditional allies, Germany and the Vatican, may have been expected, surprisingly strong support that would come from Washington was a result of Croatia's efforts on the public relations front.

CROATIA WINNING THE PUBLIC RELATIONS WAR

In Washington, the Tudjman government turned Yugoslavia's internal ethnic struggle into an image of war of democracy versus communism, good versus evil. The U.S. media quickly picked up the spin circulated by Croatia in its official rhetoric. With Western media based in Croatia, the efforts of the Croatian government to appeal to foreign journalists would ultimately pay off. The HDZ party exerted enormous efforts to boost its information-generating industry. The size of Croatia's Ministry of Information tripled in comparison to that of Serbia, while HDZ strengthened its influence over Croatian television, radio, and print media. Press releases promoting official government propaganda were readily available to foreign correspondents in Zagreb. Reporters based in Zagreb accepted Croatian government reports and avoided traveling to Serb-populated areas of Krajina or Slavonia where the conflict was taking place. Reporters were often accompanied by Croatian drivers and translators provided by the government who were in a position to influence reporters' views of the situation, setting a precedent for similar coverage of the Bosnian war in years to follow.

The Croatian government lobbied intensely for support in its push toward independence. In fighting a war of words in Washington, Croatia needed effective communicators. Early in the conflict, Tudjman recognized the value of Croatian nationals in the United States. He offered the former governor of Minnesota, Rudy Perpich, an ethnic Croat, the position of foreign minister of Croatia at a time when Croatia was still a Yugoslav republic. Perpich told Tudjman he declined the position "with regret and a heavy heart" after the U.S. State Department said the job would jeopardize his U.S. citizenship.[28] Other foreign nationals, however, were welcomed by Tudjman. An ethnic Croat from Canada, Ivica Mudrinic, became Tudjman's trusted adviser and was later appointed Croatia's minister of communications to present the "right" message to the West.[29]

Tudjman sought other professional help in his public relations campaign against the Serbs. In the Summer of 1991, Croatia hired a Washington-based public relations firm, Ruder Finn, Inc., whose services included "developing and implementing strategy and tactics for [the government of Croatia in] communicating with members of the U.S. House of Representatives and Senate; officials of the Executive Branch of the U.S. government including those in the State Department, National Security Councils and other relevant departments and agencies of the U.S. government; and U.S. and international news media."[30] A two-pronged public relations strategy was launched in Washington. Based on what Ruder Finn reported to the U.S. Justice Department, the first image to be conveyed in Washington was that the Tudjman regime was a "freely elected democratic government" and Serbia was an instigator of a "military intervention on

Croatian sovereign territory, to oppose Croatia's move toward democracy."[31]

Serbia's public relations effort, on the other hand, was nonexistent. The Milosevic government sought no public relations firm to help deliver its political message in Washington. While Tudjman nurtured relations with Croatian immigrants in the United States, Canada, Australia, and elsewhere, Milosevic's deep mistrust of the mostly anti-Communist Serbian diaspora formed a permanent divide between Serbia and its nationals abroad. Another obstacle in the public relations battle was the Serbian government's open disdain for the Western press. Serbian officials failed to see the benefits of scheduling regular interviews and press conferences, and they rarely issued press releases in English. Although the Serbian Ministry of Information was created in 1991 to monitor and document anti-Serb practices in Croatia, its publications were seldom read by the U.S. press and they were disregarded by the State Department. The mechanism of disseminating important facts and figures about Yugoslavia required public relations professionals in Washington, which Serbia did not have.

Deteriorating relations with U.S. diplomats were also particularly damaging to the Serbs in the 1990–1991 period. President Milosevic refused to meet with U.S. ambassador Zimmermann for an entire year in the early days of the crisis. Zimmermann, who held a key position in Belgrade as Washington's eyes and ears on Yugoslavia, developed a particular disdain for Milosevic whom he called "an ambitious and ruthless communist party official, that clawed his way to power."[32] Zimmermann started making friends elsewhere—notably, with the shadow leader of pro-separatist Albanians from Kosovo, Ibrahim Rugova, whose views would henceforth seep into Washington. Although Zimmermann described Croatia's Franjo Tudjman as a man "obsessed by nationalism" and personally witnessed Tudjman's government officials "revile Serbs in the most racist terms," Zimmermann appeared to dislike Milosevic more than Tudjman. "His [Tudjman's] saving grace," according to Zimmermann, "is that he really wants to be a Western statesman and listens to Western expressions of concern and criticism and often does something about them." This view of Tudjman arose largely because the Croatian leader was able to mask his true ambitions.

Even when Tudjman was honest about his territorial aims, Washington's view of the Croat leader was none the worse. When Tudjman talked of Izetbegovic and the Muslims as "dangerous fundamentalists" in an effort to convince Zimmermann that the United States should support Croatia's territorial designs on Bosnia, Zimmermann asked, "how can you expect the West to help you get back the parts of Croatia taken by the Serbs when you yourself are advancing naked and unsupported claims on a neighboring republic?" Although Tudjman did not respond, the answer was clear. Tudjman would continue to maintain the appearance of being cooperative with Washington, while secretly working on achieving his aims in Bosnia-Hercegovina.

AS FIGHTING INTENSIFIES, MEDIA BIAS GROWS

The image presented by the Croatian government was that of a nation besieged by the more powerful, Serb-dominated Yugoslav army. All of the Serbs's ethnic contenders in Yugoslavia described Serbs as Communists in their effort to make friends in the West, who in turn would help them achieve independence. When a coup was averted in Russia in August 1991, Slovenia's president Kucan, Croatia's president Tudjman, and Bosnian Muslim leader, Alija Izetbegovic, claimed that Russia's coup would give a pretext for "Marxist leaders in Serbia" and the Yugoslav federal army to move against their governments.[33] Yet the growing crisis in Yugoslavia was a dispute over ethnic interests, not between clashing political philosophies. Nevertheless, Washington's mind-set was already showing signs of siding with the Serbs's contenders.

The evolving anti-Serb bias in the media was evident through a number of subtle reporting techniques. Cases of violence or attacks by Croatian police against Serbs were often ignored or reported at a later date when the issue had lost its immediate impact. When Croatian forces attacked the Serb-populated town of Pakrac in mid-August 1991, it was not until a week later that the *Washington Post* reported the incident inconsequentially toward the end of an article that briefly mentioned that reporters visiting Pakrac "said troops from the Croatian Interior Ministry invaded the town of 10,000, evacuated it of all but one Croat man and leveled many buildings."[34] The article did not emphasize that Croatian attacks resulted in Serbian casualties, Serbian refugees, and destruction of Serbian homes. Several techniques were at work here: downplaying the facts in choice of words, and placing of the facts sympathetic to Serbs at the end of the article.

By choice of descriptive words, media coverage of clashes in Krajina took on an increasingly negative tone against the Serbs. When an ethnic Croat shot dead a Serbian neighbor, an event that triggered violence on May 2, 1991 in the Serb-populated town of Borovo, the *New York Times* was unsympathetic to the Serbs, using phrases such as "Croatian police was capable of crushing the Serbian insurgents," and the region was "controlled by the Serb militants," organized by "Serbian extremists," and "occupied" by the Yugoslav army.[35] The article left an impression that Croatia was a sovereign country—even though the events were taking place one full year before the United States even recognized Croatia.

U.S. media coverage helped obscure wrongdoings and discriminatory policies by the government of Croatia and its forces against local Serbs.

More remarkably, the U.S. press ignored Croatia's anti-Jewish activities as well. Relevant facts of what was taking place in the developing Yugoslav conflict were more readily seen in the European press. An entire article of the London *Independent* printed in October 21, 1991, was devoted to reasons for Jewish anxieties in Croatia. It pointed out that leaders of Croatia's Jewish community were drawing parallels between Croatia's World War II Nazi-era government and Tudjman's strongly nationalist regime. It also reported that a Jewish community center and cemetery were damaged by explosives in August of 1991 in the Croatian capital, Zagreb, while local Jews in the city were subjected to death threats and other forms of intimidation. In stark contrast, an August 20, 1991, *Washington Post* article only briefly mentioned the explosion at the Jewish center and cemetery, and it immediately supplied the Croat government's explanation by quoting one of their officials who said the blast was an attempt by Serb "terrorists" to sabotage Jewish-Croatian relations.

The media's increasing use of the term *occupied* was also misleading. As early as January 6, 1992—months before the United States recognized any new states in Yugoslavia—the *Chicago Tribune* referred to the Serbian Krajina regions that were inhabited for hundreds of years by generations of ethnic Serbs as "Serb-occupied regions of Croatia." The expression, eliciting images of an outside occupation, was increasingly used by the U.S. media only in reference to Serb-controlled areas—both in Croatia and later in Bosnia-Hercegovina. The image of Serbian "occupation" went hand in hand with accusations of Serbs committing "aggression"—another misnomer implying a cross-border invasion rather than civil war. Although the Serbian independence movement in Croatia originated as a local popular uprising against discriminatory policies of the Tudjman regime, the Croatian government continuously pointed to the growth of volunteers in Serbia willing to fight on behalf of the Krajina Serbs as evidence of an "outside aggression." Croatia's ability to sell the idea that Milosevic was "Serbia's Communist strongman" made the image of an outside Serbian aggression plausible to Washington elites.

Accusations of "Serbian aggression" were first launched by Croatian officials, but came to be accepted and repeated by the U.S. press far earlier than the U.S. State Department began to use the term. Secretary of State Baker did not first use the expression, until September 1991, whereas major U.S. newspapers began using it early in the year—although only as a direct quote from Croat officials or in op-eds written in support of the Croat cause. On February 7, 1991, the *Los Angeles Times* quoted Croatia's defense minister, Martin Spegelj, describing the Yugoslav army's moves in Croatia as an "aggression." An August 6, 1991, *Los Angeles Times* article again quoted Tudjman as saying Croatia would "resist aggression and occupation." And an August 23, 1991 *New York Times* article quoted Tudjman as saying Croatia considered "Yugoslavia's presidency directly responsible for the aggression on Croatia's territory." The term first appeared in the *Washington Post* on June 26, 1991, quoting Tudjman's accusations against "continuing threats and [Serbian] aggression." It also appeared in a report that cited Slovenia's leadership accusing the Yugoslav federal army of "ruthless aggression," as well as an accusation by Ante Markovic, a Croat and Yugoslavia's prime minister, who said Serbia was committing an "aggression of one republic on another."[36] Other quotes from Croatian sources followed, such as Stipe Mesic's call on the United Nations "to stop Serbia's war of aggression on Croatia" in September 1991.[37] A spokesman for Croatian President Franjo Tudjman was also quoted as saying the Yugoslav army was committing "total *aggression* on Croatia."[38] Use of the phrase by the Serbs's political contenders included Bosnian Muslim leader, Alija Izetbegovic, who was quoted in the *Washington Post* as describing what he called "Serbian aggression"[39] in Croatia.

These accusations, initially made by the Serbs's political adversaries in Yugoslavia, would slowly become part of Washington's media jargon and assumptions about the conflict. By late Summer of 1991, foreign correspondents covering events in Yugoslavia began to make the leap from merely reporting Croat, Slovene, and Bosnian Muslim accusations against Serbs to reiterating the claims as fact. In a first direct reference to Serbian *aggression* in the *Washington Post*, Blaine Harden wrote in an August 7, 1991, article that "Serbian guerrillas [in Croatia] have been the primary aggressor in the war."

The often repeated Croatian accusations of Serbian *aggression* were accompanied by claims that the Serbs were trying to form a Greater Serbia by uniting Serb-populated regions of Croatia. Some of the first references to Greater Serbia in major U.S. newspapers appeared as early as August and September of 1991 in the *Washington Post, New York Times, Los Angeles Times, Chicago Tribune*, and *San Francisco Chronicle*. The headline of a September 8, 1991, editorial by William Pfaff of the *Los Angeles Times* read: "Aggression must not be rewarded in Yugoslav crisis." In the piece, Pfaff repeated the often-claimed Croatian version of events that "the Yugoslav crisis is the product, first, of Serbia's attempt to create a 'Greater Serbia' by annexing those portions of modern Croatia populated by a Serbian minority." Opinion editorials of other newspapers followed along similar lines. Media coverage of the Yugoslav crisis increasingly resembled the kinds of trends described by Edward S. Herman and Noam Chomsky, who observed that "propaganda themes quickly become established as true even without real evidence," when "articles are written in an assured and convincing style, are subject to no criticisms or alternative interpretations in the mass media, and command support by authority figures."[40]

Although the U.S. press was becoming more sympathetic to the Croats, the reality of the situation was not one-sided: both sides were fighting, and both sides had casualties and civilian refugees. The U.S. press was aware of this reality but chose to ignore or downplay it. Only in the last paragraphs of an August 27, 1991, *Washington Post* article was it reported that by the end of August 1991, over 300 Serbs and Croats had been killed in the fighting, more than 50,000 Serbs had fled to Serbia from Croatia's Serb-populated Slavonia and Krajina regions, while 25,000 Croats had fled to the Republic of Hungary from areas controlled by Krajina Serbs. At that time, Serbian refugees outnumbered Croat refugees. Although the conflict in Croatia took its toll on both Serb and Croat civilians, by October 1991 the International Committee of the Red Cross reported that an estimated 250,000 Serb and Croat refugees had fled the fighting, of which roughly 105,000 Serbian refugees were in Serbia.[41] In spite of this reality, the media needed and wanted to take sides in covering the Yugoslav conflict. This was most clearly demonstrated in the early coverage by the *Washington Post*—the newspaper with significant influence on U.S. policymakers and that is in turn influenced by U.S. policy. In its earlier articles on Yugoslavia, in the first half of 1991, before the conflict erupted, the *Washington Post* was more balanced in depicting the causes of Yugoslavia's problems. At this time, *Washington Post* articles depicted rising nationalism as a problem among all Yugoslav ethnic groups, and roughly equal references were made to both Serbian and Croatian leadership as "nationalist." The newspaper's use of the term, however, changed significantly in the second half of 1991 when the conflict was taking place. At that time, references to Serbian nationalism were twice those made with regard to Croatia. Events taking place in Yugoslavia itself gave no cause for this change. Nationalism was still running rampant everywhere in Yugoslavia, and it certainly did not decrease in Croatia. If anything, Croatian nationalism was on the rise at an alarming rate during the second half of 1991.

The growing bias at the *Washington Post* was most evident in its choice of photographs. The pictures accompanying *Washington Post* articles in the second half of 1991, during the first six months of conflict in Croatia, were more sympathetic to Croats and hostile to Serbs. From June to December 1991, photograph captions described Serbs "in army vehicles," Serbian "armored personnel carriers smashing through roadblocks," Serbs in "army tanks," "Serbian guerrillas" pictured with machine guns, or soldiers said to be "stalking" or participating in an "assault." In contrast, in describing Croatian forces, the *Washington Post*'s captions presented sympathetic images of Croatian soldiers "writing letters home," "comforting a woman," "taking cover" from Serbs, or participating in "defensive positions."

A similar bias was evident in the portrayal of refugees, civilians, and casualties in *Washington Post* photographs during the mid- to late-1991 period of war in Croatia. No photographs showed either Serbian civilians or refugees fleeing from Croatian attacks, or Serbs mourning for those killed as a result of attacks by Croat forces. Although one *Post* article printed in August 27, 1991, mentioned that "more than 50,000 Serbs are reported to have fled into Serbia from Croatia," there was no photograph of Serbian refugees. Instead, the accompanying photograph caption read: "Yugoslav army tanks [firing] at Croatian defensive positions during heavy fighting near the Danube river city of Vukovar"—an image that was hardly meant to draw sympathy for Serbian refugees. On October 1, 1991, when the *Washington Post* printed an article on "35 Federal soldiers killed in a Croatian attack," there were no accompanying sympathetic photographs of Serbian mourners, but rather a picture of elated "Croatian soldiers [riding] into Bjelovar on a tank captured from Federal Yugoslav troops." In contrast, during the same months, the *Washington Post* printed photographs of "mothers demonstrating in Croatia," "mourners in Croatia" gathering around coffins, a mother and son mourning the death of a Croatian policeman, a Croatian woman "praying for families who abandoned homes in a Croatian town," a "mother carrying a baby" in Zagreb, "an elderly Croatian woman" described as a victim of ethnic nationalism, and "refugees from Croatian city of Vukovar." The very existence of "displaced Serbs" was only briefly mentioned in a November 25, 1991 headline, but the caption of the accompanying photograph showed Croats leaving Osijek—no photos of Serbian refugees were shown.

U.S. media bias in choice of photographs and newspaper articles would grow as the war continued and skyrocket with the coming war in Bosnia-Hercegovina. Time would show that media-generated images of the coming conflict in Bosnia would significantly affect Washington's decision makers. The media's efforts to portray a one-sided version of events would ultimately lead to Washington's taking sides in the Croatian and upcoming Bosnian conflict.

NOTES

1. Samuel P. Huntington, *The Clash of Civilizations and the Remaking of World Order* (New York: Simon and Schuster, 1996), 67, 76.

2. Alan Ridins, "NATO Struggling to Redefine Itself," *New York Times* (September 24, 1990): 5.

3. See Philip Shenon, "U.S. Increases Its Lead in World Market for Weapons," *New York Times* (August 17, 1996).

4. "Inter-Ethnic Conflicts and War in Former Yugoslavia," *Institute for European Studies* (Belgrade, Yugoslavia, July 1992): 7.

5. Edmond Paris, *Genocide in Satellite Croatia: 1941–1945* (Chicago: American Institute for Balkan Affairs, 1961), 62.

6. Francis Ofner, "Antisemitism in Yugoslavia," *Jerusalem Post* (April 14, 1992): Opinion Section.

7. Guy Dinmore, "Dinko Sakic: History's Shadow," *Financial Times* (London, July 7, 1998): 3.

8. Efraim Zuroff, "Croatia's Trial," *Jerusalem Post* (June 2, 1998): 10.

9. Guy Dinmore, "Croatia Confronts Its Past as War Crimes Suspect Returns," *Washington Post* (June 19, 1998): A35.

10. Representatives Traficant, Hefley, Stokes, Fazio, Gutterez, Henry, Dellums, Berman, Towns, Gilman, Frost, and Schroeder to The Honorable Bill Clinton, May 13, 1993 (Washington, D.C).

11. Laura Silber, "Guerrillas Press Attacks on East Croatian Towns; Macedonian Republic Votes on Secession," *Washington Post* (September 9, 1991): A18.

12. Blaine Harden, "Yugoslav Army Takes Equivocal Stand; Military Vows to Shun Politics But Warns of Action in Civil Strife," *Washington Post* (March 20, 1991): A25.

13. Michael Montgomery, "Troops Ordered to Halt Yugoslav Strife," *The Daily Telegraph* (May 6, 1991): 1.

14. Dusko Doder, "Slovenia and Croatia Declare Independence from Yugoslavia 2 Parliaments Vote Ahead of Schedule," *San Francisco Chronicle* (June 26, 1991): A1.

15. Peter Millonig, "After 7 Centuries, Slovenia Is Free,"*New York Times* (June 26, 1991): 23.

16. Jim Fish, "Croatian Area Claims Merger with Serbia; Proclamation by Yugoslav Rebel Group Threatens Explosion of Ethnic Hostility," *Washington Post* (April 2, 1991): A14.

17. Blaine Harden, "Yugoslav Regions Assert Independence; Secession of Slovenia, Croatia Prompts Calls for Army Intervention," *Washington Post* (June 26, 1991): A1.

18. Warrren Zimmermann, "The Last Ambassador: A Memoir on the Collapse of Yugoslavia," *Foreign Affairs* 74 (March 1995): 12.

19. Blaine Harden, "Thousands of Serbs Evade Call-Ups; Young Men Hide from Military Service in Yugoslav Crisis," *Washington Post* (July 25, 1991): A27.

20. Zimmermann, "The Last Ambassador," 12.

21. Blaine Harden, "Yugoslavia's Partisan Peacekeeper; Conflict in Slovenia and Croatia Sharpens Army's Serbian Outlook," *Washington Post* (July 12, 1991): A21.

22. Blaine Harden, "Guerrillas, Army Shell Croatian City; Republics' Leaders Open Peace Talks," *Washington Post* (August 21, 1991): A8.

23. "Serb-Croat Cease-Fire Announced; Both Sides Accept Presidency's Plan," *Washington Post* (August 7, 1991): A1.

24. Harden, "Yugoslavia's Partisan Peacekeeper," A21.

25. "30 Reported Dead in Croatia After Night of Battles," *Washington Post* (July 28, 1991): A30.

26. Samuel P. Huntington, "The Clash of Civilizations,"*Foreign Affairs* (Summer 1993): 30.

27. Peter Maass', "Pope Gives Moral Aid to Croatia; Independence Move Called 'Legitimate'," *Washington Post* (August 18, 1991): A29.

28. Maralee Schwartz, "Minnesota Ex-Governor Declines Croatian Post," *Washington Post* (April 31, 1991): A5.

29. General Lewis MacKenzie, *Peacekeeper: The Road to Sarajevo* (Vancouver, British Columbia: Douglas & McIntyre, 1993), 114.

30. U.S. Department of Justice, *Foreign Agents Registration Statement*, "Agreement Between the Republic of Croatia and Ruder Finn, Inc." (Washington, D.C., August 21, 1991): 6.

31. Ibid., 2.

32. Zimmermann, "The Last Ambassador," 3.

33. Blaine Harden, "Three Yugoslav Republics Fear Crackdown: Leaders Say Soviet Coup Could Be Pretext for Army Move," *Washington Post* (August 20, 1991): A8.

34. Blaine Harden, "Clashes in Croatia Escalating; Army Pullout Deadline Looms," *Washington Post* (August 24, 1991): A11.

35. Marcus Tanner, " '35 Killed' in Croatian Clashes,"*New York Times* (May 3, 1991): 14.

36. Laura Silber, "Army Sends More Tanks into Croatia; 35 Federal Soldiers Reportedly Killed in Raid on Garrison," *Washington Post* (October 1, 1991): A15.

37. Laura Silber, "EC Observers Admit Failure in Croatia; Serbs' Forces Threaten Adriatic Ports," *Washington Post* (September 14, 1991): A13.

38. Blaine Harden, "Army Offensive in Croatia Draws European Warnings," *Washington Post* (August 27, 1991): A1.

39. Blaine Harden, "Bosnia Braces for Arrival of Ethnic Violence; Yugoslav Republic Feels Threatened by Serbian Nationalism, Plans Referendum on Secession," *Washington Post* (August 23, 1991): A14.

40. Edward S. Herman and Noam Chomsky, *Manufacturing Consent: The Political Economy of the Mass Media* (New York: Pantheon Books, 1988), 34.

41. Robert Marquand, "Serb Refugees in Flight from War Find Reunion," *Christian Science Monitor* (October 9, 1991): 4.

Chapter 4

Ethnic Conflict Spreads to Bosnia-Hercegovina (October 1991 to mid-1992)

FIGHTING INTENSIFIES IN CROATIA, TENSIONS RISE IN BOSNIA-HERCEGOVINA

While armed clashes were taking place between Croat and Serb paramilitary and civilian groups, Serbian President Milosevic attempted to convince Bosnia's chairman of the seven-member presidency, Alija Izetbegovic, that Bosnia-Hercegovina should remain part of a new Yugoslavia that would include non-Serbian regions of Croatia. The new Yugoslav federation would have 14 million people, two-thirds of whom would be Serbs. An alliance with Serbia, however, was out of the question for Izetbegovic. By remaining in a Yugoslav state, Izetbegovic would be a negligible political player compared to Milosevic, with a significant Serbian constituency. Instead of Bosnia's 1.9 million Muslims being a minority in Yugoslavia, Izetbegovic wanted Muslims to be the largest and most dominant ethnic group in a newly independent Bosnia. To accomplish his goal, he needed powerful allies.

During his Summer 1991 visit to the United States, Izetbegovic aggressively courted Washington elites in meetings with top U.S. State Department officials, newspaper editors, reporters, and members of the U.S. Congress. His message to Washington was that Bosnian Muslims would ally themselves with the republic's Croats, not Serbs. Although Izetbegovic spoke of his government's democratic and multiparty ideals during his stay in Washington, he stressed his Islamic beliefs while soliciting support from Muslim countries in the Middle East. Bosnian Serb members of government viewed Izetbegovic's friendship with Islamic states to be an indication of the SDA party's hostile designs against the region's Serbs. They feared it was only a matter of time before Bosnia would attempt to split away from Yugoslavia, with an Islamic-based government dominated by Izetbegovic and his inner circle of relatives, friends, and SDA party members.

Izetbegovic was monitoring the growing confrontations in Croatia in deciding when Bosnia's Muslims should make their move. As battles continued across Serb-populated regions of Croatia and Tudjman gave an ultimatum to the Yugoslav army to get out of Croatia by August 31, 1991, Izetbegovic was emboldened to announce the next day that he was scheduling a referendum throughout Bosnia-Hercegovina on secession from Yugoslavia. Bosnia's Croats welcomed the move, not because they wanted to live in a state dominated by the Muslim SDA party, but because breaking Bosnia away from Yugoslavia would ultimately allow Bosnian Croat-populated areas to be joined to Croatia. The Bosnian Croat drive for joining a "Greater Croatia" was seldom mentioned by the U.S. press during this period, while Bosnian Serb attempts to stay within Yugoslavia were depicted as supporting the expansionist aims of a "Greater Serbia."

Bosnian Serbs wanted the republic to remain part of Yugoslavia as a way of ensuring protection of Serbian political rights. Izetbegovic's call for a referendum meant that the republic's Muslims and Croats would take advantage of their combined majority and vote to secede from Yugoslavia. The Serbs protested that according to the Yugoslav constitution, decisions made in Bosnia-Hercegovina should only be undertaken via a system of agreement by consensus, not by a simple majority. This consensus system that guided Bosnia-Hercegovina for 45 years ensured that no decisions would be taken without agreement by all ethnic groups. Serbian members of parliament demanded that the referendum be withdrawn and threatened to boycott the vote if it took place. Muslim and Croat representatives ignored the Serbs's warning.

It was now clear that the Serbs could not keep Yugoslavia together. On August 23, 1991, battles escalated in Croatia, in violation of the latest of many truces between Serbs and Croats. While the Croatian government flooded the international media with allegations that it was being attacked by the JNA, Yugoslav army claims that it was only responding to offensives by Croat forces were made far less known to the public. Only at the very end of a *Washington Post* article was a Bosnian Muslim member of the Yugoslav federal commission on enforcing the cease-fire, Irfan Ajanovic, quoted as saying, "Croatia is also an aggressor . . . the cease-fire is being breached by both sides." Troops from the Croatian Ministry were by now invading the town of Pakrac, attacking Serbs, and destroying houses and other buildings.[1] In Western capitals, on the other hand, the Croat government was accusing the JNA of aggression. When the Yugoslav army responded to Croat attacks in Pakrac by attacking Vukovar a few days later, Austria, Germany, and Italy, Croatia's traditional allies, immediately voiced outrage. They threatened to recognize Croatia as an independent state. To the Serbs, history appeared to be repeating itself. Croatia was again supported by its traditional allies. Thousands of Serbs took to the streets in Belgrade chanting slogans outside the German embassy and accused Germany of supporting Croatian separation from Yugoslavia to create a "Fourth Reich."

As some Western European countries increasingly blamed the Serbs for what was happening, by August 1991, ethnic Serbs were the largest number of refugees, with 50,000 Serbs reported to have fled from Croatia's Serb-populated eastern Slavonia and Krajina region, while 25,000 Croats fled from areas controlled by the Krajina Serbs.[2] Although Serbs throughout the country supported JNA efforts to prevent further expulsions of Serbs from Krajina, Germany would recognize Croatia as an independent nation unless the Serbs ended their military resistance against the Croats. The Serbs were being forced to choose between two bad alternatives that would ultimately lead to the same situation. If the JNA allowed Croatia to defeat the Krajina Serbs, Croatia's recognition as a sovereign nation would be inevitable. The only hope for the Serbs was a military option—to defeat the Croats and force the republic either to rejoin Yugoslavia or to grant Krajina Serbs their independence.

Although the EC attempted to mediate the situation, it was increasingly unable to do so. On September 2, 1991, 80 EC monitors were sent to enforce a cease-fire between Serbs and Croats in Krajina, while negotiations were taking place. At an opening of an EC-sponsored peace conference on Yugoslavia in September 1991 where presidents of all six Yugoslav republics sat down with EC ministers to forge a solution, harsh exchanges between Serb and Croat leaders ensued. Tudjman accused Serbia of waging a dirty war aimed at conquering and creating ethnically pure areas by expelling all non-Serbian inhabitants. Milosevic denied any expansionist aims, charging that most of the refugees who were "ethnically cleansed" from Croatia were ethnic Serbs who fled from state terror and suppression waged by Croatia on Serbian citizens. During the exchange, Belgian Foreign Minister Mark Eyskens said, "as I listened to their speeches, I had the impression that this was the continuation of the Second World War."[3] At the conclusion of the conference, Dutch Foreign Minister Van den Broeck commented that there should be "no changes in existing Yugoslav borders by force or unilateral decree and the agreement of all Yugoslav parties to any such changes."[4] Tudjman and Kucan denied EC authority to revoke their republics' declarations of independence.

The failure of the European Community's first peace mission was soon evident. Only a few days later, fierce fighting erupted again around Pakrac and Kostajnica, a town 50 miles southeast of Zagreb on the Una River which had passed several times from Serb to Croatian control in earlier months of fighting. After 300 Croatian soldiers were forced to surrender to the Yugoslav army in Kostajnica, Croatia imposed a block-ade of food, water, and electricity on JNA barracks throughout Croatia. As young, mostly Serbian, recruits faced dehydration and starvation, Western European nations issued no reprimand to Croatia. With Germany as a powerful force behind the EC, Croatia had gained a powerful backer who appeared to condone its policies. To save JNA personnel from imminent death from starvation after a full week of Croat block-ade, the JNA launched a full-scale attack on September 20, 1991, breaking through Croatian military front lines in Vinkovci, Osijek, and Vukovar.

Intensified fighting in Croatia did not appear to be an incentive for Bosnia's Muslim and Croat leaders to attempt to forge a compromise with the Serbs to avoid a similar conflict in their republic. Far from attempting to diffuse tensions, Izetbegovic immediately mobilized his Green Beret forces and ordered the Yugoslav army to leave Bosnia-Hercegovina. As in Croatia, this move was made while Bosnia-Hercegovina was still a re-public of Yugoslavia—before any referendum on independence actually took place and before Bosnia was recognized as an independent nation. At the time, the *Washington Post* reported "the [Bosnian] republic's pres-idency ordered the mobilization of its territorial defense forces."[5] This seemingly unassuming phrase demonstrated the newspaper's growing bias. By stating that the "presidency" ordered the mobilization, the *Washington Post* implicitly recognized Izetbegovic and his supporters as the sole legit-imate government of Bosnia—ignoring the fact that Bosnia was headed by a joint presidency, which included Bosnian Serb members who deemed Izetbegovic's mobilization to be illegal.

Western European criticism of the JNA emboldened Bosnia's Muslims and Croats to take increasingly more hostile actions against Yugoslavia's Serbian authorities. When the Yugoslav army mobilized its forces in Bosnia-Hercegovina to join forces in preventing Croatia's continuing at-tempts to secede, and as a JNA military convoy was passing through two small Bosnian towns near Mostar, armed Bosnian Croats barricaded the road and killed a young Serbian soldier. This was to become the first casualty of war in Bosnia-Hercegovina. Anti-JNA and anti-Serbian emo-tions were similarly charged in Sarajevo where armed Croats and Muslims attempted to block a column of 35 JNA military buses and 100 armored vehicles bound for Croatia.[6] In a compromise agreement with Izetbegovic, Serbian President Milosevic promised to remove some Yugoslav federal army reserve units from Bosnia-Hercegovina, in exchange for Izetbe-govic's guarantee that Muslim paramilitary units would be disbanded. Ul-timately, neither side complied.

By the end of September 1991, Macedonia had already declared inde-pendence, Croatia was in turmoil, and the Yugoslav defense minister, General Veljko Kadijevic, announced that the federal presidency had col-lapsed and that Yugoslavia was "moving rapidly toward the maelstrom of an all-encompassing civil war and genocide against the Serbian population in Croatia."[7] Croatia, on the other hand, desperately wanted to internationalize the conflict. After the JNA attacked Vukovar, in numerous appeals and letters sent to EC ministers and to U.N. representatives, Croatia urged the world to stop what it called a "Serbian aggression." Soon after the Croatian media blitz on Vukovar, on September 26, 1991, Secretary of State James Baker for the first time singled out the Yugoslav army as committing an "aggression." Washington's shift in policy gave impetus for other forms of international reaction. On the same day that Baker declared the conflict in Yugoslavia to be an "aggression." U.N. council members voted to impose a total arms embargo on all areas of Yugoslavia, in spite of several months of debate on whether the United Nations had the right to intervene in the internal affairs of Yugoslavia. Neither rhetoric nor policy of the United States and Europe, however, addressed the real problems of Bosnia's three ethnic groups that were about to unleash a brutal war.

On October 15, 1991, Muslim and Croat members of Bosnia's government voted to declare Bosnia-Hercegovina a sovereign nation. After Bosnian Serb lawmakers called the declaration illegal, 73 Serbian delegates walked out of parliament and Momcilo Krajisnik, president of Bosnia's parliament and an ethnic Serb, declared the session closed. Western legal analysts agreed that the legality of the Muslim-Croat declaration of independence was questionable, but Washington expressed no concern over Muslim-Croat attempts to separate Bosnia-Hercegovina from Yugoslavia without Serbian consent.[8] Outnumbered and outmaneuvered by the Muslim-Croat coalition, Bosnia's Serbian representatives, mostly from the SDS party, formed what they called a new "Parliament of the Serbian people in Bosnia-Hercegovina," and on November 9, voted by an overwhelming majority that the republic should stay within Yugoslavia. The Serbs hoped not only to demonstrate the democratic will of their people, but also to warn Muslim and Croat leaders that a separation of Bosnia-Hercegovina would be met with resistance.

Impending warnings of civil war might have persuaded Bosnia's Muslim and Croat leaders to come to an agreement with the Serbs, had it not been for one crucial factor—Germany. It was at this time that Germany spearheaded a European policy to recognize Croatia, which indicated to Bosnian Muslims and Croats that recognition of Bosnia-Hercegovina would be forthcoming. It made negotiating with Bosnia's Serbs unnecessary and pushed Bosnia one step closer to war.

GERMANY SPEARHEADS YUGOSLAV DISINTEGRATION

At the moment Bosnia-Hercegovina was experiencing its greatest ethnic tensions, Germany became Europe's champion of Croatian independence.

German support for Croatia intensified further in October 1991, when fighting in the city of Dubrovnik, on Croatia's Adriatic coast, caught global media attention. Croatian forces battling the JNA in the neighboring republic of Montenegro took up positions in Dubrovnik's historic city center. This enabled them to lob shells at the JNA, believing that the JNA would not fire back and damage parts of the historic city, which would surely cause international outrage.[9] A reckless JNA response played right into the Tudjman government's hands and was used by the Tudjman government to elicit extraordinary sympathy from European states. While JNA shelling resulted in minimal damage to Dubrovnik, the Croatian government claimed massive destruction was taking place in the city's historic district. The story shocked European public opinion, especially Germans, many of whom spent summer holidays on the Dalmatian coast as tourists. In later months, members of the media went to Dubrovnik and found the city was not nearly as damaged as the Croatian government claimed.[10] At the time, however, Croatia's grossly exaggerated charges had achieved the desired effect. Germany now more than ever was ready to help Croatia.

Enthused with the fervor of its own reunification and determined to punish the Serbs, Germany pushed for the right of self-determination for Croats and Slovenes at EC meetings. Germany was largely behind a November 1991 EC decision to impose economic sanctions only against Yugoslavia—Serbia and Montenegro. When Germany became the first European state to publicly label Serbia an "aggressor" in December of 1991, the EC quickly followed with its own accusations of Serbia's "brutal aggression" against Croatia.[11] The German call to recognize Croatia stirred deep divisions within the EC. France and Britain, anxious to preserve the integrity of national frontiers, did not want to set a precedent for the dismantling of ethnically volatile nations, including the Soviet Union. They urged that recognition be delayed in order to allow more time for the deployment of U.N. peacekeeping forces separating Yugoslavia's warring Serbs and Croats. An EC panel headed by French jurist Robert Badinter was designated to review the claims of Yugoslav republics seeking independence, including each republic's record of minority and human rights protection, adherence to democratic principles, and respect for existing borders. While the Badinter Commission approved of Slovenia's record on minority rights, it was skeptical that Croatia would guarantee the rights of its Serbian population and it expressed concern for the absence of legal protection for minorities in Bosnia-Hercegovina.[12]

Germany refused to recognize the Badinter Commission findings, as Hans-Dietrich Genscher announced his country was adamant in recognizing new Balkan states and that the Badinter report was "not a condition for implementing the decision to recognize."[13] On December 23, 1991, EC members were taken by surprise as Germany became the first country to recognize Croatia and Slovenia as independent states. The German announcement came shortly after an EC summit meeting had reached an agreement on closer European political and economic unity, including a common foreign policy. Intent on maintaining a unified European policy, EC countries yielded to German pressure and recognized Croatia and Slovenia on January 15, 1992. It was the first major post–Cold War German initiative accepted by the EC. At a convention of the Christian Democratic Union party, German Chancellor Helmut Kohl called the EC decision "a great triumph for German foreign policy," while officials in Bonn boasted that they would soon win agreement from most European countries to recognize the independence of Bosnia-Hercegovina as well.[14] In ceding to Germany, the EC passed up an important opportunity to require minority rights as criteria for granting recognition to newly aspiring states. The EC accepted mere written assurances by Croatia's president, Franjo Tudjman, that his government would respect Serbian rights.

With the EC's increasing willingness to support German policy, Serbia's leadership welcomed steps to move the negotiations from the level of a regional organization to the attention of a world body—the United Nations. U.N. envoy to Yugoslavia, former U.S. Secretary of State Cyrus Vance, managed to convince Serbia's president Milosevic and Croatia's president Tudjman to allow U.N. peacekeepers to be deployed in Croatia. The Vance plan called for a complete withdrawal of Yugoslav army units as well as non-JNA Serbian militias from Croatia's borders. It also called for 10,000 U.N. peacekeepers to be brought into Croatia and the establishment of three U.N. Protection Areas in Serb-populated eastern and western Slavonia and Krajina. In signing the Vance plan, Milosevic hoped that by cooperating with the United Nations and ending the six-month war with Croatia, the international community would ultimately grant Serbs in Krajina the same kind of self-determination they appeared willing to give to Croatia. The agreement, however, became the first step toward recognizing Croatian sovereignty. It gave Croatia one less reason to negotiate with the Serbs, and in effect, it signed away Serbia's right to protect its nationals in Croatia. It would open the way for a similar dismissal of the Serbs's rights in Bosnia-Hercegovina.

AWAITING THE STORM: ETHNIC STRIFE IN SARAJEVO

In the early months of 1992, ethnic tensions were accelerating in Bosnia-Hercegovina. Having refused to acquiesce to Muslim- and Croat-dominated governments, the Bosnian Serb parliament on January 10, 1992 proclaimed the creation of its own autonomous Yugoslav state of Bosnian Serb people—the Republika Srpska. The Bosnian Serbs announced that their new state had a valid claim to 60 percent of the republic's territory, since ethnic Serbs, though constituting only 31 percent of the population, predominantly lived in Bosnia's rural areas as farmers (see Appendix 2, map 7).[15] Bosnia's Serbs were also traditionally the largest ethnic group in Bosnia-Hercegovina, until the 1960s (see Appendix 1). The Bosnian Serb parliament created its own constitution and appointed a president, vice presidents, ministers, and staff. Although Bosnian Serbs worked on creating an infrastructure for their own separate and independent government in Bosnia-Hercegovina, Bosnia's Muslim-Croat coalition ignored Serbian warnings and scheduled a republicwide vote on independence.

Bosnia became increasingly polarized. Bosnian Muslim and Croat leaders labeled the Serbs hard-line nationalists and cronies of Serbia's president Slobodan Milosevic, who was accused of harboring expansionist aims over Serb-populated areas of Bosnia-Hercegovina. Hostility toward Bosnian Serbs was evident on the front cover of a popular Bosnian Muslim youth publication, *Novi Vox*, which showed a Muslim wearing traditional dress worn in the days of the Turks stepping on the head of the Bosnian Serb leader, Radovan Karadzic.[16] The same issue presented a cut-out board game whose object was to kill as many Serbian leaders as possible. On another page, *Novi Vox* published what it called a "patriotic poem" which read, "Dear Mother, I'm going to plant willows, we'll hang Serbs from them" (referring to the World War II Ustashi slogan, "we'll hang Serbs on willows").

With such sentiment openly expressed in Bosnian Muslim publications, feelings of fear and resentment grew among the Serbian population. In the years to follow, as the Bosnian Muslim government and their supporters in Washington contended that nationalism and propaganda by Bosnian Serb leaders were the direct cause of Serbian fears and were responsible for war, it was daily events that underlay Serbian fears, without the need for prodding from their Bosnian Serb leaders. Throughout the latter half of 1991 and early 1992, Bosnian Serb businessmen and shopowners reported incidents of attacks by radical Muslim groups. Monuments to important Serbian writers and heroes of Bosnia's past were desecrated and destroyed.

The most ominous sign of the oncoming Bosnian conflict, however, occurred in late February 1992, just a few days prior to the scheduled independence referendum, when at a Serbian wedding procession in Sarajevo, Muslim and Croat gunmen shot and killed the groom's father. Wedding guests and bystanders identified two men, but they were never arrested. The Bosnian Serb public was convinced that the Muslim-dominated police were shielding the culprits. To the Serbs, it was a taste of what life would be like under a Muslim-dominated government. On February 28, 1992, the Serbs organized a protest in Sarajevo against the Serbian wedding murders and put road blocks on neighborhood streets. The protest had a greater significance as a demonstration of Serbian opposition to the upcoming referendum on independence. Road blocks continued to be erected throughout the coming days as Bosnian Muslim paramilitaries began patrolling the city.

Sporadic violence continued in Sarajevo's suburbs, and three deaths were reported on March 1, 1992, the day of the referendum on Bosnia's independence. Reporting on the matter, *Washington Post* headlines read: "Bosnians Hold Independence Referendum"—although it was not all "Bosnians" who were holding a referendum, since Bosnian Serbs boycotted the vote. The article failed to make this important revelation. It was indicative of the developing tendency to depict the mostly Muslim government or civilians in Bosnia-Hercegovina as "Bosnian" in the U.S. press. The term gave the impression that Serbs were alien to Bosnia, while the Muslims—depicted as Bosnians and their government as "Bosnian government"—had the right to be in their own country. It legitimized repeated State Department accusations yet to come against the Serbs and claims that the Serbs need to be "rolled back," as if they were invaders from another country.

Protests by Sarajevo's Serb residents on the day of the referendum evoked little sympathy from Europe. Germany's foreign minster, Hans-Dietrich Genscher, remarked that the only possible response to Serbian protests was for Germany to encourage the EC to accept the independence of Bosnia-Hercegovina. To demonstrate that the Serbs were outnumbered on the issue of independence, Bosnian Muslims and Croats launched their own demonstration by encouraging a large gathering in support of an independent Bosnian state. As masses of demonstrators filled the streets of Sarajevo, a shot was fired into the crowd of mostly Muslim demonstrators. Muslim Green Beret forces claimed that the shot came from the Bosnian Serb Democratic Party (SDS) headquarters at the Holiday Inn. They stormed into Serb offices and killed four staff members. Bosnian Serb officials claimed that the Muslims fired into the crowd as a pretext for launching an attack on SDS political leaders. Bosnian Serb representatives, including Dr. Radovan Karadzic and other Serbian Democratic party members, fled from their homes and escaped to the surrounding mountainous countryside in the suburbs of Sarajevo. They left their homes behind as well as most of their belongings. Some officials, such as Biljana Plavsic, escaped to what would later become Sarajevo's Serb-held neighborhoods. One SDS party member, Aleksa Buha, fled from his apartment five minutes before a grenade attack on his residence.

The Serbian leadership fled to Pale, a small ski village 10 miles from Sarajevo. Serbs living in the mountainous areas surrounding Sarajevo as well as in city districts mostly populated by Serbs, continued putting up barricades to block passage of Muslim forces. Ethnic tensions were spiraling out of control, much to the disbelief of its residents. Sarajevo became a divided city. As Bosnian Muslim police massed in one part of the city, armed Bosnian Serbs and ex-JNA army officers sectioned off mostly

Serb-populated suburbs. A war zone was created. Makeshift barricades put up by Sarajevo's Serb residents divided roads and buildings between neighborhoods. The river later became a dividing line in Sarajevo between Bosnian Serbs in the hills and Muslims in the inner city. Sensing impending hostilities, thousands of Sarajevo Serbs (mostly women and children) quickly gathered their belongings and caught the last flights to Belgrade. Most of the men stayed behind. Other Serbs and Muslims remained in their homes and apartments regardless of which part of Sarajevo happened to be their residence.

Many Serbs fled from Sarajevo in the midst of chaotic events in the Spring of 1992. "We left everything behind except what we could carry in our suitcases," said Radomir Lukic, who became the deputy foreign minister of the Bosnian Serb Republika Srpska. He explained to me: "I sent my wife and kids to Belgrade almost immediately. I sensed what was about to happen." After the Dayton Accords ending the war were signed in November 1995, Lukic was assigned as chief legal adviser to the government of Republika Srpska on Brcko arbitration negotiations.

I returned to Sarajevo with him for the first time after the war in the Summer of 1997. We were taken by U.N. vehicle to discuss problems that had been encountered in forming the joint Bosnian institutions called for by the Dayton Accords. As we drove past Sarajevo's city shops, people casually walking along city streets, and teenagers sitting in cafes, Lukic's face had a painful look: "This is not the same city," he said. "These are not the same people. I could never live here again." To Lukic and others who left Sarajevo, events in the Spring of 1992 marked the moment when their city was taken away from them. The decision by Muslims and Croats to vote for Bosnia's independence meant that Sarajevo was no longer a city for everyone but for Muslims and Croats only. It sowed the seeds of deep and bitter resentment among Bosnian Serbs forced to flee the cosmopolitan lifestyle of Sarajevo.

Several members of the top Bosnian Serb leadership were professors at Sarajevo's universities. The two Serbian representatives elected in Bosnia's 1990 elections, Nikola Koljevic, a Shakespearean scholar and former professor at the University of Philosophy in Sarajevo, and Biljana Plavsic, a biologist and former professor at Sarajevo's University of Natural Sciences, became vice presidents of the Bosnian Serb Republic. Aleksa Buha, former professor at the University of Philosophy in Sarajevo, became the Bosnian Serb minister for foreign affairs. Others left successful careers in Sarajevo. Radovan Karadzic, elected in 1990 as president of the Serbian Democratic party in Bosnia-Hercegovina, left a practice as a psychologist when he fled Sarajevo. Momcilo Krajisnik, former president of the Bosnian parliament and an economist and a former director of a major corporation in Bosnia-Hercegovina, became the Bosnian Serb president of parliament.

Even as deep differences developed among Serbs, Muslims, and Croats in Bosnia-Hercegovina, Bosnian Serb political leaders did not anticipate having to flee to the mountains to fight a grueling ethnic war with their former Muslim and Croat colleagues. Karadzic would later say, "it was something I could have never imagined, not even in my worst nightmares. If it wasn't for my Muslim neighbor who warned me that Alija's men were coming, I probably would not be alive today." The fact that the Bosnian Serb members of government left most of their belongings behind in Sarajevo attests to their lack of forethought of coming events. "We had to quickly leave our apartment and most of our belongings," Karadzic's wife, Ljiljana, told me in later years. "What I regret the most is leaving our family photographs and video tapes, one of which was a video from my mother's burial. I know I'll never see these things again because we heard radio transmissions of Muslim soldiers talking as they were taking apart our apartment." In the years to come, the U.S. media would sympathize with Bosnian Muslim refugees of war, but never appreciated that members of Bosnia's Serbian leadership and tens of thousands of other Serbs from Sarajevo were exiled—refugees on their own land who attempted for months and years of upcoming war to regain what was once theirs.

LISBON AGREEMENT: LAST EFFORT TO STOP A WAR

In an attempt to defuse ethnic violence in Bosnia-Hercegovina, the international community took two measures. The first was the introduction of a modest U.N. peacekeeping mission in Sarajevo on March 13, 1992, with U.N. General Lewis MacKenzie as head of the United Nations Protection Force (UNPROFOR). The second step was a series of EC-brokered diplomatic initiatives that engaged the three ethnic groups in negotiations. A meeting at Lisbon, Portugal on March 17, 1992, finally resulted in a breakthrough. On that day, all three ethnic leaders signed the Lisbon Agreement: Radovan Karadzic (for the Bosnian Serbs), Mate Boban (for the Bosnian Croats), and Alija Izetbegovic (for the Bosnian Muslims). The parties agreed in principle to an independent state of Bosnia-Hercegovina divided into three separate areas along ethnic and geographic lines between Muslims, Serbs, and Croats. The plan would give the constituent ethnic groups control over local economic and political issues, while matters pertaining to defense or foreign and monetary policies would remain under the central Bosnian government and parliament. The agreement did not, however, resolve where the new boundaries would be drawn to separate Bosnia's ethnic groups, nor did it define the authority of the police and the armed forces.

In spite of its vagueness on territorial and defense issues, the Lisbon Agreement was a first step toward settling the dispute. It called for international recognition of Bosnia as an independent state comprised of three constituent, mostly ethnic units. Although the Bosnian Serb leader Radovan Karadzic, previously rejected the idea of an independent Bosnia, he now approved a united Bosnia divided into three ethnic units. At the signing of the Lisbon Agreement, Karadzic said, "it is a great day for Bosnia . . . we can see there are no more reasons for civil war."[17] Months later, Karadzic said he was willing to compromise to avoid war. "I never wanted war to happen," he said, "I prayed to God that the Muslims would not make a tragic mistake by forcing us to fight."

The Lisbon Agreement was also a concession by Izetbegovic, who initially opposed the division of Bosnia-Hercegovina into ethnic units. By accepting the Lisbon principles, however, Izetbegovic and his supporters appeared willing to take steps to avert a war, had it not been for one key factor—the United States. After receiving encouragement from U.S. Ambassador Yugoslavia Warren Zimmermann, Izetbegovic quickly reneged on his pledge and the deal fell through.[18] It set a pattern that continued throughout the war as European diplomatic initiatives would be foiled by Washington time and again.

THE UNITED STATES RECOGNIZES NEW STATES

Lacking a clear policy and goal on Yugoslavia or direct national interests, Washington initially preferred to let the Europeans handle the crisis. The Europeans, in turn, were willing to allow Germany to take the lead and "Balkanize" Yugoslavia by recognizing the country's ethnically unstable republics as independent states. At this point, U.S. policy was ripe for Croatian and Bosnian Muslim government influence.

In almost a full year of lobbying and appealing to Washington elites, the government of Croatia was targeting certain members of Congress, foreign policy analysts, influential officials, and the media. Croatia's public relations firm, Ruder Finn, arranged what it described as "numerous contacts" between Croatian officials and Representative Susan Molinari and her staff, as well as the House Foreign Affairs Committee staff, for which the Croat representatives organized a "fact-finding trip . . . in order to facilitate U.S. recognition of, and aid to, the Republic of Croatia."[19] Another fact-finding trip was organized in February 1992 for Representative Jim Sensenbrenner, his legislative director Brian Dean, John Plashal from the House Appropriations Committee, and Mira Barratta—a Croatian American who was a key adviser to Senator Bob Dole. The Croatian government's appeals and steady, behind-the-scenes influence began to take hold in Washington by the Spring of 1992. It came as no surprise when members of Congress, including Susan Molinari, Jan Meyers, Dana Rohrabacher, Tom Lantos, and Dick Swett, who had never had any apparent interest in the Yugoslav region, now urged President Bush to recognize Croatia as an independent state.[20]

Other Balkan enthusiasts in Washington began to apply pressure on the Bush administration to change its initially cautious policy on Yugoslavia. Former U.S. ambassador to the U.N. Jeanne Kirkpatrick criticized President Bush in a March 1992 opinion editorial for not recognizing Croatia and Slovenia, arguing that the United States would be giving "adequate priority to the U.S. national interest in preserving democratic governments and extending democracy," and that the United States had a "major stake in encouraging civilized standards of respect for human rights and peaceful settlements of the issues of ethnic separatism and nationalism, [and] democratic outcomes."[21] In another editorial, Senator Alfonse D'Amato praised the government of Croatia for having "dismissed the communists and installed a parliamentary democracy."[22] Neither Kirkpatrick nor D'Amato acknowledged that Croatia's behavior toward its Serbian minority was neither democratic nor supportive of human rights. D'Amato's opinions, however, reflected the Croatian government's spin more so than his substantive understanding of Yugoslav issues. A U.S. Justice Department foreign agents report said that D'Amato's *Washington Post* editorial was written after "Senator D'Amato requested information and assistance" from Croatia's public relations firm, Ruder Finn.[23] Kirkpatrick and D'Amato appeared to base their views on Croatian claims or media reports, but not from first-hand knowledge. This trend would be repeated in years to come.

Any information about the Yugoslav conflict that did not make front-page news was as good as nonexistent to a growing group of Washington's Balkan-interventionists. U.S. press coverage of the war in Croatia increasingly depicted the Serbs as aggressors and the Croats as victims. This fueled criticism of the Bush administration's reluctance to recognize new Yugoslav states. As hawkish interventionism became the popular view of the Yugoslav conflict, those in Washington who supported the Bush administration's more cautious policy were harshly criticized. In an April 1992 editorial, Stephen S. Rosenfeld wrote that the "common media juxtaposition of 'communist' Serbia and 'democratic' Croatia" was "cartoonish," that "the Bush administration has gotten a bum rap on Yugoslavia," and that Germany's "one-sided oversimplification" in blaming the Serbs and recognizing the Croats was a misguided policy.[24] Croatia's friends in Washington quickly reacted to such assertions. Senator D'Amato lashed back in another editorial in which he rebuked Rosenfeld for "parroting the failed line of the State Department."[25]

Interventionist views eventually won the day in Washington. U.S. Ambassador Warren Zimmermann was the primary U.S. diplomat pushing for recognition of Bosnia-Hercegovina at the time. "Our view," Zimmermann acknowledged later, "was that we might be able to head off a Serbian power grab by internationalizing the problem. Our hope was the Serbs would hold off if it was clear Bosnia had the recognition of Western coun-

tries. It turned out we were wrong."[26] Zimmermann's views mirrored the
arguments made by German diplomats in previous months. If Washington
had taken a different view and had encouraged Bosnia's Muslims to accept
the Lisbon Agreement, four and a half years of tragic war could have been
avoided. Perhaps, as Stefan Halper later noted, "Mr. Zimmermann and
other would-be arbiters of property and allocators of American resources—moral and military—might have stepped back, hesitated to dive
into complex situations in which Washington has no clear direct, strategic
interests."[27]

Instead of putting the brakes on policies that would cause further tension among Bosnia's ethnic groups, the Bush administration ultimately
yielded to pressure from Washington interventionists and the German
drive for recognition. When the EC recognized Bosnia-Hercegovina as an
independent state on April 6, 1992, the next day the Bush administration
announced it would recognize all three Yugoslav republics of Slovenia,
Croatia, and Bosnia-Hercegovina as independent nations. The recognition
of a Bosnian Serb state was never even considered. If the Bosnian Serbs
were disappointed at Washington's policy, it should have come as no surprise to them. The Bosnian Serb leadership had no representatives in
Washington and made no effort to contact members of Congress, the State
Department, or the media. Since Bosnian Serbs ignored Washington,
Washington ignored them.

Unlike the Serbs, Bosnia's Muslims knew they could not achieve their
goal of independence without full support from the United States. Muslim
officials became regular visitors to Washington. They made appeals in
every possible way, directly and through influential friends. Bosnia's Islamic allies were also engaged in the struggle. In April 1992, appeals by
Bosnian Muslim Foreign Minister Haris Silajdzic to Saudi Arabia for help
seemed to yield positive results, since Secretary of State Baker immediately agreed to meet with Silajdzic, after which Baker initiated urgent calls
to European allies to help the Bosnian Muslim government.[28] For Baker,
this was a crucial period when the United States was building stronger ties
to Muslim states, which was viewed as critical to U.S. efforts in Middle
East peace negotiations.

Washington appeared to be basing its policy on the Balkans not on
clearly thought-out goals, but in response to pressures at home from activists and interventionists, and abroad from Germany, and America's Islamic allies. This was the reason behind a mistaken policy to prematurely
recognize new Balkan states. Lord Carrington, former British minister of
foreign affairs and the European Community's mediator on the civil war
in Yugoslavia, later said that the recognition of Slovenia, Croatia, and
Bosnia-Hercegovina was a "tragic error" and that he advised the EC
against recognizing Bosnia-Hercegovina, arguing that a "scenario of this
sort [was] unacceptable for the Serbs in Bosnia, [and] would lead to civil

war."[29] Such warnings were ignored in European capitals and in Washington as well.

FIGHTING IN BOSNIA: THE JNA DEPARTS UNDER ATTACK

With Sarajevo and other parts of Bosnia already the scene of growing ethnic clashes, the recognition of Bosnia-Hercegovina by the United States unleashed full-scale fighting in the region. Bosnia's Serbs were faced with a two-front conflict, with the Muslims and Croats. Between March and April 1992, at least 30 to 40 people were killed in fighting between Bosnian Serbs and Croats in towns bordering Croatia, in Mostar, and other areas of southwestern Bosnia. The Yugoslav army was playing the same role it did in Croatia—to prevent Bosnia-Hercegovina from separating, and to protect the local Serbian population. By April 8, 1992, the Yugoslav army gained control of the Bosnian town of Kupres and its military installations. The Yugoslav army also shelled the town of Zvornik across the Drina River bordering Serbia, while Bosnian Serb forces launched a ground attack on the city and eventually took over the town and suburbs. The fighting caused most of Zvornik's 13,000 inhabitants, about 60 percent Muslim and 40 percent Serbian, to flee the area. A few days later, as fighting intensified between Muslims and Serbs in Visegrad, JNA units and Bosnian Serb militiamen launched an all-out assault on the city, as Murat Savanovic, a local Muslim militia leader, threatened to blow up the Visegrad Dam and send a wall of water hurling down the river into Serbia.

In just four weeks of fighting, 500 people were killed and 500,000 displaced. Bosnian Serbs controlled almost two-thirds of Bosnia, while the Muslim-Croat coalition controlled most of Bosnia's larger cities. Sarajevo was shut down as roads were blocked by armed Bosnian Serbs. Serbs sought JNA help, still hoping that the Muslim-Croat coalition would relinquish its intention to create an independent Bosnia. With U.S. and European recognition of Bosnia-Hercegovina, however, the Muslim leadership felt justified in attempting to force all JNA units out of the region. Throughout April of 1992, Muslim forces attacked JNA personnel as they traveled within the region in buses and cars, and blockaded JNA barracks in Sarajevo and demanded their weapons.[30] Attacks on JNA recruits during this time did not arouse sympathy from abroad. Instead, on May 1, 1992, EC mediator Jose Cutileiro of Portugal suspended Bosnian peace talks and criticized the JNA and Bosnian Serbs for refusing to withdraw their artillery and blockades from around Sarajevo, and supported Bosnian Muslim demands that 100,000 JNA troops stationed in Bosnia-Hercegovina be removed. This was to become a familiar pattern of the Bosnian war: first, Bosnian Muslims would make military demands of the Serbs, second, European and U.S. officials would give support to these demands; and finally, Bosnian Muslims would interpret foreign support as a green light to take even greater military steps against the Serbs.

The strategy proved to be effective. On the day the EC demanded that JNA and Bosnian Serb forces withdraw from Sarajevo, Muslim militiamen attacked the Yugoslav army headquarters in the city, taking 60 Serbian reservists hostage. The Serbs struck back. On May 2, 1992, as Izetbegovic was returning from talks in Lisbon, the JNA took him into custody at Sarajevo airport. The next day, Muslim forces responded by attacking the JNA Officers Club in downtown Sarajevo, killing three Serbian officers, while the JNA retaliated with tank fire against the Bosnian Muslim presidency building and the mayor's office. When U.N. General Lewis MacKenzie intervened, Izetbegovic promised that in exchange for his release, his forces would allow the JNA military commander and his staff of about 400 members to leave Sarajevo. Having reached an agreement, on May 3, 1992, a convoy of 400 JNA soldiers, personnel, and their families headed out of Sarajevo, when Muslim troops suddenly split the JNA convoy in two and started shooting at Serbian recruits who had been left stranded in the back of their trucks. U.N. personnel witnessed Muslim soldiers firing through windows of JNA cars at close range. About 200 Serbian JNA soldiers were taken prisoner by the Muslim troops, and seven officers were executed.[31]

The U.S. media and State Department officials hardly took notice of the incident, and they also failed to criticize Bosnian Muslims for committing atrocities against unarmed Serbian JNA officers. The event did not make front-page news. The *Washington Post* downplayed the Muslim attack on the JNA by merely stating that "gunfire broke out" and omitting specific references to the execution of Serbian recruits in the statement that "some truck drivers and troops were fatally shot or seriously wounded."[32] Surprisingly, the *Washington Post* reported that "the number of casualties could not be confirmed from independent sources," even though U.N. General MacKenzie was personally on the scene, witnessed the shootings, and reported the exact number of Serbian casualties. This was to be one of the few incidents in the coming years of war in Bosnia that would have been easy to confirm.

The media paid equally little attention to condemnations by the U.N. Undersecretary for Special Political Affairs, Marrick Goulding, who said that JNA personnel were "killed in cold blood," with regard to which U.N. General MacKenzie would later write, "I was surprised to discover just how little media coverage Goulding's strong statement had received around the world. I couldn't help thinking that if the JNA had ambushed the TDF [Muslim ground forces], instead of the other way around, it would have been front-page news."[33] The Bosnian Muslim government was clearly skilled at downplaying its wrongdoings for the international media. On the day Goulding was scheduled to hold a press conference in Sarajevo condemning the execution of JNA personnel, he was given a car tour of the city by Bosnian Muslim president Alija Izetbegovic, during which gunfire broke out—an incident that General MacKenzie said had strong "indications that it was an orchestrated show for the accompanying media, intended to put the Serbs in a bad light."[34] As a result, the U.S. press ignored Goulding's criticism of the Muslim government, while reports of alleged Serbian attacks on the car carrying Goulding and Izetbegovic were widely reported.

Although Izetbegovic denied that he had ordered the attack on withdrawing JNA troops, clearly someone of authority in the Muslim military was responsible. In the coming years, Washington would accuse the Bosnian Serbs's political and military leadership of almost every violent act committed against Muslims, while ignoring the Bosnian Muslim role in identical activities. The atrocities committed by Muslim forces against JNA recruits in May of 1992 were among the many examples of crimes committed against the Serbs that were not addressed by the War Crimes Tribunal in the coming years.

BREADLINE MASSACRE TAKES CENTER STAGE

The first major surge of media focus on Sarajevo took place on May 27, 1992, after a mortar fell in the center of the city's Bosnian Muslim district. Seventeen people were killed as they waited to buy bread. International media converged on the spot within minutes. The horrifying scene of severed limbs and people bleeding was broadcast around the world. Continual CNN coverage showed people in severe pain and doctors scrambling in a panic to get them to a hospital. Bosnia's Muslim government immediately blamed the Serbs, as Washington officials and media pundits began a week-long barrage of accusations of barbaric Serbian behavior against innocent civilians.

Responsibility for the breadline massacre was never questioned in Washington, even though Bosnian Serb leaders denied responsibility for the shelling and blamed Bosnia's Muslim leaders for the attack. The Bosnian Serb vice-president, Nikola Koljevic, said at a Belgrade press conference that Muslim forces attacked their own people as a pretext for interrupting the European Community negotiations on the ethnic partition of Bosnia. The *Washington Post*'s Blaine Harden took a personal view on the matter by dismissing Serbian arguments as yet another claim by "Serb generals and political leaders [who] previously have accused Croats and Muslims of shelling their own cities." Harden implied that Koljevic's claim was suspect because "like all the senior Serb leaders in Bosnia, Koljevic is believed by Western diplomats to take orders from Milosevic."[35]

On television, the gruesome incident was repeated and sensationalized to such an extent that by the time the findings came out questioning the

Serbs's culpability, the issue was a moot point. The media's love affair with hating the Serbs had already begun. It was not until two months later, on August 22, 1992, that a London newspaper, *The Independent*, reported on U.N. findings that the "bread queue massacre was a propaganda ploy" and that it was a Muslim "slaughter" of "their own people."[36] The article stated that U.N. officials and senior Western military officers examining the direction of the mortar had confirmed that Sarajevo's Muslim forces were the source of the attack, and that it was a propaganda ploy to win world sympathy and trigger military intervention on their behalf. Top U.N. commander in Bosnia at the time, General Lewis MacKenzie, stated that his staff had noted a number of discrepancies during the incident, which led them to believe the incident was used as a media spectacle.[37] They noticed that the streets were blocked off and that the media was present just before the explosion, and reporters appeared immediately on the scene. By now, however, the facts of the matter were not as important in Washington, since a policy supporting the Bosnian Muslim government was already in place and was unlikely to change.

WASHINGTON CLINGS TO THE MULTIETHNIC MYTH OF BOSNIA

From the early days of war, the crux of the Muslim argument for U.S. support was the claim that it was a multiethnic government. Bosnia's Muslim officials claimed that the Republika Srpska leadership was supported by only a small following of radical nationalists, encouraged by Serbia's president Milosevic. These claims helped make the case that the war in Bosnia was an outside Serbian aggression, instigated against Bosnia's multiethnic government. Bosnian Muslim officials portrayed this image to the international media—in press conferences, in Sarajevo's government-run newspapers and radio reports, and in direct contacts with individuals representing international organizations based in the city. The message constantly circulated to foreign correspondents, diplomats, and U.N. personnel was that the mostly Muslim government was supported by all ethnic groups.

The U.S. press echoed this message. In May 1992, the *Washington Post* claimed that "Bosnia's Muslims and Croats support reorganization of the republic into a multi-ethnic state with decentralized communal authority and strong human-rights safeguards, while militant Serbs wish outright autonomy and preservation of political links with Serbia or the new two-republic Yugoslav federation it controls."[38] There was little reason to question the claim. With the vast majority of the foreign press based in Sarajevo's Muslim-held section, correspondents were operating under the premise that they were placed on the "right" side. They did not venture to counter politically correct views of the Bosnian conflict presented by their hosts in Sarajevo and accepted by their editors back home.

The "multiethnic Bosnia" argument was undoubtedly a fiction that U.S. policymakers and the media were willing to accept. Some policymakers and members of the press may have genuinely believed the claim to be true, especially in the early days of the war when there was a tentative union between Muslims and Croats. Yet even in the first weeks of the war in Bosnia, the Croatian army began pouring into Bosnian territory, assisted by local Bosnian Croat irregular forces. The aim of Bosnian Croats and their military supporters in neighboring Croatia was to establish their own government in Bosnia, which was no different than the goal of Bosnian Serbs. This fact became clearer on May 6, 1992, when only a month after Bosnia-Hercegovina was recognized as an independent state, Bosnian Serbs and Croats signed the Graz Plan at a secret meeting in Austria, where they agreed to stop fighting each other and divide Bosnia-Hercegovina without Muslim approval. The Croats were even beginning to assist the Serb military in their battles against the Muslims. Although Bosnia's three-sided ethnic divisions were becoming more evident, why were Washington's pundits, activists, and policymakers continuing the myth of Bosnia as a multiethnic state? By denying that Bosnia's Croats had similar goals as those of the Serbs, it lent credence to interventionist views against the Serbs and justified coercive measures that followed.

U.N. SANCTIONS AGAINST SERBIA: INCONSISTENT CRITERIA

In May of 1992, the United States initiated a number of policies that would not only fan the flames of Yugoslav conflict, but also stand as glaring examples of Washington's double standards in foreign policy and international law. With Bosnia-Hercegovina formally recognized as an independent state, the United Nations Security Council issued Resolution 752 on May 15, 1992, which proposed that "those units of the Yugoslav People's Army and elements of the Croatian Army either be withdrawn or be subject to the authority of the Government of Bosnia-Hercegovina, or be disbanded and disarmed." In the coming weeks, the United States imposed a series of sanctions on the Serb-led Yugoslav government. Although Great Britain asked the United Nations to consider applying sanctions not only against Serbia, but against any state that might intervene in Bosnia, such as Croatia, Washington was focused on punishing only the Serbs. The United Nations followed Washington's lead, and on May 30, 1992, the Security Council decided to impose comprehensive mandatory economic sanctions on Yugoslavia by Resolution 757.

The resolution was unjustified for several reasons. First, JNA troops were already pulling out of Bosnia as called for by the U.N. resolution.

The remaining troops were Bosnian Serbs. Even U.N. commanders in Sarajevo acknowledged that by this time most of the recruits in the JNA who were born in Bosnia-Hercegovina had left the Yugoslav army and had joined the new Bosnian Serb army under the command of former JNA General Ratko Mladic.[39] As the conflict intensified, fighting took place between Bosnian Muslim (TDF) ground forces and local Bosnian Serbs—not the JNA. Any remaining JNA troops that were attempting to pull out of the region were often delayed by frequent ambushes by Muslim troops. For example, when the last remaining JNA troops in Sarajevo attempted to pull out on May 17, 1992, they were blocked by Muslim forces and were held hostage. Furthermore, during the period JNA was withdrawing, the United Nations documented Muslim snipers regularly shooting and killing Serbs stranded in JNA barracks.[40] It was in retaliation against these attacks that the Serbs would fire from their positions into Sarajevo. In the end, the JNA was disarmed and escorted from Sarajevo under U.N. protection.

Given this situation, if a modest presence of JNA troops in Bosnia-Hercegovina by the end of May 1992 was interpreted by the U.N. Security Council as an outside intervention, then the presence of Croatian troops in Bosnia-Hercegovina would surely come under the same category. Yet U.N. Resolution 757 applied sanctions solely on Yugoslavia, even though just one month earlier, U.N. General Lewis MacKenzie and his staff noted that, while fighting was taking place between Bosnian Muslim and Serb forces on April 20, 1992, the Croatian army was invading Bosnian territory in the north and southwest.[41]

Washington's claim that Bosnia was a case of Serbian aggression was simply unfounded. To admit that Bosnia-Hercegovina was undergoing civil war would weaken the justification for intervention to fight an "aggression" and would leave Washington's interventionists with limited arguments in support of U.S. involvement in the Balkans. *Washington Post* editors would frequently claim that the war in Bosnia was a case of outside Serbian aggression, but as early as September 1991 an article from their own newspaper showed the true nature of the conflict: "all three ethnic groups [were] being organized into rival militias [in] mountain training camps."[42] The "civil war" scenario of Bosnia would be shelved as pundits and interventionists pushed for a greater U.S. role in solving the Balkan quagmire.

U.N. OBSERVATIONS CONTRADICT POPULAR VIEWS OF THE BOSNIAN WAR

By the middle of 1992, the image of the war in Bosnia that was emerging in U.S. newspapers and television news reports greatly differed from what was taking place on the ground. This difference was most readily apparent when comparing views of U.N. personnel stationed in Sarajevo and other parts of Bosnia and views presented by the U.S. media. One reason for these differing perceptions was the fact that U.N. personnel traveled to Bosnian Serb-held areas and dealt closely with all sides of the war. The media, on the other hand, was stationed primarily in the Muslim-held parts of Sarajevo and was often not allowed, unable, or unwilling to cross the dangerous front lines. As a result, the United Nations had a more realistic view of the war fought in Bosnia. Other individuals—usually military personnel—who had a better understanding of the true nature of the fighting in Bosnia similarly found their views diverging from popular myths promoted in Washington by media images. Charles G. Boyd, who spent two years as deputy commander of the U.S. European Command, put it succinctly when he wrote that the "the linchpin of America's approach to the Balkans has been the notion that this is a war of good versus evil," and the "public view of the war has come largely through the eyes of one party, the Bosnian Muslims, a people whose status as victim has been a valuable and jealously guarded tool of war."[43]

A reputable Western source for the nature of the war in Bosnia-Hercegovina during 1992 was the UNPROFOR commander in Bosnia, General MacKenzie, who has described his experiences in his book, *Peacekeeper*. Although the U.S. media perceived the war as a struggle of good against evil, MacKenzie saw no good guys in the conflict. He observed daily battles taking place between Serbian and Muslim forces. A telling example was the battle over Sarajevo airport that took place throughout June of 1992. To the Bosnian Muslims, gaining control over the airport meant that they would be able to smuggle weapons from Islamic countries more easily. The Bosnian Serbs, on the other hand, sought to deny Muslims control of the airport in order to weaken their wartime enemies and force them to negotiate a territorial division of Bosnia and Hercegovina. The military implications of controlling the airport were ignored by the U.S. press, which continued to focus solely on the humanitarian aspects of the war. The *New York Times* described the situation as one where "General Mladic's marauders [were keeping] U.N. peacekeepers from securing Sarajevo's airport and allowing desperately needed relief flights to land."[44] In another report, the *Washington Post* depicted the situation as one where the United Nations was trying "to fly in badly needed supplies of food and medicine to the besieged city" and "supervise the removal of Serb anti-aircraft guns and to prepare the runway for humanitarian flights."[45]

Serb antiaircraft guns were not the real issue here. The Bosnian Serb command was interested mainly in neutralizing the military capability of Muslim forces. As soon as the Muslim side agreed to demilitarize the area around the airport, the Bosnian Serbs agreed to place their guns under U.N. control, and the airport was open to U.N. relief flights by the end of

June 1992. Clearly, the humanitarian situation was a result of military strategies and related circumstances that occur in every war and, to greater or lesser extent, to all warring sides.

In one of my trips to Bosnia during this period, both Bosnian Serb civilians and soldiers I met told me they feared laying down their arms because Serbian concessions were invariably followed by Muslim attacks. At least one such example confirmed the Serbs's fears at the time. After diplomatic intervention by Russian Foreign Minister Andrei Kozyrev convinced Bosnian Serbs to allow the reopening of Sarajevo's airport for deliveries of humanitarian aid to the city, on June 13, 1992, Bosnian Muslims took advantage of the situation to launch an all-out attack on Serbian neighborhoods in Sarajevo. Bosnian Muslim leaders wanted more than just delivery of humanitarian aid to their part of the city: they wanted to gain a military advantage.

The reality in Sarajevo, observed by U.N. General MacKenzie but rarely addressed by the U.S. media, was that countless battles took place in the city with a "vicious circle of retaliation," where "the TDF [Bosnian Muslim forces] would initiate a minor encounter, and the Bosnian Serbs would overreact with their heavy weapons, including artillery and rocket launchers. The Serbs were outnumbered by a less well-trained TDF infantry force; however, they were fixated on their fear of being 'overrun' by the Muslim 'Green Berets,' and chose to fight them from a distance.... The vicious circle was getting worse every day as the TDF became stronger."[46] Outnumbered, Bosnian Serbs attempted to thwart Muslim assaults with heavy shelling, and the results were tragic for Sarajevo's civilian population.

The shelling of Sarajevo was negative from the point of view of the foreign press stationed in the Muslim-held parts of the city. Members of the media, frequently confined to hotel rooms and shelters during the shelling, experienced a frightening and memorable phenomenon of war. Foreign correspondents could not possibly know who fired first at any given instance. Nor could they witness the results of the battle from the perspective of the Serbian civilians on the other side. As a result, media coverage from Sarajevo exhibited the same trends noted by observers in previous years. In their book, *Manufacturing Consent*, Herman and Chomsky described the media's tendency to create "worthy victims" who were "featured prominently and dramatically" and "humanized" by providing "detail and context in story construction that generated reader interest and sympathetic emotion" and by giving ample coverage of the worthy victim with "gory details and quoted expressions of outrage and demands for justice."[47] In contrast, coverage of the "unworthy victims was low-keyed, designed to keep the lid on emotions" and described with "only slight detail, minimal humanization, and little context that [would] excite and enrage." Media coverage of the Bosnian war similarly pushed the idea that Bosnia's Muslims were "worthy victims." Bosnian Serb victims of war, on the other hand, were trivialized or ignored. Serbs were repeatedly demonized as aggressors, nationalists, or hard-liners.

This perception was particularly obvious in photographs depicting the war. From January to July 1992, out of a total of 71 photographs relating to the war in Bosnia and printed in the *Washington Post*, only three drew attention to the plight of Bosnian Serbs: one was a photograph of a dead Yugoslav soldier after a Muslim ambush in Sarajevo in May 1992; another showed Bosnian Serbs weeping after being driven from their village near Sarajevo; and the third was a photo of a Serbian refugee mother and her child.[48] In the same period, an overwhelming 31 photographs were sympathetic to Bosnian Muslims—showing refugees, women crying, Bosnian Muslims waiting for food, or mourning. At the same time, a disproportionately large number of photographs depicted Serbian soldiers. Out of 13 photographs, including an armed Serbian woman, none depicted Serb soldiers in a sympathetic manner. In comparison, out of eight photographs of Muslim soldiers, three were sympathetic—one showed a Muslim soldier carrying groceries, another assisting refugees, and another praying at a funeral. Indeed, the *Washington Post*'s choice of photos sent a clear message to the average reader: Serbs were the aggressors, while Muslim and Croat soldiers were a defensive force protecting the primary victims of the war.

Other aspects of the Bosnian war differed between U.N. observations and media reports as well. To U.N. observers on the ground in Sarajevo, a typical all-out exchange between Muslims and Serbs would involve shell detonations on both sides that went off about every 10 seconds. U.N. observers who viewed daily battles from a strategically high point often reported that firing would start everywhere at about the same time.[49] Although many U.N. reports refrained from blaming either side when they were unable to determine who started the fighting, the media frequently implied or directly accused Bosnian Serbs for most of the fighting that took place in four and a half years of war. In starkly contrasting reports, during a June 1992 battle over Sarajevo airport, the *Washington Post* reported that Serb forces "continued to fire artillery shells indiscriminately into the city center despite a cease-fire call."[50] The same incident was described by U.N. General MacKenzie as a situation in which "over fifty rounds were fired, while mortars joined in *from both sides*."[51]

In reality, it was often difficult to determine who fired first and from which direction in Bosnia, because the mortar was frequently used on all sides. To complicate matters further, in most cases, neither side would admit to firing on the other. The inability of U.N. observers to determine the exact source of mortar attacks made the mortar a preferred choice of weapon, particularly for several likely "staged" attacks by Bosnian Muslim forces on their own territories aimed at drawing Western support and military intervention against the Serbs. Evidence suggested that such attacks included the May 27, 1992 Sarajevo breadline attack, as well as later incidents, such as the August 4, 1992 explosion at a Sarajevo cemetery where two orphans were being buried, and what was called a "choreographed" mortar salvo 30 seconds after British Foreign Secretary Douglas Hurd entered a building for a meeting with Bosnian Muslim President Alija Izetbegovic.[52]

A common technique used by the Bosnian Muslim forces was to set up their weapons close to U.N. positions. This would allow them to fire at the Serbs while denying the Serbs a clear target, since they would endanger U.N. positions next to Bosnian Muslim military targets. Any counterattack would provoke international outrage with reports that the Serbs were shelling U.N. peacekeepers. A clear example occurred in July 1992, when Muslim TDF forces set up a mortar position about 60 yards from a U.N. camp in Sarajevo. At the time, U.N. general MacKenzie vehemently protested to the Bosnian Muslim vice-president Ejup Ganic: "It is against every rule ever written to set up weapons beside a U.N. position and use us as a shield."[53] MacKenzie's increasing criticisms of Bosnian Muslim military tactics, however, were not well received either by the Bosnian Muslim leadership or their sympathizers in Washington.

The U.S. press, in particular, could not bring itself to view the Bosnian Muslim government as merely a warring party with the same military tactics as any other side fighting a war. At a June 1992 press conference in Sarajevo, when General MacKenzie blamed both sides for the fighting, a reporter asked: "why did you say both sides are equally to blame, General MacKenzie? We all know who the aggressor is."[54] By now, the media's image of Bosnian Muslim as "victims" was not likely to change. The Muslim government was particularly annoyed with MacKenzie. Only toward the end of his assignment in Sarajevo did the U.N. general openly acknowledge that "it was probably a good thing that I had only a few more days to go in Sarajevo, since I was becoming much too honest in my statements to the press."[55] Predictably, after his press conference, General MacKenzie was pulled out of Sarajevo ahead of schedule. Referring to MacKenzie's criticism of the Bosnian Muslim government, U.N. General Satish Nambiar said, "You might be right, but you can't say those things."[56]

MacKenzie's quick departure from Sarajevo was a demonstration of what happened to members of international governmental and media organizations based in Sarajevo who ventured to criticize Muslim officials. It was quietly understood that personnel stationed in Sarajevo would hold a politically correct view of the Muslim government if they were to stay and continue their work. In General MacKenzie's case, his reluctance to take sides in the war, his opposition to international intervention, and his opposition to lifting the arms embargo were the basis for a Bosnian

Muslim government smear campaign against him in 1992 that made his work as head of the U.N. peacekeeping mission in Sarajevo impossible.[57] Even after he left Bosnia, slanderous attacks on him continued. In November 1992, a Bosnian-Serb soldier, Borislav Herak, arrested by the Bosnian Muslim government and charged with murder and rape, allegedly testified to seeing General MacKenzie pick up four Muslim girls who were taken to be raped and murdered.[58] Years later, it was discovered that Herak and other captives were forced to testify under torture by Muslims on this and other matters.[59] At the time, however, accusations aroused greater media attention than fact. The media would become a willing collaborator in the Bosnian Muslim government's war of words against Serbs, or anyone they viewed as opposed to the Muslim cause.

The effects of the war of words would come to full force in the coming months as a second phase of the Bosnian war was about to begin—the public relations war. In the period ending with the Winter of 1992, the Bosnian Muslim government would launch a significant public relations campaign to win the hearts of Washington elites. This would have the most significant effect on the Yugoslav conflict and would change the military situation on the ground.

NOTES

1. Blaine Harden, "Clashes in Croatia Escalating; Army Pullout Deadline Looms," *Washington Post* (August 24, 1991): A11.
2. Blaine Harden, "Army Offensive in Croatia Draws European Warnings," *Washington Post* (August 27, 1991): A1.
3. William Drozdiak, "Yugoslavs Trade Accusations as Peace Conference Opens," *Washington Post* (September 8, 1991): A31.
4. Ibid.
5. Blaine Harden, "Yugoslav Tanks Roll into Croatia; Army Launches Biggest Offensive," *Washington Post* (September 21, 1991): A1.
6. Blaine Harden, "Croatia Claims It Repulsed Tank Assault; Yugoslav Army Fails to Capture Key City," *Washington Post* (September 22, 1991): A29.
7. Ibid.
8. Laura Silber, "Bosnia Declares Sovereignty: Serbia, Croatia Set Peace Talks," *Washington Post* (October 16, 1991): A29.
9. Jamie Owen, "Dubrovnik Is Not Destroyed," *Europa Times* (September 1994).
10. Ibid.
11. Laura Silber, "EC Lifts Yugoslav Sanctions, Except Serbia, Montenegro; West European Monitors Accuse Army of Brutality; Vance to Visit Besieged Croatian City," *Washington Post* (December 3, 1991): A9.
12. William Drozdiak, "12 West European Countries Recognize Croatia, Slovenia," *Washington Post* (January 16, 1992): A21.
13. William Drozdiak, "Germany Vows Balkan Recognition; EC's Criteria for

Ties Not Binding, Genscher Tells Foreign Ministers," *Washington Post* (January 11, 1992): A14.

14. William Drozdiak, "Europeans' Balkan Stance Attests to Rising German Influence," *Washington Post* (December 18, 1991): A25.

15. Robert Marquand, "UN-EC Map for Bosnia Plan Based on Disputed Figures," *Christian Science Monitor* (February 3, 1993): 7.

16. "Bosna je Okupirana—Al' ne za dugo" [Bosnia is occupied, but not for long], *Novi Vox* 3 (Sarajevo, October 1991).

17. "Breakthrough Announced in Talks on Bosnian Independence Plan," *Washington Post* (March 19, 1992): A20.

18. George Kenney, "Steering Clear of Balkan Shoals," *The Nation* (January 8/15, 1996): 22.

19. U.S. Department of Justice, *Foreign Agents Registration Statement*, "Amendment to Registration Statement" (Washington, D.C., November 6, 1992): 2.

20. Ibid.

21. Jeanne Kirkpatrick, "What Are the President's Foreign Policy Goals?" *Washington Post* (March 16, 1992): A17.

22. Alfonse M. D'Amato, "Bum Rap on Yugoslavia?" *Washington Post* (April 18, 1992): A18.

23. *Foreign Agents Registration Statement* (November 6, 1992): 3.

24. Stephen S. Rosenfeld, "Bum Rap," *Washington Post* (April 10, 1992): A27.

25. D'Amato, "Bum Rap on Yugoslavia?" A18.

26. David Binder, "U.S. Policymakers on Bosnia Admit Errors in Opposing Partition in 1992," *New York Times* (August 29, 1993): 10.

27. Stefan Halper, "Bosnian Policy at Odds with History?" *Washington Times* (September 7, 1993).

28. David Hoffman, "U.S. Urges Europe to Protect Bosnia; Baker Maps Protest to Serb Leaders," *Washington Post* (April 15, 1992): A1.

29. Michael Colomes and Marc Roche, "Big Blunders in Yugoslavia," *Cleveland Plain Dealer* (October 19, 1992): 5-B.

30. General Lewis MacKenzie, *Peacekeeper: The Road to Sarajevo* (Vancouver, British Columbia: Douglas & McIntyre, 1993), 144.

31. Ibid., 170.

32. "Army Releases Bosnian Leader; Retreating Troops Are Attacked," *Washington Post* (May 4, 1992): A16.

33. MacKenzie, *Peacekeeper*, 179.

34. Ibid.

35. Blaine Harden, "Serb Gunners Pound Sarajevo in Fierce Attack; Dubrovnik Shelling Resumes as U.N. Debates Sanctions," *Washington Post* (May 29, 1992): A1.

36. Leonard Doyle, "Muslims 'Slaughter' Their Own People: Bosnia Bread Queue Massacre Was Propaganda Ploy, UN Told," *The Independent* (August 22, 1992): 10.

37. MacKenzie, *Peacekeeper*, 194.

38. "Army Releases Bosnian Leader; Retreating Troops Are Attacked," *Washington Post* (May 4, 1992): A16.

39. MacKenzie, *Peacekeeper*, 191, 195, 279.

40. Ibid., 192, 200.

41. Ibid., 156.

42. Blaine Harden, "Yugoslav Army Keeps Fighting Without a Country to Defend," *Washington Post* (September 27, 1991): A21.

43. Charles G. Boyd, "America Prolongs the War in Bosnia," *New York Times* (August 9, 1995): A19.

44. "The World Watches Murder," *New York Times* (June 24, 1992): 20.

45. Blaine Harden, "Shells Hit U.N. Convoy in Sarajevo; 3 Canadian Officers Injured Amid Heavy Fighting in City's Suburbs," *Washington Post* (June 21, 1992): A25.

46. MacKenzie, *Peacekeeper*, 200.

47. Edward S. Herman and Noam Chomsky, *Manufacturing Consent: The Political Economy of the Mass Media* (New York: Pantheon Books, 1988), 35, 39.

48. Marc Fisher, "Trepidation over Balkans; Europeans Fear Yugoslav War Could Spread," *Washington Post* (May 16, 1992): A1.

49. MacKenzie, *Peacekeeper*, 217–218.

50. Blaine Harden, "Shells Hit U.N. Convoy in Sarajevo; 3 Canadian Officers Injured Aim Heavy Fighting in City's Suburbs," *Washington Post* (June 21, 1992): A25.

51. MacKenzie, *Peacekeeper*, 221–222.

52. Leonard Doyle, "Muslims 'Slaughter' Their Own People," *The Independent* (August 22, 1992): 10.

53. MacKenzie, *Peacekeeper*, 309.

54. Ibid., 307.

55. Ibid., 308.

56. Ibid., 310.

57. Ibid., 328.

58. Mike Trickey, "War Propagandists for Hire: Croatia, Bosnia Use Western Public Relations Firms to Win Support," *The Spectator* (February 12, 1993): A11.

59. Jonathan C. Randal, "Serb Convicted of Murders Demanding Retrial After 2 'Victims' Found Alive," *Washington Post* (March 15, 1997): A17.

Chapter 5

War of Words, at Full Force
(June to December 1992)

PUBLIC RELATIONS WAR IN WASHINGTON

The six-month interval from the middle to the end of 1992 would prove to be a crucial period, setting the stage for all future U.S. decisions in the Yugoslav conflict. An intensified public relations effort by the Bosnian Muslim government during this time would solidify the foundation they had previously laid with U.S. policymakers and the media on assumptions about the Bosnian war. Perspectives that Washington's foreign policymakers and media elites were already exposed to during the Croatian government's public relations campaign were about to be reinforced by the Bosnian Muslim government, which hired the same public relations firm engaged by Croatia a year earlier.

The Serbs' ethnic rivals centralized their war of words in Washington. The Bosnian Muslim strategy was to depict the conflict not as a civil war but as a war of Serbian aggression. A specifically stated intention of the Bosnian Muslim government's public relations firm in Washington was what they described as the "dissemination of Bosnia's position on issues concerning the Serbian invasion of that country."[1] Bosnian Muslim representatives reinforced the idea that the war in Bosnia was—as their foreign minister, Haris Silajdzic, told American reporters at a May 1992 press conference—"purely an attack by Serbia and Montenegro . . . with the Yugoslav Army instrumental in the aggression."[2] Silajdzic later told me that he must have been in and out of taxis hundreds of times in years of visiting members of Congress and the State Department and giving interviews to the U.S. media. Several Bosnian Muslim officials spoke fluent English and were skilled at using emotional sound bites that became the daily staples of U.S. media reports. These included phrases like "Serbian hard-line nationalists," "Serbian siege," "Serbian aggression," or "Serb occupiers," as well as depictions of Bosnian Muslim forces as "Bosnian defenders," Sarajevans as "Bosnian victims," and Sarajevo as a "besieged city."

In the early months of the Bosnian Muslim government's public relations efforts, Washington's foreign policy and media elites were barraged with letters and press releases written by Ruder Finn on behalf of the Bosnian Muslim government and distributed to key members of congressional committees dealing with Bosnia, including Senators Robert Dole, Richard Lugar, Joseph Lieberman, Dennis DeConcini, George Mitchell, Claiborne Pell, Sam Nunn, Paul Simon, and Alan Simpson, as well as high-level officials, including Secretary of State James Baker and Secretary of Defense Dick Cheney. Appeals were made at the highest levels, not just in the United States, but in Europe and international bodies too, including President George Bush, British Prime Minister Margaret Thatcher, members of the European Community, and the United Nations Security Council.[3] In faxed press releases and propaganda material prepared by Ruder Finn, Bosnian Serbs were portrayed as "occupiers," "aggressors," extremists," and "hard-line nationalists," and their legitimacy was questioned by claims that most of the region's Serbs did not support them. The Bosnian Muslim government, on the other hand, was depicted as "multiethnic," "tolerant," and a "freely elected government with guarantees for all ethnic groups."[4]

Historic revisionism helped generate Bosnian myths promoted during this period. By reinterpreting history, the Muslim government hoped to undermine Serbian territorial claims in Bosnia and obscure the true nature of ethnic relations between Serbs, Croats, and Muslims. In one press release, Izetbegovic was quoted as saying, "we have lived together for hundreds of years," in an attempt to justify his government's goal to keep Bosnia together. But it was also misleading, considering that during those "hundreds of years," Bosnian Serbs had attempted to free themselves from Ottoman Turk occupying forces and their Bosnian Muslim supporters. Bosnia was presented as a long-time independent nation, the Muslim leadership referred to itself as the "Bosnian government," the region's history as "Bosnian history," its inhabitants as "Bosnians" rather than Serb, Croatian, and Muslim, and the official language as "Bosnian" rather than Serbo-Croatian. This would be comparable to a claim that Americans speak American rather than English.

On political debate shows, Bosnian Muslim representatives alleged that Bosnia had been a peaceful nation for centuries and a model of multiethnic cooperation—a skillful attempt to appeal to Washington and the American public by comparing Bosnia to the United States. During an April 18, 1994, episode of CNN's *Sonya Live*, Nedzib Sacirbey, the Bosnian Muslim Minister at Large, said, "we were together for centuries, we were together in an independent Bosnia too, because when we had elections in November of 1990, the Serbs, Croats, and Muslims together formed a presidency and government." Yet, Sacirbey knew perfectly well that Bosnia was not at all "independent" in 1990. "Yes, Muslims, Croats, and Serbs lived together in Bosnia," I replied, "but this was when it was part of Yugoslavia ... but democratically elected Bosnian Serb leaders were ousted from Sarajevo ... democracy and multi-ethnicity does not exist in Muslim-held areas of Bosnia today."

The idea that ethnic groups in Bosnia lived together for centuries was highly deceptive. Muslim officials claimed that proof of a "multiethnic Bosnia" was clear to anyone visiting Sarajevo, where one can see a Muslim mosque standing next to a Catholic church, a Serbian Orthodox church, and a Jewish temple. This idea was then touted by U.S. officials, such as former U.S. ambassador to Yugoslavia, Warren Zimmermann, who said that Sarajevo "for centuries had been a moving symbol of the civility that comes from people of different ethnicities living in harmony."[5] The media willingly repeated the claim that Sarajevo, in the words of one reporter, "was for centuries a model in Europe of ethnic cohabitation." This was far from the truth. Since the Ottoman Turk occupation of Bosnia and Hercegovina in the 15th century, Sarajevo had been the stronghold of Muslim nobles who exploited the mostly Serbian Christian Orthodox peasants.[6] The fact that different religious buildings in Sarajevo stood in close proximity to each other did not indicate a tolerant society. Quite the contrary, numbers of churches or mosques in Bosnia-Hercegovina served as indicators of political power and control that one group was able to exert over the other. When Serbian feudal lords ruled much of the region in the Middle Ages, hundreds of Serbian monasteries were built. Catholic churches were likewise built in areas dominated by Croat feudal lords. By the 15th century, Islamic dominance over Bosnia and Hercegovina was accompanied by the building of mosques. The idea that Bosnia and Hercegovina were characterized by centuries of multiethnic cooperation, however, was regularly presented in an attempt to convince Washington that the Muslim government was trying to keep Bosnia unified and multiethnic, while Serb nationalists were trying to break it apart. The strategy was effective in arousing sympathy in the West.

Having professional help in presenting its views to Western governments made the Bosnian Muslim government's tactics more likely to succeed. The public relations firm, Ruder Finn, helped promote the Muslim position by distributing news releases, writing speeches, organizing media conferences, and drafting pertinent resolutions at international conferences relating to Bosnia. The firm also regularly arranged interviews with members of the editorial boards of the *Washington Post, New York Times, Wall Street Journal, USA Today, Newsweek*, as well as producers at CNN, and NPR's *All Things Considered*, to name a few.[7] Media "stake-outs" were also frequently scheduled to promote coverage of reactions from members of Congress after meeting with Muslim officials. Duplicating strategies previously used by the government of Croatia, "fact-finding" missions were organized for members of Congress who were selectively exposed to Bosnian Muslim views and guided to Muslim-controlled areas. After returning from such trips, members jumped at the chance to speak out on behalf of the Bosnian Muslims.

Having returned from his second trip to Sarajevo, Congressman McCloskey became one of the most outspoken supporters of the Muslim and Croat position. On television, radio, and in editorials, McCloskey urged immediate U.S. military assistance to the Bosnian Muslim government.[8] Bosnia launched McCloskey from obscurity into the spotlight of CNN's *Crossfire* and other popular shows. It is difficult to say what motivated McCloskey to support aggressive U.S. intervention against the Serbs in both Croatia and Bosnia-Hercegovina throughout his congressional term. He may have done so out of genuine humanitarian concern, or because of financial support from Croatian constituents, personal sympathy for Croatian Catholics with whom he shared the same religion, or acquaintances he developed with members of the Bosnian Muslim government. Whatever his reasons, McCloskey became one of the most vocal members of the Commission on Security and Cooperation in Europe (CSCE)—an important congressional committee that dealt with U.S. foreign policy in the Balkans. McCloskey's interest in the Balkans extended well beyond his term in Congress. In 1996, after leaving Congress, he worked directly for the Bosnian Muslim government as a legal adviser. Activism by Congressman McCloskey and others on behalf of the Bosnian Muslim government demonstrated how easily Congress became yet another public relations arena for one Yugoslav warring party. Interestingly, no member of Congress visited Bosnian Serb areas until 1995.

The public relations campaign by the Bosnian Muslim government in Washington partially explained why the U.S. media frequently became a conduit of popular, though often incorrect, rhetoric on Bosnia. Articles presenting views outside the mainstream were typically published in newspapers that were less likely to be read by Washington elites. In the early days of the public relations wars, Bill Mandel of the *San Francisco Examiner* wrote that, "without a good map, a good teacher, and a good dose of patience, your view of the jaw-dropping carnage in the pieces of old Yugoslavia may come directly from the same kind of international PR firm that cooked up the famous fake Persian Gulf incubator horror . . . concocted for Kuwait by its public relations firm."[9] Another article published in a February 1993 issue of the *Atlanta Journal* observed that "Yugoslavia is an example of a less publicized playing field in the Washington lobbying game. It is the marketing of human misery. . . . If they convince Americans that their cause is just, political support, financial assistance—

even U.S. troops—may follow."[10] The public relations war during the Yugoslav conflict indeed had a significant effect on Washington, yielding political support, humanitarian aid, weapons, and even U.S. troops in later years.

HUMANITARIAN AIRLIFTS: THE SLIPPERY SLOPE TOWARD INTERVENTION

On June 17, 1992, President George Bush announced that the United States would take part in a large-scale airlift of food and humanitarian supplies to Sarajevo. Although a seemingly benevolent act, the humanitarian airlift would mark the emergence of a slippery slope that would eventually lead to extensive U.S. involvement in the Bosnian war. Interventionists supported the airlift as a step toward expanding America's role in European crises. The U.S. media and human rights advocates pushed for aid to Muslim civilians to alleviate their suffering. The Bosnian Muslim government welcomed airlifts as the first step toward drawing in U.S. military support and the covert flow of weapons, while the Serbs saw the airlift as yet another step in aiding just one side in the war.

The Serbs believed that the airlift would provide covert military assistance to the Muslims, since alongside the airlifts, airplanes from Islamic countries carrying weapons could go unnoticed. The war in Bosnia had already become a religious struggle, with Arab and Afghan *Mujaheddin* "holy warrior" fighters pouring into Bosnia-Hercegovina, apparently, with the backing of Alija Izetbegovic and his government.[11] Even U.S. newspapers such as the *Washington Post* had been reporting that arms from Islamic countries were reaching Bosnian battlefields.[12] In the Summer of 1992, Serbian military commanders were finding fragments of mortar shells lobbed from the Muslim side with Iranian insignia. They believed that Turkey and other Muslim countries were covertly delivering airdrops of weapons to Bosnia's Muslims. For this reason, the Serbs kept Sarajevo sealed off.

Ignoring the military implications of keeping Sarajevo sealed off, the media presented an image of the city as a civilian catastrophe, with Serbs maliciously preventing aid from alleviating the people's suffering. While Washington frequently expressed humanitarian concerns for Bosnia, the intent clearly was to help only people in Muslim areas, including Muslim troops. U.S. humanitarian airdrops did not target towns controlled by the Bosnian Serbs, even though Serbian civilians had just as much need of food and medical supplies as others in Bosnia. Washington was more interested in helping one side win the war than in providing comprehensive humanitarian aid.

Washington's interventionists turned Bosnia's humanitarian problem into a case for stronger U.S. involvement—a necessary step in demonstrating U.S. leadership in Europe. Years later, in a CNN interview on June 3, 1998, Richard Holbrooke, chief U.S. negotiator for Bosnia in 1995, reiterated that position by saying that the main lesson to be learned from Bosnia was that Europeans were wrong to think they could handle the Yugoslav conflict without the United States. Bosnia, according to Holbrooke, proved that the United States, as the world's only superpower, was an integral part of the process of resolving crises in Europe. Those in Washington who supported a more active U.S. role in Bosnia would get ammunition for their propaganda war in the Fall of 1992 with the breaking of the prison camp story.

IMAGES OF PRISON CAMPS: WEAPONS IN A WAR OF WORDS

The media was assuredly the most substantial source of information about the Bosnian war, for the American public, as well as for hundreds of analysts and advisers in Congress, the State Department, and other governmental agencies. Martin Bell of BBC television explained that on Bosnia, "Governments get to hear what's happening through us. People come up and talk to me—ministers, mediators, and so on. . . . they haven't the least idea what's happening because they can't be on the ground."[13] The media's effect was particularly evident in Washington, where the media played a large part in gaining U.S. support for the Bosnian Muslim government. Selectively chosen words and sound bites used in a timely manner became comparable to weapons, by eventually persuading Washington to step in with military support.

The Bosnian prison camp issue emerged in August of 1992, dramatically demonstrating the effect of sensation over substance in U.S. foreign policy. It was the beginning of some of the most emotional media coverage of the conflict. Allegations that Muslim refugees were victims of "ethnic cleansing" and that their people were kept in "death camps" were first made by Bosnian Muslim officials. Soon afterward, the U.S. press was buzzing with similar allegations, which would become part of Washington's jargon in years to come. Even though all of Bosnia's warring factions had prison camps for war detainees, the U.S. press focused solely on gruesome images in describing Serb-run camps, which they referred to as "concentration camps" and "death camps," recalling visions of Nazi Germany. Bosnian Muslim Foreign Minister Silajdzic made one of the first comparisons between Bosnian Serb and Nazi camps. In an impassioned plea during a May 1992 news conference in Washington, he accused the world of "standing on the sidelines as it had done in the face of Nazi atrocities in the 1930's." He claimed that "Bosnian towns and cities were undergoing ethnic cleansing under Serbian guns" and that "whole neighborhoods of non-Serbs were being herded" into "concentration camps."[14] Silajdzic and other Bosnian Muslim officials regularly evoked these images in an effort to influence Washington.

Not surprisingly, Jewish organizations were quite moved by the parallel between Bosnia and the Holocaust. A number of Jewish groups, including the American Jewish Committee expressed strong sympathy for Bosnia's Muslims. Committee president Richard J. Sideman, immediately published an editorial on the "brutalities in Bosnia" in which he wrote that "mass killings, deportations in cattle cars, ethnic cleansing, rape, [and] mutilation ... are words that summon the darkest memories of World War II."[15] An August 2, 1992, *Newsday* article by Roy Gutman entitled "Bosnia's Camps of Death" gave particular legitimacy to the Nazi camp comparison. Gutman's dramatic accounts of survivors' tales of systematic executions in two detention camps in northern Bosnia launched a week of publicity and energized pundits and politicians to push for an expanded U.S. role in halting the war. Gutman later wrote his most emotional rendition of events in Bosnia in his book, *A Witness to Genocide.*[16]

The State Department responded to growing media interest in Bosnian prison camps, and the Bush administration was eager to show that it was concerned about the matter. On August 4, 1992, U.S. State Department spokesman Richard Boucher singled out the Serbs and accused them of establishing detention camps in Bosnia where Muslims and Croats were being abused. On the same day, in a more even-handed tone, the head of International Committee of the Red Cross (ICRC), Cornelio Sommaruga, said that all three sides had prison camps and were refusing to open them for inspection, and he placed blame on all warring parties for terrorizing and harassing civilians, intimidating minorities, interning civilians on a massive scale, as well as "torture, deportations and summary executions." Red Cross spokesman Pierre Gathier announced that "very serious violations of internationally recognized law and practice on the treatment of civilians in military conflicts are being perpetuated by all parties," not just the Serbs.[17]

The difference between the ICRC and State Department statements exemplified Washington's increasing tendency to blame the Serbs exclusively. The State Department spokesman acknowledged receiving reports of what he called "detention centers" operated by the Muslim-led Bosnian government and Bosnian Croat militia forces, but unlike the ICRC claims, Boucher said "we do not have similar allegations of mistreatment at those."[18] Notably, one day after accusing the Serbs of committing abuses in prison camps, the State Department backtracked. Thomas M. T. Niles, assistant secretary of state for European and Canadian affairs, stated that previous reports of atrocities did not represent "substantiated information," and therefore the United States could not "confirm" that such atrocities were taking place.[19]

The State Department's note of caution was drowned out by continued allegations by the Bosnian Muslim government, intent on fanning the flames of outrage. On August 5, 1992, the Bosnian Muslim ambassador to the United Nations, Muhamed Sacirbey, charged the Serbs with running what he called concentration camps with Muslim prisoners. On the same day, a *Newsday* headline read: "Serbian 'Ethnic Cleansing' Echoes Nazi Atrocities," while a *Washington Post* headline read: " 'Ethnic Cleansing': Cunning Strategy." Highly charged allegations that originated from the Bosnian Muslim government made a considerable impact on the U.S. media, which readily accepted these accusations and relayed them to the public. Without regard to context or evidence, the prison camp allegations kicked off months of Nazi-era allusions in describing Bosnian Serb activities. On August 6, 1992, British television broadcast an image around the world showing an emaciated prisoner of war held by the Serbs. In an effort to make a sensational news story even more shocking, *USA Today* described Serbian prisoner of war centers as "scenes reminiscent of World War II death camps: emaciated prisoners, barracks and barbed wire."[20] What these reports failed to mention was that all three sides had detention centers for soldiers captured in combat, and that Serbian prisoners were held in exactly the same manner—behind barbed wire—by Croats and Muslims. The physical state of the soldiers varied, depending on their condition upon capture. Those that were captured after having spent weeks hiding out in the mountains were weak and malnourished. Others may have been mistreated during capture. The scenario, however grim, was no different than that of any other wartime situation between combatants.

The number of prisoners the Serbs allegedly held fluctuated wildly. Bosnian Muslim officials immediately claimed that 120,000 Muslim and Croat prisoners were held in Serbian camps. The next week the number was cut in half as official Croat and Muslim estimates concluded that 70,000 of their prisoners were held by Serbs in 45 camps. In spite of ample evidence available at the time, generally unreported were Serbian estimates that over 42,000 Serbs were held in 21 Muslim and Croat camps of which 6,000 prisoners had already been executed.[21] The Bosnian Serb officials delivered a statement via the Tanjug News Agency in Belgrade on August 5, 1992, presenting a list of camps run by Muslims and Croats in Bosnia-Hercegovina. The list included approximately 600 Serbs held in the town of Livno; 500 at a camp in Tomislav Grad; 700 at a factory in Bugojno; 500 in the old town fortress in Jajce; 900 at the Bihac soccer stadium; and another 1,000 at a makeshift camp in Orasje. In the town of Odjak, an elementary school served as a camp for 400 Serbs; 150 were held at a factory; 160 in the village of Pazaric near Hodjici; 800 at a soccer stadium in Ilidja; 4,000 at a stadium in Tuzla; 400 in a camp at Bosanski Brod near the Sava River; another 600 in the village of Celebici near Jablanica; and between 1,000 and 1,500 mostly Serbian women and children in a camp in Odjak's Novi Grad suburb.

Bosnian Serbs reported some of the most appalling conditions in the village of Rubici, where 300 prisoners were held at a military depot. In July of 1992, Serbian prisoners were said to have been shipped from Muslim-run camps in the villages of Poljari and Ribici, near Odjak, where the bodies of those executed were bulldozed into the ground near the town's main hospital. In the town of Konjic, 3,000 Serbian civilians were held in appalling conditions in a railroad tunnel. War crimes were reported in Zenica, where Croat and Muslim forces took a number of Serbian prisoners to the town's iron mill factory where they were thrown into the furnace. In the village of Stipari, witnesses said that at least one prisoner a day was taken out to be hanged. The Bosnian Serb leadership made a mistake in thinking that the Western press would report on the plight of Bosnian Serb prisoners without being prodded to do so. During my trips to Bosnia-Hercegovina in later months and years, I met a number of Bosnian Serbs who were held in Muslim prisons, and who told me of the torture they suffered. Although Bosnian Serb newspapers were full of photographs and stories of beatings suffered by male and female Serbian prisoners of war, the information was not readily available to the Western press. Articles were not translated into English, and the Bosnian Serb government did not actively seek out Western reporters to provide them with its point of view. Since most foreign journalists were based in the Muslim-held part of Sarajevo, it was often logistically impossible for Bosnian Serbs to contact foreign journalists. This, combined with the fact that the foreign press was not sympathetic to the Serbs, resulted in little or no information published in the Western press about the plight of Serbs in camps where they were held.

While the U.S. press published an overwhelming number of reports relating to Serb-run camps where Muslims and Croats were held, a list of camps with Serbian prisoners was never made public. Having tried to convey to *Washington Post* Foreign Editor David Ignatius the need to publish information on Serbs held in Bosnian camps, which I faxed to him on August 5, 1992, I was informed that the list would not be published. No explanation was given. One British journalist was said to have been specifically instructed by her editors not to investigate reports of Serbian prisoners, including elderly men, women, and children, held by Bosnian Croats and Muslims in a partially destroyed railroad tunnel.[22] By the time the journalist was able to verify the facts of the report several months later, the story had lost its timeliness and effect.

Only some European press, notably Russian and Greek, placed significant emphasis on the Serbian plight in the Bosnian war. Limited information, however, did emerge about the conditions of Serbian prisoners in Western sources as well. An August 10, 1992 issue of London's *Evening Standard* printed an article that described how 2,000 Serbs were held in what Western observers described as "unimaginable" conditions at a soc-

cer stadium in the Muslim-held town of Gorazde.[23] Remarkably, during
the same time, *Washington Post* articles on Gorazde made no mention of
either the existence of Muslim troops in Gorazde nor the Muslim-run
camp. Instead, an August 16, 1992, article described Gorazde as "just one
of many besieged and battered Muslim outposts in Bosnia"; an August
18, 1992, article included a photograph of a woman crying in what was
described as "Serb-besieged Bosnian city of Gorazde"; and an August 18,
1992, article referred to Gorazde as "refugee-packed city . . . shelled daily
by encircling Serb militia forces." At the same time as U.S. reporters were
willing to go to great lengths to explore Serb-run detention camps, they
almost completely ignored Muslim and Croatian-run camps.

Heinous war crimes against Serbian men and women prisoners that took
place in Celebici, including beatings, torture, rape, and starvation, were
not reported until April 3, 1997, when the U.N. War Crimes Tribunal
charged three Muslims and one Croat for the numerous incidents of torture, abuse, and murder of Serbs at Celebici. Hazim Delic, the Muslim
deputy commander of the camp, along with other members of the Bosnian
Muslim military, Esad Landzo, and Zdravko Mucic were charged with the
deaths of Serbs through torture and cruelty, including beatings of elderly
men to death with wooden planks and torture through use of pliers, acid,
electric shock, and hot pincers.[24] The press did not report these abuses
against Serbs until long after the war in Bosnia was over.

In 1992, when the prison camp issue was at its height, the international
media, U.N. personnel, and other observers in Sarajevo missed the existence of one of the most readily accessible sites for detaining Serbs—
Sarajevo's central prison, which held about 600 Serb civilians. As in the
case of other revelations, not until January 1996 did the *New York Times*
report a story told by one Serb of how his brother was "tortured to death
in a Muslim jail in Sarajevo."[25]

While the U.S. press ignored Serbs imprisoned in Muslim and Croat-
run camps, the popular labels relating to Bosnian Serb-run camps were
repeated by Washington's opinionmakers and politicians vying for attention. Democratic presidential nominee, Bill Clinton, made Bosnia a campaign issue when he declared that "the Balkans is taking on characteristics
of the Nazi extermination of Jews in World War II," and put pressure on
President Bush by joining a group of senators urging that the administration take action against reported atrocities in Bosnian detention camps.[26]
Other critics of the Bush administration used the prison camp issue. Correspondent Richard Cohen of the *Washington Post* wrote an editorial entitled "Death Camps on Bush's Watch," in which he compared World War
II Nazi camps to "Serbian-run death camps" in Bosnia.[27]

With the presidential elections of 1992 now looming, the Bush administration found itself increasingly confronted with a barrage of criticism,
and on August 7 of that year it responded. President Bush announced

measures to penalize Serbia and protect deliveries of humanitarian aid with U.S. military force if needed. Bush said he would order U.S. intelligence agencies "to use every asset available" to find out what was happening in what he called "concentration camps," a term he used even though Pentagon spokesman Pete Williams told reporters at the time that "we do not see any evidence of a program of systematic or massive killing of innocent people by any of the parties to the fighting."[28]

The rhetoric and propaganda used during the mid- to late-1992 period was stronger than that at any other time during the war and got U.S. foreign policy rolling. The impassioned rhetoric was spewed forth without regard for events actually taking place in Bosnia. Although the nature of the Bosnian conflict continued unchanged in the years to come, including daily battles between warring parties, the existence of prison camps, and reports of war crimes, the popular Nazi-era allusions used so frequently in the latter half of 1992 were rarely used toward the war's end. Nevertheless, gruesome images of Bosnian Serb prison camps would fuel interventionists for years to come. While Washington's media pundits, humanitarian activists expressed shock and concern over Serb-run camps, they virtually ignored the round-up of Bosnian Muslim prisoners by Croat forces who turned on their one-time allies in the Spring of 1993—only a few months later. Once a designated "villain" was chosen in Bosnia, nothing else that opposed this view appeared to interest Washington elites.

ETHNIC CLEANSING

The Bosnian Muslim leadership's humanitarian pleas were the key to building consensus in Washington and would ultimately lead to U.S. political and military assistance on behalf of their government. Tragedies of war needed to be turned into effective sound bites. As in the case of prison camps, the phrase "ethnic cleansing" became synonymous with the justification for humanitarian intervention in Bosnia.

The largest number of articles and editorials accusing Bosnian Serbs of "ethnic cleansing" were published in the second half of 1992 and the first half of 1993. In one of the first uses of the term in the mainstream press, the headline of a July 4, 1992 article by *Washington Post* reporter Blaine Harden read "U.S. Airlift Brings Aid to Sarajevo; Serbs Resume Policy of 'Ethnic Cleansing'."[29] The article alleged that "Serb forces began expelling all non-Serbs from a major downtown neighborhood in another round of what is known here as ethnic cleansing." Considering this was the first time the *Washington Post* mentioned ethnic cleansing, an explanation of the term might have been expected. One telling sign about the source of the article's information was the phrase, "what is known here as ethnic cleansing." Most information reported by foreign correspondents from Sarajevo came from Bosnian Muslim sources. So too was the term "ethnic cleansing" or "Serbian policy of ethnic cleansing."

The U.S. media quickly picked up the spin, and soon there were reports accusing Bosnian Serbs of "pursuing a policy of 'ethnic cleansing' by driving out all of the non-Serb population" were followed by even more sensational claims accusing the Serbs of mass extermination as well.[30] In an opinion editorial on June 23, 1992, *Los Angeles Times* editors led off with the statement that "No one knows how many people have died in Bosnia-Hercegovina in the three months since Serbian forces launched a campaign of 'ethnic cleansing' in the multicultural republic. Bosnian officials now put the figure at 40,000, while other, perhaps more objective sources put it at a little more than 7,000."[31] The article's divisive wording combines the idea of people dying in Bosnia with accusations of "ethnic cleansing" to give an impression of Nazi-era systematic extermination. In a June 1992 commentary, *New York Times* editors claimed that Bosnian Muslims were subjected to "ethnic cleansing reminiscent of the Nazis."[32] The former U.S. ambassador to the United Nations, Edward Perkins, went so far as to describe what he called the Bosnian Serbs' "vile policy of 'ethnic cleansing,' " which he said was "actually ethnic extermination."[33] The ethnic cleansing hype was a driving force behind a sense of urgency in Washington and other Western capitals. On August 10, 1992 the U.N. Security Council agreed on a resolution to authorize the use of force to deliver humanitarian aid to Bosnia-Hercegovina.

Although policymakers favored more active steps in Bosnia based on widespread accusations of "ethnic cleansing," the term itself was seldom defined and was often misused by Washington's policymakers and media alike. Ethnic cleansing was a term used to describe Nazi Germany's attempt to remove any trace of its Jewish population—a group of people that was neither armed nor threatened the German nation in any way. The term, however, was inapplicable to the Bosnian scenario, where all sides were armed and whose populations were potentially hostile and dangerous to each other. The same scenario existed in Vietnam, where U.S. soldiers—often unable to recognize friend from foe and soldier from civilian—were bulldozing and burning entire villages suspected of harboring the Viet Cong. U.S. efforts to "clear" areas of Vietnam became a standard strategic maneuver. When U.S. soldiers attempted to secure the infamous "Iron Triangle," having fought hundreds of battles with the Viet Cong, American commanders ordered the removal of tens of thousands of Vietnamese who were placed in camps. The wartime removal and displacement of populations in both Vietnam and Bosnia were entirely different from Hitler's plan to "cleanse" German society.

In Bosnia "ethnic displacement" was pursued to greater or lesser degree by all three sides—Serbs, Muslims, and Croats—in a war effort to gain control over territories which each group sought to wrest from their enemies. "Ethnic displacement" has been a recurring and perhaps an inevitable phenomenon, particularly in civil war, and it occurs when people are fleeing from fighting or due to forced emigration, population exchange, or deportation. The Nazi campaigns in the 1940s were much more than "ethnic cleansing." The Holocaust combined elements of deportation, expulsion, population transfer, massacre, and genocide. Similarly, Croatian fascist Ustashi forces launched a campaign during World War II designed to have Croatia "thoroughly cleansed of Serbian dirt," which entailed killing one-third of the Serbs, expelling another third, and converting another third to Catholicism and having them meld into Croats.[34] Ironically, the Serbs, who were so virulently accused by the media of instigating ethnic cleansing in the 1990s, were the victims of an enormous ethnic cleansing in Europe during World War II. They were ethnically cleansed by Croatian Ustashi in Krajina, Slavonia, Bosnia, and Hercegovina where over 750,000 Serbs were murdered. The Serbs were also ethnically cleansed from Serbia's northern region of Vojvodina by occupying Hungarian forces allied with Hitler, who in one day alone executed 15,000 Serbian civilians in the city of Novi Sad on Serbian Orthodox Christmas on January 7, 1942. Serbs were also ethnically cleansed from southern Serbian regions when occupying Albanian forces allied with fascist Italy drove as many as 200,000 Serbs from Kosovo in the 1940s.[35] The profusion of articles and editorials accusing Serbs of ethnic cleansing in the 1990s, however, made no mention of the ethnic cleansing and extermination of Serbs during World War II. Pundits and policymakers apparently wanted Serbian guilt for Bosnia to be viewed in isolation, both past and present.

The reality of Bosnia was that "ethnic displacement" was taking place on all sides, both as a matter of military strategy and as a natural occurrence of war. The property of Muslims and Croats who fled or were forced from areas controlled by the Serbs was repopulated with Serbian refugees. Serbian homes abandoned or forcefully vacated in Muslim and Croat-held areas were given to Muslim and Croat refugees. Consolidating land, property, and population denied the enemy the ability to gain control over a particular territory—a basic strategy of civil conflict. This reality, however, was not reflected in Washington's rhetoric on Bosnia. Alongside accusations of ethnic cleansing and war crimes, the media was intent on making every battle and incident of war in Bosnia into a case against the Serbs.

In late August 1992, the focus was on Gorazde, where as already noted Bosnian Serbs were rebuked for preventing humanitarian aid from going to allegedly starving Muslim civilians. Serbian claims that Muslim forces might use U.N. convoys to smuggle weapons and ultimately launch attacks on Serb civilians in the area were frequently dismissed by Washington. Indeed, as soon as the Serbs allowed humanitarian convoys into Gorazde at the end of August 1992, Muslim forces launched an attack that led to the expulsion of thousands of Serbian civilians from the area. But the incident was not described as ethnic cleansing of Serbs. On the contrary, an August 31, 1992, *New York Times* article described the Serbian exodus from Gorazde in a positive light by depicting the situation as an "effort to break the siege" of Gorazde; "Bosnian Government troops had driven off the Serbs in combat"; and Bosnian Muslim forces had "liberated Gorazde."[36] No mention was made of attacks on Serbian civilians. Similarly, *Washington Post* articles at the time reported that Bosnia's Muslim-led forces "liberated Gorazde" and "had broken the siege of Gorazde," and that the Serb militia was withdrawing from positions around the "besieged city of Gorazde."

This image of Gorazde emphasized Muslim civilians but completely neglected Bosnian Serb civilians in the area. Only in the last paragraph of an August 31, 1992, article did the *Washington Post* even acknowledge these Serbs by mentioning that "7,000 to 10,000 Serb civilians from villages north of Gorazde left in convoys during the past few days." The article quoted a Serbian woman who said, "The Muslims are advancing . . . we are expecting attacks soon . . . in three days my house will probably be burned down by the Muslims."[37] The *Washington Post* did not report attacks on these Serbs until a few days later, on September 2, 1992, when Serbian "combatants and civilians" were said to have been "streaming from the area" and "attacked by Muslim-led forces as they withdrew."[38] Notably, the article was on page 26, while a less important story about the daily routines of the Bosnian Muslim newspaper, *Oslobodjenje*, made front-page news. Conspicuously absent from the *Washington Post* coverage were photographs of Serbian civilians, wounded, bleeding, in hospital beds, or crying—the kinds of photographs that typically accompanied articles about Muslim casualties. Instead, *Washington Post* editors chose a photograph of a seated Serbian soldier armed with ammunition strapped over both of his shoulders, with the caption reading "A Serb militiaman lays down his machine gun and stops to eat near Gorazde." This was hardly an image to arouse sympathy for Serbian civilians gunned down or forced to flee by Muslim forces. No one in Washington voiced concern over the forced expulsion of Serbs from Gorazde. The title of victim was reserved exclusively for Bosnia's Muslims.

MUSLIM-CROAT FIGHTING IGNORED

Washington's policy on Bosnia was based on the idea of a single, multiethnic government. The Serbs appeared to be the only obstacle to this concept. Although Bosnian Croat leaders had already declared their own, independent state of Herceg-Bosnia as early as July 1992, events taking place in Bosnia that countered Washington's view were ignored or downplayed. To admit the existence of the self-declared Bosnian Croat state would add a complex dimension to the war that would undermine the U.S. position. Vocal segments of the Washington establishment continued to espouse the view that the Muslim government in Sarajevo was supported by a multiethnic union.

By October of 1992, however, a split in the Muslim-Croat alliance and ensuing fighting were too great to ignore any longer. As Bosnian Croats pounded Muslims with mortar and howitzer fire in the town of Prozor, Croatian commando squads spread throughout the city outfitted with black masks, sniper rifles, and serrated hunting knives, armed for what they referred to as "hunting Muslims." In the end, the town was shattered. Visiting journalists said no Muslim or Serb inhabitants were left.[39] During the fighting, Bosnian Croat forces cut off food and fuel supplies to both Muslim fighters and civilians and prevented Muslim vehicles from using a vital supply link, which resulted in depriving Muslim civilians of desperately needed food. Croat forces also expelled 3,000 Muslims from Prozor in what was acknowledged even in the *Washington Post* as the first significant case of Croats engaging in ethnic cleansing against Muslims.[40] When a Croat soldier was asked what happened to the Croat-Muslim alliance, he laughed and replied, "it was an illusion." A few days after the battle in Prozor, ultranationalist Croatian militia forces of the Croatian Defense Council (HVO) imposed martial law and held Bosnian Muslims captive within the encircled city.

Washington perhaps could have concluded that the multiethnic Bosnia argument was a myth and that the region was experiencing a three-sided civil war. All wartime misdeeds that Washington accused the Serbs of committing were repeated by Croat forces in Prozor, Mostar, and other towns they occupied while battling against their former Muslim allies. This included the shelling of civilian areas, forceful expulsion of civilians or ethnic cleansing, and denial of humanitarian relief to Muslim civilians. While Croatian military actions demonstrated that ethnic groups in Bosnia used similar methods to achieve their territorial aims, no accusations against Bosnian Croats were made, nor were there punitive measures against their protégés in Zagreb. The U.S. press was relatively quiet on the Muslim-Croat conflict. Only a few articles and news stories discussed the fighting compared to vast numbers of articles and television reports covering fighting between Muslims and Serbs. Sarajevo was frequently depicted as a "besieged capital," a "Serb-besieged town," a town "besieged by Bosnian Serb nationalists," or a "brutal Serb siege." But the Croatian takeover of Mostar and surrounding areas was never described in similar terms. Neither was the often-repeated phrase "Serb-occupied" or "Serbian occupation" applied to territories taken over by Bosnian Croats.

There were no accusations of "outside Croat aggression against Bosnia," even though Bosnian Croats were following military orders from neighboring Croatia. Their soldiers were receiving their salaries from Cro-

atia, the Croatian flag was flying over buildings in areas of Bosnia controlled by the Croats, Croatian currency (the kuna) was being used, and
Croatian political appointees headed government offices in Bosnian Croat-
held areas. While this information was reported in U.S. press sources, it
received little or no editorial commentary, and was never emphasized by
the White House or State Department. The Security Council passed no
resolution to impose sanctions against Croatia for supporting Bosnian
Croat war efforts, as it did against Serbia with U.N. Resolution 757. In
late October 1992, when fighting between Croats and Muslims prevented
U.N. humanitarian airlifts from reaching Sarajevo, Washington was surprisingly reluctant to blame Croatian political and military command, as
it had so often blamed the Bosnian Serbs. The double standard was clear.
Those in Washington supporting the Bosnian Muslim government favored
coercive action justified by humanitarian rhetoric only against Serbs, not
against any other warring party in Bosnia-Hercegovina.

The double standard was the product, in part, of a continuing effort by
the Croatian government and its Croatian-American supporters in the
United States to whitewash events in Bosnia-Hercegovina. On a December 24, 1992, episode of *CNN & Company*, when I questioned the role of
Croatian troops in Bosnia, a Croatian-American representative angrily insisted that "Croatia has allied forces with Muslims in Bosnia, and they are
in solidarity in the effort against the same occupier, against the same aggressor." The Croation American defended the Tudjman regime by saying
that the Croatian president "was among the first to establish diplomatic
relations with Bosnia and recognize the integrity and sovereignty of its
territory, and we [Croatians] do not hold any claims to it, if anything, we
are standing with our Muslim brothers against an aggressor." Neither
CNN anchor Bobbie Battista nor guest Johanna Neuman of *USA Today*
challenged the Croatian American's claim. The extent of most journalists'
understanding of what was happening in Bosnia did not go far beyond the
sound bites aired on a daily basis through television reports and newspaper
stories. With fighting between Muslims and Croats virtually ignored,
Washington's pundits and policymakers focused on the good-versus-evil
struggle in Sarajevo that dominated headlines.

NO-FLY ZONE: HUMANITARIAN AID OR MILITARY STRATEGY?

At the onset of the first winter of the war, Bosnia activists and pundits
generated dire scenarios of humanitarian disasters about to take place in
Sarajevo. To resolve this possible situation, U.S. participation in patrolling
a no-fly zone over Bosnia was urged. The media inundated the American
public with images of human suffering, which were designed to show that
America had a moral responsibility to prevent the starvation of Bosnian

civilians. Estimates of how many people would die in Bosnia varied wildly and were based more on emotion and Bosnian Muslim government claims than on real data. The CIA claimed up to 150,000 civilians, most of them Muslims, could die in the Winter of 1992 from exposure and lack of food. International aid officials claimed 400,000 people would die of starvation.[41] The U.N. Refugee Agency said as many as 1 million were at risk.[42] The U.N. High Commissioner for Refugees predicted that the Winter of 1992 would bring mass starvation in Sarajevo.[43]

As was the case of Bosnian prison camps, the media's statements of alarm again pressured the Bush administration to do something. On October 2, 1992, President Bush announced that the United States would be willing to participate in enforcing a no-fly zone over Bosnia. The policy to block Serbian aircraft from flying over Bosnia went beyond previous limits the Bush administration had tried to set for U.S. military involvement in the Balkans. The decision to enforce the no-fly zone launched a heated debate among top officials. General Colin L. Powell, chairman of the Joint Chiefs of Staff, argued against the move. President Bush, however, chose to listen to Secretary of State Lawrence Eagleburger, who argued in favor of what he described as "imperatives of trying to stop an awful slaughter now when we see winter coming and a lot of people potentially about to starve to death."[44] On October 9, 1992, the United States, Britain, and France agreed on a compromise U.N. resolution banning Serbian airplanes from flying over Bosnia but stopping short of calling for use of allied military power to enforce it.

Only after the U.S. enforcement of the no-fly zone was decided on was it reported that earlier estimates of how many people would die in Bosnia were exaggerated.[45] Adequate U.N. truck and air deliveries were already being made into Sarajevo, and at the end of November 1992, deliveries *exceeded* the city's daily needs of 270 metric tons. The need for humanitarian aid was not the only motivating factor behind the imposition of a no-fly zone. The most important reason was that the Bosnian Muslim government would gain strategic benefits with the enforcement of a no-fly zone. Without air-reconnaissance capabilities, Bosnian Serbs would not be able to monitor the movements of Bosnian Muslim forces, or the delivery, location, and content of Bosnian Muslim military vehicles as well as U.N. and other foreign aid deliveries to Bosnian Muslim areas. This was a particular concern to the Serbs, who were aware of increasing amounts of smuggled weapons. On September 6, 1992, for instance, the United Nations intercepted an Iranian air force cargo plane delivering 4,000 machine guns and 1 million rounds of ammunition to Bosnian Muslims, in violation of the U.N. weapons embargo.[46] Such weapons were being smuggled in crates alongside U.N. food shipments that went into Muslim-held areas. After such food deliveries, the Bosnian Serb com-

mand noted an increased level of Muslim provocations from these enclaves.

In late November 1992, Bosnian Serbs stopped several U.N. food convoys they suspected of delivering weapons to Muslim forces in the strategically sensitive towns of Gorazde and Srebrenica. The Serbs tried to
inspect U.N. trucks from Sarajevo which they suspected of being used to
smuggle weapons, since the trucks were driven by armed Bosnian Muslim
soldiers who could have easily hidden arms next to boxes of food. The
United Nations' response was to halt food aid to Bosnian Serb civilians
so that the Serbs would be forced to allow U.N. food convoys to proceed
unhindered.[47] Although the United Nations repeatedly condemned the
Serbs for stopping food convoys, no apparent dilemma existed in suspending food deliveries to 100,000 Bosnian Serb civilians. When Bosnian
Serbs eventually allowed U.N. convoys to go through in exchange for food
for Serbian civilians, Serb women and children blocked U.N. convoys,
angered by the double standard in U.N. policy. As Serbian residents gathered in the streets, they chanted that food should not be allowed to reach
their enemies and that they were hungry too.

The U.S. media had little sympathy for Serbian demonstrators. A *Washington Post* article dismissed the Serb protests as "a novel method to block
U.N. convoys." This, they claimed, was a ploy of the Bosnian Serb government, which was accused of deliberately organizing the Serb women
and children to block the highway leading to Muslim towns.[48] The *Washington Post*'s bias was clear when compared to later reports of "demonstrating Croat women and children" blocking U.N. convoys in the Mostar
area. These convoys were blocked because of concerns that "U.N. aid
vehicles would deliver food and possibly weapons to the Muslim soldiers
battling them in the fiercely divided city." Similarly, when Muslim civilians
blocked a U.N. convoy, the *Washington Post* justified it by explaining that
"Muslims feared that Croats would start killing them again if the United
Nations left."[49] Neither case mentioned that Croat or Muslim leadership
staged the protests, as claimed in the Serbian case.

This familiar pattern of media coverage of the Bosnian war—eliciting
sympathy for one side and condemnation for the other—was merely a
part of the war of words whose main thrust came in mid- to late 1992.
Images implanted in this early period would have a cumulative influence
throughout the following years. In the next two years, an increasing number of weapons smuggled to Bosnian Muslim forces would tilt the military
balance in their favor, while repeated attempts to reach a negotiated solution by U.N. and European negotiators would be repeatedly foiled by
Washington's support for the Muslim-led government. The result would
ultimately lead the United States toward military intervention.

NOTES

1. U.S. Department of Justice, *Foreign Agents Registration Statement*, "Supplemental Statement" (Washington, D.C., November 30, 1992), 3, 8.

2. Barbara Crossette, "Bosnian, in U.S. to Seek Aid, Assails Inaction," *New York Times* (May 20, 1992): 5.

3. U.S. Department of Justice, *Foreign Agents Registration Statement*, 5.

4. U.S. Department of Justice, *Foreign Agents Registration Statement*, Dissemination Report, Bosnia-Hercegovina Fax-Update, Nos. 27, 28, 29 (June 25, 1992).

5. Warren Zimmermann, "The Last Ambassador: A Memoir on the Collapse of Yugoslavia," *Foreign Affairs* 74 (March 1995): 20.

6. Stephen Clissold, *A Short History of Yugoslavia: From Early Times to 1966* (London: Cambridge University Press, 1966), 67.

7. U.S. Department of Justice, *Foreign Agents Registration Statement*, 8.

8. Frank McCloskey, "U.S. Air Strikes on Serb Positions Urged by Indiana Rep. McCloskey," *Washington Post* (November 20, 1992): A48.

9. Bill Mandel, "Spin Doctors at Work in Bosnia War,"*San Francisco Examiner* (August 14, 1992): A-4.

10. Matthew C. Vita, "Secret Weapon: U.S. Public Relations Firm Sells Serbs as Bad Guys." *Atlanta Journal/Atlanta Constitution* (February 28, 1993): A-17.

11. Andrew Hogg, "Arabs Join in Bosnian War," *Sunday Times*, London (August 30, 1992): 1. See also Francis Chipaux, "Bosnians 'Getting Arms from Islamic Countries,' " and "Arab Volunteers Joining the Fight," *Guardian Weekly* (August 30, 1992): 16.

12. Blaine Harden, "Middle Eastern Muslims Helping Bosnian Defenders Against Serb Forces," *Washington Post* (August 27, 1992): A22.

13. Roland Keating, "When Reporters Go over the Top," *The Guardian* (January 18, 1993).

14. Barbara Crossette, "Bosnian, in U.S. to Seek Aid, Assails Inaction," *New York Times* (May 20, 1992): 5.

15. Richard J. Sideman, "Brutalities in Bosnia," *San Francisco Chronicle* (July 30, 1992): A24.

16. Roy Gutman, *A Witness to Genocide* (New York: Macmillan, 1993).

17. Don Oberdorfer, "U.S. Verifies Killings in Serb Camps; State Dept. Spokesman Repeats Condemnation of 'Horrible' Abuses," *Washington Post* (August 4, 1992): A1.

18. Ibid.

19. Don Oberdorfer, "State Dept. Backtracks on Atrocity Reports; Calls for Action on Serb Camps Rise," *Washington Post* (August 5, 1992): A1.

20. Sandra Sanchez, "Horror in Serbian Prison Camps," *USA Today* (August 7, 1992): 4A.

21. See Andrew Bell-Fialkoff, "A Brief History of Ethnic Cleansing," *Foreign Affairs* 72 (Summer 1993): 110, and Laura Silber, "Serbs Agree to Allow Red Cross into Camps," *Washington Post* (August 9, 1992): A1.

22. Peter Brock, "Anti-Serbian Bias Cited in Coverage," *Washington Times* (February 14, 1994): A15.

23. Paul Cheston, "Atrocity Fears for 2,000 Serb POWs," *The Evening Standard*, London (August 10, 1992): 7.

24. Marlise Simons, "A War-Crimes Trial, But of Muslims, Not Serbs," *New York Times* (April 3, 1997): A3.

25. Chris Hedges, "Serbs in Bosnia See No Peace for Their Dead," *New York Times* (January 16, 1996): A6.

26. Don Oberdorfer and Helen Dewar, "Clinton, Senators Urge Bush to Act on Balkans," *Washington Post* (August 6, 1992): A1.

27. Richard Cohen, "Death Camps on Bush's Watch," *Washington Post* (August 7, 1992): A21.

28. Don Oberdorfer, "Bush Shifts Toward Force to Aid Bosnia," *Washington Post* (August 7, 1992): A1.

29. Blaine Harden, "U.S. Airlift Brings Aid to Sarajevo; Serbs Resume Policy of 'Ethnic Cleansing' " *Washington Post* (July 4, 1992): A1.

30. Maurice Carder, "Letter: The Serbian Contribution to the Conflict in Bosnia," *The Independent*, London (April 20, 1992): 16.

31. "Yugoslavia: Carnage Must Stop; Baker Is Right—It's Time to Weigh Collective Action, Presumably by NATO," *Los Angeles Times* (June 23, 1992): 6.

32. "The World Watches Murder," *New York Times* (June 24, 1992): 20.

33. Trevor Rowe, "U.N. Approves Use of Military Force for Bosnia Aid, Seeks War Crime Data," *Washington Post* (August 14, 1992): A1.

34. Ibid.

35. See Raju G. C. Thomas and H. Richard Friedman (eds.), *The South Slav Conflict: History, Religion, Ethnicity, and Nationalism* (New York: Garland Publishing, 1996), 342; Alex N. Dragnich and Slavko Todorovich, *The Saga of Kosovo: Focus on Serbia-Albania Relations* (New York: Columbia University Press, 1984), 138.

36. Chuck Sudetic, "15 Killed by Artillery Shell in a Busy Sarajevo Market," *New York Times* (August 31, 1992): A6.

37. Peter Maas, "Serbs Pulling out from Besieged City; Bosnian Forces Say They Broke Blockade," *Washington Post* (August 31, 1992): A12.

38. Peter Maass, "Serb Forces Vacate Gorazde After 4-Month Siege; Withdrawing Militiamen Say They Were Attacked by Muslims While Leaving Bosnian City," *Washington Post* (September 2, 1992): A26.

39. Peter Maass, "Conflict Between Croats, Muslims Plays Out in Streets of Bosnian Town," *Washington Post* (October 25, 1992): A34.

40. Peter Maass, "Bosnian Muslims Face Fight with Supposed Allies: Croats; Three-Way Division of Ex-Yugoslav Republic Is Feared," *Washington Post* (October, 29, 1992): A25.

41. Mary Battiata, "Promised Western Aid Effort for Bosnia Falling Short as Frigid Weather Looms," *Washington Post* (October 14, 1992): A1.

42. Blaine Harden, "Moynihan Sees Sarajevo Siege for Himself," *Washington Post* (November 26, 1992): A56.

43. John M. Goshko, "U.S., in Shift, to Accept Balkan War Refugees," *Washington Post* (October 27, 1992): A25.

44. John M. Goshko, " 'No-Fly' Zone Needed to Protect Aid, Eagleburger Says, A Reluctant Expansion of Policy," *Washington Post* (October 11, 1992): A51.

45. Blaine Harden, "Two UN Relief Convoys Fail to Reach Isolated Muslim Towns," *Washington Post* (November 26, 1992): A57.

46. "Iran Supplies Arms to Croatia, U.S. Says." *Washington Post* (September 10, 1992): A20.

47. Blaine Harden, "UN Halts Food Aid to Serbs," *Washington Post* (November 24, 1992): A17.

48. Ibid.

49. Kim Murphy, "Muslims Block Convoy Leaving Mostar," *Washington Post* (August 27, 1993): A30.

Chapter 6

Push Toward Intervention (December 1992 to February 1994)

BUSH ADMINISTRATION PRESSURED TO ENFORCE NO-FLY ZONE

By the end of 1992, the Bosnian war was one of the most talked about foreign policy issues in Washington. With 24-hour-a-day CNN updates and newspapers with two or three daily articles and numerous op-eds on the war, the emerging picture of the Bosnian conflict was a struggle between Bosnian Muslim victims and Serbian aggressors. The reality was quite different: the conflict had turned into a three-sided civil war between Muslims, Serbs, and Croats. Each side was fighting to stake a claim to its own, separate territories. Serbs in Slavonia and Krajina regions controlled areas of Croatia where Serbs were a majority, whereas neighboring Bosnian Serbs controlled roughly 70 percent of a crescent-shaped area in the east, northeast, and northwest (see Appendix 2, map 10). From their stronghold in Mostar, Bosnian Croats controlled southern regions, while Bosnian Muslims controlled most of Sarajevo and central Bosnia. This reality was obscured by media-driven images that would pressure the Bush administration to adopt a more aggressive U.S. policy in the Balkans—one that would be pushed incrementally further over the next two years by the incoming Clinton administration and culminate in the first use of U.S. and NATO forces in Europe since World War II.

Months of intense Bosnian Muslim lobbying from the start of the war until the Winter of 1992 produced virulent anti-Serb rhetoric and promises of humanitarian aid by the Bush administration—far less than the U.S. military intervention the Bosnian Muslims had hoped for. By December 1992, however, the Bosnian Muslim strategy to push Washington toward greater action appeared to be having an effect. Some of the pressure was applied through Congress. At the end of November 1992, having returned from his second visit to Sarajevo and talks with Bosnian Muslim officials, Congressman Frank McCloskey urged immediate U.S. air strikes against Bosnian Serb positions. As one of the most fervent supporters of U.S. involvement in the three-sided Bosnian war, McCloskey's anti-Serb rhetoric and frequent media appearances in support of the Bosnian Muslim government grew more strident.

Other members of Congress who had never expressed interest in the Balkans suddenly became enthusiastic supporters of the Bosnian Muslim cause. Soon after McCloskey returned from Sarajevo, Senator Patrick Moynihan went on a fact-finding mission to Bosnia. He visited Muslim-held areas and met with Croatian officials in Zagreb, but he saw no Bosnian-Serb officials. In Sarajevo, Moynihan was hosted by Izetbegovic who told him that 130,000 Muslims were killed in seven months of war.[1] The figure was intended to dramatize the Bosnian Muslim's plight at a time when Washington needed a jolt to act. One month later, Izetbegovic significantly lowered the number, estimating the number of deaths at about 17,000.[2] As the war went on, the Bosnian Muslim government raised casualty figures, until they culminated at 200,000. This figure was frequently cited but could not be substantiated. Its primary purpose was to arouse international sympathy. At the time of Moynihan's visit to Sarajevo, these exaggerated claims of Muslim casualties of war had their intended effect. At a Boston University speech on November 12, 1992, Senator Moynihan advocated U.S. military strikes on the Serbian capital, Belgrade, arguing this would stop Serbian advances in Bosnia—repeating another false claim of the Muslim government.[3]

The Congress's urgent pleas were followed by pressure from a Bosnian Muslim supporter and an important U.S. ally in the Middle East—Saudi Arabia. Recalling the Bush administration's intense lobbying of the Saudis in 1990 to win approval of U.S. use of force in the Persian Gulf War, the Saudis now wanted Washington to return the favor by supporting U.S. military intervention in Bosnia. Following months of appeals to President Bush, in December 1992, Saudi King Fahd again urged Washington to allow weapons into the Muslim-led Bosnian state, a move that the Saudis felt could only be achieved through U.S. pressure on the United Nations to lift the arms embargo.[4] The Saudi statement came after Izetbegovic had pleaded for military help from Islamic states at a December 1, 1992, meeting of the Organization of the Islamic Conference, where he claimed that "weapons would help repel aggression aimed at obliterating the Muslim people [in Bosnia]."[5]

A few days after the Islamic conference, Egyptian Brigadier General Hussein Abdel Rezek, commander of U.N. forces in Sarajevo, declared the U.N. humanitarian mission was a failure and called for immediate military intervention. Interventionists among the U.S. mainstream media echoed his demands. The *Washington Post* immediately printed an op-ed supporting Rezek's view, while no comments were issued in support of a December 12, 1992, warning by UNPROFOR commander Lieutenant General Satish Nambiar, who said Western military intervention would cause more problems than it would solve.[6] Nambiar claimed that humanitarian aid was successfully getting through to nearly all parts of Bosnia-Hercegovina and that threats of military intervention would unnecessarily endanger the situation. Ignoring reality, Washington's news media, activists, and former U.S. officials pushed for U.S. enforcement of the no-fly zone in Bosnia—a move viewed by Bosnia hawks as a way of getting the United States headed down a slippery slope toward even stronger action.

Perhaps some of the most important pressure on the Bush administration to spearhead U.S. military involvement in Bosnia came from a veteran foreign policymaker, former Secretary of State George Shultz. At a December 7, 1992, speech in New York, Shultz expressed outrage over what he considered an inadequate U.S. response to the "Serbian rape of Bosnia." He compared Serbian war crimes to Nazi atrocities against the Jews in World War II and called for the United States to take out Bosnian Serb military targets. In an unusual meeting of minds, the *Washington Post*'s op-ed writer, Jim Hoagland, applauded Shultz's urgings by saying, "George Shultz is right. Aerial strikes on Serb military targets must now be considered.[7] Shultz next went on PBS's *MacNeil-Lehrer Newshour* and several other television programs to emphasize his calls for tough U.S. action. A transcript of Shultz's entire interview on the *MacNeil-Lehrer Newshour* was reprinted in the *Washington Post* a few days later. The media was more than happy to publish and promote views favoring greater involvement in Bosnia, while ignoring contrary viewpoints. George Bush could not now ignore the concerted efforts by pro-Bosnia interventionists and his former colleagues.

In a December 12, 1992, conference, Secretary of State Eagleburger announced a toughening of U.S. policy on Bosnia. In addition to a stricter enforcement of the no-fly-zone, the administration now for the first time favored selective removal of the arms embargo against Bosnian Muslims. Eagleburger stepped up the rhetoric by accusing Bosnian Serb leader, Radovan Karadzic, General Ratko Mladic, and Serbia's president, Slobodan Milosevic, of being responsible for war crimes in Bosnia—an accusation that Eagleburger later said was meant to put pressure on the Serbs to back down prior to the oncoming Winter. Two days after Eagleburger announced the change in U.S. policy, Washington pushed for a Security Council resolution to authorize strict enforcement of the U.N.-mandated no-fly zone over Bosnia-Hercegovina. Washington spearheaded a new role for NATO as formal plans were drawn up for NATO enforcement of the no-fly zone. By December 15, 1992, Pentagon officials were already planning for possible air strikes against Serbian targets. With a new, aggressive approach, by December 17, 1992, Washington was able to convince the U.N. Security Council to use NATO in enforcing the ban on Serbian military flights over Bosnia.

The U.S. administration, however, still remained divided on the issue of enforcing the no-fly zone. The Defense Department was opposed to using U.S. aircraft in Bosnia, which they described as costly, risky, and dangerously open-ended, while the State Department pressed for stronger U.S. action.[8] As the incoming Clinton administration was about to take the reins of power in Washington, Secretary of State Eagleburger was presented with a last opportunity to leave his short term in office with a record as a man of action. The Bush administration decision to shift policy was said to have been based on intense frustration with the continuing war in Bosnia, failure to remedy the situation through international mediation and sanctions on the Serbs, and greater public and political support in the United States and Europe for taking action to stop the televised horrors in Bosnia.[9] Other factors, however, weighed in on the decision—including pressure on Washington from Islamic allies, pressure from increasingly interventionist U.S. media and Bosnia activists, and active lobbying by Bosnian Muslim officials. Another, more cynical reason for the shift was that the soon-to-depart Republican administration had no incentive for caution. In response to months of criticism by Bill Clinton against the administration's lack of action in Bosnia, President Bush may have decided to go ahead and do what Clinton wanted. Stepped-up U.S. military involvement in Bosnia would mean the new Clinton administration would have to deal with the consequences—much as Johnson left a legacy of greater involvement in Vietnam for Richard Nixon. Richard Holbrooke, the U.S. negotiator on Bosnia, later wrote: "if there were a change in Administrations, Bosnia would be the worst kind of legacy imaginable—it would be George Bush and Larry Eagleburger's revenge if Clinton wins."[10]

SOUND BITES TO SUPPORT POLICY

The announcement of the new, more aggressive U.S. policy sent Bosnian Muslim officials rushing to Washington to ensure that the U.S. administration followed through on its promises. In his three-day visit to Washington, Bosnian Muslim Prime Minister Haris Silajdzic made an all-out effort to tackle the media as Bosnian activists in Washington supported his efforts. Representative Frank McClosky joined Silajdzic on CNN's *Larry King Live* on December 18, 1992, to urge more than just a U.S. enforcement of the no-fly zone, but also a lifting of the arms embargo and selective U.S. air strikes against the Serbs.

Public relations activities organized by Ruder Finn for the Bosnian Muslim government were crucial at this time, including a December 17, 1992, lunch briefing with leading journalists and important foreign policy analysts at the American Enterprise Institute; a December 18, 1992, news briefing at the Carnegie Endowment for International Peace; news media stake-outs after meetings with the Clinton transition team; as well as media interviews and appearances for Silajdzic on NBC's *Today Show*, PBS's *MacNeil-Lehrer Newshour*, *John McLaughlin's One-on-One*, *McLaughlin Group*, CNN's *Larry King Live*, *CBS News*, *ABC Evening News*, *ABC Morning News*, ABC's *This Week with David Brinkley*, the *Washington Post*, the *New York Times*, *USA Today*, *Newsweek*, *Time Magazine*, and *U.S. News and World Report*.[11] The vast majority of views presented on national television during this time centered either on those of Bosnian Muslim officials or those of activists who supported U.S. military intervention in Bosnia.

After the producers of CNN's *Larry King Live* invited me to present a counter-perspective alongside Bosnian Muslim Prime Minister Haris Silajdzic, CNN suddenly withdrew the invitation and decided to allow the Muslim official to go on alone. I was told Silajdzic refused to appear on the program with a guest with an opposing view and demanded that I be excluded. Similarly, after being invited by producers of *McLaughlin's One-on-One*, I was told Silajdzic threatened he would "walk out" if I was invited. Again, he was allowed to appear by himself, and again his views went unchallenged. After I was invited to participate with Bosnian Muslim representative to the United Nations, Muhamed Sacirbey, on a popular Washington-based National Public Radio show, the *Derek McGinty Radio Hour*, Sacirbey was furious at the show's producers for not informing him that I would be participating. Although the program's producers were happy to present a well-balanced show that allowed both perspectives to be heard, Sacirbey avoided appearing with me ever again. Several times in the coming months, I would be invited by PBS's *MacNeil-Lehrer Newshour* to appear with Sacirbey, but each time after he insisted on appearing alone, *Newshour* producers withdrew their invitation to me. It was not surprising that Bosnian Muslim officials did not want their perspectives to be challenged or their legitimacy as the sole recognized government of Bosnia-Hercegovina to be questioned. More surprising, however, was the relative ease with which producers of major U.S. television programs were willing to allow foreign representatives to dictate the nature of their shows and accept a one-sided presentation of such a complex issue as Bosnia.

In the case of CNN, I would appear on dozens of CNN programs in years to come with numerous guests but never with official Bosnian Muslim representatives. CNN tried to accommodate requests by Bosnian Muslim officials to appear alone. Sometimes CNN would attempt to avoid criticism by Bosnian Muslim officials by interviewing them separately from me. At one of a number of my appearances on Canadian Broadcasting

Corporation (CBC) news programs, Bosnian Muslim ambassador in Washington, Sven Alkalaj, was angered when he heard that CBC was broadcasting his interview, followed by a separate interview with me. He originally thought that CBC would air only his views. I was clearly encroaching on one of the most important battle zones of the Bosnian war—television, the most effective and instantaneous vehicle for fighting the war of words.

The effects of several factors were now coming together to silence the Serbs. The lack of an effective Serbian public relations campaign prevented adequate responses to rapidly unfolding events and the ensuing media blitz was skillfully encouraged by the Muslims. Recognition of Bosnia's Muslims as the "legitimate" government gave credence to their demands to appear on shows without opposing points of view. Finally, the U.S. government was now completely won over by the Bosnian Muslim view of the conflict and was desperate for a solution to the crisis.

IMAGES OF "STARVATION" AND "RAPE" CONQUER REALITY AT GENEVA

By the end of 1992, while Washington was headed down the path of an intensified pursuit of aggressive action in Bosnia, European diplomats believed that negotiations would be impossible if the Bosnian Muslims expected the United States to come in on their side of the war. European negotiator, Lord Owen, who came to Sarajevo in December of 1992, said to the Muslims, "Don't live under this dream that the West is going to come in and sort this problem out."[12] U.N. officials also attempted to bring some semblance of neutrality to the organization's activities in Bosnia. When U.N. Secretary General Boutros Boutros-Ghali visited Sarajevo in January of 1993, he appealed to Bosnian Muslims in a public speech and called on them to participate in negotiations rather than wait for a foreign military intervention. In response, about 200 Muslim protestors shouted abuses at Boutros-Ghali, while one man was quoted saying, "the old bastard should be killed."[13] To the Bosnian Muslim leadership and civilians alike, no one was neutral in a war; there were only friends and enemies. Either the United Nations was with them or it was against them. Under pressure from Washington, the United Nations would ultimately compromise its originally neutral role. As Washington was heading down the path of military intervention in Bosnia, it was forcing the Europeans and the United Nations along with it.

At the time, however, Europeans still hoped the conflict could be settled through diplomacy. When European negotiators finally convinced the Bosnian Muslims to come face-to-face with the Bosnian Serbs for the first time since the war began, they organized the Geneva Peace Talks on January 3, 1993. In Geneva, the three parties were presented with the

Vance–Owen plan, which envisioned the creation of 10 Bosnian provinces (see Appendix 2, map 8). The provinces would be based largely on ethnicity, but their organization was to also take into account the region's geography, economic characteristics, and transportation routes. The proposal intended Sarajevo to be an open city in which all three ethnic groups would be represented, and the 10 provinces would be linked by highways patrolled by the United Nations. Bosnian Serbs were to negotiate the transfer of some of the territory they held to Muslims and Croats, leaving the Serbs with 40 percent of the territory as compared to the 70 percent they controlled at that time.

One great factor stood in the way of peace in Bosnia—Muslim anticipation of U.S. support to alter the military balance and help them win the war. The Bush administration's promise that U.S. military power would be used in enforcing the no-fly zone gave little incentive for the Muslim leadership to negotiate. This began a pattern in which Washington's support would lead Bosnian Muslims to refuse to negotiate, which would foil the European negotiators' attempts to end the war. While European mediators pressed the Bosnian Muslim leadership to accept less than all of Bosnia, the Muslims turned to Washington for help. Bosnian Muslim President Izetbegovic left the negotiations and flew to Washington. U.S. officials met with Izetbegovic, in spite of warnings by U.N. envoy Cyrus Vance that hopes of attaining increased U.S. support for military intervention into Bosnia would discourage Izetbegovic from negotiating in Geneva. After talks with members of the incoming Clinton administration, including Vice President Al Gore, Izetbegovic was even further encouraged that U.S. military support was forthcoming.

More than just winning over the new administration, Izetbegovic needed to gain the hearts of Washington's opinionmaking and foreign policymaking elites. He found the humanitarian angle of the Bosnian war always effective. At a January 8, 1993 speech at the Carnegie Endowment for International Peace, Izetbegovic made an emotional appeal by claiming that an end to his people's suffering could only come about with U.S. military assistance. Surely, the war could have been ended immediately if Bosnia was divided between ethnic groups, but rather than having to compromise an end to the war, Izetbegovic wanted a military victory. In a meeting with the main editors and reporters of the *Washington Post*, Izetbegovic admitted he would be willing to forgo U.N. assistance if American forces would hit Serbian airfields in Bosnia or Serbia.[14] The U.S. press, however, downplayed Bosnian Muslim military aims. The spotlight was kept on hunger and the suffering of civilians during the first Winter of war in Sarajevo. At the time, a *Washington Post* headline read: " 'Help Us, or We Will All Die,' Aged Sarajevans Beseech U.N.' "[15] News reports coming out of Sarajevo almost exclusively depicted the plight of Bosnian Muslims, even though the Winter affected everyone in Bosnia. Almost no mention was made of Bosnian Serb deaths from severe cold which took a particular toll on the elderly, sick, and wounded.

The media was a willing participant in the Muslim public relations campaign during negotiations. While mediators Vance and Owen pressed Bosnia's ethnic rivals to end the war, the Muslim government launched several weeks of desperate shortwave radio transmissions that reported hundreds of people were dying from hunger and exposure in Zepa. Washington was soon ablaze with anti-Serb calls for U.S. military action. However, U.N. personnel traveling with a food convoy that reached Zepa on January 18, 1993, said that Muslim reports were considerably exaggerated. Although supplies were low, the Muslim population of Zepa was not undernourished and certainly was not dying from hunger.[16] Washington's Bosnia advocates, however, were not about to retract their calls for a tough anti-Serb policy, even though these calls were based on inaccurate reports. The means justified the ends, and Washington was convinced of the rightness of the Bosnian Muslim cause.

Muslim officials successfully manipulated other tragedies of war to vilify the Serbs during crucial moments in the Geneva negotiations. A European Community team was intentionally invited to Sarajevo during the negotiations to investigate allegations of rape in Bosnia. The task of EC investigators was not to find out how many women were raped on all sides during the Bosnian war, but instead to focus exclusively on Muslim women. Although members of the EC committee admitted that exact numbers were difficult to quantify, on January 9, 1993, they concluded that Serb forces raped up to 20,000 Muslim women and girls in Bosnia as part of a systematic policy of terror designed to intimidate, demoralize, and drive them from their homes.

The rape allegations again set the media ablaze. In late 1992, as Linda Grant of the London newspaper, *The Guardian*, observed, "rape in Bosnia was the hottest story of the new year," with the Croatian capital, Zagreb, "teeming with foreign journalists, scouring refugee camps with a revival of that familiar wartime phrase: 'Anyone here been raped and speak English?' "[17] But in spite of the EC estimate, in months to come, Grant observed, no one was able to come up with any reliable figures for the numbers of women actually raped, and at least one member of the EC mission who was originally convinced that rape was part of a policy of ethnic cleansing later expressed doubts.[18] While the media was quick to publish allegations of rape whose numbers jumped from 20,000 to as high as 60,000, some journalists began to question the logic of the claims. At the time, Jacques Merlino, deputy news editor at the French television network, France 2, said he questioned the enormity of the figures and the suddenness of their appearance.[19] He noted that his colleagues working on Yugoslav issues also questioned the figures, but no one wanted to do so publicly.

The conclusions presented in the EC report were suspect for a number of reasons. The investigation was brief, and the 20,000 figure was an arbitrary number, derived from estimates based on information provided by representatives of the Croat and Bosnian governments and the heads of the Catholic and Muslim religious communities. No direct testimony of the women raped was recorded. Furthermore, the EC team did not investigate rapes of Serbian women in Bosnia to get a balanced view of the situation. They did not travel to any Bosnian Serb-held areas, nor did they examine information provided by Serbian organizations in Belgrade that gathered evidence of war crimes and victims of rape among Bosnian Serb refugees who fled to Serbia. If the EC team had put the rape issue into context, it could reasonably have been concluded that rape was not part of what was described as an expansionist attempt to create a "Greater Serbia" through expulsion and ethnic cleansing. Rather, it was a tragic phenomenon of war that occurred on all sides and at a level much lower than claimed. This reasoning, however, did not suit the Bosnian Muslim government's political purposes: it was using rape allegations to maintain pressure on the Serbs during the Geneva negotiations.

While the press kept a spotlight on rape and civilian suffering in Sarajevo, it was not until January 12, 1993, when the Geneva talks were already completed, that an obscure statement found its way to a back-page *Washington Post* article. It reported that Muslim forces had "begun to demonstrate a capacity for effective, and sometimes brutal, attacks on Serb militia forces and Serb civilians." In previous weeks of negotiations in Geneva, however, the *Washington Post* did not mention these same "brutal attacks" by Muslim forces. Neither did the newspaper print articles on another significant development in Bosnia—fighting between Muslims and Croats in central Bosnia. Only when the Geneva negotiations had faltered did the *Washington Post* report that "Croats have battled Muslims in central Bosnia around the towns of Jablanica and Travnik," and "cut off international aid supplies to Muslim-held towns" in an attempt to solidify claims over central Bosnian territory, while Croatian officials harassed international relief workers, confiscated their vehicles, and denied humanitarian aid to Muslims.[20] In mid-January, Croat pressure on U.N. aid deliveries was so severe that UNHCR closed its offices in Jablanica, Prozor, and Gornji Vakuf in central Bosnia.

While the U.S. press battered the Bosnian Serbs with anti-Serb articles during the Geneva negotiations, more balanced facts about what was happening in Bosnia were reported only after the Geneva negotiations had failed. Washington was prepared to turn a blind eye to Croat transgressions because it believed that Croats were the only hope the Muslims had in winning the war—since all food and weapons to Muslims had to go through Croatian-held territory. The Bosnian Muslim government itself downplayed its problems with the Croats. To admit that Bosnia was split in a three-way fratricidal war would negate the "Serbian aggression" argument and would deny Bosnian Muslim officials their main justification for international intervention—that this was a war of aggression. Maintaining the "aggression" label was particularly important during Geneva negotiations when Muslims were being pressured to divide Bosnia along ethnic lines.

U.N. and EC negotiators Cyrus Vance and David Owen were openly frustrated with Washington's views. Vance issued a public warning that any talk of military action by Washington "makes it harder" to reach an agreement with the Muslim side which believed it had more to gain by stalling or even breaking off the conference.[21] Negotiators also blamed U.S. threats against the Serbs for encouraging the Croats to violate a year-old truce, breaking through a U.N. protected buffer zone, and launching a series of offensives against the Krajina Serbs. Washington, on the other hand, believed its threats were coercing the Serbs into submission. On January 11, 1993, Bosnian Serbs accepted the Vance–Owen plan, dropped their insistence on a distinct state of Republika Srpska, and agreed to control 42 percent of Bosnia-Hercegovina. A week later, the Bosnian Serb government and Republika Srpska Assembly voted on and accepted the plan. While Washington was convinced that threats of use of force were effective against the Serbs, the Bosnian Serb leadership was bowing to pressures from Serbia's president Milosevic, who believed the plan was the best the Serbs could hope for. U.N. and EC negotiators were pleased to have secured the plan in hopes of averting calls for lifting the arms embargo against Bosnia's Muslims—a move Europeans believed would intensify and spread the conflict.

At this moment, the Bosnian war could have been stopped, but interventionist forces in Washington would not allow it. The election of Bill Clinton signified to the Muslim-led government that the United States would ultimately enter on their side of the war. As new players entered the White House, they brought a change in ideology with regard to America's role abroad. The Clinton administration's new foreign policy team had a vision of an active, interventionist U.S. role in dealing with conflicts around the world. This view would come to the forefront—first in Somalia and then in the Balkans. In months to come, although the new secretary of state, Warren Christopher, would take a somewhat cautious view of the Balkan crisis, it was U.S. Ambassador to the United Nations Madeleine Albright and National Security Adviser Anthony Lake who had the president's ear on Bosnia. Their belief in active U.S. involvement in the region helped them build credibility and prestige with the new president. Albright's strong anti-Serb rhetoric on Bosnia would soon make her a favorite with the U.S. media.

Bosnian Muslim government officials had their hands on the pulse of the new administration. They believed it was only a matter of time before the United States would come in on their side. On January 30, 1993, Bosnian Muslim forces launched an all-out attack on Serbian positions in Sarajevo. This was followed by a rejection of the Vance–Owen plan by Bosnian Muslim officials, who argued the plan would give their side only one-fourth of the republic while they represented 44 percent of Bosnia's population. The U.N. negotiating team felt that the Serbs's willingness to drop to 43 percent of Bosnian territory was a significant compromise, since Bosnian Serbs lived on 60 percent of Bosnian land prior to the war—a figure that U.N. spokesman Fred Ekhart said was based on maps of Bosnia-Hercegovina's ethnic dispersal from the 1991 census.[22] International mediators believed the real reason Bosnian Muslims rejected the Vance–Owen plan was because they hoped U.S. officials would persuade the Security Council to lift the arms embargo against them and because they anticipated NATO military actions to help in their war efforts against the Serbs.[23] The Serbs were becoming suspicious of Muslim intentions as well. With renewed Muslim provocations in Sarajevo, the Bosnian Serb leadership was convinced that the Muslims were not serious about negotiating and decided to withdraw their initial support for the plan.

U.N. NEGOTIATIONS IN NEW YORK AMID THREATS FROM WASHINGTON

With the collapse of the Geneva negotiations, European negotiators recognized that Washington's support for Bosnian Muslim demands was an impediment to a compromise. One way of getting the U.S. administration to have a more realistic appreciation of Bosnia's problems was to get the United States directly involved in the negotiating process. Mediators Vance and Owen believed that switching the peace talks to the U.N. headquarters in New York would provide a better vantage point from which to convince the Clinton administration to support the peace process and press the Muslims to do the same. Moving the new round of negotiations to New York, however, would have the opposite effect. It would shift the policy focus from a European to a U.S.-led approach. While British and French diplomats knew Geneva had failed because of Washington's meddling on behalf of the Bosnian Muslims, the Clinton administration was under the mistaken impression that the failure of the warring parties to come to an agreement was the result of insufficient U.S. pressure on the Serbs. For Washington, it was time for Europe to step aside and let the United States take the lead. Clinton administration officials viewed the Vance–Owen plan with skepticism and as a sellout to "aggressors."[24] Instead of backing the peace plan, Clinton administration officials were set on providing military support to the Muslims to gain a better negotiating position. Ostensibly the New York negotiations were meant to reach a solution to Bosnia's ethnic problems. Yet Washington was conducting interagency studies on how much military force would be needed to assist Bosnian Muslim forces to break through Serbian military positions around Sarajevo.

On February 5, 1993, in an atmosphere of conflicting goals and policies between Clinton administration and European officials, all three warring factions arrived at U.N. headquarters in New York for negotiations to end the Bosnian war. The Serbs quickly found themselves pressured from all sides—by Washington's threats of greater coercive measures, and in Sarajevo, by a series of attacks by Muslim forces during several rounds of negotiations that took place in New York from February to April.

As soon as the Bosnian Serb delegation arrived, U.S. officials and Bosnian Muslim government representatives began a series of vocal threats designed to pressure the Serbs to accept Bosnian Muslim terms for a peace settlement. Izetbegovic immediately urged the Clinton administration to launch air strikes against the Serbs, arguing that this was a "more speedy way" to end the war.[25] At this time, however, surely a faster way to end the war would have been for the Muslim leadership to sign the Vance–Owen plan. The reasons Izetbegovic refused to do so were outlined at the very end of a *Washington Post* article, which received little attention, stating that "Izetbegovic's government [would] have to relinquish the power it currently holds in Sarajevo" and transfer his presidency to a nine-member council made up of three representatives from each ethnic group.[26] This would have brought back true multiethnic power sharing in Bosnia which was present before the war and was wholly acceptable to Bosnian Serbs. Bosnian Serb leader, Radovan Karadzic, issued a statement encouraging the United States to support the peace plan. "This plan is not perfect," he said, "but we don't have anything better."[27]

Clinton administration officials, skeptical of the plan, firmly backed the Bosnian Muslim hard-line position. On February 6, 1993, during a meeting in Munich, Germany, with six key American allies, U.S. Defense Secretary Les Aspin supported tougher measures to pressure the Serbs. The emerging Clinton administration plan was a two-track approach that combined new diplomatic efforts with threats of military intervention. It was intended to shift the balance of power in favor of Bosnian Muslims, while diplomatic initiatives were aimed at coercing the Serbs to accept their demands. Bosnian Muslim Islamic allies welcomed the new Clinton administration policy, and as in previous crucial moments in U.S. decisions on Bosnia, applied pressure on Washington to move in a direction of intervention. During U.N. negotiations in New York, President Clinton received Turkish President Turhut Ozal, who reiterated Bosnian Muslim demands and urged that the United States launch military actions against the Serbs.[28] On the same day, the Clinton administration announced the greatest policy shift to date in favor of intervention. Washington was now prepared to offer U.S. ground troops and to push for a stronger NATO role in enforcing a Bosnian peace plan. The Clinton administration named a special U.S. representative, Reginald Bartholomew, whose previous position as U.S. ambassador to NATO was well suited to the new approach in pushing for a stronger U.S.-led NATO role in Bosnia.

Apart from threatening gestures from Washington, Serbs were put under more pressure from events on the ground in Bosnia. In the middle of the New York negotiations, on February 11, Bosnian Muslim forces launched an attack on the Serbian suburb of Ilidza in Sarajevo, resulting in numerous Serbian casualties. When two French U.N. soldiers were wounded, United Nation humanitarian flights to the area were suspended.[29] While U.N. Secretary General Boutros Boutros-Ghali vociferously protested to the Bosnian Muslim government, the State Department issued no condemnation of the attack, in spite of appeals issued just days earlier by Secretary of State Warren Christopher for all sides to silence their heavy weapons. At the same time, a *Washington Post* article prominently featured a large front-page photograph of Muslim civilians taking cover in Sarajevo just several days earlier. References to the Muslim attack on the Serbian part of the city were buried in an article with no photographs of Serbian casualties or civilians fleeing the attack.[30]

Clinton administration officials ignored sporadic offensives launched by Muslim forces in Sarajevo and instead continued their tough rhetoric and threats of impending use of force to coerce the Serbs to abandon their dream of a separate state. It brought home the message to international mediators that unless they made a deal quickly, the United States would take unilateral action. Officials from British and other U.N. missions in New York desperately tried to avoid a scenario where their government's policies would openly conflict with U.S. military action. They repeatedly appealed to the Bosnian Serb delegation and told them to take what they were offered or face U.S. military intervention. "Time is not on your side," said one British representative in a meeting with Karadzic. Clinton administration officials even refused to meet with the Bosnian Serbs, since the Republika Srpska government was not officially recognized by the United States. This attitude in Washington prevailed in years to come as Richard Holbrooke, then the head of the State Department's European Bureau, pressured one member of Congress not to meet with Bosnian Serb leader, Radovan Karadzic, in the Spring of 1995. But in 1998, when Albanian separatism flared up in Serbia's southern region of Kosovo, Holbrooke was eager to negotiate with leaders of the Kosovo Liberation Army—a guerrilla group even State Department officials described as "terrorists."[31]

By refusing to meet with Bosnian Serb delegates during the 1993 negotiations and at other times during the war, Clinton administration officials intentionally shut out the views of one party in a negotiating process. When contrasted to the Middle East peace process, which has required

that both Israelis and Palestinians talk to each other, Washington's treatment of the Bosnian Serbs and their representatives was not constructive.
In contrast, Bosnian Muslim representatives regularly met with U.S. officials during the New York negotiations and beyond. As their views became a staple of national television and radio reporting, Washington
continued to be overwhelmed with only one view of the Bosnian war—
one that sought and would ultimately attain U.S. military intervention.

U.S. INTERVENTION IN BOSNIA BECOMES CASE FOR NATO STRENGTH

When the Clinton administration presented its new two-track approach
for Bosnia, some segments of the Washington establishment disagreed
with the policy. In February 1993, the Pentagon opposed the Clinton administration proposal to shoot down Serbian planes, arm the Muslims, and
launch air strikes against Serbian targets. While testifying before the Senate Armed Services Committee, the operations and intelligence directors
of the Joint Chiefs of Staff stated that enforcing the no-fly zone would
make no appreciable military difference and that providing arms to Bosnian Muslims would only make for continued chaos. During the hearings,
intelligence director, Rear Admiral Mike W. Cramer, asserted that Bosnia
was not viable as an independent state and that "the only solution ultimately [would] be when the Serbs and the Croats achieve their military
objectives."[32]

France, Great Britain, and Russia were even more skeptical of U.S.
proposals for military intervention in Bosnia. Russia was especially
alarmed by implications of an expanded NATO role in the Balkans, which
would set a precedent for allowing NATO to pick and choose military
interventions. Russian President Boris Yeltsin was increasingly pressured
by members of his parliament to take a stand. On February 18, 1993, the
Russian parliament voted almost unanimously to ask the United Nations
to lift sanctions on Serbia and impose them on Croatia. A week later, on
February 24, 1993, the Russian government unveiled its new Balkan peace
initiative which called for a more evenhanded approach to the Serbs. The
eight-point plan suggested a tightening of the arms embargo on all parties,
U.N. sanctions to be imposed on Croatia if attacks were not stopped
against Serb-populated Krajina, and inclusion of conditions for lifting U.N.
sanctions against Serbia and Montenegro within the Vance–Owen plan.

Russia had little political influence, nor did even the British and French,
in preventing Washington's drive toward military intervention in Bosnia.
The Clinton administration was concerned first with boosting NATO's image under U.S. leadership, and second with strengthening U.S. relations
with Islamic allies by showing solidarity with Bosnian Muslims. To maintain a strong U.S. presence in Europe, U.S. political and military capability

would need to be demonstrated to affirm its key role in NATO. Bosnia provided a fortuitous opportunity to demonstrate U.S. leadership. This strategy included enlarging NATO to include Eastern European countries, including Poland whose concern about German domination would ensure their continued support for a U.S.-led, rather than German-led, NATO.

In preparation for what U.S. military planners realized was the likelihood that America's role in NATO would increase in the coming years, in 1993 the most significant reorganization of NATO's force structure was undertaken since NATO's creation in 1949. This process was overseen by U.S. General John M. Shalikashvili, supreme allied commander of NATO forces. It involved the breakup of large anti-tank formations from the Cold War era into highly mobile, multinational units capable of responding quickly to sudden crises. This would allow the United States to conduct effective special operations in the coming years. Shalikashvili observed that "NATO is the only organization with the command structure, training, and experience capable of performing the tough jobs, which has established its future importance to European security."[33]

Although America's European allies were concerned that an aggressive U.S. intervention would intensify the Bosnian conflict, they also realized that their own resources were insufficient to sustain their security needs. They needed the United States to be engaged in Europe. As one European diplomat acknowledged, "there is no alternative to dependence on American troops and technology for years to come, and with a recession coming on and defense cuts getting deeper, that reliance may become even greater."[34] NATO fulfilled a mutual U.S.-European interest as an element of stabilization. This mutual goal of maintaining a strong U.S.-led NATO would give the Clinton administration free reign in setting military and political strategy in Bosnia, and later in Kosovo.

WASHINGTON ABANDONS DIPLOMACY, PREPARES FOR INTERVENTION

In the Spring of 1993, as all three Bosnian warring parties went back and forth several times to New York throughout ongoing negotiations, the Europeans were still the main strength behind international attempts to find a diplomatic solution to the war. Although the Bosnian Muslim government publicly expressed its willingness to accept the Vance–Owen plan, it was a tactic of negotiations and did not reflect its true agreement to the plan. They calculated that they ultimately would not accept the plan's requirements, since U.S. military intervention was likely to come. The Bosnian Croats, who had similar misgivings about the Vance–Owen plan as the other parties, consented to what they viewed as a temporary solution to their own territorial aspirations. Bosnian Serbs, angered with being singled out as the only party threatened by U.S. air strikes unless they accepted the plan, reacted with defiance. On April 2, 1993, the Bosnian Serb parliament rejected the Vance–Owen plan, arguing that the 10-province division of Bosnia would leave them a powerless minority in each province, while the plan's noncontiguous distribution would leave them vulnerable to attack.

The U.N. Security Council responded with a carrot-and-stick approach. A modification of the Vance–Owen plan was offered, which provided a six-mile-wide corridor linking Serb-held enclaves across northern Bosnia— a move meant to address Bosnian Serbian security concerns. At the same time, additional economic sanctions were threatened against Yugoslavia to encourage Serbian President Milosevic to pressure the Bosnian Serbs. Although the Bosnian Serb leadership accepted the amended plan on April 25, 1993, the next day the Bosnian Serb Assembly rejected it. This prompted new U.N.-imposed trade sanctions against Serbia and Montenegro that took effect on April 27, 1993, including a worldwide freeze on all Yugoslav financial assets, seizure of all Yugoslav planes, ships, trucks, and other vehicles on foreign territory, and a strictly enforced embargo, except for food and medicine, on all land, water, and air commerce with Serbia and Montenegro.

Although the Europeans still believed in a mediated solution to the Bosnian war, on April 28, 1993, Clinton administration officials announced their intention to pursue a two-point strategy that combined air strikes on Serbian positions with the lifting of an arms ban on the Muslim-led government. U.S. military planners drafted a NATO peacekeeping plan for Bosnia that would begin with U.S. Marines landing in the Adriatic and U.S. Army paratroopers taking control of Sarajevo airport, followed by a quick deployment of 12,000 combat troops from the 1st US Armored Division based in Germany. An estimated 60,000 multinational troops were said to be required to enforce a peace agreement in Bosnia, with about one-third of these coming from U.S. forces based in Europe. The Clinton administration threatened strong military action against the Bosnian Serbs if their assembly rejected the Vance–Owen plan for the second time. By now, members of all levels of the Bosnian Serb government and parliament were outraged by what they perceived to be open U.S. favoritism toward the Muslims, disregard for the national security needs of the Bosnian Serb people, and unfair singling out of Serbs as targets of intimidation and propaganda. In a show of resistance to foreign coercion, on May 6, 1993, the Bosnian Serb assembly voted for the second time to reject the Vance–Owen plan.

The Clinton administration was now prepared more than ever to use force against the Bosnian Serbs. U.S. officials prepared to sell the idea to a skeptical American public. Although polls at the time showed that most Americans opposed U.S. military intervention in the Balkans, President Clinton was determined to pursue an aggressive new policy. "Before I agree to put one American soldier there," Clinton told reporters at a May 3, 1993 conference, "I will obviously speak not only to you [the media] but directly to the American people about it."[35] A senior Clinton campaign aide acknowledged at the time that President Clinton was not as much moved by a passion to save the Bosnian Muslims as by "the need to offer a more activist approach to solving the problems of the post–Cold War world," by moving away from former President Bush's cautious approach and portraying himself as a leader of a new world in which the United States exerted moral and international leadership.[36] In portraying this image, Clinton aides attempted to rally Washington's interventionists and the American people by pointing to the humanitarian and geopolitical stakes in the Balkans. One Clinton aide said that the president's focus on U.S. involvement in Bosnia was based on humanitarian arguments because Americans have traditionally responded well to idealistic reasons for getting into wars.[37] Knowing that he could not convince the American public to support U.S. intervention in Bosnia for strategic reasons, Clinton set out to sway the public with humanitarian arguments.

The first part of the strategy, lifting the arms embargo against the Muslims, would be justified as a necessary step to "level the battlefield," a claim that peace could be made only when the Muslim side was better armed. This was an odd claim since the front lines had not changed significantly in months. While Great Britain, France, and Russia argued that lifting the arms embargo would widen the war, the Clinton administration was already covertly undertaking what it could not do openly—arming the Muslims.[38] A May 9, 1993, *Washington Post* article revealed that U.S. officials had already begun to assemble a multinational coalition to finance and supply arms to the Bosnian Muslim government. The Clinton administration intended to play a "brokering role in which the governments sympathetic to the Muslims—Saudi Arabia, in particular—would buy weapons and ammunition from other countries and arrange for their delivery to the Bosnian Muslims."[39] U.S. officials expected the Saudis to spend $100 million on the weapons delivery project. To ensure that arms delivered to Bosnia's Muslims would be compatible with their current supplies, the administration devised a scheme to buy Soviet-made weapons from Eastern Europe to be delivered to Bosnia. Clinton administration officials believed this approach would serve U.S. foreign policy goals in two ways. First, American hard currency would help provide an economic boost to new U.S. allies in countries such as Czechoslovakia, Poland, and Hungary, and second, these countries would be encouraged to sell their Cold War arsenal to Bosnian Muslims instead of countries like Syria or Iran. Another U.S. ally, Egypt, was also a promising weapons provider because of its substantial stock of Soviet-built equipment.[40] Having conducted an analysis of what equipment the Bosnian Muslims would need, how much it would cost, and how long it would take to arm them, Clinton administration officials said they would provide anti-tank missiles as well as small weapons such as mortars and ammunition for machine guns.

At the time, revelations of the U.S. plan to deliver covert arms to Bosnian Muslims in violation of the U.N. weapons embargo did not disturb Washington's advocates of international law. When dealing with a warring party that interventionists felt morally justified in supporting, it was apparently acceptable to subvert international law. Four years later, a Senate Foreign Relations Committee investigating the Clinton administration's knowledge of arms deliveries to Bosnian Muslim forces was reluctant to place clear blame for violating the arms embargo. Yet the Clinton administration's plan was not only reported by the media, but was an integral part of the two-point strategy frequently reiterated throughout early 1993. Richard Holbrooke would later write that the administration was not entirely opposed to arms flowing to Bosnian Muslim forces and that "for the United States to have continued to object to such assistance without providing something to replace it would in my opinion have been unconscionable."[41] Although U.S. officials publicly denied their involvement with covert weapons deliveries to the Muslims in Bosnia, it would not be until February 1996 that Saudi Arabia—in an effort to take credit for helping Bosnian Muslim war efforts away from rival Iran—openly disclosed the extent of U.S. participation. The Saudis admitted to funding a $300 million covert operation to channel weapons to the Muslim-led government between 1993 and 1996, with the knowledge, cooperation, and consent of the United States that began under President Bush and became much greater under President Clinton.[42] Clearly, Washington had the intent to provide military assistance in one form or another to Bosnia's Muslim-led government, at least as early as the Spring of 1993. The pretext for direct U.S. military intervention, however, would take more time to establish. Creating "safe havens" was a start.

THE PUSH FOR "SAFE HAVENS"

The Muslim leadership continued to direct emotional appeals at Washington while making tangible military gains on the ground. The creation of safe havens accomplished this goal. It provided a moral justification for U.S.-led air strikes against Bosnian Serbs—actions that would ultimately help Muslim forces. The military advantage of safe havens was clear to the Muslim side at least as early as the Spring of 1993. At the time, as Muslims and Serbs battled over the town of Srebrenica, U.N. General Philippe Morillon was about to play an integral part in the Bosnian Muslim strategy against the Serbs. After meeting with Muslim commanders, Morillon was prevented from leaving the town by hundreds of Bosnian Muslim civilians who surrounded his vehicle and confronted the general with a moving scene of Bosnian Muslim women crying, while others begged for

U.N. help. Yet, the mass gathering was not as spontaneous as it had appeared. As Bosnian Muslim official, Murat Efendic, later acknowledged: "I had sent a coded message to our commander to hold Morillon in Srebrenica until he guaranteed the safety of our population."[43] The Muslim leadership's use of the plight of its civilians for military gain was yielding results. After being held for two days in Srebrenica's post office, Morillon emerged from the building to announce to the crowd that he had decided that the United Nations would from now on protect Srebrenica. His promise contradicted the United Nations's neutral policy in Bosnia and was a great surprise to diplomats at U.N. headquarters in New York. Morillon's statement obligated the United Nations to defend Bosnian Muslim positions in Srebrenica, while the town's Muslim forces remained armed. The term *safe havens* was a deceptive one. How could a safe haven for civilians simultaneously be a stronghold for thousands of armed Muslim soldiers?

Although Clinton administration officials stressed the idea of Muslim-held safe havens as a necessary step in protecting Muslim civilians, the more important reason for their creation was absent from public debates. The proposed safety zones were strategically important to the Bosnian Muslim government for two reasons: first, they gave Muslim fighters cover from which to launch attacks on Serbs, and second, they provided legal grounds for justifying future U.S.-led NATO interventions. The legal grounds came on May 6, 1993, when the Clinton administration convinced the U.N. Security Council to pass Resolution 824 making the six Muslim-held towns of Sarajevo, Tuzla, Zepa, Gorazde, Bihac, and Srebrenica and their surrounding areas "safe areas"—areas free from attacks and from any other hostile act. If the Serbs moved against these towns, the United Nations would react. This was the first U.N. resolution providing a clear impetus for future U.S. military intervention in Bosnia. It was followed by Resolution 836 on June 4, 1993, which called for the enforcement of safe areas by extending the mandate of UNPROFOR to enable it to protect the zones. The resolution did not call for protecting Bosnian Serb areas from Muslim or Croatian attacks. "Safe havens" were created solely for Muslim-populated towns whose front lines were held by thousands of armed Muslim soldiers, with U.N. troops stationed on Muslim front lines. Therefore, any military action taken by Serbs against Muslims would be interpreted as an attack on the United Nations, and a U.S.-led NATO military response would be initiated. It also gave Muslim forces the ability to launch attacks on Bosnian Serbs from safety zones with impunity, while a Serbian response would trigger NATO air attacks.

In reality, the concept of safe havens was a misnomer. As long as there was no settlement of the war, there was no safety for civilians anywhere. Knowledge that U.N. and NATO forces would protect safe areas encouraged the Bosnian Muslim military command to leave its civilians in key strategic towns rather than seek shelter in other, better-stocked areas of

Bosnia. As such, Muslim forces were partially using civilians as a shield. During a May 1995 visit to the nearby town of Bratunac, a U.N. medical officer told me that the situation in Srebrenica was "disastrous." But, she said, "the Muslim leadership did not want a stampede of people leaving the town, because this would deny them justification for U.N. protection." This, in turn, would threaten Bosnian Muslim control of key strategic areas wedged within Bosnian Serb-held territory. By 1995, Srebrenica was so militarily crucial to the Muslims, according to the U.N. medical officer, that Srebrenica's Muslim mayor ordered an execution of two Muslims who tried to leave the town without permission.

The U.S. media ignored the military reality of safe havens—either deliberately or because it was misunderstood. The popular rhetoric of the day obscured what was really happening in the region at a crucial time when the idea of protecting Muslim safe havens was being discussed. Prior to an April 16, 1993, *CNN & Company* show on which I participated, CNN played a statement from an interview with former British prime minister, Margaret Thatcher, who said in a melodramatic voice, "if we had not had the planes with which to defend ourselves in the Battle of Britain not only we would have perished but freedom would have perished in Europe, and because we fought, we defeated the tyranny in Europe and rescued the rest from it." Her comparison of what was happening in Bosnia to the Battle of Britain and "protecting Europe from tyranny" was grossly overstated. It was a good sound bite, however, and one that appealed to media and human rights interventionists alike.

The comparison of the civil war in Bosnia to the Jewish Holocaust was another preposterous idea that was reiterated at this time. To bring home the need for safe havens, the Bosnian Muslim government drew parallels between what was happening in Srebrenica and the Nazi genocide of the Jews. Washington readily accepted the comparison. As Muslim and Serbian forces battled in Srebrenica, on an April 16, 1993, show of *CNN & Company*, Mary Tillitson said to me, "there is a Holocaust museum that opens in Washington next week, [and] there are people who are comparing what is going on between Serbs and Muslims to what went on when Adolf Hitler rounded up and killed Jews, the Muslims this time being in the role of the Jews. Do you buy that comparison?" "No, I don't at all," I replied, "and I think it is an insult to the Jewish people, and to the Serbian people, who suffered through their own Holocaust in Bosnia-Hercegovina itself during World War II, where up to one million Serbs were killed." But the comparison of Bosnia to the Holocaust energized Washington at a time when crucial decisions were made on safety zones. The comparisons even aroused Auschwitz survivor Eli Wiesel, who said to President Clinton during the April 22, 1993, opening of the Holocaust museum, "We must do something to stop the bloodshed in that country."

The political rhetoric in Washington in relation to the Yugoslav war was making a mockery out of the idea of the Holocaust. Perhaps the most amazing example of the power of images, propaganda, and historic revisionism in modern-day Washington was the appearance of Croatia's president Tudjman—the same person who minimized Croatia's war crimes against Serbs and Jews during World War II—as a guest at the opening of the Holocaust Museum in Washington, D.C. Ironically, representatives of the Serbs, the people who suffered extermination in Yugoslav regions alongside the Jews, and the only people in the Yugoslav region who opposed Hitler and defended the Jews, were not even invited.

SAFE HAVENS FAIL TO ADDRESS THE MUSLIM-CROAT FIGHTING

The establishment of enclaves protecting Muslims did not address the fighting between Muslims against Croats and Muslims against Serbs. As safe havens were being created, none included towns where some of the most brutal fighting and human rights abuses were taking place at the time during the Muslim-Croat battles in the Spring of 1993. On April 16, as many as 500 Muslim villagers of Ahmici were killed by Croat forces, and the village was set ablaze.[44] U.N. troops found 89 bodies, mostly elderly Muslims as well as women and children, massacred by Croat forces with high-powered rifles at close range, as Croat militia went house to house, shooting their victims and sometimes pouring gasoline on them and setting them on fire while they were still alive. The Ahmici incident was not reported in the *Washington Post* at the time it occurred; only two months later did the newspaper give the details of the massacre. Even then, the article did not make the front page, and no photographs accompanied the text.

As Muslim-Croat fighting continued, on May 9, 1993, Bosnian Croat forces launched an all-out attack on the Muslim-held areas of Mostar. The *Washington Post* quoted U.N. observers reporting that Croat militiamen were "forcing Muslims from their homes and herding women and children into a soccer stadium." Even after 10 days of fighting around Mostar between Croats and Muslims, the U.S. press was hardly moved, and Washington did not call for the creation of safe havens to protect Muslim civilians in Mostar. On May 21, the *Washington Post* casually reported that Croat forces released 1,000 Muslim "detainees" under U.N. supervision.[45] As gruesome reports of maltreatment and torture of Muslims in Croat camps emerged, Washington's opinionmakers and foreign policymakers were not alarmed by Croat-held camps for Muslim prisoners. Unlike earlier claims against Serbs, Croatian prison camps were not called "death camps" for Muslims.

While Washington rejected Bosnian Serb claims that prison camps were necessary to disarm and detain Muslim troops, it appeared willing to accept the same explanation by Bosnian Croats. Bosnian Croat General Praljak argued that Croat-run camps were necessary in "the process of disarming [Muslim] men [since] we had to put prisoners somewhere."[46] In one Bosnian Croat-run camp, Muslim men were held in unbearably hot, half-buried underground fuel tanks which had only a small hole through which the men could breath—and many died. Although news of Serb-run camps just nine months earlier caused Washington to frantically accuse Serbs of war crimes, Croat-run camps hardly caused a ripple. Television news shows were not overflowing with scenes of emaciated Muslim men in Croat camps seen in one Discovery Channel episode of *Yugoslavia: Death of a Nation*, but not until December of 1995, when the war was over.

In the Spring of 1993, the Clinton administration, the U.S. press, and even the Bosnian Muslims downplayed the situation. On May 15, 1993, thousands of Bosnian Muslims and their supporters gathered in front of the White House urging the United States to launch air strikes only against Bosnian Serbs, not against Croats. Conveniently ignoring the three-sided civil war in Bosnia, Muslim government officials continued to lobby Washington for weapons to fight the Serbs, while remaining silent on the Croats. In an interview in early May 1993, Haris Silajdzic was still saying that his government would use the weapons "to liberate our country from an invader."[47] At a June 15, 1993 U.N. World Conference on Human Rights, Silajdzic again directed his rhetoric exclusively against the Serbs, accusing them of "genocide" against his people, while failing to mention one of the most brutal attacks by Croat forces on Muslims in Ahmici that took place a mere one month prior to his speech.

While ignoring Croat offensives against Muslims, Washington was even less concerned with renewed attacks against Serbs in Sarajevo. On May 21, 1993, a *Washington Post* headline read, "Serbs Fight to Keep Their Only Enclave in Muslim Sarajevo," which for the first time brought greater attention to attacks from Bosnian Muslim forces on Sarajevo's Serbian suburbs. The article stated that mortar fire from Muslim forces killed two Serbian children and four soldiers and that their heavy shelling "terrorized Serb civilians," of whom about 45,000 lived in the Serb-held suburbs of Sarajevo.[48] The Muslim targeting of civilians was not limited to Serbs. On June 9, 1993, after one of the bloodiest battles with Bosnian Croats, Bosnian Muslims took control of the key city of Travnik, and U.N. relief workers witnessed Muslim forces firing at Croat civilians and forcing thousands of Croats from their homes.[49] By June 16, U.N. officials reported that Bosnian Muslim forces had rampaged through several Croat villages northwest of Sarajevo where they looted Croatian areas and forced over 10,000 Croat villagers from their homes.[50] The Clinton administration made no accusation of "ethnic cleansing" by Muslim troops of Croats. During the same period, Croat and Muslim troops turned against the U.N. as well. On June 10, troops from the Muslim-led army northwest of Sarajevo halted two armored U.N. vehicles at gunpoint, forcing their British crews to lie on the road while they stole all of their equipment, bulletproof vests, automatic weapons, and heavy machine guns.[51] A day later, U.N. troops were forced to shoot and kill two Croat militiamen who were attacking them, signifying the first combatants killed by U.N. personnel in the 14-month-old war.

Still, Muslim and Croat offenses raised no viable questions in the minds of Clinton administration officials and media as to why the United States was providing support to warring parties that appeared to behave no differently than Bosnian Serbs. Given these reports, Washington's 14-month-long portrayal of the Bosnian Muslims as victims should have provoked some skepticism. If some individuals in Washington recognized the inconsistency of the situation, their views almost never made it in the press. The vast majority of editorials called for more assertive U.S. actions against the Serbs.

EUROPEAN PLAN TO DIVIDE BOSNIA: OWEN–STOLTENBERG

With intense battles taking place between Muslim and Croat forces throughout the Spring and Summer of 1993, it was becoming increasingly difficult to argue that Bosnia's three ethnic communities wanted to live under a shared government. The Muslim side continued to believe that Washington's support and covert weapons from Islamic countries would help them win control over all of Bosnia, while Bosnian Serbs felt that self-rule in their domain was the only way to ensure their safety. On June 17, 1993, in a significant turnaround during meetings in Vienna, EC mediator Lord Owen urged Bosnian Muslims to accept a partition of Bosnia into three separate ethnic divisions (see Appendix 2, map 9). Changing views of what could realistically end the war in Bosnia even began to be seen in Washington. President Clinton indicated that he would accept a partition if all parties would agree. Shortly thereafter, a CIA briefing concluded that dividing Bosnia into three states would be the most reasonable solution, and a senior U.S. State Department official confirmed that the United States was willing to let realities on the ground dictate a resolution of the conflict. Secretary of State Warren Christopher, in justifying the new U.S. approach, delivered the Clinton administration's first open criticism of Germany by saying that "there were serious mistakes made in the whole process of recognition, and the Germans bear a particular responsibility in persuading their colleagues and the European Community [to recognize Croatia and Bosnia-Hercegovina]. . . . The beginning of the problems we face here today stem from [that] recognition."[52]

Hoping that the international community would accept the same sort of ethnic division in Croatia that they appeared willing to accept in Bosnia, on June 20, 1993, Krajina Serbs held a two-day referendum and over-whelmingly voted in favor of unifying the Republic of Krajina with Bosnian Serb areas of Republika Srpska. While the Serbs were sending one message to the international community to recognize the right of self-determination for ethnic Serbs in Croatia and Bosnia, the Bosnian Muslim government was sending another: we need weapons. At a conference in Copenhagen held on June 21, 1993, Alija Izetbegovic made an emotional appeal to European representatives to lift the arms embargo against his government. Izetbegovic was tenaciously holding out against the division of Bosnia, in spite of pressure from European Community mediators and even from another surprising source—members of his own Muslim-led government in Sarajevo. While Izetbegovic refused to attend the next round of negotiations in Geneva to discuss a three-way split of Bosnia, several members of his government secretly voted to go to Geneva to discuss terms of the partition plan. On June 24, 1993, seven of the ten members of the Bosnian Muslim wartime government in Sarajevo split with the hardliners headed by Izetbegovic and attended negotiations in Geneva. One of the members who came to Geneva, Fikret Abdic, was a leader of the Muslim-held northwest Bihac region. In Geneva, Abdic an-nounced that diplomatic recognition of the new group by European ne-gotiators meant that the international community accepted them as Bosnia's true government. The legitimacy of the Izetbegovic-led faction was now more questionable than ever. With added pressures within his own government, the ability of Izetbegovic and his supporters to regain crucial U.S. military backing was to become the most remarkable turna-round of the war—not in the field of battle but in Washington.

On July 8, 1993, Izetbegovic announced that he and his supporters would reject the plan to partition Bosnia-Hercegovina proposed in Ge-neva. Instead, the Muslim leadership demanded that the United Nations first disarm Serbs around safe havens. In Washington, policy was still fo-cused on the plight of civilians in Sarajevo and other Muslim-held areas. Bosnian Muslim calls for the United States to pressure the Serbs to with-draw heavy weapons from around Sarajevo appeared justified. From the Bosnian Serb perspective, heavy weapons were the only thing holding off the more numerous Muslim troops, and by removing these weapons, the Serbs would be vulnerable to attack. Convinced that protecting Muslim civilians was not Washington's true concern, the Serbs called their bluff and demanded that Bosnian Muslim safe havens be completely disarmed. The Bosnian Muslim government would not agree to this demand.

On July 26, 1993, Izetbegovic suddenly consented to participate in direct discussions with the Bosnian Serb and Croat leaders, Radovan Karadzic and Mate Boban, respectively. International mediators were encouraged. It appeared that the Muslim government would finally agree to create a loosely confederated state of three separate ethnic entities. The new plan presented by EC representative Lord David Owen and U.N. envoy Thorvald Stoltenberg differed from the previous 10-province Vance–Owen plan in that it called for a communally based, three-way federation of largely independent republics. Each republic would have its own constitution and the right to apply for membership in the United Nations and other international organizations. No central national army or national police force was envisioned, and the plan did not call for a central bank but rather provided for three different currencies. Bosnian institutions were to consist of a three-person presidency comprised of leaders of the three republics rotating every four months as chairman. All decisions were to be made by consensus. Bosnian Serbs suggested that the city of Sarajevo be divided between two neighboring cities for Muslims and Serbs.

The Owen–Stoltenberg plan proposed in Geneva at the end of July 1993 was one of the most realistic proposals to date for ending the Bosnian war. It called for preserving the region as a multiethnic union while at the same time allowing each group relative freedom and self-government. The agreement to partition Bosnia into three ethnically based republics could have brought an end to the war. Yet at this crucial moment, Washington's threat of force and its backing of the Izetbegovic government would again prevent a negotiated solution to the conflict.

THREATS OF U.S. AIR STRIKES UPSET NEGOTIATIONS

At the end of July 1993, just as Bosnian Muslims, Croats, and Serbs were about to sign the Owen–Stoltenberg agreement on partitioning Bosnia, the Clinton administration announced that the United States was considering using air strikes against the Serbs in order to break their military hold on Sarajevo. At last the Muslim leadership was hearing what it needed to hear: the United States would provide military support. Washington's announcement eliminated any possibility that the European-led plan would be signed.

This decision, like many others before it, was made by the Clinton administration outside the scope of what was really happening on the ground. At the time, U.N. convoys were prevented from getting into Sarajevo, not because of the Serbs but because of fighting between Muslims and Croats. Instead of working on stopping the Muslim-Croat battles, Washington was again focused on pursuing a more aggressive policy against the Serbs. A cable warning of a desperate situation about to engulf the Balkans sent by the U.S. ambassador in Croatia, Peter Galbraith, was said to have made a particularly strong impact on Secretary of State Warren Christopher at the time.[53] In his cable, Galbraith went so far as to compare Sarajevo to Auschwitz and spoke of horrors about to befall the city, such as typhoid, rampant dysentery, starvation, and an extremely cold winter. The U.S. ambassador's emotional drive was characteristic of what was happening in Washington at the time. State Department personnel described the evolving U.S. policy in favor of bombing Serbian positions to have been driven more by a sense of crisis and determination to help the Muslims than by broader principles of foreign policy.

As the media increasingly criticized Clinton's Bosnia policy as ineffective in stopping the war, and after Galbraith's desperate plea, Christopher began to ally himself with the more interventionist camp of the Clinton administration—National Security Adviser Anthony Lake and U.N. Ambassador Madeleine Albright—who supported air strikes around Sarajevo. Warding off months of growing criticism from his colleagues against his mild approach, Christopher now presented more forceful arguments. He made urgent appeals in both letters and phone calls to his counterparts in Europe, arguing that not only was Sarajevo at stake but also the future of NATO. President Clinton added more weight to the new U.S. appeal by sending a letter to U.N. Secretary General Boutros Boutros-Ghali on July 30, 1993, urging U.N. authorization for U.S.-led air strikes. A flurry of diplomatic activity was initiated to get British and French officials to drop the Owen–Stoltenberg plan and to support U.S. military action in Bosnia.

Domestically, Clinton administration officials worked on building a consensus among skeptical Pentagon officials. When on July 13, 1993, the Clinton administration asked the Pentagon to present military options in Bosnia, the Joint Chiefs of Staff estimated that the United States would have to deploy 80,000 logistical and combat troops. National Security Adviser Anthony Lake and Secretary of State Christopher believed the Pentagon presented a politically impractical option in order to ensure that the plan would be rejected. The two immediately lobbied the Pentagon for a military proposal supporting their aims. The revised Pentagon option would give Lake and Christopher what they wanted. It estimated that only 25,000 U.S. troops would be needed in Sarajevo if support was given to Bosnian Muslim troops through U.S.-led air strikes. President Clinton embraced the air strikes option, and a U.S. military role in the Balkans became a reality. Publicly, Lake and Christopher argued that air strikes would help the negotiating process; in reality, their goal was to strengthen the Muslim strategic and negotiating position. As a final step, Washington also applied increased pressure on the Europeans to back the plan. At a meeting in Brussels on August 3, 1993, Clinton administration officials were able to convince NATO to support a U.S. plan to use air strikes against Bosnian Serbs in Sarajevo.

Following a familiar pattern, U.S. threats to use force in Bosnia led the Muslim government to pull out of the peace talks. When NATO announced it was putting together a target list for Bosnia, Bosnian Muslim leader Alija Izetbegovic issued a letter to international mediators on July

31 demanding substantive changes to the plan he had accepted just a few days earlier. Bosnian Muslims now wanted Serb forces to pull back from two key strategic mountain positions they held around Sarajevo. The new demands were bolstered by Islamic allies. On August 13, 1993, representatives of Islamic countries, including Turkish Foreign Minister Hikmet Cetin, met in Washington with Secretary of State Warren Christopher and urged the United States to reject the peace plan and launch air strikes against the Serbs.

Such calls were echoed by Washington interventionists and the media. In an August 9, 1993, *Washington Post* editorial, Jeanne Kirkpatrick called the situation "our first great post–Cold War failure." A day later Jim Hoagland's editorial called the plan "Lord Owen's betrayal." At the time, the *Washington Post* urged the Clinton administration to take greater unilateral steps to directly help the Bosnian Muslim government. Although 70 percent of the American public felt that the United States should not act alone in carrying out air strikes against Bosnian Serbs, it was the media's views that had a greater impact on Clinton. Richard Holbrooke later noted that "the press was merciless in its coverage of the administration [on Bosnia], and was likely pressuring Clinton to act more aggressively."[54] A State Department analyst working on Bosnian issues at the time told me that the administration was "pushed into backing the Muslims by the media" because "people on all levels at the State Department wanted to get good reviews by actively doing something on Bosnia."

While the Clinton administration was preoccupied with media images, European mediators continued working on a mediated solution. In August 1993, they convinced the Bosnian Serbs to withdraw from their positions above Sarajevo, in the hopes of inducing the Muslim government back into negotiations. At the same time, international mediators offered the Bosnian Muslim government a division of Sarajevo into two cities as part of an overall peace settlement. When Bosnian Serb forces agreed to withdraw from the strategic high ground in Sarajevo, talks resumed in Geneva, and the warring parties further agreed to demilitarize Sarajevo by placing it temporarily under U.N. control. NATO again threatened Bosnian Serbs, and predictably, Izetbegovic began to make new demands for additional territory from Serbs and Croats during an August 19, 1993, meeting in Geneva.

While negotiations continued, fighting between Muslims and Croats intensified in Mostar to the point where the United Nations reported the city's 55,000 Muslim population was close to starvation. As Bosnian Croat troops encircling Mostar blocked U.N. aid deliveries, they created a far more dire humanitarian situation than in Sarajevo. U.N. officials visiting Croat detention centers for Muslims reported that they were the worst camps they had seen in the 16 months of civil war in Bosnia-Hercegovina.[55] The Bosnian Croat blockage of food deliveries was neither admonished nor punished, even though Ambassador Albright warned at a Hague press conference that "the United States intends to consider interference by any of the three warring Bosnian factions in the delivery of emergency food supplies a violation of international humanitarian law that should fall under the jurisdiction of the War Crimes Tribunal."[56] Washington issued no calls for air strikes against Bosnian Croat forces if they did not withdraw from Mostar or give up their weapons as was required of Serbs in Sarajevo. Few, if any, members of the media questioned Washington's one-sided policies.

The Bosnian peace talks reached a critical point by early September 1993. After Izetbegovic had apparently failed to move French and British U.N. Security Council representatives to approve air strikes, Albright was angered into a public show of outrage. Her speech, following that of Izetbegovic, demanded that the Serbs and Croats yield more territory to the Muslims or face air strikes. Her message was directed only against the Serbs. Washington never seriously contemplated using force against the Croats. Although the Foreign Relations Committee of the U.S. Congress told Izetbegovic not to expect U.S. military support to turn the tide of the war, the Bosnian Muslim government had friends among top levels of the Clinton administration who would ultimately send U.S. forces in 1994 and 1995 to intervene on his government's behalf. The U.S. administration announced that NATO would act if Sarajevo came under attack or if U.N. convoys were stopped from reaching the city. Emboldened by U.S. support for their territorial claims, on September 29, 1993, the Muslim-dominated Bosnian parliament rejected key terms of the U.N.-sponsored peace plan and insisted that Bosnian Serbs give up even more land. U.S. Special Envoy Charles Redman supported the Muslim decision, but European mediators were greatly disappointed.

Convinced that Muslim negotiating tactics were merely aimed at extracting a continuing number of concessions from the Serbs, without compromising their own position, the Bosnian Serb parliament withdrew all concessions it made earlier reducing Serbian territory from 70 percent to 52 percent as called for by the peace plan. The Serbs now refused to allow Muslims access to the Sava River and part of the city of Brcko, while Bosnian Serb president Radovan Karadzic announced that his government would not accept the presence of NATO troops in Bosnia, only U.N. monitors. In addition to refusing to bow to Izetbegovic's new demands, Bosnian Serbs were beginning to feel that the Muslim position was weakening from internal struggles. In October of 1993, the unity of the Bosnian Muslim government in Sarajevo was greatly undermined by one of the Muslim members of government, Fikret Abdic. His breakaway faction declared autonomy in the northwestern region of Bihac and signed a peace pact with the Bosnian Serbs. Abdic believed that the hard-line position presented by Izetbegovic and his supporters was encouraging a continuation of the war at the expense of Muslim civilians.

The U.S. media paid little attention to the split in the Bosnian Muslim government at the time it took place. References to Abdic's breakaway Bosnian Muslim faction did not appear until July 4, 1994, in the *New York Times*, nine months later. The issue was again briefly mentioned in two *New York Times* articles in the following year, after fighting between the two Muslim factions intensified to such an extent that it could no longer be ignored. The *Washington Post* did not even mention the breakup. The Bosnian Muslim government specifically avoided the topic in interviews. They did not want to endanger U.S. military intervention by acknowledging that their government, the alleged model of multiethnicity, was now rejected not only by Bosnia's Serbs and Croats, but by a significant number of Muslims as well.

With a somewhat more realistic view of what was happening in Bosnia, the Europeans continued to push for a division. At a November 28, 1993 meeting of the European Community in Paris, 12 nations of the EC called for lifting economic sanctions against Yugoslavia in return for Bosnian Serb territorial concessions, while Croatia's cooperation was sought through promises of financial assistance. Washington, on the other hand, continued to build a consensus for use of force in Bosnia. At a January 9, 1994, NATO summit in Brussels, President Clinton pledged American leadership in building a "new security" in Europe by bonding the established democracies of the West to the emerging democracies of the East through a web of military, economic, and democratic links. During the conference, NATO made demands on Bosnian Serbs to lift the siege of Sarajevo and allow the opening of the airport in the northeast Bosnian city of Tuzla.

The Europeans were not pleased with Washington's sabre-rattling. U.N. Secretary General Boutros Boutros-Ghali told the Security Council that he was opposed to NATO air strikes because they could endanger the entire humanitarian relief operation in Bosnia. The Clinton administration, however, was more focused on Bosnian Muslim strategic goals than genuine humanitarian concerns. By now, Bosnian Muslim forces were making military gains due to the increased flow of weapons from Islamic countries. Believing they could eventually use armed force to take what they could not get in negotiations, the Bosnian Muslims rejected the peace proposal again on January 23, 1994. This latest rejection of a negotiated settlement would launch a 19-month period of joint Bosnian Muslim and Croatian attacks on Bosnia's Serbs, aided by U.S.-led air attacks, which would last until just before November 1995, when the Dayton peace plan was signed.

NOTES

1. Blaine Harden, "Moynihan Sees Sarajevo Siege for Himself," *Washington Post* (November 26, 1992): A56.

2. John Pomfret, "Bosnian Makes Plea for Help," *Washington Post* (January 9, 1993): A12.

3. Charles A. Radin, "Moynihan Sounds Warning on Ethnicity," *Boston Globe* (November 13, 1992): 12.

4. Caryle Murphy, "Fahd Urges Arms Aid for Bosnia," *Washington Post* (December 2, 1992): A37.

5. Ibid.

6. Blaine Harden, "U.N. Commander in Bosnia Opposes Intervention," *Washington Post* (December 13, 1992): A38.

7. Jim Hoagland, "Empty Threats, Balkan Savagery; It's Time for the West to Put Up or Shut Up about Bosnia," *Washington Post* (December 14, 1992): A23.

8. Don Oberdorfer, "Clinton: Enforce 'No-Fly Zone' in Bosnia; President-Elect's Call Is Echoed by French Military Chief," *Washington Post* (December 12, 1992): A19.

9. Don Oberdorfer, "Eagleburger's Last Lap: All Eyes Still Look to America," *Washington Post* (December 20, 1992): C1.

10. Richard Holbrooke, *To End a War* (New York: Random House, 1998), 39.

11. U.S. Department of Justice, *Foreign Agent Registration Unit*, Supplemental Statement, Attachment A, Question 12 (May 31, 1993).

12. Discovery Channel's *Yugoslavia: Death of a Nation*, December 1995.

13. Peter Mass, "UN Leader Reviled in Sarajevo," *Washington Post* (January 1, 1993): A1.

14. John Pomfret, "Bosnian President Accuses Serbs of Playing Games with Talks," *Washington Post* (January 8, 1993): A9.

15. Peter Maas, " 'Help Us, or We Will All Die,' Aged Sarajevans Beseech U.N." *Washington Post* (January 7, 1993): A21.

16. Peter Maass, "Convoy Brings Food, Hope to Besieged Bosnian Town," *Washington Post* (January 19, 1993): A14.

17. Linda Grant, "Anyone Here Been Raped and Speak English?" *The Guardian*, London (August 2, 1993): 10.

18. Ibid.

19. Jacques Merlino, "Rapes, Figures in Question," *Le Point* (March 13, 1993).

20. Jonathan C. Randal, "Croats Move to Solidify Claims on Bosnian Land," *Washington Post* (February 3, 1993): A20.

21. William Drozdiak, "Intervention Threats Said to Slow Bosnian Talks," *Washington Post* (January 26, 1993).

22. Robert Marquand, "UN-EC Map for Bosnia Plan Based on Disputed Figures," *Christian Science Monitor* (February 3, 1993): 7.

23. John M. Goshko, "U.S. Officials Resist Pressure to Endorse Bosnia Peace Plan," *Washington Post* (February 4, 1993): A16.

24. Ibid., A14–A16.

25. Christine Spolar and Julia Preston, "Rivals Vie on Balkan Role of U.S.," *Washington Post* (February 5, 1993): A27.

26. Julia Preston, "U.N., EC Mediators Ask U.S. to Clarify Its Bosnian Policy," *Washington Post* (February 3, 1993): A20.

27. Spolar and Preston, "Rivals Vie on Balkan Role of U.S.," A27.

28. Daniel Williams and Julia Preston, "U.S. Wants New Talks on Balkans Plan; Clinton to Name Envoy," *Washington Post* (February 9, 1993): A18.

29. Julia Preston, "U.S. Options Slim in Balkan Morass," *Washington Post* (February 12, 1993): A32.

30. See photograph in Don Oberdorfer, "A Bloody Failure in the Balkans," *Washington Post* (February 8, 1993): A1, compared to Preston, "U.S. Options Slim in Balkan Morass," A32.

31. Chris Hedges, "With Kosovo's Rebels: A Growing Confidence in Battle," *New York Times* (June 29, 1998): A3, and *Washington Post* (June 25, 1998): A1.

32. Barton Gellman, "Allies Preview Emerging U.S. Plan for Balkans," *Washington Post* (February 7, 1993): A26.

33. Jane Perlez, "Blunt Reason for Enlarging NATO: Curbs on Germany," *New York Times* (December 7, 1997): 17.

34. William Drozdiak, "NATO Is Forced by Events into More Assertive Role," *Washington Post* (March 28, 1993): A24.

35. John M. Broder and Paul Richter, "Laying U.S. Lives on Line in Bosnia Will Be a Tough Sell," *Los Angeles Times* (May 4, 1993): 4.

36. Ann Devroy, "Trying to Level the Battlefield: Immediate U.S. Goal Is to Equalize Bosnia's Muslim, Serbs," *Washington Post* (May 9, 1993): A27.

37. Broder and Richter, "Laying U.S. Lives on Line in Bosnia Will Be a Tough Sell," 4.

38. Devroy, "Trying to Level the Battlefield," A1.

39. Ibid., A27.

40. Ibid.

41. Holbrooke, *To End a War*, 51.

42. "Official Says Saudis Gave $300 Million in Arms to Bosnians," *Washington Post* (February 2, 1996): A25.

43. Discovery Channel's *Yugoslavia: Death of a Nation* (December 1995).

44. Jonathan C. Randal, "Ahmici Massacre—Bosnian Turning Point," *Washington Post* (June 20, 1993): A29.

45. "Bosnian Croats Free Muslim Detainees," *Washington Post* (May 21, 1993): A28.

46. Discovery Channel's *Yugoslavia: Death of a Nation* (December 1995).

47. Devroy, "Trying to Level the Battlefield," A27.

48. John Pomfret, "Serbs Fight to Keep Their Only Enclave in Muslim Sarajevo," *Washington Post* (May 21, 1993): A28.

49. "Bloody Battle Leaves Muslims in Control of Key Bosnian City," *Washington Post* (June 9, 1993): A27.

50. James Rupert, "Muslim Forces Plunder Bosnian Croat Villages," *Washington Post* (June 17, 1993): A33.

51. James Rupert, "British U.N. Troops Kill 2 Croat Gunmen," *Washington Post* (June 12, 1993): A15.

52. "Three-Way Partition of Bosnia: Realities of War Come to Force," *Washington Post* (June 19, 1993): A12.

53. Daniel Williams, "Grim Balkans Outlook Affected U.S. Position: Policy

Based on Emotion, Not Broad Principle," *Washington Post* (August 19, 1993): A1, A24.

54. Holbrooke, *To End a War*, 56.

55. Lee Michael Katz, "Muslims in Bosnia City Near Starvation," *Washington Post* (August 23, 1993): 5A.

56. David B. Ottaway, "U.S. Warns Serbia on War Trials," *Washington Post* (January 17, 1994).

Chapter 7

War of Force: U.S. Intervention in Bosnia (February 1994 to November 1995)

SARAJEVO'S MARKET EXPLOSION DRAWS U.S. INTERVENTION

After a two-year push for intervention, by February 1994, the Clinton administration had fully committed itself to enter into the Yugoslav conflict on the side of Bosnia's Muslims. It was the start of a period lasting a year and a half in which a series of NATO air attacks on Bosnian Serbs and increasing attacks by Muslim forces would seriously weaken the Bosnian Serbs. This, combined with several offensives by Croatian forces on Krajina Serbs, would ultimately lead to the signing of the November 1995 Dayton Peace Accord by the warring parties.

The initiative during this period of greater international intervention came from Washington. Buckling under pressure from the Clinton administration to approve the use of military force in Bosnia, U.N. Secretary General Boutros-Ghali gave the go-ahead on January 28, 1994, for NATO aircraft to be used in the event U.N. peacekeepers were attacked. The introduction of NATO aircraft in the Bosnia peacekeeping scenario was a key part of the U.S.-led military intervention. Having additionally secured reluctant French and British support to allow NATO aircraft to back U.N. peacekeepers in Bosnia, the Clinton administration was now in a position to execute the second part of its two-part strategy announced in April of 1993—air strikes against the Serbs.

With Washington elites itching to punish the designated culprits of war, the scenario for justifying air strikes against the Serbs would soon be in place. The linchpin was provided on February 5, 1994, when a mortar exploded in Sarajevo's Markala market, killing 68 people. CNN was on the scene in a matter of minutes bringing live footage of wounded civilians being frantically rushed to hospitals. Reporters immediately blamed the Serbs, although Karadzic vehemently denied Bosnian Serb involvement, arguing that the Serbs had absolutely no logical reason to commit an act that would bring NATO reprisals at such a crucial time. He stated that the mortar attack likely came from the Muslim side, which hoped to gain international sympathy and give NATO the final push to bomb the Serbs. Although clear proof of which side fired the mortar was not publicly disclosed, the Bosnian Serbs had the most to lose by launching an attack that would serve no military purpose but would instead draw NATO reprisals.

After investigations were conducted, the United Nations could not place blame on either side; some U.N. personnel even stated they believed the mortar was fired from Muslim positions.[1] Regardless of who launched the mortar, it was perfectly timed to bolster the political and military aims of the Bosnian Muslim government. Aware of Washington's hypersensitivity to media images, Bosnian Muslim officials made an all-out effort to use the mortar explosion to their advantage. Izetbegovic quickly called a news conference after the Market Square incident, describing the tragedy as evidence that the arms embargo against his government should be lifted. The Bosnian Muslim foreign minister, Haris Silajdzic, gave Peter Jennings of ABC News an emotional exclusive interview, taking advantage of the disaster to argue against pressures from the international community on his government to sign the Owen–Stoltenberg peace proposal that would divide Bosnia into loosely confederated ethnic states.[2]

With CNN broadcasting an endless loop of scenes of death, destruction, and human suffering, the question of who fired the mortar quickly became a moot point. Predictably, Washington geared up to respond to the media hype with a commitment to protect Bosnia's Muslims. The Clinton administration set in motion a NATO ultimatum that gave Bosnian Serbs a 10-day deadline either to withdraw their heavy weapons 20 kilometers from the center of Sarajevo, to hand them over to U.N. control, or to face air strikes. The ultimatum was portrayed by the press as an effort to lift the so-called siege of Sarajevo. As the U.S. media focused exclusively on the plight of Bosnian Muslim civilians in Sarajevo, the NATO ultimatum against the Serbs appeared justified. The media ignored Serbian claims that Bosnian Muslim forces were a threat to Serbian security. Serbian civilians killed by Bosnian Muslim shelling and snipers in Sarajevo were never presented on television or the front pages of newspapers.

Few voices were heard in Washington opposing these media-generated views which appeared to be moving U.S. policy inexorably toward intervention in Bosnia. One dissenter, columnist Charles Krauthammer, criticized the Clinton administration's policies as being based largely on "TV pictures . . . of the massacre at the market." He warned that "foreign policy by CNN may be psychologically satisfying, but it is very dangerous" because it leads to the kind of U.S. support for one side in a civil war, resembling U.S. involvement in Vietnam.[3] *New York Times* columnist A. M. Rosenthal blamed the United States and the West for having encouraged conditions for war in Bosnia by prematurely recognizing new states, and he cautioned U.S. foreign policymakers that peace would be attained in Bosnia not through U.S. bombing but through U.S.-led negotiations to partition the country.[4] Such views, however, were a small minority among journalists and opinionmakers. Rosenthal aptly described the challenge of presenting an opposing view in Washington by saying: "On Bosnia I am a minority among more fearsome colleagues, and now their target, but here I stand."

The sober judgments of these individuals were mirrored by those of diplomats in Europe who opposed air strikes. EC mediator Lord Owen warned that NATO air strikes could divide the international community, with Russians coming in on the side of the Serbs. After British Prime Minister John Major met with Russian President Boris Yeltsin in Moscow, both leaders publicly criticized the Clinton administration's aggressive move toward military intervention in Bosnia. Michael Rose, British U.N. general and head of U.N. peacekeeping forces in Bosnia, agreed that air strikes would set a dangerous precedent that would make his large contingent of British U.N. soldiers vulnerable to Bosnian Serb reprisals. But the Clinton administration appeared to be set on bombing Bosnian Serbs in spite of criticism against such action by negotiators and U.N. personnel on the ground in Bosnia.

In an attempt to avoid a confrontation with the Serbs, U.N. General Rose initiated a number of meetings with Bosnian Serb political and military leaders and finally convinced them to follow through with requirements of the NATO ultimatum and avoid air strikes. The Bosnian Serbs agreed to withdraw heavy weapons from around Sarajevo, but only on the condition that the Bosnian army withdraw its infantry from front-line positions. Muslim leaders refused, knowing they had the United States behind them. Several days before the ultimatum was about to expire, the Russians came up with a compromise solution. They offered to send troops to areas from which the Bosnian Serbs were supposed to withdraw. The Serbs accepted Russia's offer and complied with NATO's ultimatum.

It appeared as if a small breathing space had been created in which Washington could reevaluate its policy and back what was now a largely British effort to push warring parties toward a diplomatic solution. Instead, Clinton administration officials argued for a greater U.S. role in Bosnia and rejected further diplomatic moves, in light of the opportunity created by the Markala market incident which now provided moral justification for attacking the Serbs. The incident that actually triggered the first military clash in NATO's 44-year history occurred on February 28, 1994, when American F-16 fighters shot down Serbian planes bombing a Bosnian

Muslim munitions plant. This NATO action demonstrated that Washington was willing to go beyond merely defending U.N. personnel and would defend Bosnian Muslim military targets as well. At the same time, NATO was unwilling to defend Bosnian Serb military targets from Muslim attacks. No NATO forces were called in at the end of March 1994, when Bosnian Muslim forces launched a massive attack on Bosnian Serbs in Maglaj killing 70 Serbian soldiers. The attack was not widely reported in the U.S. press. The *Washington Post* published only a small blurb from Associated Press wire services describing the incident.[5]

GORAZDE: PEACEKEEPING TURNS INTO MILITARY INTERVENTION

The Clinton administration had worked hard to get NATO involved in Bosnia and to move the international operation from a strictly neutral U.N. peacekeeping mission to one where force could be used against the Serbs to change the military balance of war in favor of the Muslims. In Gorazde, U.S. forces would be used in another incremental step toward getting involved in Bosnia's war. NATO air power would be deployed for the first time during battles between Muslim and Serb forces, in a mission that influenced the military balance on the ground. What really happened in Gorazde in March and April of 1994 would be revealed only after the United Nations was able to investigate the matter and with the publication of a May 4, 1994, congressional analysis by the House Republican Research Committee entitled "The Truth about Gorazde." The report, which detailed Muslim military activities and propaganda campaign designed to draw in U.S. military intervention in Gorazde, received surprisingly little attention in Washington. It also showed how the kind of scenario that lent popular support in Washington for NATO intervention was created, even though the crisis was initiated not by the Serbs but by Muslim military forces.

Throughout years of war, the U.S. media did little to put Gorazde into context. Although they frequently referred to Gorazde as a "Muslim enclave," they seldom mentioned how this situation was created. In the Fall of 1992, the town's Serb inhabitants increasingly fled the area after being regularly attacked by small highly trained groups of Islamic guerrillas—a combined force of Bosnian Muslim volunteers and fighters from Afghanistan. Without adequate Bosnian Serb forces to protect them, the Serbian population left Gorazde, while a primarily Muslim population remained. Muslim forces quickly consolidated their hold over the town and made it into a military stronghold. This situation remained throughout the war.

In March 1994, the Bosnian Muslim army reorganized its Gorazde forces in preparation for launching a Spring offensive against the Serbs.

At the time, there were over 12,000 armed Bosnian Muslim men in the area, comprised of a large number of *Mujaheddin* and Islamic commandos, 5,000 regular Bosnian Muslim troops, 5,000 militia and Interior Ministry troops, and armed volunteers. Neither the U.S. media nor the State Department emphasized the extent of Bosnian Muslim military power in Gorazde. The town was generally described as a beleaguered enclave and as a symbol of Serbian siege and aggression waged against Bosnia's Muslim population. Very few, if any, references were made to the fact that Gorazde's Muslim soldiers frequently shelled Serbian civilians in surrounding hillside villages.

Major U.S. media sources also failed to report that the newly reorganized Muslim army in Gorazde had violated a cease-fire and had launched a major attack on Bosnian Serb positions between Foca (Srbinje) and Cajnice on March 20, 1994. By the end of March, as the attacks grew into a major Muslim offensive, the Bosnian Muslim government anticipated a Serbian response. It was at that point that Muslim officials began a propaganda campaign accusing Serbian forces of attacking civilians in Gorazde—an accusation that drew international attention and ultimately, NATO intervention. On March 30, both Madeleine Albright and General Shalikashvili arrived for their first visit to Sarajevo in a show of unprecedented support for the Bosnian Muslim government. In press conferences and interviews, the Muslim leadership made emotional claims that civilians were being killed by Serbian shelling of a Gorazde hospital and that Serbian attacks were part of a policy of genocide against Muslims—a claim that the media appeared readily willing to accept. The press never mentioned the fact that the Serbs were responding to Bosnian Muslim forces, who were using Gorazde's hospital roof and other tall buildings as observation posts and command centers for directing attacks against Serbian positions. The Muslim army also positioned heavy machine guns in a five-story building occupied by UNPROFOR in Gorazde from which they fired at Serbian troops in the hillsides—a clever tactic, since a Serb response would elicit accusations that they were attacking the United Nations, and would potentially draw NATO reprisals.[6]

While the Muslim-led government in Sarajevo was adept at generating images of Gorazde surrounded and pummeled by Serbs, in the first week of April of 1994, the Muslim military launched a series of offensives in many directions to destabilize Serbian troops surrounding the town. One Muslim offensive took place northward toward Zepa, another westward toward Sarajevo, and still another attacked a Bosnian Serb convoy of 30 trucks advancing from Foca, as a detachment of Bosnian Muslim Special Forces, including Afghan *Mujaheddin*, participated in the fighting.[7] The Serbs responded by adding infantry reinforcements, many of whom were recruited from destroyed Serbian villages in the immediate area, which had been overrun by Muslim forces in 1992. These Serbian recruits, who typically harbored the strongest resentment against Muslim troops in Gorazde, were said by Bosnian Serb commanders to be the most difficult to restrain from violating cease-fires.

Following fierce infantry clashes, Serbian troops broke through Muslim defense lines and took over a strategic high ground above Gorazde by April 8, 1994. Again, Bosnian Muslim officials claimed that this act was an aggression and urged U.S. military intervention to help defend Muslim civilians in Gorazde. The United Nations deployed eight soldiers to the Gorazde battle zone, providing a legal pretext for NATO air strikes should Serbs "attack" U.N. personnel. The fact that UNPROFOR personnel sent to Gorazde were members of a special British unit equipped to direct air strikes was not a coincidence.[8] When U.S. aircraft under NATO command bombed Bosnian Serb positions around Gorazde on April 10–11, UNPROFOR's British units directed the attack.[9] Although NATO commanders claimed they were protecting U.N. personnel from a Serb tank fire into Gorazde, and additionally justified the action under U.N. Resolution 836 allowing U.N. troops to deter aggression against safe areas in Bosnia, NATO's intent was to help the Muslim side fight a war. The air strikes also appeared to have been conducted in close coordination with Bosnian Muslim forces, as the Serbs intercepted Muslim radio transmissions in Gorazde and Sarajevo communicating the details of NATO attacks several hours before they occurred.[10] Aware of what was about to happen, Muslim forces were deployed to front-line areas in Gorazde, in anticipation of a chance to launch attacks on Bosnian Serb forces reeling from NATO bombing raids. Muslim troops were clearly on the offensive, with close coordination with NATO. After UNPROFOR arranged a cease-fire between the two sides, Muslim troops launched several additional surprise attacks against Serbian positions.

A pattern that now emerged in Gorazde would later be seen elsewhere in Bosnia. First, Bosnian Serbs would agree to a U.N.-mediated cease-fire, then Muslims forces would provoke the Serbs, Serbian forces would respond, Bosnian Muslim leadership would feed international media with reports that Serbs were shelling civilians, and this would prompt U.S. and NATO military actions against the Serbs. The goal of this tactic was clear even to U.N. General Rose who, in an interview for French television, said that Muslim forces would "shoot on the Serbs to step up the pressure and to obtain a fresh intervention from NATO."[11] Predictably, in mid-April 1994, when the Bosnian Muslim government intensified their allegations that hundreds of civilians were being killed by Serbian shelling on Gorazde, NATO presented the Serbs with an ultimatum to withdraw to 3 kilometers from center of town, pull their heavy weapons back 20 kilometers, and allow U.N. and other humanitarian convoys to travel into Gorazde, notably, without inspection.[12]

Having advanced to almost the center of town, the Bosnian Serb leadership now surprisingly bowed to NATO demands. The Serbs were unable to take hold of a vital Muslim stronghold, even with a superiority of weapons on their side. The reality of what happened in Gorazde was obscured by the refusal of Clinton administration officials to openly acknowledge Muslim military aims in Bosnia and by the media's failure to be forthcoming on the facts. As a result, the war of words by the Bosnian Muslims, combined with Muslim attacks and NATO air power, convinced the Serb army to withdraw from Gorazde. It succeeded in bringing U.S., U.N., and NATO military intervention on behalf of the Bosnian Muslims and pointed the way to victory.

The truth about Gorazde was not evident until the end of April 1994, when UNPROFOR personnel were deployed on the dividing line between Serbian and Muslim forces in the area. After inspecting the town, they immediately saw that casualty and damage levels were far lower than those reported by the Muslim leadership. Initial UNHCR reports, based primarily on Bosnian Muslim government sources, claimed that 715 people were killed and up to 2,000 wounded in Gorazde. At the time, UNHCR stressed that most casualties in Gorazde were civilian. The United Nations later found, however, that there were only 200 fatalities and 200 seriously wounded, of which 80 percent were Muslim soldiers—not women and children as was previously reported.[13] Damage to Gorazde's hospital and other buildings was also far less than what the United Nations was led to believe based on Muslim radio reports. Contrary to Muslim claims that the Gorazde hospital was almost entirely destroyed, one U.N. officer said that the hospital was still functioning and "what was basically needed was a broom to clear up the rubbish."[14]

After going on an inspection tour of Gorazde, U.N. General Rose criticized the Bosnian Muslim government for exaggerating the situation to induce NATO military intervention. Rose was surprised to find that Bosnian Muslims who were airlifted by U.N. helicopters from Gorazde in allegedly critical condition included "young men who hopped off the stretchers and went into town."[15] Another senior U.N. officer who visited Gorazde, General Bertrand de Lapresle of France, said that "a false impression was given to the international community to help stir the vision of the Bosnian Serbs as the enemy, and unfortunately, all this very nearly went out of control." He went on to say that "The problem is that the Muslims believe they can bring the Americans into the war. A dangerous overreaction was stirred up in international capitals. The talks of wider use of NATO airpower [against Bosnian Serbs], hitting ammunition dumps and infrastructure went well across the line that would have turned the U.N. forces here into combatants."[16] Both U.N. generals blamed Washington for the continuation of war in Bosnia by encouraging the belief that U.S. military support would be given to the Bosnian Muslims.

In normal circumstances, criticisms by U.N. generals against the Clinton administration's heavy-handed approach in Gorazde should have caused Washington to reexamine its views on Bosnia. In this case, however, Ambassador Albright filed a formal complaint to the U.N. secretary general "in the strongest possible terms" against the criticism and reprimanded U.N. officials for failing to support aggressive actions against Bosnian Serbs.[17] Albright and other Bosnian Muslim government supporters within the Clinton administration actively targeted anyone opposing their views. After U.N. Special Representative Yasushi Akashi described the Bosnian Serb president, Radovan Karadzic, as "a man of peace," Clinton administration officials accused Akashi of having a personal friendship with Karadzic and being too conciliatory to the Serbs.[18] The administration threatened to press for the removal of Akashi and French and British U.N. military commanders who criticized U.S. policy. U.N. Secretary General Boutros Boutros-Ghali made immediate promises to Ambassador Albright to have Akashi conduct a full inquiry to ensure that criticisms against the United States would not be voiced again.[19]

Relations between the United Nations and Washington were now more strained than ever before. Neither U.N. generals nor U.N. officials could alter the fact that Gorazde had changed the United Nations's role from peacekeeper in Bosnia to combatant due to Washington's drive toward military intervention in the region. This new U.N. role in Bosnia would become a significant factor in helping what would become increasing Muslim offensives against Serbs in the coming year.

THE RESULTS OF "LEVELING THE BATTLEFIELD"

Between the Spring of 1993, when the Clinton administration decided to stand behind the Bosnian Muslim cause, and the Spring of 1994, the front lines between the warring parties remained basically unchanged. Throughout that time, Bosnian Muslim officials visiting Washington repeatedly told U.S. policymakers and lawmakers: "We don't need American soldiers to fight our war, we have plenty of our own soldiers, we just need weapons." Washington was generally sympathetic to this view and frequently reiterated the need to "level the battlefield" so that the Bosnian Muslims could "defend" themselves. After a full year of covert weapons smuggling to Muslim forces, by the Spring of 1994, the Muslim army was ready to go on the offensive against the Serbs on multiple fronts. The effort began in Gorazde, where U.S.-led NATO attacks on Serbs demonstrated how bombings, combined with offensives by Muslim forces on the ground, could be an effective method in gaining a military advantage over the Serbs. In the next year, Muslim forces would launch a number of intensified offensives against Bosnian Serb forces, with Washington giving full support. The so-called leveling the battlefield resulted in an intensified war in Bosnia as Muslim forces launched an unprecedented number of attacks on Serbian positions and as the Muslim leadership made greater demands for more territory during negotiations. Although still willing to negotiate, the Bosnian Serb leadership was unwilling to accept peace proposals in the face of Muslim attacks.

In April of 1994, Bosnian Muslim military commanders prepared for an all-out offensive on areas of the Serb-held town of Brcko—a vulnerable, thin corridor of land that linked the western and eastern half of Serbian territory.[20] In an effort to help the Muslim offensive, Clinton administration officials began to plan for how a Bosnian Serb military response could be thwarted. With the Gorazde safe haven scenario viewed as a successful method of fighting the Serbs, Secretary of State Warren Christopher and other U.S. officials contemplated declaring Muslim-held areas surrounding Brcko as a safe haven, hence providing a pretext for NATO attacks on Serbs. The safe haven scenario became unnecessary when U.N. troops were stationed in Muslim-held areas around Brcko. As in Gorazde, the United Nations's position on the front lines adjacent to Muslim troops provided justification for U.N. retaliation against any Serb military action.

On April 29, 1994, when Muslim forces from nearby Tuzla shelled Serbs in Brcko, U.N. observers did nothing but watch the attack from the Muslim side. With U.N.–U.S. relations at a low point as a result of Gorazde and U.N. generals' criticism of Clinton administration policies, the U.N. command would become more cooperative with Washington's views and would not impede attempts by Muslim forces to take over a key strategic position. When Serbian forces returned fire on Muslim positions in Tuzla, U.N. peacekeepers turned into combatants and began shelling the Serbs. That day, Brcko experienced the strongest clashes between U.N. and Bosnian Serb forces since the war had begun. U.N. peacekeeping forces fired 72 shells at Bosnian Serb positions, killing nine soldiers and wounding four. Although U.N. commanders in Tuzla claimed that they returned fire after being fired on by Bosnian Serbs, the Serbian attacks were clearly directed not at the United Nations but at Muslim forces. As Muslim forces continued to launch a series of offensives against Serb positions in Brcko throughout May 1994, and NATO was not called in to stop the fighting, a sharp diplomatic dispute flared up between Moscow and Washington, as Russia accused the United States and NATO of pursuing a double standard.

At the end of June 1994, Muslim forces launched another attack by breaking a cease-fire and shelling the Serbian town of Doboj. The expulsion of 4,000 Serbian villagers due to the 10-day Muslim offensive was hardly mentioned in the U.S. press. Far from sympathizing with Serbian civilians, the *Washington Post* called the Muslim offensive at Doboj "the most ambitious attack ever on Bosnian Serb forces."[21] No NATO threats against the Muslims ensued at Doboj. Nor was there a NATO response to another Muslim offensive during this time directed against Serbian positions in the Ozren region in an attempt to link Muslim-held Tuzla and Zenica. In the Ozren attack, no Serbian civilians were expelled, thanks not to U.N. protection, but to the ability of Serbian forces to repulse the Muslim advance.

It was becoming increasingly evident that the results of leveling the battlefield were to encourage more Muslim offensives and to harden the Muslim leadership's negotiating position by insisting on more territory. In view of increasingly bolder Muslim military actions against Serbs, a new partition plan was presented to warring parties in Geneva in July 1994 that accommodated Muslim demands for more territory. The so-called Contact Group plan offered the Muslim-Croat alliance control over 51 percent of territory and 49 percent to Bosnian Serbs. The plan also required the Serbs to cede a land route connecting the Muslim enclaves of Gorazde, Zepa, and Srebrenica (see Appendix 2, map 11). Pleased with the plan's territorial distributions, on July 18, 1994, the Bosnian Muslim parliament voted overwhelmingly to approve it, while the Bosnian Serb parliament rejected the proposal. The Serbs argued that the plan would have pushed them back to 49 percent of mostly rural, undeveloped land with few industrial areas or natural resources and would have allotted areas to the Muslim-Croat alliance, which included larger, wealthier cities. Serbia's president, Slobodan Milosevic, failing to convince the Bosnian Serb leadership to accept the plan and bring about the removal of international sanctions against Yugoslavia, announced on May 6, 1993, that Serbia was cutting off all political and economic ties and closing its border with Republika Srpska. The split was serious. Without support from Serbia, Bosnian Serbs were now more isolated than ever.

Sensing the Bosnian Serbs were weak, Muslim forces continued their offensives against Serbian positions, this time in areas southeast of Sarajevo. The Serbian military response aroused predictable reactions in Washington. In what was now a familiar pattern of war, NATO struck back with an air attack that destroyed a Bosnian Serb anti-tank vehicle in Sarajevo. In effect, NATO forces were increasingly taking on the role of an air force for the Muslim-led government. An August 8, 1994, *Washington Post* headline correctly summed up the cycle of events in Bosnia: "Bosnian Drive Riled Serbs, Who Then Provoked NATO." In the coming months, intensified Bosnian Muslim attacks on Serbian positions were quietly encouraged by their Washington supporters, while NATO reprisals were demanded against Serb military activities. The media trivialized, or did not even report, attacks launched by Bosnian Muslims, while a Serbian response was invariably presented as an assault against Bosnian Muslim civilians.

Washington's policymakers and the media showed a complete lack of concern that increasingly stronger Muslim forces resulted not in greater peace in Bosnia but in more instances of expulsion of Bosnian Serb civilians and an increasing number of human rights violations against the Serbs. One example of this disregard for human rights violations against

Serbs was the media coverage of an October 6, 1994, attack by Muslim forces which killed 16 Serbian soldiers and 4 nurses, whose mutilated bodies were found in the outskirts of Sarajevo. The *Washington Post*, discreetly reported the incident in the bottom corner of page 28.[22] U.N. personnel who discovered the bodies found that the victims' throats were slit and that some of the bodies were burned. Muslim offensives and accompanying war crimes were not vocally reprimanded by Clinton administration officials, nor were they followed by NATO reprisals or threats of war crimes prosecutions. A week after the incident, Muslim troops launched two commando attacks from Mount Bjelasnica and Mount Igman in the vicinity of Sarajevo—which were supposed to be U.N. demilitarized zones.[23] Again, there was no response from Washington. Instead, Clinton administration officials appeared more pleased with Muslim military advances than distressed with intensified hostilities.

Washington continued to be an avid supporter when Muslim forces launched a two-day offensive on October 27, 1994, that swept through surrounding Bosnian Serb lines in the Bihac pocket of northwestern Bosnia, sending 10,000 Bosnian Serb civilians into flight.[24] The *Washington Post* described the situation as the Muslim government's "biggest victory against Serbs" and stated that large numbers of Serbian civilians had been forced to flee by the "successful Bosnian offensive."[25] Although Washington waited with anticipation to see how well ongoing Muslim offensives would do against the Serbs, U.N. peacekeepers stationed in Sarajevo were becoming increasingly fearful that the war was about to spiral out of control. With Muslim offensives intensifying, the United Nations again tried to take on a more neutral role and put the brakes on the conflict. U.N. officials began publicizing breaches of the peace by Muslim forces. On October 29, 1994, the United Nations said that Muslim forces "deliberately directed artillery and mortar fire . . . onto the U.N. observation post," in a demilitarized zone near Sarajevo, using the area to launch an attack on Serbian positions.[26]

The Muslim forces' direct attack on the United Nations resulted in the first threat from the U.N. command of a NATO air strike against the Bosnian Muslim army, yet no NATO air strike came. On the contrary, Muslim forces continued their unfettered attacks on Serbs, launching several offensives on Serbs in central Bosnia, capturing 35 square miles of territory, and causing the flight of several thousand more Serbian refugees. The incident was only briefly mentioned well after the fact in a *New York Times* article.[27] Similarly, in early 1995, when a Croatian offensive in the Medak pocket resulted in the execution of at least 50 Serbian civilians, the fact was not reported until months later and was inconspicuously mentioned in the last paragraph of an unrelated *New York Times* article.[28] The media continued to write predominantly stories that presented the Serbs in a negative light and few or no stories that depicted Bosnia's Muslims as anything other than victims.

In February 1995, important evidence of U.S. military involvement was revealed, when U.N. personnel in the Muslim-held town of Tuzla discovered that the United States was backing a secret operation delivering high-tech weapons to Bosnian Muslim forces in violation of the U.N. arms embargo. The United Nations identified two transport planes whose nightly visits to the Tuzla airport occurred on at least four occasions during the month. The planes parachuted bundles of weapons onto a runway, and Bosnian Muslim troops rushed the weapons into bunkers in the forest north of the airport. When attempting to investigate the situation, the United Nations was denied access to the runway by Muslim forces. Although the entire story was explored in great detail in a March 1, 1995, British Independent Television News (ITN) report, CNN and other major U.S. networks were surprisingly uninterested in the story, and major newspapers buried the story in their back pages. Almost no public attention was given to the matter in the United States, but the allegations caused a major uproar at NATO headquarters in Brussels. NATO officials denied any knowledge of weapons deliveries, but U.N. personnel said there was no doubt that the operation was induced and coordinated by the United States. When U.N. General de Lapresle reported that the clandestine deliveries contained high-technology weapons, modern anti-tank guidance missiles, and surface-to-air missiles, NATO officers demanded that the United Nations withdraw its reports.[29] There was no call to investigate the veracity of the reports or to punish the arms embargo violator.

It was now abundantly clear that the policy of the U.S.-led NATO command was diverging from that of the United Nations. NATO was actively involved in helping one side in a civil war, while the United Nations was still trying to maintain some semblance of neutrality. As Washington talked of leveling the battlefield as a pretext for helping defend Bosnia's victims, the battlefield was already level—with a larger number of weapons already in Muslim hands, combined with greater numbers of Muslim troops. In reality, Clinton administration officials wanted to help Bosnian Muslims not just to "defend themselves," but to become a formidable military force. It was not a coincidence that soon after the Tuzla weapons deliveries in February, in early April 1995, Muslim forces launched another attack from Tuzla and Bihac on Serb positions. This tied down much of Bosnian Serb forces who were unable to help neighboring Krajina Serbs in what was about to become the largest Croat offensive and the beginning of the endgame in Bosnia.

CROAT WAR CRIMES IN WESTERN SLAVONIA

During this heightened period of force used against Serbs by increasingly well-armed Muslim forces, Croatia had similarly strengthened its military forces and was prepared to begin a series of attacks on Krajina Serbs. As in the case of Muslim attacks, the oncoming Croat operation on western Krajina would demonstrate the same double standards by Washington's policymakers and the media's low level of attention to Croat transgressions.

On May 2, 1995, in violation of a regionwide cease-fire, Croatian forces broke through the U.N. buffer zone to launch an all-out assault against Krajina Serb positions. During the attack, Croat gunners seriously wounded three U.N. peacekeepers, but no NATO airplanes were called in to protect U.N. personnel. The only action taken was 2,000 U.N. soldiers fleeing to their barracks as the Croat offensive continued.[30] On the morning of May 4, 1995, on CNN's *Morning News*, a guest described the situation as a "case of Serbian aggression." Attempting to put the situation into context, I explained that Krajina Serbs "could not accept living under a Croatian government where Serbs cannot hold jobs, where one cannot say that one is a Serb, where Serbian homes are confiscated and where civilians are killed." When the CNN host asked me, "But hasn't the Croatian government offered the Serb minority population guarantees?" I replied, "That guarantee is only on paper. If you look at what Croat troops are doing to Serbs right now as 5,000 refugees are fleeing Croat troop attacks, as they have gunned down 200 women and children, it does not seem to me that minority rights of Serbs are being upheld in any way." To this, the Croatian guest responded, "It is absolutely untrue . . . the U.N. has just verified this morning that there are absolutely no atrocities committed against the Serbian population in the fighting in western Slavonia."

Several days later, however, a U.N. report was released detailing Croatian war crimes against Serbs. While parts of the U.N. report were revealed in a May 8, 1995, *Washington Post* article, it was not until May 25 that a more complete report on U.N. findings was printed in the *New York Times*. A few weeks later, on July 10, the *New York Times* printed another article on the U.N. findings, reporting that U.N. soldiers saw bodies of Serbian civilians scattered along the routes of the Serbs' retreat from western Slavonia. In three days following the Croat offensive, the Croat forces were said to have blown up more than 100 Serbian homes. In order to cover up the extent of Serbian civilian casualties, Croatian authorities had the bodies removed in refrigerator trucks, which witnesses saw leaving western Slavonia on May 3, 1995.[31] U.N. officers also received reports of looting, physical abuse, intimidation of Serbs by Croatian soldiers, and beatings of Serbian men between the ages of 16 and 65 who were rounded up and taken into custody by Croat forces.[32] In a tiny article on the bottom of the page, the *New York Times* reported two mass graves of Serbs killed in the towns of Okucani and Pakrac, after Croatian troops attacked western Slavonia.[33]

At the time of the Croatian coverup, the Tudjman government barred foreign journalists from entering the region. By the time a CBS News team entered the scene of the massacre of Serb civilians, all they found were Croatian authorities covering up much of the forensic evidence, spraying chlorine on streets from where the bodies had been removed.[34] While Western reporters demonstrated themselves to be increasingly adept at gaining access to Serb-held areas of Bosnia and reporting on alleged war crimes against Muslims, they were surprisingly unmotivated to go beyond Croat restrictions and reveal what happened to Serbs in western Slavonia. At the time, the *Washington Post* and *New York Times* printed photos of civilians wounded in Zagreb as a result of the Krajina Serb military response to Croatian attacks and photos of weeping mothers of dead Croatian soldiers. There were no photographs of the vastly larger number of Serbian soldiers who died defending Krajina and several hundred massacred women and children. The media's apathetic coverage of the incident was mirrored by the initial State Department conclusion that the overall record of Croatian troops during the attack "was good"—a claim that was never retracted or revised following U.N. discoveries of war crimes against Serbs in Krajina.[35] Far from being appalled at Croat actions, Washington was willing to continue committing NATO forces to help Muslim and Croat offensives.

SREBRENICA: SERBS RESPOND TO YEAR-LONG MUSLIM OFFENSIVE

Having failed to report on a number of offensives against the Serbs throughout a year-long period between the Spring of 1994 and the Spring of 1995, the media's sudden focus on events in the Muslim enclave of Srebrenica in the Summer of 1995 did not put the issue into the context of what was happening militarily on the ground in Bosnia at this time and in previous years.

Before the war started in Bosnia, Srebrenica had a population of 36,292, of which about 25 percent were Serbs.[36] Serbs living in the villages surrounding Srebrenica made up a majority of the population in the countryside. In the early months of the war, in March and April of 1992, the Bosnian Muslim paramilitary force began to grow in Srebrenica, and as greater hostility toward Serbs was felt, they began to leave. With the outbreak of fighting between Muslims and Serbs, an even greater number of Serbs left Srebrenica and fled to surrounding villages where they felt safer. As a large number of Serbs fled the area, Muslim soldiers and refugees from other parts of Bosnia-Hercegovina poured into Srebrenica. By 1995, the Muslim population in Srebrenica nearly doubled to approximately 42,000.

A visit to the town of Bratunac, on the outskirts of Srebrenica, in May of 1995 showed me how little the media covered the war outside the limited perspective of Sarajevo. In Bratunac, I met people who were overflowing with heart-wrenching stories of what happened to Serbs in Srebrenica and the surrounding areas during Muslim offensives between the Spring and Fall of 1992. During this time, as many as 26 mostly Serb-populated villages in the Srebrenica area were attacked, damaged, or destroyed by advancing Bosnian Muslim forces. These attacks resulted in the forced expulsion, or "ethnic cleansing," of up to 5,500 Serbs. Out of the total number of 9,390 Serbs who lived in the Srebrenica proper, less than 10 percent remained. The residents of Bratunac estimated that over 1,200 Serbian villagers were killed during attacks by Muslim forces in 1992. Dozens were executed or burned alive in their homes, many were tortured to death, a number of women were raped, and most homes looted and burned.

One Serbian village I drove through showed scenes of almost complete destruction. Kravice, in the vicinity of Srebrenica, once a pleasant village surrounded by picturesque hills, was now a scene of empty houses—many completely leveled, others charred—and abandoned fields. There was not a single person in sight. In Bratunac, whom I met two young Bosnian Serb volunteers from Kravice, brothers, whose entire family had been killed by Muslim forces, and who vowed to avenge their parents' deaths. Some residents of Bratunac whom I met knew exactly which Muslim soldiers in Srebrenica were responsible for the carnage against the Serbs in 1992. Bosnian Serb leader, Radovan Karadzic, would later say, "It was these elements of the Bosnian Serb forces, in the Srebrenica area that were most difficult to control. They really wanted to get at the Muslim soldiers sitting in Srebrenica who had committed these crimes." The U.S. media never explained this aspect of Srebrenica's significance to the Serbs, and they also obscured a number of important events that occurred just prior to the Srebrenica battle.

By May 1995, Bosnian Muslim forces were continuing their multifrontal attacks on Bosnian Serb lines. As part of this ongoing offensive, Muslim troops launched a barrage of mortars at Serb-held areas of Sarajevo, timed to take advantage of the Croat assault on Serbs in western Slavonia.[37] When Bosnian Serb forces responded by shelling Sarajevo, it gave a pretext for another NATO bombing raid against the Serbs, this time at their main headquarters in the small mountain town of Pale, just outside Sarajevo. To the latest NATO attack, the Serbs resorted to desperate measures. They detained about 100 U.N. peacekeepers and even provided video footage of one U.N. peacekeeper handcuffed to a post at a location near their headquarters in Pale. Bosnian Serbs wanted to bring home the message that NATO could not act as an air force on behalf of the Muslims and expect U.N. peacekeepers to be viewed as neutral. Although U.N. peacekeepers were not mistreated during their short detention by the Bosnian Serb command, the resulting image of a handcuffed U.N. soldier backfired on the Serbs. It was an unsophisticated, impulsive response against overwhelming Western force. The hostage-taking incident proved a field day for the media and was interpreted by Washington's interventionists as a direct Serbian challenge to NATO.

Bosnian Serbs detained the United Nations for strategic reasons: to discourage NATO attacks on their territories. In the coming weeks, Bosnian Muslims pursued similar actions, yet without arousing the same degree of concern. When the United Nations attempted to withdraw its personnel from Muslim enclaves at the end of May 1995, Bosnian Muslim forces detained 76 Ukrainian U.N. peacekeepers in Gorazde. The incident was downplayed in the *New York Times* in the last of several articles on Bosnia that day—in the last paragraph, at the very bottom of the page.[38] Another important issue received little attention by the U.S. press. An August 1, 1995, *New York Times* article reported U.N. discoveries that Muslim snipers were not only targeting their own people in Sarajevo but were shooting at U.N. vehicles in the city as well.[39] U.N. findings supported claims made by Bosnian Serbs for years that Muslim forces were firing on their own civilians in order to arouse international intervention on their behalf. Apart from the *New York Times* article, in Washington hardly anyone was aware of the United Nations's findings. The United Nations was said to have been reluctant to publicize the information, which they described as too "politically sensitive."

Continuing the pattern of downplaying or ignoring ongoing attacks on Serbian positions, the U.S. media and Clinton administration officials made no public mention of a violation of Srebrenica's safe haven status when Muslim forces launched an attack against several surrounding Serb-populated villages. In the village of Visnjice, Muslim forces murdered dozens of mostly elderly Serbs, and hundreds of civilians fled. U.N. personnel stationed in Srebrenica were either not monitoring Muslim troop movements adequately or were willing to step aside and ignore Muslim attacks on Serbs. When Serbian forces responded, Muslim troops fell back to their positions in Srebrenica. To the latest Muslim assault in Srebrenica, the Serbs responded with overwhelming firepower.

Only when Serb forces attacked Srebrenica was media attention aroused. The *Washington Post* immediately publicized what it called the "Serbian assault on Srebrenica."[40] With U.N. troops stationed right next to Muslim forces in Srebrenica, the Serbs were accused of attacking "United Nations peacekeepers and civilians in Srebrenica."[41] No major U.S. newspaper mentioned the initial Muslim attacks on Serbian villages. Nor did any comment that the so-called safe haven of Srebrenica was not solely a refuge for Muslim civilians, but a strategic stronghold for Muslim government troops.

The media continued to provide a cover for what was happening in Srebrenica. When on July 9, 1995, Bosnian Muslim forces killed a Dutch U.N. peacekeeper during an exchange of fire with Serbian forces, the headline of a *New York Times* article at the time read "Dutch Peacekee-per Killed in Serb Assault," while the article benignly mentioned that "the soldier was hit by fire from Government forces."[42] NATO did not react to protect U.N. peacekeepers in Srebrenica, to what they must have con-sidered a "friendly-fire" incident. Only when Bosnian Serb troops ad-vanced toward the edge of Srebrenica did NATO authorize air strikes if Serbs were to attack U.N. positions in the town. Clearly, NATO was more concerned with possible Serbian military gains than with protecting U.N. personnel. As Bosnian Serbs troops took over parts of Srebrenica's sub-urbs, they detained 30 U.N. peacekeepers—partly to prevent a replay of the Gorazde scenario when U.N. personnel directed NATO air strikes against the Serbs and partly to get the U.N. troops out of the way so that their possible injury would not be used to justify air strikes. However, another 60 Dutch U.N. troops moved into positions at the only entrance to the town, in an effort to stop the Serbian advance against Muslim forces. On July 11, 1995, Bosnian Serb forces continued into Srebrenica past U.N. peacekeepers, and NATO warplanes attacked and hit two Serbian tanks but failed to stop their advance.

In mid-July 1995, after Bosnian Serb forces took over Srebrenica, it was the start of a media flurry of accusations of war crimes allegedly committed by Serbian forces against Muslim men and civilians in Srebrenica. Re-ported numbers of men missing and presumed to have been executed varied significantly—from several thousand to six thousand and higher. When Bosnian Serb forces moved into Srebrenica, as many as 30,000 Mus-lim civilians who gathered in the nearby suburb of Poticari were told by Bosnian Serb General Ratko Mladic that if they wanted to leave, they could do so by trucks and buses provided by the Bosnian Serb military. The exodus of Muslims from Srebrenica, over half of whom were refugees from other areas of Bosnia, was described by the UNHCR spokeswoman in Zagreb, Ilemka Lisinska, as "a forced movement and [we] condemn it strongly."[43] Yet the same *Washington Post* article that quoted the UNHCR spokeswoman also printed photographs of U.N. personnel calmly drinking with Bosnian Serb General Ratko Mladic, while other pictures showed U.N. officers helping Muslim refugees waiting for a Serbian truck convoy. While many of the Muslim refugees who chose to leave Srebrenica were likely to have done so in fear of Bosnian Serbs, U.N. assistance in the process implies that they were not forcefully "expelled." Instead, it was the same unfortunate and tragic process of war that was taking place on all sides as ethnic groups sought safety among their own people.

The fate of Muslim men detained by the Bosnian Serb military com-mand in Srebrenica was a different matter. Muslim soldiers and men of fighting-age were separated from the women, children, and elderly. A number of Muslim men were likely mistreated, and others were probably killed in the days following the battle over Srebrenica. To what extent these acts were committed by Bosnian Serb volunteers from Srebrenica's surrounding villages seeking revenge or by regular Serb soldiers may never be determined. The media reports were overflowing with accusations that thousands of Muslim men were executed and buried in mass graves, which became the subject of intense scrutiny. Bosnian Serbs explained that these graves contained between 1,000 and 1,500 Muslim fighters who died in the takeover of Srebrenica and had to be buried. The media and the U.S. government rejected this claim out of hand, without conducting an investigation.

The discovery of the mass graves was the career-making story for *Christian Science Monitor* reporter David Rohde. It was the subject of a front-page story accusing Serbs of mass extermination of Muslim men in Srebrenica and later for Rohde's book *Endgame: The Betrayal and Fall of Srebrenica, Europe's Worst Massacre Since World War II*. Shortly before Rohde was to print his story on mass graves, he called from Zagreb and asked me for more information on Srebrenica. I faxed him descriptions of what happened to Serbian villages in the Srebrenica municipality at the start of the war. To my dismay, none of the articles Rohde was to publish on Srebrenica made any attempt to put Srebrenica into context by mentioning the massacres of Serbs in 1992 or any other important information he received from me. Instead, Rohde's articles, like those of other correspondents on Bosnia, placed unwavering blame on Serbs as the sole "aggressors" and ignored Serbian victims. This impression would prove to be particularly crucial during this time, since the demonization of Serbs following the Srebrenica takeover would eliminate any sympathy in Washington for the victims of what was to be the largest "ethnic cleansing" in the entire Yugoslav conflict: the Croatian assault against Krajina Serbs.

SECOND CROAT OFFENSIVE TURNS WINDS OF WAR AGAINST SERBS

From July to October 1995, the largest and most overwhelming offensives against Serbs in Krajina and Bosnia were launched by Croat and Muslim forces that ultimately changed the course of the Yugoslav war. The first of these offensives began on July 28, 1995, when the Croatian army crossed the border into Bosnia-Hercegovina and struck the town of Grahovo, which was 90 percent Serbian prior to the war. The Croatian strategy was to encircle Krajina Serbs by going around them through Bosnia and attack the main Serbian headquarters in Knin. Washington gave tentative approval of the operation, through Ambassador Galbraith who told Croatia's president Tudjman that the Croatian takeover of Krajina would be tolerated if the battle was "short and clean."[44] In the first week of August 1995, Croatian forces put "Operation Storm" into action and shelled numerous Serbian towns in Krajina. Although the Clinton administration halfheartedly urged Croatia to stop its offensive, top U.S. officials were clearly in favor of the action.

Washington not only condoned the Croatian offensive, but even helped in its execution. Retired U.S. military officers trained the Croatian forces in planning the operation, and on August 4, 1995, as Croatian forces shelled Serbian civilian and military targets in Knin, NATO warplanes bombarded Serbian communications systems.[45] Almost two years would pass before the editors of the *New York Times* would acknowledge that "Mr. Tudjman and his party own much to the West, which built up Croatia's military to fight the Serbs," with the help of "retired American soldiers [that] trained Croatia's army."[46] Washington expressed no concern about what the Croatian offensive would do to Krajina Serb civilians, but only about the possibility that the Yugoslav army might come to the Serbs' rescue. "The abandonment of the Croatian Serbs by Milosevic," Richard Holbrooke later wrote, "eliminated one of our greatest fears—that Belgrade would re-enter the war."[47]

Overall, the Croatian offensive resulted in the exodus of over 300,000 Serbs from Krajina. It was the largest single forced movement of civilians in Europe since World War II. CNN showed footage of long columns of Serbian refugees streaming out of Croatia, many wounded by Croatian shelling as they fled. After two days of merciless Croat attacks on the Serbian city of Knin, U.N. officials found what they described as "quite significant number of bodies in the streets," many of them women and children.[48] In the months to come, Croatian forces began a campaign of burning and looting Serbian homes, and out of a total of 600,000 Serbs who lived in Krajina before the war, only 120,000 would remain. Elderly Serbs who stayed behind were tortured and murdered. A U.N. report at the time said that one elderly lady was tied by fish net, and a tire was put around her neck before she was set on fire and her husband's burned body was found a few yards from hers.[49] Other Serbs fleeing from Croatia toward the Bosnian Serb town of Banja Luka were killed after being attacked by Muslim soldiers. Soon after Croatia's assault on the Serbs, the Croatian parliament passed a housing law permitting Croats from outside Croatia to take over properties of Serbs who had fled the region.[50] Through a combination of intimidation, violence, and government policy, it was clear that the Tudjman regime did not want Krajina Serbs to return. Carl Bildt, the European Union's mediator on the Yugoslav conflict, said that the killing of Serbian civilians and the Croat shelling of the Serbian city of Knin would cast "a dark shadow over Croatia for a long time to come." Nonetheless, no action was ever taken to punish Croatia.[51]

NATO issued a warning that attacks would be imminent if Croat forces harmed U.N. peacekeepers, but even when Croats killed a Danish peacekeeper and wounded two others, no U.S. calls for NATO reprisals followed. On the contrary, in the months and years to come, Croatia's actions were met with Washington's approval. Holbrooke praised the Croatian offensive as a "complete success"—a term that would never have been applied, for example, to Bosnian Serb takeovers of Srebrenica and other strategically important towns.[52] Columnist Charles Krauthammer disapprovingly explained U.S. policy as "simple realpolitik" where the Croatian atrocity was conveniently fixing the map—"It solves Croatia's Serb problem, neatly cleanses the Croatian state, removes an ethnic pocket . . . [that] might make a Balkan settlement more possible."[53]

What the United Nations was calling the largest instance of ethnic cleansing in the Yugoslav conflict was glossed over by the U.S. State Department and the media.[54] Washington's pundits and moralists fell unusually silent. Krauthammer rightly asked, "Where were the moralists who for years have been so loudly decrying the ethnic cleansing of Bosnia's Muslims? Where were the cries for blood, the demand for arms, the call to action on behalf of today's pitiful victims? Where were the columnists, the senators, the other posturers who excoriate the West for standing by when Bosnian Muslims are victimized and are silent when the victim of the day is Serb?"[55] Clinton administration officials, who for two and a half years talked of America's moral imperative to protect Bosnian Muslims, were now unmoved by the Croat offensive on Krajina Serbs. U.S. Ambassador Madeleine Albright was quick to deny that ethnic cleansing was taking place against Serbs in Croatia.[56]

The media's double standards were also coming to the surface. The largest ethnic cleansing of the Balkans war and war crimes against Krajina Serbs by Croatian forces was accompanied by a remarkably quiet week of news, devoid of debates on the matter. Having been a frequent guest on dozens of CNN programs during the flurry of media interest when Bosnian Muslims were being attacked, I noted an appalling lack of interest in covering Croatian attacks on Krajina Serbs. A *Washington Post* news analysis on the day Croatian forces launched their attack on Krajina Serbs said the operation "may have done what four years of diplomacy failed to do: laid the foundations for resolution of the Balkans crisis."[57] If the Serbs had launched a massive attack on Sarajevo and had expelled hundreds of thousands of Muslims in an effort to end the war, Washington's pundits would hardly have touted the act as one that "laid the foundations for resolution of the Balkans crisis." Demonstrating an incredible lack of sensitivity and gross historic revisionism, *Washington Post* correspondent John Pomfret described the expulsion of the last generation of Krajina Serbs, whose ancestors made up the core of Krajina history and culture for centuries, as an end to "more than 500 years of Serb *occupation* of the Krajina region."[58] By using the word "occupation," Pomfret seemed to be implying that the Serbs had no business being in Krajina in the first place. *Washington Post* editors, though acknowledging that Croatia was practicing "its own ethnic cleansing" against Krajina Serbs, did not call for immediate use of force as they did in the case of Srebrenica and numerous other battles. Instead, in response to massive attacks against Krajina Serbs, the editors urged Washington to get Croats and Serbs immediately "to the bargaining table, at once."[59] In contrast, Serb attacks on Muslim areas were never followed by urgent calls to get Muslims "to the bargaining table." As Washington maintained a low-key response to the ethnic cleansing of Serbs in Krajina, a single explosion in Bosnia was about to reenergize Washington's pundits against the Serbs.

TWO WEEKS OF BOMBINGS HELP CROAT-MUSLIM OFFENSIVE

On August 27, 1995, CNN's *Morning News* was again overflowing with coverage of a mortar shell that fell into a Sarajevo marketplace and killed 37 people. The incident was almost a mirror image of the shell that fell on the Sarajevo marketplace in February 1994. As in the previous incident, the Bosnian Serb leadership accused the Muslims of launching the mortar against their own people in order to draw in NATO air power against the Serbs at a critical moment. Some members of the United Nations in Sarajevo disputed the claim that the mortar came from Serbian positions, but by now, verification of facts did not seem to matter. Washington's interventionists wanted justification for their final drive against the Serbs. Richard Holbrooke later wrote that the incident "had given us an unexpected last chance to do what should have been done three years earlier."[60] Some dissenting voices tried to put the brakes on a spiraling U.S. policy. In a column published in the *New York Times*, Charles G. Boyd, who spent two years as deputy commander of the U.S. European Command, pointed out that while the United States says it wants peace "we have encouraged a deepening war" and that the United States was supporting "the legitimacy of a leadership [Bosnian Muslim Government] that has become increasingly ethnocentric in its makeup, single party in its rule and manipulative in its diplomacy."[61] Such views rarely appeared in the press, and at this late date, they were unlikely to change Washington's momentum.

The day that NATO was about to launch attacks against the Serbs, Bosnian Muslim forces attacked Ilidza, a Serbian suburb of Sarajevo, killing a number of Serbian worshipers at a local church. When I pointed out the lack of media attention to the Muslim offensive on Ilidza on BBC International radio that evening, the BBC reporter hosting the show appeared equally surprised and asked me, "Yes, why wasn't that covered?" I replied, "Because the press does not want to arouse sympathy for Serbian civilians killed by Bosnian Muslim forces at a time when NATO is about to launch attacks against the Serbs." Other media sources wanted to keep any perspectives that might support the Serbian view out of the news. On the day before NATO started its attacks, CNN invited me to appear on the next morning's news show. Early next day, CNN retracted its invitation and explained that it had been informed that NATO was about to launch attacks on Bosnian Serbs. It appeared that CNN producers did not want a debate on the issue, which would only serve to "confuse" matters.

In the following two weeks, NATO launched sustained, heavy air strikes against Bosnian Serb targets. By the time NATO finished its attacks, a significant number of Bosnian Serb military and communications facilities were destroyed. A hospital on the Serbian side of Sarajevo was hit, and the Bosnian Serb government estimated that 100 to 150 Serbian civilians, including hospital patients, were killed as a result of NATO attacks. In Washington, pundits and foreign policy analysts alike said that the bombing campaign was intended to show the Serbs that NATO was serious about protecting safe havens—including Gorazde and Sarajevo. Others said that NATO action was a proportional response to the marketplace explosion in Sarajevo. *Washington Post* editors commended the attacks as "necessary . . . to avenge the 37, and useful to send a message to the Bosnian Serbs."[62]

The most likely cause of NATO action, however, was not talked about in the mainstream media, except for an August 30, 1995, news show, FX's *Under Scrutiny*, where former U.N. commander General Lewis MacKenzie raised doubts about NATO's motivations and pointed out that Bosnian Serbs had been ready to negotiate for the past six months but were not invited to do so. As I pointed out on the show, "the fact that NATO chose this time to attack the Bosnian Serbs rather than allow a peace settlement to take place leads one to believe they wanted to destroy the Bosnian Serb military command before Bosnian Serbs actually sit down and sign something—so obviously, the intent was to destroy the Serbs." To this observation, host Jane Wallace asked General MacKenzie, "Do you really think the intent was to destroy the Serbs militarily?" MacKenzie replied, "There is a distinct possibility that when they [Bosnian Serbs] sit down at a table somewhere, I would imagine they would want them at a distinct military disadvantage and that's why they've been attacking command and control centers, radar sites, and so on . . . probably the Bosnian-Croat coalition will take advantage of the moment of opportunity and go on the offensive."

MacKenzie's observations were correct. On September 12, 1995, as the Serbs were being attacked by NATO, Croat and Bosnian Muslim forces launched a massive offensive against Serb-held northwestern territories in the area of Gornji Vakuf, just south of the largest Serbian town of Banja Luka. As Gornji Vakuf fell to Croat and Muslim forces, International Committee of the Red Cross (ICRC) representatives reported that 40,000 to 50,000 Bosnian Serb refugees were fleeing in the direction of Banja Luka. By October 13, 1995, Croat and Muslim forces launched yet another all-out attack on Bosnian Serb positions at Sanski Most. That day, CNN reported that a cease-fire was broken at Sanski Most but avoided blaming the Muslim-Croat forces for the attack. The offensive forced another 40,000 Bosnian Serbs to become refugees, for a total of 100,000 in 1995 alone.[63] When Muslim and Croat forces reached as far as only 30 kilometers from Banja Luka, now it was the Serbs who were calling for NATO air strikes against advancing Muslims and Croats. Not surprisingly, NATO ignored their calls for help.

With the Clinton administration turning a blind eye to the ethnic cleansing of Serbs from Croatia and Bosnia, Croat and Muslim forces were unhindered in removing nearly all Serbs from regions they were taking over. If Washington had wanted Serbs to remain in Croatia and northwestern Bosnia, a strong NATO threat or substantial bombing would have stopped the offensive, just as NATO bombings prevented the Serbs from taking Gorazde in the Spring of 1994. On the contrary, by refusing to act, Washington condoned the Muslim-Croat offensive. When Western Europeans called for a cease-fire, the Clinton administration's chief negotiator on Bosnia, Richard Holbrooke, opposed it because "the trend on the battlefield was, for the first time, favoring the Bosnians" and "the Croatian offensive was valuable to the negotiating process."[64] It seemed that ethnic cleansing and war crimes were acceptable as long as they favored U.S. client states.

RESULTS OF THE WAR: THE FINAL COUNT

Now it was possible to calibrate the results of the Clinton administration's decision to reject the European Owen–Stoltenberg plan to divide Bosnia and end the war in the Fall of 1993, and to back a year and a half of attacks on Serbs by Muslim and Croat forces. What did Washington achieve by supporting a continuation of the war? It created an almost ethnically pure Croatia as over 300,000 Serbian civilians fled the region during this period. In Bosnia, the war continued longer than it should have and caused another 100,000 Bosnian Serbs to flee from areas taken over by Bosnian Muslim and Croat forces in the Summer of 1995.

Clinton administration officials argued that a massive combined force of Muslim, Croat, and NATO attacks against Serbs forced them to sign the Dayton Peace Plan. But the Serbs were willing to sign the Owen–Stoltenberg plan in the Fall of 1993 which had nearly identical provisions as the Dayton plan. If Washington had encouraged the Muslims to do the same, it would have avoided 18 months of war and hundreds of thousands of additional Serbian refugees. The Clinton administration was clearly not interested in human suffering when it came to the Serbs, but instead was determined to help Muslims fight their war and gain a better negotiating position.

While Washington's foreign policymaking elites and media pundits had been pushing for the need to "level 'the battlefield," ostensibly for humanitarian reasons, by the Fall of 1995, Bosnian Muslim and Croat forces had achieved military superiority over the Serbs, which they used not as a defensive measure but offensively. Although the Muslims jealously guarded their status as "victims" throughout years of war, the results of their hidden efforts to create a powerful military force came to fruition. The international community that rallied behind Bosnian Muslim victims was now astonished by the speed and brutality of attacks conducted by these same "victims."

Croatia emerged a clear victor in the war. "We have resolved the Serbian question," Tudjman declared to his generals, adding "There will never be 12 percent of Serbs" in Croatia, as before the war.[65] By November 1995, Croatia had not only ethnically cleansed most of its Serbs from Krajina and Slavonia regions without suffering any punitive measures from the international community, but was also able to establish a close relationship with the Bosnian Croat region which increasingly behaved like it was part of Croatia. The U.S. media did little to expose Croatia's military aims. Although Croat troops were pouring into Bosnia as early as 1992 in support of the self-declared Bosnian Croat state of Herceg-Bosnia, by 1998, only 51 articles in major newspapers referred to "Greater Croatia," while over 764 articles used the term "Greater Serbia." Ironically, although Washington's pundits and interventionists aroused fears that a "Greater Serbia" would be created unless the West took action, the resulting situation was far from this scenario. Serbia sent no forces to protect Krajina Serbs nor Bosnian Serbs, while Croat troops poured into Bosnia and regularly fought alongside Bosnian Croats.

Throughout the war, when the Serbs time and again claimed they were defending themselves out of fear that Muslims and Croats would slaughter them as they did during World War II, journalists implied that the Serbs were suffering from delusions or paranoia. As the total number of Serbian refugees in the Fall of 1995 rose to over 1 million, the U.S. media persisted in its lack of sympathy for the Serbs. The vast majority of photographs of refugees in the U.S. press were of Bosnian Muslims, thus supporting the claim that Muslims were the greatest victims of ethnic cleansing. Out of 593 photographs of refugees printed throughout the war in major newspapers whose captions included the terms "Serbian refugee," "Bosnian or Bosnian Muslim refugee," and "Croat refugee," only 6.4 percent were of Serbs and 6.1 percent were of Croats, while an overwhelming 87.5 percent were of Muslim refugees. This did not correspond with the actual numbers of refugees on each side.

Most observers would be surprised to find that by the end of the war in Croatia and Bosnia-Hercegovina, Serbian refugees from Krajina and Bosnia-Hercegovina totaled 1.354 million, an extraordinary number to be virtually ignored by the press. In December 1995, UNHCR reported a total of 874,000 Bosnian Serb refugees and displaced persons, which included 544,000 Bosnian Serb refugees displaced within Bosnia and Hercegovina and 330,000 in Yugoslavia (Serbia and Montenegro). In Croatia, up to 480,000 Krajina Serbs had left the region.[66] From a total of 1.9 million Serbs living in Croatia and Bosnia-Hercegovina before the war, by the end of 1995, up to 69 percent of these Serbs had become refugees. In comparison, Bosnian Muslim refugees totaled 753,000 in Bosnia-Hercegovina, plus 30,000 in Croatia, and several hundred thousand estimated to be living elsewhere in Europe, for an estimated 1.091 million refugees.[67] Croatian refugees totaled 433,000 from both Bosnia-Hercegovina and Krajina and Slavonia regions.

The lack of media attention to the existence of Serbian refugees supported a popularly held misperception that the greatest number of refugees resulting from the Yugoslav conflict were Muslim. The method of quoting refugee numbers explains how these misrepresentations emerged. UNHCR estimates of refugees from all ethnic groups in Bosnia-Hercegovina were lumped together into one number and simply labeled "Bosnian" refugees. The term "Bosnian" refugees conveniently inflated the perceived number of Muslim refugees and was often used in accusations of "ethnic cleansing" against the Serbs. On an August 30, 1995 program of *CNN & Company*, Jeanne Kirkpatrick, former U.S. ambassador to the United Nations, justified NATO bombings of Bosnian Serbs by claiming that Serbs were engaged in "ethnically cleansing and creating 3 million refugees." This claim was preposterous since the total number of Muslims in Bosnia-Hercegovina before the war was only 1.9 million. I tried to explain this discrepancy to Kirkpatrick after our participation on the show, but she refused to listen—apparently angered by any information that threatened the Bosnian Muslims' "victim" status. Such misperceptions continued in Washington, justifying use of force against the Serbs and laying the basis for a U.S.-led peace plan that would deny Bosnian Serbs the right of self-determination, divide Serbian lands, and cement the status of a permanently "ethnically cleansed" Croatia.

NOTES

1. Laura Silber and Allan Little, *Yugoslavia: Death of a Nation* (New York: Penguin Books, 1997), 379 n.2.

2. Ibid., 309.

3. Charles Krauthammer, "Intervention Lite: Foreign Policy by CNN," *Washington Post* (February 18, 1994): A25.

4. A. M. Rosenthal, "Bosnia: The Real Lessons," *New York Times* (February 22, 1994): 21.

5. "Government Forces Attack Serbs in Northern Bosnia," *Washington Post* (March 28, 1994): A16.

6. Yossef Bodansky and Vaughn S. Forrest, "The Truth about Gorazde," Task Force on Terrorism and Unconventional Warfare, House Republican Research Committee, U.S. House of Representatives, Washington, D.C. (May 4, 1994), 6.

7. Ibid., 18.

8. Ibid., 10.

9. John Pomfret, "Two U.N. Officials Accuse U.S. of Prolonging War in Bosnia," *Washington Post* (April 30, 1994): A18.

10. Bodansky and Forrest, *The Truth about Gorazde*, 12.

11. Ibid., 14.

12. Ibid., 20–21.

13. For the 80 percent figure, see report by U.N. French officer in "French Officer Says World Was Hoodwinked on Gorazde," *London Times* (May 3, 1994).

14. John Pomfret, "Two U.N. Officials Accuse U.S. of Prolonging War in Bosnia," *Washington Post* (April 30, 1994): A18.

15. James Bone in New York and foreign staff, "Rose Condemns Muslims for Failing to Defend Gorazde," *London Times* (April 28, 1994).

16. Roger Cohen, "U.N. Military Aide Says Plight of Gorazde Is Exaggerated," *Washington Post* (April 30, 1994): 3. See also Pomfret, "Two U.N. Officials Accuse U.S. of Prolonging War in Bosnia," A18, and Paul Lewis, "U.S. Says U.N. Officials in Balkans Lack Will to Block Serbs," *New York Times* (May 2, 1994): 7.

17. Lewis, "U.S. Says U.N. Officials in Balkans Lack Will to Block Serbs," 7.

18. Ibid.

19. "U.N. Letter on Bosnia," *New York Times* (May 3, 1994): 12.

20. Roger Cohen, "12 Serbs Dead in Two Fights with the U.N.," *New York Times* (May 2, 1994): 7.

21. John Pomfret, "Bosnians Keep Faith in Fighting," *Washington Post* (July 11, 1994): A1, A12.

22. Roger Cohen, "Mutilated Serb Bodies Found Outside Sarajevo," *New York Times* (October 7, 1994): A7, and "Bodies of Serbs Found Mutilated Near Sarajevo," *Washington Post* (October 7, 1994): A28.

23. Joel Brand, "U.N. Threatens Airstrikes Against Bosnian Government Army," *Washington Post* (October 30, 1994): A33.

24. "Surging Bosnia Government Forces Attack Serbs on Two Fronts," *New York Times* (October 30, 1994): 14.

25. Roger Cohen, "Bosnian Government Army Wins Its Biggest Victory Against Serbs," *Washington Post* (October 28, 1994): A1.

26. Joel Brand, "U.N. Threatens Airstrikes Against Bosnian Government Army," *Washington Post* (October 30, 1994): A33.

27. Roger Cohen, "Bosnian Offensive Draws UN Warning," *New York Times* (March 28, 1995): A3.

28. Roger Cohen, "Croatia Hits Serb-held Area After Violating UN's Lines," *New York Times* (May 2, 1995): A8.

29. Independent Television Network (ITN), March 1, 1995.

30. Cohen, "Croatia Hits Serb-held Area After Violating UN's Lines," A8.

31. Stephen Engelberg, "UN Report Accuses Croatian Troops of Killing Refugees," *New York Times* (July 10, 1995): A3.

32. Mike O'Connor, "Croatian Troops Said to Brutalize Serbs in Retaken Area," *New York Times* (May 25, 1995): A14.

33. From Associated Press, "UN Reports Croat Atrocities," *New York Times* (May 25, 1995): A14.

34. John Pomfret, "Serb Refugees Were Fleeing Army Attack," *Washington Post* (May 8, 1995): A18.

35. Engelberg, "UN Report Accuses Croatian Troops of Killing Refugees," A3.

36. 1990 Statisticki Godisnjak Jugoslavije (Belgrade, Yugoslavia: Sazveni zavod za statistiku, 1990), 627.

37. See Christopher S. Wren, "New Fighting in Sarajevo, UN Blames Both Sides," *New York Times* (May 17, 1995): A6.

38. Roger Cohen, "U.S. Set to Offer Aid to Reinforce U.N. Bosnia Troops," *New York Times* (May 31, 1995): A8.

39. Mike O'Connor, "Investigation Concludes Bosnian Government Snipers Shot at Civilians," *New York Times* (August 1, 1995): 6.

40. Samantha Powers, "Bosnian Serbs Seize 'Safe Area'," *Washington Post* (July 12, 1995): A1.

41. From Associated Press, "Dutch Peacekeeper Killed in Serb Infantry Assault," *New York Times* (July 9, 1995): 8.

42. Ibid.

43. John Pomfret, "Serbs Start Expelling Muslim Civilians from Seized UN Enclave," *Washington Post* (July 13, 1995): A1, A20.

44. Silber and Little, *Yugoslavia*, 360.

45. Ibid.

46. "Croatia's Dangerous Extremism," *New York Times* (April 28, 1997): A24.

47. Richard Holbrooke, *To End a War* (New York: Random House, 1998), 73.

48. Raymond Bonner, "Croat Army Takes Rebel Stronghold in Rapid Advance," *New York Times* (August 6, 1995): A1.

49. Silber and Little, *Yugoslavia*, 358, 360.

50. Chris Hedges, "Croatia Resettling Its People in Houses Seized from Serbs," *New York Times* (May 14, 1997): A9.

51. Steven Greenhouse, "U.S. Criticizes Croatia, But Only Halfheartedly, for Attack on Serbs," *Washington Post* (August 5, 1995): A14.

52. Holbrooke, *To End a War*, 72.

53. Charles Krauthammer, "Ethnic Cleansing That's Convenient," *Washington Post* (August 11, 1995): A23.

54. James Rupert, "Croatia Accused on 'Ethnic Cleansing'," *Washington Post* (August 9, 1995): A15.

55. Krauthammer, "Ethnic Cleansing That's Convenient," A23.

56. PBS's *MacNeil-Lehrer Newshour*, August 11, 1995.

57. John Pomfret, "Battle Could Hasten Long War's Conclusion—on Fighters' Terms," *Washington Post* (August 5, 1995): A1.

58. John Pomfret, "Croatia Seizes Stronghold of Serb Rebels," *Washington Post* (August 6, 1995): A25.

59. Editors, "Croatia Attacks," *Washington Post* (August 5, 1995): A18.

60. Holbrooke, *To End a War*, 92.

61. Charles G. Boyd, "America Prolongs the War in Bosnia," *New York Times* (August 9, 1995): A19.

62. "Answering the Bosnian Serbs," *Washington Post* (August 31, 1995): A22.

63. United Nations High Commissioner for Refugees, *Implementation Report*,

UNHCR Special Operation for Former Yugoslavia, SOFY (January to December 1995), 3.

64. Holbrooke, *To End a War*, 86.

65. Raymond Bonner, "Croatia Branded as Another Balkans Pariah," *New York Times* (March 3, 1999): A6.

66. United Nations High Commissioner for Refugees, *Implementation Report*, UNHCR Special Operation for former Yugoslavia, SOFY (January to December 1995), 8. See also the same UNHCR report, section "Who Is Where?" for ethnic makeup of refugees. For less than 120,000 Serbs left in Krajina, see also Silber and Little, *Yugoslavia*, 360.

67. Calculation includes the UNHCR figure of 753,000 Muslim refugees in Bosnia-Hercegovina, 30,000 in Croatia, and out of 700,000 refugees in Europe, using an estimated 44 percent to be Muslim, 308,000 yields a total of 1.091 million Bosnian Muslim refugees.

Chapter 8

War of Influence: Dayton and Beyond (November 1995 to 1998)

DAYTON: WAR AGAINST SERBS BY OTHER MEANS

Following weeks of NATO bombing raids and Croat and Muslim offensives in northwestern Bosnia, by the Fall of 1995, Bosnian Serbs were experiencing significant military setbacks. Knowing they could not stand on their own against two ethnic enemies backed by U.S. military might, they reluctantly agreed to allow Serbian President Milosevic to represent their government during U.S.-led negotiations at Wright-Patterson Air Force Base in Dayton, Ohio. The resulting Dayton Plan and its implementation would signify a continuation of war against Bosnian Serbs, by means other than direct military attacks. It was the start of Washington's war of influence in an attempt to coerce, convince, or entice Bosnian Serbs to give up their state within a state in Bosnia.

In November 1995, representatives from all warring parties met under U.S. supervision during several days of grueling negotiations to hash out a plan that would establish territorial and political divisions. The most critical discussions took place between U.S. Special Representative Richard Holbrooke and Serbian President Milosevic. Bosnian Serb representatives later complained that Milosevic did not inform them of substantive territorial concessions he made on their behalf, which they discovered only when they were presented with the final map. Although the Bosnian Serb delegation was determined not to sign away their rights to some form of independence in Bosnia, Milosevic believed that Bosnian Serbs were in a weak negotiating position and needed to compromise. Other than committing Yugoslav army forces to intervene on behalf of Bosnian Serb nationals which would lead to full-scale war with NATO itself, Milosevic saw no other choice for the Bosnian Serbs but to accept whatever peace plan Washington envisioned. On November 21, 1995, Milosevic wrote to the acting secretary general of NATO, Sergio Silvio Balanzino, "I wish to assure you that the Federal Republic of Yugoslavia shall take all necessary steps, consistent with the sovereignty, territorial integrity and political independence of Bosnia and Hercegovina, to ensure that the Republika Srpska fully respects and complies with commitments to NATO."[1] The government of Croatia conveyed similar assurances to NATO.

The Dayton Peace Plan was formally signed by all parties in Paris, France, on December 14, 1995. It called for a unified Bosnia-Hercegovina made up of two entities: the Muslim-Croat Federation, with 51 percent of the country, and the Bosnian Serb entity Republika Srpska, with 49 percent (see Appendix 2, map 12). Although Dayton envisioned two, interrelated entities, the situation on the ground was still one of three, separate ethnically held territories. What clinched the agreement was the fact the all sides believed they were signing a document that looked one way in theory, but whose outcome would in reality be determined by each ethnic leadership's policies. The Bosnian Serbs were convinced that the idea of a unified Bosnia-Hercegovina was unrealistic, because it would allow the Muslims to dominate Bosnia—the scenario that they fought several years of war to avoid. Instead, they hoped that by going along with Washington's plan, they could avoid further military actions against them, while continuing to maintain their own governmental structures and policies that would permit them, for all intents and purposes, to act as if they were an independent state. Bosnian Croats thought along the same lines. They would agree to a unified Bosnia, but they knew that in reality they would continue to have full control of the southern Bosnian areas of Herceg-Bosnia and maintain close ties with neighboring Croatia.

The interests of the Bosnian Muslim leadership and Washington were the same. The Muslims believed that the Dayton plan would allow them, in time, to dominate Bosnia's politics and eventually, gain control over Bosnian Croat and Serb areas. This was the reality behind the rhetoric of the "multiethnic" Bosnia argument heard frequently in Washington and the accompanying claims that the international community should not reward the "aggressor" by dividing Bosnia along ethnic lines. Now, with the fighting over, the Clinton administration's strategy in the Balkans appeared to be following the Muslim government's second strategic phase of coercing the Serbs into submission by manipulating Bosnia's internal affairs and weakening the Serbs in four major ways—territorially, militarily, politically, and economically. The Dayton agreement set this policy in motion, but its success would be determined by Washington's resolve to implement the plan's goals.

To weaken Bosnian Serbs territorially, the Dayton plan required the Serbs to give up all of their part of Sarajevo to the Bosnian Muslim government. It denied the Serbs any part of Bosnia's capital city and major source of resources—what the Serbs were fighting for during years of war. It would ensure that Bosnian Serbs would never again have control of the hub of Bosnia's political and international activity. Another way that Dayton would weaken the Serbs territorially was the decision to make the status of the Bosnian Serb town of Brcko, the key bottleneck corridor linking the eastern and western halves of Republika Srpska, uncertain; its final status would be determined at a later date by arbitration.

The move to postpone the decision on Brcko effectively gave Clinton administration officials power over the Bosnian Serb leadership in the coming months, for the status of Brcko was used as a way of coercing the Serbs on a number of issues. Washington also carefully chose the main arbiter on Brcko, Roberts Owen, who could hardly have played a neutral role in the arbitration process. He was the State Department's top adviser on Yugoslav policy and chief mediator in the Washington-led effort to create the Muslim-Croat federation in February 1994.

What mattered to the Muslim government was that future arbitrations would take Brcko away from the Serbs and even further weaken the Bosnian Serb republic by splitting them territorially. This would make them militarily vulnerable and put their economy under the control of the Muslim central government. The Serbs argued that the decision to leave the status of Brcko up to arbitration contradicted the ideas behind the Dayton agreement in two ways. First, the Dayton plan recognized the Republika Srpska as a single entity and hence as a contiguous territory in Bosnia. This idea would be violated if Brcko were designated under other than Bosnian Serb control since the town constituted an essential link between the western and eastern sections of the Serb Republic and was vital in maintaining the economic viability of the Bosnian Serb region. Second, the 49 percent territory allotted to the Serbs at the Dayton negotiations included Brcko. If Brcko were taken away from the Serbs, the percentage would be lower. Most importantly, the Serbs resented the fact that in contrast to its decision on Brcko, the Dayton agreement simply gave the Muslims control over a route connecting Gorazde to Sarajevo without any future arbitration on the matter. Brcko would ultimately be taken away from Bosnian Serb control in 1999.

By handing over the Serb-held part of Sarajevo to the Muslim-led government, Clinton administration officials believed Bosnia's Serbs, Muslims, and Croats would be forced to integrate in a unified Bosnia-Hercegovina. The foremost tenet of the Dayton agreement was to promote multiethnic coexistence and power-sharing in postwar Bosnia. After three and a half years of horrible war, the idea that Bosnia's three ethnic groups could live together again reflected wishful thinking more than reality. This reality became evident with the transfer of Sarajevo to Muslim control, which would shatter the notion that the Izetbegovic government was interested in a "multiethnic" Bosnia—although few in Washington would notice it.

DAYTON'S MULTIETHNIC EXPERIMENT FAILS AS SERBS LEAVE SARAJEVO

The first move under Dayton was to eliminate Serbian control of areas in and around Sarajevo, which were handed over to the Bosnian Muslim government. Clinton administration officials and the U.S. press welcomed what they perceived as a long-awaited "liberation" of Sarajevo. In the months to follow, the Muslim-led government would take over tens of thousands of homes from Serbs who fled the city, in what the United Nations described as "the worst ethnic cleansing since the Balkan war ended," violating the word and intent of the Dayton peace agreement.[2]

Almost immediately after the Muslim takeover was announced and the Serbs started to leave, some families even dug up the graves of their relatives to take away with them, knowing they would never return. Although the U.S. press for years ignored the reasons for Serbian fears of allowing their part of Sarajevo to come under Muslim control, at last a *New York Times* article detailed one Serb's reasons for leaving Sarajevo. He said he came to the Serbian cemetery in Sarajevo's suburb of Ilidza to take away the remains of his youngest child, his son who was killed by a Muslim sniper a year earlier.[3] He also said he had not seen his wife for three years because Muslim authorities in Sarajevo refused to allow her to leave, even to attend their son's funeral.

The Serbian civilians who lived during several years of war on the Serb-held side of Sarajevo feared not only that they would not have physical safety under Muslim control, but also that they were likely to be discriminated against and harassed in a primarily Muslim city. A February 1996 *Washington Post* article outlined these reasons and pointed out that the Serb exodus from Sarajevo and the takeover by Muslim police were accompanied by wholesale looting. The article also made references to never-before revealed information about the true nature of Bosnia's Muslim government—Sarajevo's increasingly Islamic-dominated school system and society. When one Serbian woman who worked in a Sarajevo company asked her Muslim boss if she could go back to work, he said "First the Muslims will get the jobs, then the Croats, then maybe the Serbs."[4]

The Bosnian Muslim government refused to acknowledge this reality. They continued to promote the myth that their government was supported by all ethnic groups. They said that Serbs living in these parts of Sarajevo were welcome to stay, and they blamed what they called propaganda by the Bosnian Serb leadership in Pale, which was said to be intentionally frightening Serbian civilians into leaving. Reflecting these new efforts by the Muslim leadership to portray their own view of what was happening in Sarajevo, the headline of a February 23, 1996 *Washington Post* article read: "Thousands of Serbs Flee Sarajevo Suburbs; Exodus Precedes Arrival of Multiethnic Police." The article claimed that the new police force was "theoretically made up of Muslims, Croats, and Serbs," and was supposed to be a step on the way to a multiethnic society. The article also claimed "the Bosnian Serb media have pounded out a message of fear" to Serbs living in Sarajevo, and it quoted one UNHCR spokesman as saying, "There's a propaganda hype in Pale media, and the show masters of this whole operation want these people to leave. It's a fairly cynical political manipulation."[5]

No doubt, some U.N. personnel believed that Sarajevo's Serbs, who spent three years on the other side of the war, would now welcome their enemies with open arms. Yet, as Sarajevo's northern suburb of Vogosca was about to be taken over by a 44-member "multiethnic police force," the same U.N. official said he was surprised that no Serbs had applied to join the force. This demonstrated the Bosnian observers' great naivete, wishful thinking, or desire to perpetuate the fiction that Sarajevo was "multiethnic." When one Serbian refugee was asked why she did not trust U.N. assurances that the new "Bosnian" police force would protect their human rights, she replied, "The U.N. has never protected the rights of Serbs in this war."[6]

Events that took place on March 6, 1996, would demonstrate that the United Nations was not willing to protect Sarajevo's Serbs nor was the incoming police force "multiethnic." When the Serbs began to leave Sarajevo, local Croats did not join the ranks of "Bosnian" police, but rather continued their wartime policy of trying to take more territory for themselves. As soon as Serb civilians abandoned the Hadzici suburb of Sarajevo, Bosnian Croat forces tried to grab control of the area for themselves before the Muslim police moved in. Only when NATO threatened to take retaliatory action did the Croats allow the suburb to be handed over to the Muslim police. Far from enjoying protection from the United Nations, by mid-March, in Sarajevo's previously Serb-populated suburb of Ilidza, the *New York Times* reported that hundreds of Muslim thugs began wandering the streets with guns, knives, and grenades, claiming ownership of Serbian homes, carting off people's belongings, and intimidating the 3,000 or so Serbs, mostly the elderly or those too ill to travel, who were still in Sarajevo.[7] Muslim officials in Sarajevo had little sympathy for the Serbs. Mehmed Kaltak, Sarajevo's official in charge of taking over 70,000 Serbian apartments under the direct control of the government, commented: "No one expelled people from Sarajevo. Those who left abandoned their homes of their own free will, so they have lost them."[8] The Muslim government passed a law that received little attention in December 1995, decreeing that any Sarajevo residents who were outside the city had 7 days to reclaim their homes if they were in Bosnia-Hercegovina, and 14 days if they were out of the country. As a result of this law, over 130,000 mostly Serbian homes and properties were confiscated. It was not reported until months later in the *New York Times*, but received no attention in Washington.

Although the actions and policies of the Muslim-led government were reported by the U.S. press, any attempts to arouse sympathy for the Serbs was frequently met with skepticism. "It was Karadzic's fault for spreading all that propaganda and scaring the Serbs," said one top associate of the Carnegie Institute for Peace during a meeting with members of the Republika Srpska delegation in September 1996. Radomir Lukic, deputy foreign minister to the Bosnian Serb Republic, was amazed at the accusation and protested, "I have to say this is not true. In fact, I was the one instructed by my government to convince Serbs to remain in Sarajevo," he said. "We wanted our people to stay in the city because we were hoping that after signing the Dayton plan, we could negotiate some kind of autonomous status for Serbs in this part of the city. Besides, we were not capable of housing a new wave of up to 100,000 new Serbian refugees. We wanted them to stay in their homes. But during a meeting with local Sarajevo Serbs, a man stood up and asked me, 'Would you want your children to stay in Sarajevo?' and I said in all honesty, I would fear for my children's lives. In fact, I took my family out of Sarajevo as soon as the war began. The man then said to me, 'Now you know why we want to leave also.' This is why Serbs left Sarajevo in the Spring of 1996. To say it was our government's policy is absurd."

Only time would show the Bosnian Muslim government's real attitudes toward Serbs in Sarajevo. As late as the Fall of 1998, the Serbs had already allowed over 8,000 Muslim refugees to return to the Serb-held town of Brcko, but the Muslim government made no significant effort to allow the Serbs expelled from Sarajevo to return. Although international observers criticized the Muslim government for obstructing the return of Serbian refugees, few in Washington openly condemned the policy. Washington would continue its military, political, and economic support for the Muslim government and ignore any negative behavior by the Muslim government that might raise questions about that support.

AS U.S. WEAPONS FLOW IN, MUSLIM-LED GOVERNMENT SHOWS TRUE NATURE

As part of the post–Dayton effort to weaken the Serbs militarily, Washington began openly arming the Muslim army with high-tech weapons and providing military training so as to ensure that the Bosnian Serbs would never be able to put up resistance to the central Muslim government. Now that the war was over, the United States was firmly committed to arming the Muslims. Talk of a multiethnic Bosnia and democratic values was not as necessary as when the Izetbegovic government was trying to draw U.S.-led NATO air power to help fight the Serbs. It was at this time that the Muslim-led government in Sarajevo would show its true colors.

The first demonstration of this began with the ethnic cleansing of Serbs from Sarajevo. After that, Izetbegovic and his supporters displayed increasing political intolerance within their own government, as well as their more radical side through relationships with countries like Iran. In 1996, Izetbegovic accepted over $500,000 in cash from Iran for use in his reelection campaign.[9] His party was reported to have been involved in a December 1996 beating of a Bosnian Muslim political opponent, while his government refused to grant a license for Bosnia's first independent television station. Izetbegovic also exhibited increasing intolerance to anything non-Islamic in Bosnia, even going so far as to discourage the idea of "Grandfather Frost," a popular holiday figure in the former Yugoslavia among Serb, Croat, and secular Muslim children. Although examples of the more intolerant and radical side of the Bosnian Muslim government were reported in major U.S. newspapers, Clinton administration officials took no notice and continued to provide unquestioning support to their Bosnian allies.

Western governments, which for years had seen the Muslim government as a victim of Serbian aggression, now expressed dismay at the direction in which Bosnia was moving. One Western diplomat, a staunch supporter of the Bosnian Muslims during the war, was led to remark that "As far as I am concerned, the gloss is off the Bosnian government.... I have tried to help these guys out, but now frankly I am tired of their talk."[10] Western perceptions were no longer nearly as important to the Muslim government as they had been in the early part of the war when they needed to convince the West, particularly the United States, of their tolerance and support for democracy. Whatever the West thought of them now was almost irrelevant. The Muslim leadership had accomplished its goal of drawing U.S.-led NATO forces on their side of the war in Bosnia and defeating Serbian efforts to create their own independent state in Bosnia.

Clinton administration officials, concerned by possible congressional and public criticism of U.S. backing of Bosnian Muslims, emphasized that in spite of the Muslim-led government's ties to Iran, Izetbegovic had adopted a pro-Western stance overall. Neither the Muslim government's "ethnic cleansing" of Serbs from Sarajevo nor its openly undemocratic tendencies resulted in a change of policy. The Clinton administration's promise to provide arms to the Muslims would be kept. To admit a policy failure at this point and to reevaluate the situation in the Balkans would show a remarkable flexibility in U.S. foreign policy that was unlikely to occur at this point.

Washington's willingness to grant the Bosnian Muslim government the long-anticipated weapons they had lobbied for throughout years of war coincided with the Clinton administration's desire to expand America's role as the world's largest arms dealer. Since 1994, Commerce Secretary Ron Brown had been an outspoken advocate of overseas arms sales as a way of countering widening trade deficits and cuts in Pentagon spending.[11] The State Department had instructed U.S. embassies around the world to promote U.S. weapons sales overseas, while congressional legislation passed in the Spring of 1994 increased the amount in loan guarantees for arms exports. Undaunted by concerns that such a policy would in the long run promote regional conflicts and potentially endanger American security, the Clinton administration pursued its weapons connection to Bosnia.

Before Clinton administration officials would give the Bosnian Muslim government weapons, they insisted first, that the Izetbegovic government would have to break off its connection to Iran and radical Islamic fighters, and second, that the Muslim government would be required to cooperate with the Croats. Washington officials explained that these conditions were necessary so that the Islamic fighters would not pose a security risk for U.S. troops scheduled to be stationed in the town of Tuzla. This exposed yet another double standard in U.S. policy. Although Washington's policymakers discounted Bosnian Serb claims during the war that Islamic fundamentalists were dangerous to Serbian security, when it came time for U.S. soldiers to be placed in Tuzla, U.S. commanders were seriously concerned about their presence in the region and sought to remove them from Bosnia before committing U.S. troops.

U.S. concerns about potential threats from radical Islamic groups were to be expected. The threat of terrorism has been one of the most pressing concerns to U.S. policymakers throughout the post–Cold War period. What was surprising, however, was the Clinton administration's willingness to support the Bosnian Muslim government, even though it continuously reneged on its promises to break its ties with Iranian and other *Mujaheddin* fighters. After signing the Dayton agreement in December 1995, Izetbegovic promised to remove a thousand *Mujaheddin* soldiers from the town of Tuzla who had been based there throughout the war. By mid-January 1996, Islamic fighters were still in Bosnia, including about 200 members of the Iranian Revolutionary Guard.[12] When U.S. intelligence reports revealed that they were planning attacks against American targets, Secretary of State Warren Christopher threatened to cut off military and financial aid to the Muslim-led government unless Islamic fighters were expelled from Bosnian territories.[13] Seven months later, by July 1996, Izetbegovic still had not made good on his promises.

Mujaheddin were not only still present in Bosnia, but they were taking over abandoned Serbian apartments and houses in Muslim-held areas of Bosnia and were even kidnapping Muslim girls and forcing them into marriage. Izetbegovic was said to be reluctant to expel these Islamic fighters, since they served as a personal paramilitary guard.[14] Some Muslim officials acknowledged that foreign Islamic fighters in Zenica and the surrounding central Bosnian towns were allowed to remain so that they could be used to terrorize political opponents, harass Serbs and Croats, and intimidate Muslims who did not support Izetbegovic. This was the kind of government that Washington continued to commit U.S. taxpayer money to provide military and financial aid. Although Washington expressed mild verbal rebukes, weapons shipments flowed into Bosnia throughout August of 1996.

When in the Fall of 1996 Washington again threatened to cut off the remaining $98.4 million in promised weapons unless the Izetbegovic government ended its relations with Iran, Izetbegovic removed from office the deputy defense minister of Bosnia's federation, Hasan Cengic, who was also an Islamic cleric and had strong ties with Iran. But the man nominated to replace Cengic, Sakib Mamuljin, also maintained close ties with radical Islamic regimes. As commander of Bosnian Muslim troops in the central Bosnian town of Zenica during three and a half years of war, Mamuljin was responsible for several thousand foreign Islamic guerrillas based there under his command. After receiving assurances from Izetbegovic that Mamuljin was not a "hard-line" Islamic radical, State Department officials seemed to relent.

Clinton administration officials were willing to downplay the Izetbegovic government's ties to radical Islamic groups, because they wanted to avoid admitting they had made a mistake and that their four-year patronage was not necessarily in U.S. interests. At an October 10, 1996 congressional hearing, Republican members criticized the Clinton administration for allowing Iran to gain a foothold in Europe, send weapons to the Bosnian Muslim government, and permit the largest concentration of Iranian fighters to remain outside the Persian Gulf. These criticisms received little attention in the press, which appeared as interested as ever in defending the Bosnian Muslim government as "moderate."

Obscuring the reality of what was happening in Bosnia from public scrutiny did not ultimately serve a greater good. European military experts argued that U.S. weapons deliveries had dangerously tipped the military balance in the Muslims' favor. The results of the inflow of U.S. weapons to the Muslim army merely encouraged a series of armed provocations against the Serbs at a time when the Dayton Accords were meant to bring peace and stability to the region. In July and August of 1996, Muslim forces attacked the villages of Dugi Deo, Jusici, and Mahala—territories which Dayton had designated as Serbian. The occupation of these villages threatened to completely split the Serbian territories in half. While these and other similar incidents indicated flaws in Washington's policy of arming the Muslims, it did not arouse greater calls for caution among Clinton administration officials. On the contrary, Washington was ready to take on an increasingly more intrusive role in Bosnia.

WASHINGTON'S HAND IN BOSNIA'S INTERNAL AFFAIRS

The signing of the Dayton Accords was followed by months of elation among Clinton administration officials who publicized their success in getting the three Bosnian warring parties to end almost four years of war. Those in Washington who had argued for years that Bosnia should become a symbol of American leadership pointed to Dayton as an example of how the United States could successfully intervene in ethnic struggles. Now, Washington's interventionists needed to make Dayton work in spite of the realities that contradicted the plan's stated goals.

The Clinton administration originally promised that U.S. troops introduced in Bosnia as part of the Implementation Force (IFOR) in December of 1995 would be withdrawn by the end of 1996. When the end of 1996 came, the fact that Bosnia was no closer to the multiethnic utopia envisioned by Washington did not dissuade interventionist-minded elites. The U.S. presence was extended under a new multilateral mission, the Stabilization Force (SFOR), whose smaller contingent of 35,000 included 8,500 U.S. troops. With SFOR's presence and authority visible throughout all of Bosnia, it was clear that an outside power was in control of the region. Reminiscent of the period when Ottoman Turks, and later Austrians, occupied Bosnia and Hercegovina in previous centuries, the United States, it seemed, was becoming the new overseeing force to contend with in the region. As the overseer of the Dayton peace plan and the main impetus behind NATO, Washington was in a leading position to make its mark on Bosnia's internal affairs on all key issues. Now Washington could implement its strategy of weakening Bosnian Serbs both politically and economically.

The wartime leadership of Radovan Karadzic was perceived as the major obstacle to the Dayton plan's integration of Serbs within a unified Bosnia–Hercegovina. The idea of "war crimes" was an effective way of getting Karadzic out of power. As the only leader in Bosnia to have been accused of war crimes, Clinton administration officials were determined to get SFOR troops to aggressively pursue and capture Karadzic and other indicted Serbs. Although the U.S. military resisted direct involvement in hunting down alleged war criminals, political pressure from Washington ultimately led U.S. forces within SFOR to become increasingly active in monitoring movements by Bosnian Serb officials. Karadzic saw no choice but to cede power on July 2, 1996, to Biljana Plavsic, the former biology professor and Bosnian Serb vice president, who would play a significant role in the development of post–Dayton Republika Srpska.

Clinton administration officials believed that by destroying Karadzic and his supporters, they would bring multiethnic coexistence back to Bosnia. This view was based on Washington's rogue-regime oriented view of the region's problems rather than on a realistic understanding of Bosnia's underlying characteristics. The results of the September 1996 elections demonstrated that all three Bosnian ethnic groups continued to favor their own national leaders. The same three ethnic nationalist parties were reinstated as Bosnia's Muslim leader Alija Izetbegovic, Serb Momcilo Krajisnik, and Croat Kresimir Zubak headed a three-member presidency. Now, an increasing number of U.S. policymakers and the media began to acknowledge that nationalism, corruption, and bigotry were rampant among *all* ethnic groups in Bosnia. The region was described by one American reporter as "overrun by Serbian, Muslim, and Croatian nationalist leaders who dismiss abuses of authority by evoking the suffering of their own people and who have little use for free debate or the rule of law."[15]

Discrimination and other problems were present in all parts of Bosnia, but Clinton administration officials set out to eradicate only the influence of what they frequently described as Bosnian Serb "nationalists." Nationalism among the Bosnian Muslim and Croat political leaderships, on the other hand, was not even a source of minimal concern to Washington. Evidently, Washington was not interested in "nationalism" and "democracy" in and of themselves. Instead, the Clinton administration was determined to keep Bosnia unified in order to illustrate the administration's successful policies in the Balkans. Aware of this mind-set, Bosnian Muslim officials constantly reiterated the message to U.S. officials that a unified Bosnia could not be achieved with Karadzic still in power. This was one reason the Clinton administration was so intently moving against solely the Bosnian Serb SDS party, even though all three of Bosnia's political and national parties pursued similar policies.

The new Bosnian Serb leader, Biljana Plavsic, was just as nationalistic as anyone else in the Karadzic government, yet she was at least nominally willing to cooperate with the United States. Washington saw Plavsic as an excellent opportunity for a new Bosnian Serb leadership to emerge—one that would cooperate with the United States at some level. In what was to be the first meeting between a high-ranking U.S. official and the head of the Bosnian Serb government in June of 1997, Secretary of State Madeleine Albright visited Plavsic in Banja Luka. Although Albright found Plavsic to be an ardent supporter of Serbian interests, she considered Plavsic a trustworthy person. Plavsic criticized her former ally, Radovan Karadzic, and accused his government of corruption, but she refused to denigrate Karadzic on the issue of war crimes. When Albright asked Plavsic if she thought Karadzic was a war criminal, Plavsic replied: "He is as much of a war criminal as I am or any of us were, for that matter." As

Karadzic's vice president throughout years of war, Plavsic was privy to almost all discussions and policies of the Bosnian Serb government. War crimes indeed took place on all sides in the Bosnian war, yet Plavsic thought it was unreasonable to assume that such actions were part of any kind of policy. "We were fighting a war," she said to Albright, "just like Muslims and Croats were." State Department officials, though not willing to accept Plavsic's explanation of the war, were at least willing to work with her.

Plavsic's overtures toward the United States introduced a period of thawing relations between Washington and the Bosnian Serb Republic. Economic sanctions had already been removed against the Bosnian Serbs in February 1996, and in conjunction with changing State Department policy, an increasing number of organizations, such as the World Bank, International Monetary Fund (IMF), and other private investors, began dealing with the Bosnian Serb government. Although Republika Srpska received only 1 percent of all foreign economic aid given to Bosnia-Hercegovina in the 1996–1997 period, Washington promised that larger amounts of aid would be forthcoming with greater Serbian cooperation.

In August 1997, believing that the means justified the ends, the Clinton administration, in an unprecedented intervention into Bosnia's internal affairs, gave the go-ahead for U.S. troops within SFOR to help Plavsic in her internal political struggle against Karadzic's supporters. Critics argued that American troops were being needlessly endangered in risky operations; for their part, interventionists in Washington condoned the act. On August 18, 1997, NATO forces helped Plavsic by taking over police stations in Banja Luka in search of evidence of electronic eavesdropping by Plavsic's opponents. A few days later, NATO soldiers surrounded all police stations in Banja Luka held by Plavsic's opponents and confiscated a significant cache of weapons. NATO troops even took over a pro-Karadzic TV station near Bosnian Serb headquarters in Pale. All these actions aroused a sense of defiance among the Bosnian Serb population, particularly among Karadzic supporters. As American SFOR troops continued to help Plavsic secure her political power, Bosnian Serb civilians threw stones at U.S. soldiers in Brcko, who in turn shot back at the crowd. Five Bosnian Serb civilians were wounded and two American soldiers were hurt. U.S. soldiers were now fighting Serbian civilians in Bosnia, as America's role and objectives in the region were becoming increasingly ambiguous.

U.S. policies in Bosnia differed markedly from its policies toward other troubled regions of the world. In the same month that U.S. troops were helping Plavsic in her internal political struggles, Secretary of State Madeleine Albright said in a speech regarding the Arab-Israeli dispute, "The United States is not a party to the Arab-Israeli conflict. We do not assume the same risks and responsibilities as parties struggling with the issues of political identity and physical survival. As a consequence, we cannot, should not, and will not impose solutions."[16] The rationale was apparently limited to the Middle East. Washington was willing to meddle in Bosnia while holding back on other international disputes for clear reasons. In Bosnia, the overwhelming U.S. military advantage over the Serbs gave Washington interventionists a free hand in testing out their theories of social engineering and U.S. influence over the domestic affairs of states.

With relations between Washington and the Bosnian Serbs on an upswing, the U.S. media now seemed more interested in reporting on previously undisclosed and more negative information relating to the Bosnian Muslim government. *New York Times* reporter Chris Hedges, led the way in a number of revealing articles regarding the Bosnian Muslim government that came out between 1996 and 1997. One report focused on Bosnian Muslim war crimes committed against Serbian civilians in Sarajevo, and reported on a mass grave discovered in the outskirts of the city where Muslim soldiers were said to have tortured and killed dozens of Serbian civilians.[17] Another article revealed how the Bosnian Muslim government—far from promoting multiethnic values—had actually been teaching historical revisionism and ethnic segregation.[18] Yet another article reported discoveries that the Bosnian federal treasury was losing millions of dollars to corruption and misappropriation of funds by Muslim officials in Sarajevo.[19] The modest change in the media coverage of Bosnia and Croatia after the war had ended demonstrated that it takes some time for the whole story on foreign events to become publicly revealed. When policymakers soften their rhetoric on a foreign issue, and when it becomes less important for the U.S. government and the media to pursue politically correct views, the press is freer to pursue investigative reporting, and the truth begins to come out. This trend was noticeable with regard to Croatia as well.

REPROACHING CROATIA: TOO LITTLE, TOO LATE

Throughout the Yugoslav crisis, both Washington's policymakers and the media dismissed the authoritarian tendencies of Croatian President Tudjman and his ruling HDZ party. Even before the Yugoslav war began, the Tudjman-led government maintained a tight, authoritarian grip on the nation's media, economic resources, judicial system, and industry. Throughout the war, the HDZ party's open nostalgia for Croatia's World War II fascist past, its right-wing ideology, and discrimination and harassment of minority Serbs were virtually ignored by foreign correspondents based in Zagreb, whose Western governments supported Croatia. As the conflict in Croatia and Bosnia-Hercegovina raged on, the media focused on war crimes committed by Serbs and failed to expose Croatian war crimes and undemocratic practices. It was not until November 1997 that the *Washington Post*'s editors acknowledged that "Croatia has led somewhat of a charmed life since Yugoslavia broke up. The heaviest criticism, and for the grossest misdeeds, has fallen on Serbia; Croatia's transgressions have been played down."[20]

By the end of 1996 and into 1997, Washington's attitude toward the Tudjman government was changing to some degree, partially in response to the increasingly vocal criticism of the HDZ initiated by opposition forces within Croatia itself. On November 21, 1996, in what was the largest protest in Croatia since the country declared independence, more than 100,000 people gathered in Zagreb to protest the Croatian government's shutdown of its nation's only remaining independent radio station, Radio 101.[21] By the Spring of 1997, the Clinton administration was becoming annoyed by Croatia's refusal to allow hundreds of thousands of Serbian refugees to return to their homes in the Krajina and Slavonia regions of Croatia. The arguments mounted in previous years by Richard Holbrooke and U.S. Ambassador to Croatia Peter Galbraith, that the expulsion of Serbs from Krajina was a temporary evil, were clearly flawed. Croatia had no intention of allowing the Serbs to return to Krajina. Just weeks after signing on to the Dayton peace plan's "multiethnic" vision for Bosnia, when it came to Croatia, Tudjman said that "Any mass return [of Serbs to Croatia] would be out of the question."[22]

No member of the U.S. press seemed to be alarmed by Tudjman's statement, although Croatia's true intentions and demeanor were discussed somewhat more openly—particularly in the *New York Times*. Editors of the *New York Times* finally acknowledged that "the danger in Croatia" comes from the country's sophisticated mainstream government which has a "desire for a larger, ethnically pure Croatia."[23] Reports of acts of violence by Croats against Serbs were also more publicly discussed during this time. One *New York Times* article cited UNHCR reports that Bosnian Croats set fire to 25 homes formerly inhabited by Bosnian Serbs in an attempt to discourage Serbian refugees from returning to Drvar, a Croat-controlled town in western Bosnia.[24] Another *New York Times* article featured a rare front-page photograph of two elderly Serbs who remained after the Croat takeover of Krajina and were robbed and beaten by Croat forces. The article also reported that the Croatian government had confiscated tens of thousands of Krajina Serb houses and settled ethnic Croats from Bosnia and Serbia in seized properties. In addition, over 90 percent of the approximately 2,000 Serbs who tried to come back to Croatia were denied access; they found their homes taken over by Croats or destroyed in highly suspicious fires.[25]

Relief officials and Western diplomats expressed impatience with Croatia's lack of cooperation in the resettlement program. Washington, however, still appeared to be in the dark as to Croatia's true intentions to permanently ethnically cleanse the region of Serbs. Peter Galbraith, an old friend of the Tudjman government, expressed confusion. "It seems strange to us that the Croatian Government would rebuild a house that belongs to a Croatian citizen and hand it over to someone who is not a citizen of Croatia," by which he meant Croats from other former-Yugoslav republics.[26] Washington's show of disapproval caused hardly a ripple. Although Secretary of State Albright delivered a strong message of protest to Tudjman during a Washington meeting in mid-May 1997, Tudjman managed to remain on good terms with Washington. He was invited to meet with President Clinton in August of 1997, and later, both Tudjman and his defense minister, Gojko Susak, who orchestrated the brutal Krajina offensive against the Serbs, were received as honored guests in Washington during Tudjman's visit for a medical treatment at a U.S. military facility.

Tudjman's visits to Washington coincided with increasingly violent measures taken against the Serbs in Croatia. At the end of May 1997, Serbs returning to their homes in Gornji Bjelovac were attacked by more than 100 Croat thugs who beat them up, seized their few belongings, and threatened to set their houses on fire, along with them and their children.[27] In a June 1997 visit to Croatia, Albright, for the first time, had the opportunity to visit two Serbian refugee families in Prevrsac who had been beaten while attempting to return to their homes. After the Croat reconstruction minister, Jure Ganic, downplayed the incident by saying that the Serbs had brought the violence upon themselves, Albright exclaimed: "You should be ashamed of yourself" and said that she was "disgusted" by the Croat government's failure to prevent violent attacks against Serbian refugees.[28] Albright quickly back-tracked, however, after returning to Washington. She sent a letter to Tudjman which was described by the Croatian press as having the "taste of apology."[29]

Albright's mild reaction to the Tudjman government's treatment of ethnic Serbs was far from the moral outrage and military threats she made against Bosnian Serbs in response to allegations of mistreatment of Bosnia's Muslims. In the months to follow, Washington's denial of some financial aid to Croatia in 1997 because of its treatment of Serbs was no more than a slap on the wrist. Washington continued to be silent on Croatia's humanitarian record in years to come. In March 1999, when the Organization for Security and Cooperation in Europe (OSCE) came out with a damning report against Croatia (emphasizing that very few Serbs who were "ethnically cleansed" from Croatia had returned, and that "there had been no progress in improving respect for human rights, the rights of minorities, and the rule of law" in Croatia), Clinton administration officials made no public statement against the Croat government.[30] Western diplomats acknowledged that the European Union and United States were tempering their criticism of Tudjman because his cooperation was perceived to be vital to NATO peacekeeping operations in neighboring Bosnia.

Following the course of Clinton administration policy, the U.S. media was slow in drawing attention to Croatia's transgressions. It was not until 1997 that Croatia's undemocratic policies finally came to light. One *New York Times* article graphically illustrated the lack of political freedom in Croatia. It described how Vlado Gotovac, a political opponent of Tudjman and a vocal critic of the decision to prohibit Serbian refugees from returning to Croatia, "was punched and whipped with a belt by a man in an army uniform" at a public political meeting.[31] Another *New York Times* article featured a photograph of Croatia's right-wing fascist party, the Party of Rights, with members giving a "Sieg Heil" salute reminiscent of Croatia's World War II Ustasha regime, and described the party as "the closest ally of Mr. Tudjman."[32] The article corroborated many of Tudjman's policies and affinities toward Croatia's fascist past which lay the foundations for Serbian grievances in the previous years of war. Interestingly, this article was not printed until April 1997, although right-wing rallies had taken place in Croatia throughout the war.

The truth about Croatia was again exposed in November 1997 when both the *Washington Post* and the *New York Times* editors expressed outrage at the Tudjman government's court in Zagreb for convicting the George Soros Open Society Institute of falsifying official records and threatening to close its offices. The *Washington Post* blasted Tudjman, calling his behavior "old-style Communist" and describing his actions as "dirty stuff [that] Mr. Tudjman must not be allowed to get away with it."[33] *New York Times* editors scolded Tudjman for his blatant disregard of democratic concepts such as "free elections, respect for ethnic minorities, and tolerance of dissent," as well as for Croatia's new laws "setting criminal penalties for anyone criticizing top officials, or spreading what the Government defined as state secrets and false information."[34] The editors finally acknowledged years of virulent right-wing anti-Serb propaganda by reprinting sections of Tudjman's speech to the HDZ's youth wing in which he described the Serbian people as "our enemies, who come from stagnant water of negative heritage" and criticized the "various fools, crack-pots, dilettantes, ignoramuses, and simply those who sold their souls, [who] want to denigrate the magnificent revival of Croatian freedom and independence, and the glorious and thunderous Croatian victories." To this, the *New York Times* editorial remarked, "No more need be said."[35]

Much more should have been said, and a lot sooner too. Had it not been for Croatia's single demonstration of bigotry against an American philanthropist, George Soros, neither the *New York Times* nor the *Washington Post* would have cared to present a true picture of Tudjman. The media's brief unveiling of what the Serbs had had to contend with for years in Croatia was thanks not to the media's investigative reporting but to Soros's misfortunes in Croatia. Articles published in 1996 and 1997 exposing the negative tendencies of Bosnian Muslim and Croatian government officials were continually deemphasized during the height of the war. Ironically, it was during the war that these points should have been made. Foreign correspondents who were able to travel to the Bosnian and Croatian areas of conflict could have been a constructive element, in providing well-rounded facts at a time when they were important. Instead, their biased coverage of wartime events encouraged Washington to back two warring parties in the Yugoslav civil war and blinded U.S. policymakers from the realities in the region. The unfortunate result was contradictory U.S. goals and policies in the Balkans which continued as ethnic turmoil erupted once again in Serbia's southern province of Kosovo.

NOTES

1. Slobodan Milosevic to Sergio Silvio Balanzino, Acting Secretary General, North Atlantic Treaty Organization, November 21, 1995 (Wright-Patterson Air Force Base, Ohio).

2. Chris Hedges, "Muslims in Sarajevo Take Over Homes of Serbs Who Fled War," *New York Times* (June 1, 1996): A1.

3. Chris Hedges, "Serbs in Bosnia See No Peace for Their Dead," *New York Times* (January 16, 1996): A6.

4. John Pomfret, "Many Serbs Pulling Up Stakes in Sarajevo Suburbs," *Washington Post* (February 3, 1996): A14.

5. Christine Spolar, "Thousands of Serbs Flee Sarajevo Suburbs; Exodus Precedes Arrival of Multiethnic Police," *Washington Post* (February 23, 1996): A1.

6. Stephen Kinzer, "Serbs on Trek: Weighed Down and Terrified," *New York Times* (February 23, 1996): A1.

7. Kit B. Roane, "Sarajevo Suburb Changes Hands, Muslim Scavengers Reign," *New York Times* (March 11, 1996): A5.

8. Hedges, "Muslims in Sarajevo Take Over Homes of Serbs Who Fled War," A1.

9. Walter Pincus, "Iranian Cash to Bosnia's Muslim President May Complicate Lake Hearings," *Washington Post* (January 1, 1997): A24; and "As Bosnian Muslim Divide Deepens, Santa Becomes Contentious Symbol," *Washington Post* (December 26, 1996): A41.

10. John Pomfret, "Sarajevo Acts to Boost Party, Silence Dissent," *Washington Post* (February 1, 1996): A18.

11. Bruce Allen and Michael Closson, "Arms Trading Is No Substitute for Real Defense Conversion," *St. Petersburg Times* (May 10, 1994).

12. Chris Hedges, "Fearing Attack, U.S. Is Tightening Security," *New York Times* (January 24, 1996): A1.

13. John Pomfret, "Vendettas Highlight Horrors of Bosnian POW Drama," *Washington Post* (January 24, 1996): A24.

14. John Pomfret, "Mujaheddin Remaining in Bosnia," *Washington Post* (July 8, 1996): A1, A10.

15. Chris Hedges, "Stoically, a Rival Tilts at Croatia's Leader," *New York Times* (June 7, 1997): 6.

16. "Blunt Words by Albright to Players in Mideast," *New York Times* (August 8, 1997): A9.

17. Chris Hedges, "Postscript to Sarajevo's Anguish: Muslims Killing of Serbs Detailed," *New York Times* (November 12, 1997): A1, A6.

18. Chris Hedges, "In Bosnia's Schools, 3 Ways Never to Learn from History," *New York Times* (November 25, 1997): A1, A4.

19. Chris Hedges, "Gangs Are Skimming Millions from Bosnia's Federal Treasury, European Auditors Say," *New York Times* (November 30, 1997): 16.

20. "Mr. Tudjman's Vendetta," *Washington Post*, Editorial Section (November 24, 1997): A24.

21. David B. Ottaway, "Croatian Leader Displays Discontent with U.S.," *Washington Post* (December 22, 1996): A31.

22. John M. Goshko, "Security Council Presses Croatia to Stop Atrocities Against Serbs," *Washington Post* (January 10, 1996): A13.

23. "Croatia's Dangerous Extremism," *New York Times* (April 28, 1997): A24.

24. Croats Reportedly Burn Serbian Homes in Bosnia," *New York Times* (May 5, 1997): A7.

25. Chris Hedges, "Croatia Resettling Its People in Houses Seized from Serbs," *New York Times* (May 14, 1997): A1.

26. Ibid., A9.

27. Jonathan C. Randal, "Croatian Mob Tried to Keep Refugees Out," *Washington Post* (May 22, 1997): A33.

28. "Disgusted in Prevrsac," *Washington Post* (June 3, 1997): A18; and "The Albright Idiom," *New York Times* (June 3, 1997): A24.

29. Raymond Bonner, "Croatia Branded as Another Balkans Pariah," *New York Times* (March 3, 1999): A6.

30. Ibid.

31. Hedges, "Stoically, a Rival Tilts at Croatia's Leader," 6.

32. Chris Hedges, "Fascists Reborn as Croatia's Founding Fathers," *New York Times* (April 12, 1997): 3.

33. "Mr. Tudjman's Vendetta," A24.

34. "The Tudjman Tirade," *New York Times* (November 27, 1997): A38.

35. Ibid.

Chapter 9

Washington Fans the Flames of War in Kosovo (1998 to 1999)

KOSOVO CRISIS BRINGS YUGOSLAV PROBLEMS FULL CIRCLE

The November 1995 Dayton peace plan may have stopped the fighting in Croatia and Bosnia-Hercegovina, but it did not end Yugoslavia's ethnic problems. Ethnic strife had gone full circle and was now looming in Kosovo and Metohija (often referred to simply as Kosovo) the southernmost region of the Republic of Serbia. Rather than quieting the restive Albanian separatist movement, when Serbia reinstated full control and revoked Kosovo's autonomy in 1989, ethnic problems in the province were only put on hold while conflicts were taking place in Croatia and Bosnia-Hercegovina. Kosovo's pro-separatist Albanians were merely waiting for the right moment to launch a full-scale war of independence.

Throughout the 1990s, a guerrilla army calling itself the Kosovo Liberation Army (KLA) was organized with the support and encouragement of Albanian nationalists outside Yugoslavia who hoped to make Kosovo a part of "Greater Albania." Illegal weapons shipments poured into Kosovo, carried over by Albanian volunteers who regularly crossed the border into Yugoslavia. During the wars in Croatia and Bosnia-Hercegovina, the KLA conducted various forms of terrorist activities as it sporadically targeted and killed Yugoslav police, members of government, and Serbian civilians in Kosovo. This included placing fire bombs in Serbian residences, ambushing Yugoslav police, and other forms of intimidation. In 1995, tens of thousands of Serbian refugees expelled by Croat forces from Krajina fled to refugee centers in Kosovo—only to be attacked by armed Albanian militants. In February 1996, Albanian militants bombed several Kosovo camps housing Serbian refugees from Croatia and Bosnia-Hercegovina.[1] In July 1996, armed Albanian thugs barged into a bar and killed two Serbian refugees from Krajina. Increasing violence against Serbs compelled another several hundred Krajina Serbs to leave refugee centers in Kosovo. I met one of these families in Belgrade who described their ordeals to me, first in Croatia and then in Kosovo, where an increasing number of incidents of Albanian attacks impelled them to leave. The husband told me, "If Albanians think that by attacking us they will force us to flee, they're right. I simply cannot risk having my children killed."

From 1991 to early 1998, the Yugoslav government reported over 200 attacks by Albanian militants on local Serbian police and civilians in Kosovo, resulting in the deaths of 40 people.[2] Over 100 Albanian members of the KLA had been arrested. Throughout these years, although the leader of the Kosovo Albanian separatist movement, Ibrahim Rugova, did not voice support for an armed insurgency, he continued to fan the flames of Albanian nationalism by promoting the idea of an independent Kosovo. Rugova and his supporters refused to abide by Yugoslav government laws; they encouraged Albanians to not pay their taxes, boycott public schools, and not to participate in Yugoslav national elections. The refusal of Kosovo's Albanian leadership to integrate ethnic Albanians into Yugoslav society, as well as the Yugoslav government's inability to stop the flow of weapons and volunteers from Albania, strengthened support for KLA rebels.

The KLA's largest and most organized campaign against Yugoslav authorities began in February 1998, as the guerrilla group intensified its attacks against Yugoslav police and civilians. The new attacks were directed against Serb-populated villages of Klina, Decani, and Djakovica, and a refugee camp in Babaloc. On February 28, the KLA ambushed and killed two Serbian policemen on patrol on the road between Glogovac and Srbica. In response, Yugoslav police attempted to capture the KLA leader, Adem Jashari, and other members of his guerrilla group. In the process, the police killed Jashari and 20 KLA members, as well as many of Jashari's relatives and a few Albanian civilian bystanders who were barricaded within Jashari's military compound. None of the previous instances of KLA attacks on Serbs in Kosovo motivated the U.S. media to cover what was taking place in the region. Only when the Yugoslav police responded to increasing KLA attacks in February 1998, and after the Jashari incident did the media take notice. Kosovo was showing signs of becoming the new focus of Washington and the U.S. media, as Bosnia had been before.

SELECTIVE MEDIA COVERAGE, AGAIN

As the Yugoslav police continued to crack down on KLA guerrillas, killing dozens of Albanian militants and some civilian bystanders, many residents took to the hills to escape the fighting. Taking lessons from the Bosnian Muslims' successful war of words in getting U.S. support for their cause, Albanian groups in the United States accused the Yugoslav police of committing "massacres" and "genocide," and immediately called for U.S. intervention. By March 1998, the U.S. press was beginning to mirror these calls, exhibiting the same trends as seen in its coverage of the war in Bosnia. As fighting between the Yugoslav police and the KLA intensified, causing both Albanian and Serbian civilians to flee areas of Kosovo, sympathetic photographs of Albanians flooded the nation's newspapers, and almost none included Serbian civilians. Articles covering the growing Kosovo crisis that focused on police attacks on Albanians were featured prominently on front pages; few, if any, references were made to Albanian attacks on Serbs. Only a small section of a *New York Times* article acknowledged that "in the last year the rebel Kosovo Liberation Army has mounted a series of bold attacks against police, Serbian officials, and ethnic Albanians accused of collaborating with Belgrade, leaving some 50 dead."[3]

By the end of June 1998, not a single article in the *Washington Post* had discussed the KLA attacks on Serbian civilians, although dozens of attacks had been reported by the Serbian Orthodox Church and the Information Center in Kosovo. Chris Hedges, the *New York Times* correspondent who published most of the revealing stories in 1996 and 1997 on Bosnia-Hercegovina, now seemed to be the only reporter writing about KLA attacks against Kosovo Serbs. On June 24, he mentioned that KLA rebels had been kidnapping "Serbian civilians in an apparent effort to drive them out of their villages," that "five Serbian villages and many small hamlets and farms in the agricultural region around Klina have been seized by armed rebels after gun battles with Serbian inhabitants," and that "the village of Bica, three miles north of Klina, is one of the last Serbian villages staving off rebel bands in this corner of Kosovo."[4] Although the article showed no photographs of Serbian refugees or civilians, it went on to say that bodies of dead Serbs had begun turning up near Serbian settlements, including the body of a Serb, Zivojin Milic, who was shot in the head six times by the Albanian rebels. Although the report was not published until the end of June, it mentioned that in April the KLA had kidnapped three young Serbs from the town of Klina and that since that time, KLA rebels had been taking potshots at Serb villagers.[5]

Newspaper stories published in the early days of the Kosovo crisis mentioned that the latest fighting had been initiated by the KLA, with its February 1998 offensive, and that the Yugoslav police had responded to it. As the mood in Washington began to shift in favor of placing the blame on the Serbs, however, the media would increasingly claim that a "Serbian offensive" was responsible for unleashing the fighting. The same trends that had prevailed throughout the Bosnian war would soon come to bear in media coverage of the Kosovo crisis. It was only a matter of time before the familiar sound bites—"ethnic cleansing," "aggressor," and "victims"— would again be used to describe an internal civil dispute.

HYPOCRISY ON "ETHNIC CLEANSING"

Throughout the post–Cold War period of the 1990s, Washington's missionary zeal to punish the perpetrators of so-called ethnic cleansing in Bosnia-Hercegovina was not equally pursued against all Yugoslav warring parties, or in relation to other conflicts in and around Europe. With respect to Croatia, Washington did not respond to the single largest "ethnic cleansing" of the Yugoslav conflict that occurred in the Spring of 1995 when 300,000 Krajina Serbs were forced to flee the region. Ethnic cleansing in other conflicts in and around Europe were similarly ignored. When Turkish government forces launched a fierce counterinsurgency against its Kurdish rebels in July 1994, over 5,000 Kurds were forced to flee their lands, and in March 1995, a Turkish offensive forced another 1,700 Kurds to flee to a refugee camp in northern Iraq.[6] Thousands more fled in July 1995 after Turkish forces dropped bombs on civilian-populated areas of northern Iraq.[7] Although the U.S. government restricted its military aid to Turkey in November 1994 owing to what the administration called a "campaign to *depopulate* Kurdish regions through forced evacuation of hundreds of remote villages," at no time was the term *ethnic cleansing* used.[8] Washington's attitude toward Turkey was mirrored elsewhere. Little attention was paid to the 1992 war in Tajikistan between pro-Russian government forces and insurgents funded and supported by Afghanistan and other Muslim countries. After Tajikistan's government forces recaptured the capital of Dushanbe from the rebels, a process of ethnic cleansing followed as opposition refugees and insurgents were forced to retreat into Afghanistan. Yet Washington was silent.[9]

In Kosovo, when ethnic Albanians fled from towns where battles were taking place between Yugoslav police and KLA guerrillas, immediate accusations of ethnic cleansing were made by members of the U.S. State Department and the media. *Washington Post* editors called on the United States to employ "force to stop the ethnic cleansing."[10] The newspaper's editors made no effort to condemn KLA attacks on Kosovo's Serbian civilians or to react to the paper's own report revealing the goals of Albanian KLA guerrillas who vowed to "fight until the Serbian authorities, and implicitly the Serb minority of 150,000 people in Kosovo, are driven out of the province."[11] The *Post* repeatedly claimed that Albanians were "driven from their homes," or "ethnically cleansed" from Kosovo, but it described decades of harassment, attacks, and violence against the Serbs in Kosovo by Albanian extremists and the resulting exodus of over 300,000 Serbs as merely a "departure of Serbs."[12]

The State Department demonstrated a similar double standard. Serbian attacks on KLA military bases in Kosovo towns and villages were characterized as ethnic cleansing by State Department spokesman James P. Rubin, who described the term as "a determined effort to focus a military campaign against one ethnic group, to move people out of villages, [and] to use heavy firepower against one ethnic group."[13] Although the State Department was quick to condemn Serbian actions in June 1998 during a time when KLA guerrillas were losing a strategic hold on parts of Kosovo, it suddenly fell silent when the KLA gained control of 40 percent of Kosovo. Washington's policymakers, opinionmakers, and activists—who have so often expressed support for human rights—now ignored the KLA's kidnapping and murdering of Serbian civilians and police, holding entire Serbian villages hostage, and targeting Serbian residential areas with terrorist activities aimed at driving the Serbs out of the area. The State Department did not describe these KLA activities as "ethnic cleansing" of Serbs, although these activities seemed to meet the definition.

DOUBLE STANDARDS ON USE OF FORCE
ENCOURAGED KOSOVO INSURGENTS

U.S. policy on Kosovo demonstrated that Washington had learned surprisingly little from the Yugoslav conflict. In the oncoming Kosovo crisis, Clinton administration officials would again base their policies and rhetoric not on principles of international law or the reality of events in Kosovo, but rather on media images, political expediency, and unbridled interventionism. The same mistakes were repeated, the same media biases flooded the news, and the same double standards were applied.

Perhaps Washington's most dangerous double standard involved the use of force. While U.S. forces were committed to thwart Serbian attempts to create mini-states in Croatia and Bosnia-Hercegovina, Washington was now far less critical of the KLA's attempt at a violent land-grab of Serbia's southern province of Kosovo. As the KLA occupied 40 percent of Kosovo by the Summer of 1998 and the Yugoslav government claimed the right to exercise self-defense against an armed Albanian insurgency, Washington threatened to implement NATO air strikes—not against the KLA but against the Serb-led Yugoslav government. This action was in stark contrast to the lack of NATO threats and actions in other conflicts around the world.

After separatist rebels in Georgia's northern region of Abkhazia began an offensive in July 1993, over 1,000 people were killed in the first month of the war alone—a far greater number of casualties than the number killed in one whole year of fighting in Kosovo. Yet no NATO action was initiated.[14] A conflict that raged throughout the early-1990s between Orthodox Christians in Armenia and Muslims in Azerbaijan over the

Nagorno-Karabakh enclave also elicited low levels of interest among Washington's policymakers, while NATO planners appeared willing to let the two sides sort it out between themselves. In the Winter of 1992–1993, while Washington was calling for NATO air strikes in response to Bosnian Serb refusals to allow U.N. convoys into Muslim-held areas, the Turkish government blocked food and other supplies from getting to Armenia during its war with Azerbaijan—whose government was supported by Turkey. This brought the population of Armenia to the verge of famine in the Winter of 1992–1993, yet NATO refrained from threatening Turkey.[15] Most notably, NATO never sought to intervene in the brutal 14-year war the Turkish government waged against its Kurdish separatists.

The Clinton administration's willingness to use force solely against the Serbs throughout the 1990s Yugoslav conflict had far-reaching effects in the Balkans. It led the Albanian separatist group to believe that Washington would eventually accept and assist their takeover of Kosovo. A local leader of the Albanian Democratic League of Kosovo party reiterated this belief by saying: "We hope that NATO will intervene, like it did in Bosnia."[16] With an abundance of weapons pouring in from northern Albania to KLA guerrillas, the only thing the KLA needed was an air force—which they would eventually attain by getting the United States to bomb Yugoslavia.

Washington appeared oblivious to the consequences of growing KLA strength in Kosovo, but the ability of Albanian rebels to gain more ground was viewed differently by European diplomats. On June 29, 1998, 15 countries of the European Union called on Kosovo Albanians to reject "violence and acts of terrorism," after receiving reports that KLA rebels had been kidnapping and firing on Serbian civilians, driving Serbs out of rebel-controlled areas, blocking Serb-populated towns, and taking over facilities. For instance, the KLA occupied a huge open-pit coal mine and in the process kidnapped several Serbian mine workers, halting all production.[17]

The KLA's occupation of large areas of Kosovo in the Summer of 1998 did not lead to threats or reprimands against the Albanian separatists by U.S. officials but instead bolstered Washington's support. Earlier statements by U.S. special envoy on Yugoslav matters, Robert Gelbard, dismissing the KLA as a "terrorist organization," were contradicted in late June, when the Clinton administration indicated it was prepared to talk with the rebels.[18] The KLA military successes led U.S. officials to offer them a place at the negotiating table—something Washington never offered to the Bosnian Serbs when they were winning the war in 1992. By the end of June 1998, Richard Holbrooke, at the time a nominee for the position of U.S. ambassador to the United Nations, welcomed meetings with KLA guerrillas. He even posed for a photograph with a fully-armed and uniformed leader of the KLA, featured on the front page of the *Washington Post*, on June 25, 1998. Remarkably, during most of the Bosnian war, Holbrooke refused to meet with the Bosnian Serb leader, Radovan Karadzic, and discouraged other members of the U.S. government from even communicating with him. The State Department policy at the time was to refuse to talk to the Bosnian Serb government of Republika Srpska, whose legitimacy the United States did not recognize. Washington's double standard and readiness to deal directly with the KLA was sending a message to the rebels that their cause was just. The anti-Serb bias which developed in Washington during the years of Yugoslav conflict continued to mire U.S. policymakers' views with regard to Kosovo.

DOUBLE STANDARD ON "AGGRESSION" ENCOURAGES CONFLICT IN KOSOVO

As civil war raged in Bosnia-Hercegovina throughout the 1990s, Washington accused the Serbs of being "aggressors," largely due to the presence of Yugoslav army troops in Bosnia in the early days of war and later to military and other assistance provided by Serbia to Bosnian Serb nationals. If providing assistance to ethnic or religious groups in "foreign territories" was the standard offense for being branded an "aggressor," then the criterion was applied differently with respect to other nations. In the case of Croatia, although the Tudjman government provided financial and military support for the Bosnian Croat war against the Muslims, Croatia was never named an "aggressor." Outside Yugoslavia, Washington was also willing to forego labeling Turkey an "aggressor" for assisting its allies in Azerbaijan during a war against Armenia over the disputed region of Nagorno-Karabakh. Nor was Turkey reprimanded for funneling money and weapons to Bosnian Muslims, in spite of a U.N. arms embargo on Bosnia-Hercegovina.

Since the start of the Kosovo crisis in 1998, Albania had openly supported an armed insurgency in Yugoslavia in clear violation of international law. The former president of Albania, Sali Berisha, had taken on the role of a northern Albanian warlord and had forged close links with the KLA guerrillas to whom he funneled arms and money. The mountains of northern Albania bordering Serbia's southern province of Kosovo were controlled by Berisha and his supporters, and served as a sanctuary and training base for KLA terrorist activities. From these areas, observers saw "groups of 200 uniformed Kosovo Liberation Army fighters along with 20 or 30 pack horses loaded with mortars, rocket-propelled grenades, and ammunition boxes crossing nightly" into Kosovo.[19] These weapons had been used in Yugoslavia to kill members of the Yugoslav police, Serbian civilians, and Albanians opposed to KLA activities. Washington neither held Albania accountable for its support of the KLA nor branded Albania an "aggressor." Washington policymakers and the media, which repeatedly accused Serbs in Bosnia and Croatia of fighting to establish a

"Greater Serbia," expressed surprisingly little concern about Berisha's statements vowing to annex Kosovo and create a "Greater Albania," or about the statements by KLA rebels who told even the *New York Times* that they were fighting to create "a Greater Albania that stretches into Macedonia and Montenegro."[20]

As Yugoslav police tried to cut off the flow of weapons smuggled from Albania to rebels in Kosovo, NATO could have deployed its troops along the border between Albania and Yugoslavia. But as one NATO official said, "If you send in NATO troops to Albania and Macedonia and tell them to stop the flow of arms and guerrillas across the borders, it would probably be the biggest favor we could do for Milosevic."[21] Considering that NATO's expressed role in the 1990s has been to stop cross-border aggressions, this official's statement reflected a growing disregard for principles and a continuing obsession with Milosevic as the designated "rogue regime."

PUBLIC RELATIONS WAR ON KOSOVO

Since the late 1980s, the leader of the Kosovo Albanian separatist movement, Ibrahim Rugova, and his supporters invested considerable time and money to develop a presence in Washington. They hired the same public relations firm, Ruder Finn Inc., that represented Croatian and Bosnian Muslim governments, and for years they attempted to appeal to members of the U.S. Congress, the White House, the State Department officials, and the media. Although in 1998 Rugova effectively disassociated himself from the KLA, his political goals were clearly the same. Some of the largest Albanian-American financial supporters of Rugova's party also supported the KLA.[22] When the president of a local chapter of Rugova's party, Gani Shehu, was asked whether he and his party members were members of the KLA guerrilla movement, he replied: "Everyone is a member."[23] Nevertheless, Washington was prepared to deal with Rugova, and the State Department doors remained open to him.

When the crisis in Kosovo re-ignited, Rugova already had his supporters in place in Washington, with an organized ethnic Albanian activist base in the United States and important friends—including former Senator Bob Dole, who, as noted earlier, had established close relations with the Albanian community in 1989. Bob Dole had continued to be active on Balkan issues as chairman of the International Commission for Missing Persons in the Bosnian and Croatian Wars—an organization whose views were strongly supported by both the Bosnian Muslim and Croatian governments. With Kosovo once again coming to a head, Dole immediately set out to make his voice heard. In a July 1998 editorial, he was quick to call for NATO actions against the Serbs in Kosovo—the first in a line of emotional commentaries he would write in support of the Albanians.[24] He asked the assistant secretary of state for democracy and human rights, John Shattuck, to accompany him on a tour of Kosovo where Albanians welcomed an opportunity to convince the State Department official that human rights violations against Albanians warranted U.S. military intervention.

KLA supporters in the United States also sought to make an impression in Washington by working through the Albanian-American Civic League lobbying group, which maintained contacts with a number of influential lawmakers. In 1998 alone, they collected pledges for over $120,000 for campaign contributions to sympathetic members of Congress up for re-election.[25] Representative Eliot Engel from New York, who headed the Albanian Issues Caucus, expended considerable efforts on the Kosovo Albanian cause. In an October 1, 1998, appearance on CNN's *Crossfire*, Engel openly acknowledged that his close relationship with Albanian immigrants motivated him to get involved with the issue and take three trips to the Kosovo province. The Albanian lobby also made other friends in Washington, such as lobbyist and former Senator Larry Pressler, who spent the better part of 1998 conveying the views of Albanian Americans to congressional leaders and their aides.[26] While most Republicans in Congress opposed further U.S. entanglement in the Balkans, by June of 1998, efforts to induce U.S. support for KLA activities in Kosovo were already noticeable. At the time, Senator Chuck Hagel, a Nebraska Republican on the Foreign Relations Committee, said: "I detect a shift on the Republican side on this. We're probably going to have to put NATO troops in there."[27]

This renewed public relations war in Washington over Balkan affairs helped obscure the real picture in Kosovo. The fight to win the heart of Washington on Kosovo was reminiscent of the war of words on Bosnia. Just as the Bosnian Muslim government described itself as "Bosnian," which effectively conveyed the image that the Serbs had no business being in the region, so the novel term "Kosovar" made its way into the jargon of Washington's opinionmakers and policymakers. It was a newly invented description of Albanians from Kosovo that contrived to give the appearance that "Kosovars" were different from "Yugoslavs." Again, the implication was that Serbs had nothing to do with Kosovo, whereas "Kosovar" Albanians were indigenous to the province. Interestingly, the term "Kosovars" was never used to describe Serbs, the centuries-old inhabitants of the region. As in Bosnia, historic revisionism and lack of knowledge of the region made Washington susceptible to rhetoric that did not reflect reality. A telling sign among members of Congress who supported the Albanian separatist movement in Kosovo was their use of the word "Kosova," the Albanian name for the region, instead of "Kosovo," the name the Serbs gave to the region before the Middle Ages. Just prior to the onset of NATO bombings of Yugoslavia, Washington sent a message of support to the Albanian separatist movement as President Clinton began pronouncing the name of the region "Kosova." He made an additional effort to pronounce the name with an Albanian accent after meeting with Albanian-American supporters of the KLA at the White House in March 1999.

Apart from obscuring reality, the Albanian public relations effort in Washington encouraged the continuation of violence in Kosovo. Washington's display of sympathy aroused even more violent KLA attacks in the hopes of forcing Yugoslavia to relinquish Kosovo. This in turn led to greater Serbian crackdowns. The cycle of violence continued as Kosovo's Albanian separatists believed they would increasingly gain the sympathy and political support in Washington that would ultimately lead to NATO attacks and allow them to create an independent state of Kosovo, or a Greater Albania.

DEPICTING KOSOVO AS A SERBIAN WAR AGAINST "CIVILIANS"

The same humanitarian sympathies that helped motivate Washington to intervene in Bosnia would become a useful strategy for pro-separatist Albanians in Kosovo. Repeating the all-too-familiar "victim–aggressor" theme of the Bosnian war, Bujar Bukoshi, the prime minister of a group calling itself Kosovo's Albanian government in exile, said in one interview that Washington must not "press the victim instead of the aggressor."[28] While the KLA battled against Yugoslav police, the idea that Serbs were killing Albanian "civilians" would be constantly reinforced.

The U.S. media was key in promoting this theme. By October 1998, both the *New York Times* and the *Washington Post* were once again printing large, heart-wrenching photographs of Albanian civilians who were described as "driven from their homes" by "Serb terror," while there was a lack of similar photographs of Serbs, no mention of KLA attacks on Kosovo Serbs, or of the fact that Serbs from Kosovo had also been forced from their villages and had become refugees.[29] An October 2, 1998 *Washington Post* editorial said: "Serbian strongman Slobodan Milosevic waged a war of terror against the civilian population of Kosovo." A *Washington Post* article printed the same day, however, reported a more balanced view of the situation. The article mostly described Yugoslav police action against Albanian fighters, not civilians, and mentioned that "guerrillas have tortured and executed Serbian prisoners."[30] Continuing on the theme of Serb army against Albanian civilians, the familiar cast of characters lined up to give their opinions on the latest crisis in the Balkans. As a barrage of accusations were launched against the Serbs, Jim Hoagland described the situation in Kosovo as an "organized Serb massacre of Kosovar civilians."[31] Bob Dole described the situation as "a war against civilians" and as "Serb-instigated attacks on Kosovo."[32] He also accused Serbia of being "engaged in a major, systematic attack on the people and territory of Kosovo," and he noted that "the war in Kosovo has many of the worst characteristics of the war in Bosnia [where] the primary victims of Serbian attacks are civilians."

Allegations that the war was against "civilians" were bolstered by KLA supporters in Kosovo who welcomed foreign journalists and flooded the U.S. press and international observers with allegations of atrocities. Albanian men who died in battles were said to have been executed, and journalists were convinced that Yugoslav police killed "civilians" because the dead Albanian men were not in uniforms. Reporters rarely stopped to think what "uniforms" KLA terrorist groups would be wearing in the first place. In an armed uprising or civil strife, all men of fighting age are potentially engaged in fighting. They could go into battle with tennis shoes but would still be considered "soldiers" as long as they had a weapon.

The KLA's strategy of fighting while pretending to be civilians was an effective way of combating the Yugoslav police. In an October 25, 1998, *60 Minutes* segment, reporters and cameras went to what was described as a "refugee camp" in Kosovo, where Albanian civilians were said to be hiding, afraid to return to their homes. Within the confines of the "refugee camp," *60 Minutes* interviewed an Albanian man who used to work as a cook in the United States but was now a KLA volunteer. He was wearing sneakers, a leather jacket, and looked like any average male, except that he was a member of the KLA. In response to the claim by a Serbian official from Kosovo that KLA members have used Albanian civilians as cover by hiding in villages and refugee camps, the *60 Minutes* correspondent said, "but these people are just farmers." If a former cook working in the United States could turn into a KLA member, why not a farmer? Washington's naivete about the reality of fighting was first evident in Bosnia and was now again operative in Kosovo.

IGNORING REALITIES OF WAR, WASHINGTON PRESSURES SERBS

Even though the military goal of the Yugoslav police was to destroy the KLA guerrilla movement, not the Albanian people, Washington's policymakers continued to spread the misguided view of Kosovo as a war on "civilians." A lack of understanding, or choice to ignore the realities of warfare, led to contradictory statements by the Clinton administration. When asked why the U.S. administration chose to intervene in Kosovo while avoiding other internal struggles in Europe and elsewhere, Richard Holbrooke replied, "For two reasons: one, because in Kosovo you have attacks against civilians, and two, because of implications with regard to Albania and Macedonia."[33] Holbrooke's reasoning was clearly flawed. Kosovo was not the exception when it came to civilian casualties. In no conflict around the globe are soldiers the only casualties of war. U.S. intervention in Somalia in 1993 resulted in the deaths of 1,000 Somali civilians who got caught in the cross-fire of street-to-street battles with U.S. soldiers. Civilian casualties and destruction to urban areas occurred in Chechnya, Turkey, Nagorno-Karabakh, and elsewhere. Perhaps from Washington's vantage point, it is easy to forget that terrorist groups, guerrilla armies, or any other kind of armed group do not attack their opponents in a single-file regiment on an open field of battle. This kind of warfare has long ceased to exist.

Instead, armed insurgents fire from buildings, houses, schools, or hospitals converted into battle zones. During the war in Croatia, strategically tall objects such as church towers were used by Croat gunners sniping at passers below. In Bosnia-Hercegovina, especially Sarajevo, the tops of high-rises and hospitals were used as military positions. In Kosovo, KLA guerrillas have sought refuge in farm houses and villages from which they could launch attacks and from where they were difficult to extract without hurting civilians. While Yugoslavia's police was criticized for not taking adequate precautions to safeguard Albanian civilians when responding to Albanian terrorist attacks, attempts to fight against dangerous, armed guerrillas moving among civilians are likely to lead to unintended results, as U.S. soldiers discovered in Vietnam. An added problem was the difficulty in distinguishing between KLA guerrillas and civilians as the separatist movement grew larger and drew in larger numbers of Kosovo's Albanian youths and elderly alike. U.S. military experts were well aware of the realities of civil war and for this reason tended to be reluctant to support the interventionist views of Washington's political elites with regard to U.S. action in Bosnia, as well as Kosovo. It was President Clinton and his political advisers that pushed a skeptical U.S. military to intervene on both accounts.

Claims made by Holbrooke and others that the United States needed to intervene in Kosovo because of the negative effects the crisis may have on Albania and Macedonia were also contradictory. Instead of discouraging problems in these two neighboring countries, Washington was encouraging a wider Balkans war. The Clinton administration's willingness to participate in friendly negotiations with KLA guerrillas and its opposition to the Yugoslav government's attempts to stop the KLA takeover of Kosovo sent a message to Albanians in Macedonia and Montenegro that Washington would accept a violent uprising and eventual independence for Albanian minorities elsewhere. In Macedonia, where Muslim Albanians comprise over 22 percent of the country's 2.2 million people, Albanian-populated parts of western Macedonia began calling for independence, particularly in Macedonian towns close to the country's border with Albania where ethnic Albanians outnumber the country's other ethnic groups.[34] With the KLA already claiming responsibility for a series of bomb explosions in Macedonia, officials there said that "our biggest problem is the Albanians living here."[35] KLA rebels made their goals clear to the West, which as one KLA rebel described, was "to liberate all Albanians, including those in Macedonia, Montenegro, and other parts of Serbia." "We are not just a liberation army for Kosovo," said these new friends of the U.S. establishment.[36] Instead of expressing concern about expansionist KLA goals, Washington again turned its attention to putting pressure on Serbia.

When the Yugoslav government opened 15 relief centers for tens of thousands of Albanian refugees in October 1998, Holbrooke insisted this was not enough.[37] He wanted Milosevic to withdraw Serbian police from Kosovo, arguing that their continued presence was keeping Albanians from returning to their homes. On the other hand, it could have been argued that it was the KLA that was preventing Albanians from returning to their homes, since their continuing attacks on Serbs could not be met with anything other than a police response. At the time Holbrooke was making demands on the Serbian leader, four bodies of Serbs in civilian clothing were found near a former KLA hideout on Grebnicka Mountain. Representatives of Human Rights Watch said one of the skulls had a bullet hole in it, presumably from an execution.[38] A *New York Times* article that reported the incident also briefly mentioned that Serbian authorities discovered 34 bodies of mostly Serbian civilians killed by the KLA and dumped in a canal at Glodjane. The *Times* printed a brief reference in the last paragraph of the same article on the discovery of another site at Klecka in Kosovo from late August where the KLA burned 22 Serbs in a lime kiln.

Ignoring what was happening to Serbs in Kosovo, on October 6, 1998, Washington preferred to step up threats against the Serbs. As in Bosnia, Secretary of State Madeleine Albright led the way against the Serbs on Kosovo, urging NATO members to authorize the use of force against Yugoslavia. Albright was steadfast in her determination to punish Milosevic. Buckling under pressure from Washington, Milosevic agreed in mid-October to an accord allowing 2,000 international observers and NATO reconnaissance flights to monitor promised reductions in Yugoslav troops and police from Kosovo. Concessions from Milosevic were not likely to encourage the KLA to stop their attacks. As testament to this reality, in the last paragraph of a *New York Times* article was an acknowledgment that "Western diplomats concede that while they have been able to persuade the Yugoslav government at least to begin reducing forces, they have little with which to threaten the guerrillas, who are dispersed in small units and often intermingled with civilians."[39] So why was Washington so intent on pressuring just the Yugoslav government when little substantive good would come out of it? Again, media images had a great deal to do with it. At the time, the Clinton administration acknowledged that it was under congressional and public pressure because of widely publicized atrocities against Albanians.[40] Atrocities against Serbs, on the other hand, were not prominently featured by the media and aroused little concern in Washington.

In mid-December 1998, in Kosovo's town of Pec, KLA rebels, in a calculated act of terrorism stormed into a bar and machine-gunned six Serbian teenagers. A few days later, the body of the Serbian mayor of Pristina, who was shot between the eyes, was found along a road. The renewed wave of violence by KLA rebels was followed by a strong Yugoslav police response. It was not the KLA murders that prompted any international attention. Instead, it was a crackdown on the KLA's rebel stronghold in Podujevo by the Yugoslav police that prompted accusations that Serbs were violating the October cease-fire. As battles between Yugoslav police and the KLA continued, in mid-January 1999, the bodies of 45 Albanian men were found in the town of Racak. International monitors and Albanians immediately claimed these were "massacres" of Albanian civilians. The Yugoslav government maintained these were mostly KLA members killed in battle.

Nevertheless, with sound bites taking precedence over facts, a new round of media blitzes on alleged "massacres" would prompt Washington's interventionists to raise the alarm. Once again, cries of genocide and ethnic cleansing sounded through Washington to bolster interventionists' arguments. James Hooper from the Balkans Action Council, calling for "Presidential leadership," described Kosovo as a "test of American leadership and NATO's credibility."[41] Washington yet again pushed NATO threats against the Yugoslav government. No threats were issued to the KLA for their several weeks of attacks on Serbs in Kosovo. At the time, U.S. General Wesley Clark of NATO command said he expected Mr. Milosevic to withdraw his forces and "respect normal peace-time policing practices" in Kosovo.[42] General Clark's demands on the Yugoslav government were misplaced. Perhaps normal police practices would be appropriate in a state that was at peace, but Kosovo was at war—with tens of thousands of KLA rebels armed with sophisticated weapons smuggled from abroad, and the desire to take over the region.

DEMANDS ON BELGRADE—PRECURSOR TO EXPANDED WAR

When Russia initiated bombing raids on its separatist-minded region of Chechnya in 1994, White House officials stated that it was an internal matter.[43] There was no outside intervention or demands that Russia resolve the problem by granting autonomy to the region. Instead, a peace agreement was signed in May 1997, which did not resolve Chechnya's status but managed to end the destructive 20-month war.[44] Similarly, Washington dismissed Turkey's 14-year-struggle against its Kurdish minority as Turkey's internal affair. No special guarantees for Kurds or the autonomy of Kurdish regions was called for by either Europe or the United States. Even frequent Turkish incursions into Iraq throughout the 1990s, with tens of thousands of troops and bombing raids on Kurdish PKK rebel bases, were condoned by Washington as legitimate attempts by Turkey to ward off outside support for a Kurdish insurgency, described by the State Department as Turkey's "right of self-defense."[45]

One could only imagine how Washington would react if Yugoslavia entered northern Albania to destroy KLA terrorist camps. Would Washington support Yugoslavia's sovereign right to destroy advocates of violent insurgency in Kosovo? Would Washington acknowledge that Kosovo was an internal matter, as it did in the case of Chechnya or Turkey? The answer to all of these questions was clear when Washington demanded that Yugoslavia withdraw its forces from Kosovo—its own territory. Surely this was akin to asking Yugoslavia to surrender Kosovo to KLA guerrillas. In previous years, U.S. officials said they would recognize new Soviet republics as independent nations "once that government is in effective control of its territory and capable of entering into and fulfilling international obligation."[46] With such a policy, it is logical to conclude that the withdrawal of Yugoslav police from Kosovo and the handing-over of Kosovo to separatist Albanian KLA forces would pave the way for U.S. recognition of the region as an independent state or as part of Greater Albania.

Far from staying out of Yugoslavia's domestic affairs, as it did in Chechnya and Turkey, the Clinton administration called on Serbia to grant autonomy to Kosovo. U.S. envoy Christopher Hill insisted in early February 1999 that "Yugoslavia must accept some form of self-rule in Kosovo."[47] These demands were not only unrealistic, but even if met, would not solve Kosovo's problems. With Kosovo Albanians making up almost 90 percent of the local population, autonomy would mean that Albanians could again dominate all political, educational, judicial, and police positions as they did in the 1980s. This was the reason that over 300,000 Serbs left the province in the first place, since Serbia lacked jurisdiction and power to stop violence by Albanian separatists. This time, if complete autonomy was granted to Kosovo and KLA took over the region, who would protect Kosovo's several hundred thousand remaining Serbs? What would prevent the KLA from continuing their violence to break Kosovo away from Serbia and join a Greater Albania? The KLA had unequivocally rejected anything less than independence for Kosovo. Autonomy would scarcely slow down its efforts. The U.S. envoy further opened the door to Albanian independence in his February statement when he said that Washington favored a three-year interim status for Kosovo, which might lead to independence.[48]

Washington's increasingly supportive statements implying an acceptance of ultimate Albanian independence in Kosovo was setting a dangerous precedent in other parts of former Yugoslavia. If Albanians, by virtue of their majority in Kosovo, were allowed to join a Greater Albania, what would prevent Bosnian Croats from splitting areas where they made up the largest ethnic group to become part of Greater Croatia, or Bosnian Serbs from splitting their regions and joining Greater Serbia? Washington seemed to be consciously and rapidly accelerating the Balkans towards another round of war. Again, as with Bosnia, the Clinton administration saw intervention and use of force as the only solution to Yugoslavia's internal matters. Few reasonable minds in Washington questioned the wisdom of wanton threats of bombing a sovereign country. "If we attack Serbs inside their own country, do Serbs have a right to attack us in ours?" asked syndicated columnist Pat Buchanan, who recommended that "Before we use air power, that night stick of the New World Order, we should ask: What is it we hope to accomplish?"[49]

The question was well put, but with Washington's record of basing policies in the Balkans on images and emotion rather than on a realistic assessment of America's role in the region, the question was unlikely to be answered before increasingly greater steps were taken. U.S. Secretary of Defense William Cohen, after weeks of opposing Secretary of State Madeleine Albright on sending more U.S. troops to the Balkans, gave in to interventionist pressures and announced on February 3, 1999 that the United States might send between 2,000 to 4,000 American troops as part of a NATO operation in Kosovo. All the familiar steps for another round of U.S. entanglements were coming to fruition, as was the likelihood that billions of dollars would again be used to support an ongoing U.S. military presence in ethnic struggles in the Balkans.

Only a political solution could have ended the war. Instead, Washington's increasing enthusiasm for using force against the Serbs would turn the Kosovo crisis into a U.S.-led NATO war. Without sober reasoning by those in Washington willing to confront its ongoing double standards and contradicting values in the Balkans, Kosovo became yet another popular cause that Washington's interventionists were reluctant to give up.

RAMBOUILLET TALKS: PRELUDE TO ANOTHER WAR

As support grew among Clinton administration officials for U.S.-led NATO forces to be introduced into Kosovo, a peace plan was being formulated by the State Department to be presented in early February 1999 during talks between Yugoslav government officials and Kosovo Albanian representatives at Rambouillet, France. The State Department's 40-page draft document, which Secretary of State Madeleine Albright took to Rambouillet, mirrored KLA demands that Kosovo be given the status of an international protectorate and that a referendum on independence be held to determine its final status at the end of three years. The plan gave Kosovo the highest degree of autonomy for three years, including the right to create a new assembly that could elect a president and prime minister, pass new laws, and form new courts, police, and municipal governments. The plan also required 25,000 Yugoslav troops to be withdrawn from Kosovo, except for 2,500 of its security forces and 1,500 army troops, while the KLA rebel forces would be expected to disarm within three months. However, the plan did not specify how this would be accomplished. There was no requirement that NATO troops disarm the KLA. Under this plan, a likely scenario was that a NATO takeover of Kosovo would allow KLA guerrillas and weapons to flow over the border from Albania, enabling the KLA to launch more attacks on Yugoslav authorities and Serbian civilians living in Kosovo.

The Rambouillet talks were not negotiations, but rather represented an ultimatum to the Serbs. Albright had already secured NATO authorization to attack Yugoslavia if its government refused to sign the document. The intent of the State Department proposal was clear to both U.S. policymakers and the media alike. The headline of a February 3 *New York Times* article correctly observed that the "Draft Peace Plan for Kosovo Would End Serbian Control." In the weeks to follow, President Clinton and U.S. officials continually justified forthcoming NATO attacks on Yugoslavia as a reprisal for Serbia's refusal to grant autonomy to Kosovo. The major source of contention at Rambouillet, however, was not Yugoslavia's refusal to grant autonomy to Kosovo, but rather whether Kosovo was to be, in effect, occupied by NATO. As one *Times* reporter wrote at the time, "the outcome of the peace effort here is likely to come down to one major factor: will the Yugoslav President, Slobodan Milosevic, accept foreign troops on Serbian soil and allow them to turn Kosovo into a quasi protectorate?"[50]

The Rambouillet conference exposed growing differences among Western powers on how to deal with Kosovo. French and Russian officials maintained that deployment of NATO peacekeepers in Kosovo would need to be backed by a U.N. Security Council resolution. Their position was consistent with Chapter VIII, Article 52 of the U.N. Charter, which required regional organizations, such as NATO, to "make every effort to achieve pacific settlement of local disputes . . . before referring them to the Security Council," and Article 53, which states that "no enforcement action shall be taken under regional arrangements or by regional agencies without the authorization of the Security Council." The Clinton administration, however, flatly rejected U.N. authorization for NATO action, arguing that NATO should be able to act on its own. In Bosnia, the conservative government of Prime Minister John Major often put the brakes on the Clinton administration's interventionist policies. In contrast, the liberal government under Prime Minister Tony Blair—a close ally of Clinton—backed the U.S. calls for unhindered NATO attacks on Yugoslavia.

During the Rambouillet talks, President Clinton gave his weekly radio address to the American people in support of the administration's call for NATO troops in Kosovo. In his speech, Clinton demonstrated that he either lacked substantive understanding of what was happening in the Balkans, or was deliberately attempting to obscure the real reasons for U.S. involvement. "Bosnia taught us a lesson," in that "violence we fail to oppose leads to even greater violence we will have to oppose later, at greater cost . . . World War II taught us that America could never be secure if Europe's future was in doubt."[51] Clinton should have drawn entirely different lessons, however, from both conflicts. In Bosnia, a civil war was encouraged by hasty U.S. recognition of new nations, and its resolution was drawn out by U.S. support for one warring party—Bosnia's Muslims. The equally inappropriate and overused World War II analogy suited Clinton's strategy of applying simplistic and emotional analogies that the American public could readily understand, but in no way had anything to do which what was happening in the Balkans. Hitler's forces committed cross-border aggressions against a number of sovereign nations, whereas Kosovo was an entirely internal ethnic problem. It was a police action by Yugoslav authorities against an armed KLA insurgency—not unlike what was happening between the Turkish government and Kurdish guerrillas. Clinton failed to mention the lack of involvement by the United States in other civil conflicts during the 1990s, including Armenia and Azerbaijan, Chechnya, Turkey, Basque region of Spain, and Northern Ireland, none of which lead to "greater violence" or put "Europe's future in doubt." The Clinton administration was clearly groping in the dark to justify U.S. policy on Kosovo. A further justification for U.S. intervention added to his speech was that U.S. troops were needed to "return self-government to Kosovo." However, the only time Kosovo had "self-government" was from 1974 to 1989, resulting from attempts by Yugoslavia's former Communist leader Tito to separate the province from Serbia. Now, it appeared the U.S. goal in the Balkans would be one of reinstating policies created by former Communist dictators.

There were other indications that the administration was not in touch with reality on Kosovo. During the Rambouillet negotiations, Secretary of State Albright tried to convince the Serbs that by losing control over Kosovo, they would not be losing their sovereignty. Sovereignty on the eve of the 21st century, she claimed, was different than what it was 100 years ago. Yet Albright's proposals were violating the very essence of Yugoslav sovereignty. In Kosovo, it was a simple case of who would control the land—the Serbs, the KLA, or NATO? The Serbs believed the answer was being sent loud and clear by Washington that a NATO-led and KLA-dominated alliance would control Kosovo, and not the Serbs. The Rambouillet meetings would provide even greater cause for the Serbs' suspicions. KLA representatives were given increasing support from Washington as members of foreign policy think tanks and Congress began visiting the Albanian delegation at Rambouillet. Far from discouraging the KLA insurgency, kidnapping, and terrorism, Senator Mitch McConnell, visiting the Albanian delegation at Rambouillet, expressed his "concern" that the plan required the KLA forces to be dismantled.[52] By the time Rambouillet talks began, Washington had already abandoned the more moderate Albanian leader, Ibrahim Rugova, in favor of the KLA guerrilla leader, Hashim Thaci. Contacts between the U.S. State Department and Thaci became increasingly cordial. According to one U.S. official, Thaci and Albright's top aide, James Rubin, developed a "good rapport" during Rambouillet, and the State Department in later weeks sent Rubin to personally deliver an invitation to Thaci and other KLA members to visit the United States.[53] In contrast to Turkey, where U.S. officials claimed that as long as the Kurdish PKK guerrillas continued to engage in "terrorism" the U.S. would not support them, the Clinton administration embraced the KLA and was largely responsible for pressuring Yugoslavia to allow KLA participation at Rambouillet.

The interests of the KLA and the United States appeared to be merging. Bosnia taught leaders of Kosovo's Albanian separatist movement that Washington wanted to dominate Balkan affairs. Those ethnic groups that welcomed a U.S. military presence would benefit from the relationship. In exchange for Washington's support for the political and territorial aspirations of the Muslim government, U.S. military presence was introduced in Bosnia, where it continued for a fourth year. Similarly in Kosovo, Washington believed a U.S.-led NATO presence would be beneficial since it would extend NATO's influence to yet another part of the Balkans, while Albanian separatists welcomed NATO—convinced that the United States would ultimately help them take Kosovo from Serbia and call their own.

If Washington's only interest at Rambouillet was to ensure minority rights for Albanians within Yugoslavia, the issue could have been resolved immediately and peacefully. The Yugoslav government was willing to negotiate on minority rights. What was more important to the Clinton administration was to ensure that NATO, not the United Nations, emerged as Europe's policeman in Kosovo. Washington kept pressing for the implementation of U.S. and NATO troops in Kosovo, with vast policing powers that would go well above those of Yugoslav authorities. NATO would have free reign not just in Kosovo, but throughout Serbia and Montenegro. Yugoslavia could never accept this situation if it wanted to preserve its sovereignty. Clinton administration officials were less than forthcoming on their reasons for wanting U.S. troops in Kosovo. It was argued that the conflict could not be resolved by any other means. "There is a zero chance that the Kosovar Albanians will sign on to this deal if the U.S. does not participate in its implementation," Albright argued repeatedly at Rambouillet.[54]

While Washington supported the KLA during the Rambouillet talks, pressure was intensified on the Serbs as U.S. representatives continuously repeated the threat that NATO planes would attack Yugoslavia if talks failed. Washington's interventionists, obsessed with destroying Milosevic, whom they blamed for the wars in Slovenia, Croatia, and Bosnia, were itching to witness a long-awaited retribution against Serbia. *Washington Post* editors praised the possibility of NATO military intervention as "the right thing to do."[55] On the other hand, the *Washington Times*, the *Post*'s conservative competition, published far more critical editorials against the administration's policy on Kosovo. One *Washington Times* op-ed accused the Clinton administration of making Rambouillet nothing less than "a third partition of Yugoslavia."[56] Another *Washington Times* op-ed criticized U.S. policy as "captive to inflammatory rhetoric, based on propaganda, and used to demonize the Serbs over the last eight years in order to rally domestic political support."[57]

Even as Rambouillet negotiations were taking place, events in Bosnia would foreshadow to the Serbs what would happen if NATO were allowed to take over Kosovo. In March 1999, the town of Brcko, the only link between two sections of the Bosnian Serb republic, was taken from the Serbs. The town was made into a "neutral zone" and given "international supervision" by a decision of an American arbitrator. An even greater number of American NATO forces were quickly moved into Brcko to secure the area. The practical result of the decision was to split Bosnian Serb territory and subjugate the Serbs to Bosnia's central government and the will of NATO. In practical terms, Bosnian Serbs were under foreign occupation. By now, the bottom-line decisions on Bosnia's internal affairs, particularly security issues, were guided by the central Muslim-Croat government and their American overseers—with Europeans acquiescing to U.S. policy. NATO's military presence in Bosnia meant that local Serbs had no say in what oftentimes appeared to be arbitrary decisions imposed by foreign powers.

Foreign meddling in Bosnia's internal affairs culminated in an incident in March 1999 when Carlos Westerndorp, a senior international mediator on Bosnia, dismissed the democratically elected Bosnian Serb president, Nikola Poplasen. Although Bosnian Serbs strongly protested against what they called Westerndorp's gross abuse of his mandate, the situation proved yet again who was really in charge in the region. NATO soldiers took unusual security precautions in order to prevent any unrest by patrolling the streets of Brcko and setting up rigorous roadblocks. At the time, a U.S. soldier shot and killed a local Bosnian Serb Radical party official. Although the act was presumed to have been a possible case of mistaken identity, Bosnian Serb authorities had no say over the matter. It demonstrated that U.S. soldiers policing a foreign country were completely unaccountable for their actions to local authorities. The lack of ability to control one's territory and to impose law, order, and punishment on one's own land constituted a clear loss of sovereignty.

Like in Bosnia, Milosevic knew that once NATO was in Kosovo, there was no stopping the U.S.-led military alliance from completely controlling the region, imposing any number of decisions on local affairs, and even expanding its actions to include hunting down alleged war criminals throughout Serbia and Montenegro. Apart from Kosovo's great historical, cultural, and religious significance to the Serbs, the Yugoslav and Serbian leadership knew that by giving up Kosovo, they would be giving up control over their sovereign territory.

By the end of February 1999, as an increasing number of U.S. warplanes were sent to NATO bases in Europe to back up NATO's threat against Yugoslavia, the Yugoslav army massed thousands of heavily armed troops in northern areas of Kosovo in preparation for a confrontation with KLA rebels and to counter a possible NATO invasion. Anticipating that an oncoming NATO air attack would strengthen the KLA's military position, KLA guerrillas intensified their attacks on Yugoslav police and Serbian civilians. The *New York Times* reported that in early March 1999, KLA guerrillas killed two Serbian brothers in northern Kosovo and began "performing hit-and-run ambushes and shootings" against Yugoslav police of which several were killed and 11 injured, just in the first week of March.[58] The Yugoslav army responded by cracking down on KLA strongholds throughout Kosovo. As fighting escalated, 1,400 unarmed monitors of the Organization for Security and Cooperation in Europe (OSCE) left Kosovo. U.S. personnel were withdrawn from the Belgrade embassy as NATO prepared for attack.

Just days before the U.S.-led NATO bombardment of Yugoslavia, President Clinton said that "in dealing with aggressors in the Balkans, hesitation is a license to kill."[59] In the Clinton administration's ongoing moralistic approach to foreign affairs, the perception of an impending human tragedy in Kosovo was sufficient to give NATO the legal justification to bomb a sovereign country. Clinton branded Yugoslavia an "aggressor," a country conducting military action on its own soil to defend itself against an armed insurgency sponsored externally from Albania, whereas imminent U.S.-led NATO cross-border attacks against a sovereign nation were deemed by Clinton to be justified. This absurd scenario received little public debate among Washington's legal scholars. Again, as in the case of U.S. support for sending arms to the Bosnian Muslims in violation of the

U.N. arms embargo several years earlier, the ends seemed to justify the means in the Washington mindset.

As senators debated the role of the United States in a NATO bombing campaign of Yugoslavia, a few dissenting voices were heard. "If we start a massive bombing campaign, we [would be] going to war" said Republican Senator Don Nickles of Oklahoma. Texas Republican Senator Kay Bailey Hutchison criticized the Clinton administration for not seeking congressional approval for the bombing campaign and cautioned that the U.S. would be "picking sides in a civil war where U.S. security interests are not clear."[60] Interventionist forces in the Senate trumpeted the familiar calls of sensationalism in pushing for U.S. action. "It's about genocide and ethnic cleansing," rang the familiar tune in support of U.S. military action from Senator Joseph R. Biden, Jr. of Delaware, the ranking Democrat on the Foreign Relations Committee.

Clinton continued his propaganda campaign to rally the American public and Congress behind his war against the Serbs on the eve of bombing. At a speech to a labor group on March 23, he compared Milosevic to "Hitler," talked of "ethnic cleansing," and urged Americans to "stand up to brutality and the killing of innocent people."[61] Ironically, it was the United States, under Clinton's command, that was poised to kill a large number of innocent people as the U.S.-led NATO bombing campaign over Yugoslavia would bring death and destruction to thousands of Yugoslavs. After a strong public appeal by Clinton, the U.S. Senate gave in to emotional arguments of the president and voted to support the air campaign without a thorough debate. The vote was taken even though many members were still astonishingly misinformed about the complexities of Kosovo, and even its location. Some members of the Senate contacted at the time were unaware that Kosovo was in fact part of Serbia.

NATO BOMBS FALL ON YUGOSLAVIA

With the Yugoslav government refusing to sign an agreement at Rambouillet that would cede Kosovo to NATO, and ultimately to the KLA, Washington prepared for war. The first goal of NATO air strikes was to destroy Yugoslavia's integrated air defense system, followed by attacks on Serbian military targets. The Clinton administration refused to concede that the United States would be acting as an air force of the KLA. However, it was clear whose side NATO was on—at least to the KLA. The KLA was not only supportive of the bombing, but also appealed to NATO to provide heavy weapons to help their guerrilla forces fight the Yugoslav army and reestablish their military supply lines from neighboring Albania—cut off by Yugoslav special forces. In the coming weeks, KLA guerrillas helped NATO forces locate Serbian targets in Kosovo.[62] The government of Albania had already recognized an independent "Kosova"—as it was called by the KLA. Albania would drop its pretense of neutrality even further as President Rexhep Mejdani officially asked the United States to arm the KLA rebels at an April 1999 NATO summit meeting in Washington.[63]

NATO's decision to attack a sovereign nation for the first time in its 50-year history was a dramatic transformation of the organization's original purpose of protecting Western Europe against a Soviet invasion. At a time when NATO was debating its future strategic interests, its military operation in Yugoslavia would test Washington's ability to control NATO and the willingness of its member nations to follow the U.S. lead. Although the Clinton administration initially stated that primary targets were fixed Yugoslav military installations, by March 23 NATO commanders said their strikes against Serbia would be broader and more punishing than originally envisioned. The Supreme Allied Commander, U.S. General Wesley K. Clark, was given authority to strike at any targets he chose after the bombing started.

With NATO air strikes imminent, the Yugoslav government declared a state of emergency and thousands of military reservists were called up for duty. The first attack came on March 24, 1999, as NATO cruise missiles pounded air defenses near Belgrade—the first time the city was bombed since Hitler's attacks in World War II. The operation was predominantly an American one, including U.S. stealth bombers, fighters, cruise missiles, and military strategists. As air raid sirens sounded in the Yugoslav capital, residents huddled in basements and bomb shelters, while many were left without electricity. The bombing unleashed anger at the United States within Yugoslavia and throughout Europe. Although Washington believed NATO bombings would intimidate Milosevic and erode his public support, instead of turning against their leader in the face of NATO attacks, the Serbian public rallied behind their commander-in-chief. Milosevic was perceived as the undisputed protector of the Serbian people—both against KLA terrorism in Kosovo and now against a U.S.-led NATO aggression. While acknowledging NATO's overwhelming power over their small country, Yugoslav defense forces stood their ground. On March 28, Washington was astonished when Yugoslav missiles downed a stealth F-117A Nighthawk designed to be nearly invisible to radar. The Serbian people answered U.S.-led NATO attacks with defiance. Hundreds of thousands of residents of Belgrade rallied in the streets and ignored air raid sirens to attend the "music against bombs" rock concerts organized in protest of NATO attacks. Defiant Serbian teenagers wore t-shirts printed with a large target symbol to show their disgust that such awesome power was being used against their small country.

Demonstrators around the world joined anti-NATO bombing demonstrations. In Moscow, angry protesters fired a grenade at the U.S. embassy. The Russian government recalled its NATO delegate to protest the raids.

Angry protesters vandalized the American embassy in Skopje, Macedonia, and people took to the streets in Greece and Italy to show their support for Yugoslavia and anger at NATO. In Australia, thousands of pro-Serbian protesters who held signs comparing President Clinton to Adolf Hitler attacked the U.S. Consulates in Sydney and Melbourne. From Paris, to London, to Athens, to Washington, D.C., Serbs living in the diaspora, Greeks, and other opponents of the bombing raids showed anger and sadness at the American-led war in Europe.

The Clinton administration fought criticism by launching an intense public relations campaign in its continuing war of words against the Serbs. The administration dominated the nation's airwaves with dawn-to-midnight arguments in support of the policy to bomb Yugoslavia. The media campaign focused on what Clinton called a moral imperative and national self-interest in halting Yugoslav president Milosevic's "aggression" in Kosovo. Clinton's speech, made just hours before he sent U.S. bombers over Yugoslavia, was meant to explain his reasoning to the American public but ended up being what one syndicated columnist described as "a disgraceful performance" due to its "incoherence and simple-mindedness, for disorganization and sheer intellectual laziness."[64] Having just come out of a year-long scandal covered by the media 24 hours a day that resulted in his impeachment, Clinton was anxious to get media pundits focused on another issue. In a private conversation relating to Clinton's sudden switch to fighting a war against Yugoslavia, one Democratic member of Congress said off the record, "I don't think he cares for anything but himself . . . he desperately wanted to look presidential after the impeachment trial brought such embarrassment to his presidency."

At about the same time as the White House launched its public relations campaign, Albanian supporters of the KLA in the United States launched a campaign of their own. In late March, pro-KLA Albanian activists in the United States were putting out allegations against the Serbs faster than anyone could counter them. One of the first of these charges was the claim made repeatedly by Albanian representatives on American television that only women and children were coming out of Kosovo, and that the Yugoslav army was executing the men. At the same time, although the Associated Press reported what was happening to many Albanian men of fighting age, the information received little attention in the mainstream media. The report said that KLA rebels set up checkpoints along the main road near the Albanian border and were "stopping ethnic Albanians as they fled the province and sending men back to fight the Serbs."[65] Albanian television apparently regularly carried statements by the KLA ordering all Kosovo Albanian men to join ranks within one month or face reprisals by the KLA "police." In the months to come, as international media flocked to refugee camps in Albania, journalists reported that refugee camps in northern Albania were "a recruiting ground for the KLA."[66] According to a May 5 *Washington Post* article, some Albanian

KLA guerrillas were sending their family members, including their wives and children, to safety in Albanian refugee camps, while they remained to fight against the Yugoslav army.[67] Yet claims of "missing Albanian men" would be reiterated by the White House, State Department, and Pentagon throughout the weeks to come.

NATO ESCALATES WAR, YUGOSLAV CIVILIAN CASUALTIES MOUNT

With Serbs not willing to back down, the only option the White House had to offer was to drop more bombs, broaden the NATO assault, and step up the propaganda war. As NATO bombing intensified against Yugoslav army troops in Kosovo, KLA rebels took advantage of the opportunity to launch even more attacks. The KLA, operating on the outskirts of the provincial capital of Pristina, increased their sniper attacks on Serbs in Pristina and battled Yugoslav security forces in one neighborhood where Serbian civilians took up arms to fight against the KLA alongside government troops.[68] The newest confrontations between the KLA and Yugoslav government forces, as well as NATO attacks on Kosovo towns and villages including Pristina, Novi Badovac, Susica, and Livadje, led to a new wave of refugees from Kosovo.[69] Some Albanian refugees headed for other parts of Yugoslavia, while most left the country for Albania and Macedonia where many had relatives. U.N. reports estimated that 260,000 Albanians were displaced in Kosovo itself, 60,000 crossed into Albania, 22,000 fled to Macedonia, and 30,000 sought safety in the Yugoslav republic of Montenegro. Over 100,000 Serbs from Kosovo were also displaced— almost half of the pre-war Serbian population in Kosovo. It seemed that by escalating the crisis, the White House was creating an even greater number of refugees—the opposite of the stated goal of the bombing.

The exodus of Albanians from Kosovo fueled the Clinton administration accusations that "ethnic cleansing" was being committed by the Serbs. Some media reports appeared to support Washington's claims, but their sources were suspect. Although one *Washington Post* article said that Yugoslav "government troops have ordered the evacuation of whole suburbs of Pristina," a *Washington Times* report noted the source for the claim was the KLA rebel leader, Hashim Thaci, who said that "Serbian forces rounded up 100,000 people in the center of Pristina" and "were trying to force people out of the town."[70] Thaci's sources of information were secondhand at best, given the fact that he had fled the country several weeks earlier. The Clinton administration often echoed such KLA claims. Countering this were less publicized news statements, such as a *Washington Times* article that said "most residents of the provincial capital say they were leaving of their own free accord and [were] not being forced out at gunpoint, as residents of several western cities and villages in Kosovo claimed has been happening to them."[71] The *Washington Times* revealed

also that the claim by NATO spokesman Jamie Shea that Pristina had
been "almost totally destroyed" was countered by Albanian residents
from Pristina who made their way into Macedonia at the time and said
"their city was still largely intact."[72] Most likely, while there may have
been some Yugoslav army attempts to move ethnic Albanian communities
in an attempt to flush out the KLA, Albanian civilians, like Serbian civilians from Kosovo, mostly fled due to fear for their lives in a war situation
and lack of adequate food, electricity, and water, which was disrupted by
NATO attacks. With Kosovo's Serbian population blaming the Albanians
for NATO's attacks on Yugoslavia, vengeful acts undoubtedly occurred,
causing Albanians to flee the expected wrath of angry Serbian neighbors.
Although such harassment and looting surely occurred in this chaotic, wartime situation in Kosovo, there was no evidence it was happening as a
part of a policy of Yugoslavia's professional army.

The Clinton administration and the U.S.-led NATO military command,
however, searched for every possible incident to exaggerate the humanitarian crisis and demonize the Serbs. Sensationalist KLA propaganda
played into Washington's need to justify its policy as a moral imperative.
With NATO attacks not delivering the desired results, the Clinton administration pressed for escalating the conflict. General Wesley K. Clark was
given a mandate to widen the attack to "command and control centers"
and military infrastructure across Yugoslavia, including downtown Belgrade.

While humanitarian concerns for Albanians in Kosovo were the staple
of Clinton administration rhetoric, the destruction of Yugoslavia was virtually ignored. By April 1, NATO warplanes had launched over 1,000
attacks on Yugoslavia, resulting in the deaths of dozens of civilians and
hundreds of serious injuries as houses and apartment buildings were leveled. Hospitals and medical centers were hit in the cities of Nis, Leskovac,
Djakovica, and other towns. Yugoslavia closed most of its schools and
universities after NATO missiles damaged or destroyed several dozen elementary schools, high schools, and universities in the cities of Belgrade,
Nis, Novi Sad, Leskovac, and towns in Kosovo. When NATO missiles hit
a storage facility for chemicals, fertilizers, and other hazardous material
in the eastern Serbian town of Pancevo, thousands of people were exposed
to poisonous fumes and the soil was contaminated in the surrounding
countryside—an important agricultural region for Yugoslavia. NATO missiles also fell on television and radio broadcast buildings located in densely
populated areas. Attacks on Yugoslav industries, which included bombing
of factories manufacturing household appliances in Urosevac, Pancevo,
Cacak, Pristina, and other areas, left thousands of Yugoslavs without jobs
and unable to support their families.

NATO's campaign of bombing bridges in the following weeks resulted
in the destruction of almost all bridges in and around Belgrade, some of

which dated back to the early part of the century—bridges that even Hitler had spared during World War II. The Clinton administration and the American general commanding NATO forces justified their action as bombing of military targets because bridges, highways, and railroads could be used to transport military equipment and soldiers. But these are also used by cars, buses, and trains filled with people going to work, shopping, and visiting their friends and relatives, or farmers bringing their produce to the market in town. The Yugoslavs could not simply stop living because NATO decided to bomb their country. Residents of Belgrade hoped to save some of the city's bridges by standing on them and turning themselves into human shields. To the Serbs, the bridges that NATO was mercilessly bombing were no less important than San Francisco's Golden Gate bridge is to Americans. The bridges in Belgrade were both historical monuments and the lifeline of the city.

By April 3, NATO attacked a heavily populated area of downtown Belgrade for the first time, setting ablaze two government buildings, the Ministry for Internal Affairs and Ministry of the Interior of the Republic of Serbia housing the Serbian police headquarters. The buildings stood close to a major university medical complex, forcing doctors and nurses to move patients to bomb shelters. A senior Clinton administration official said at the time that the NATO targets, including bridges and Yugoslav government buildings, were "deliberately chosen and timed to maximize their psychological impact and leave the Yugoslav authorities uncertain of what and where the next strike will be."[73] A *Washington Post* article on NATO missiles hitting downtown Belgrade was dwarfed by several large photographs of thousands of Albanian refugees in Macedonian refugee camps. Constant pictures of the plight of Albanians were to be used in the coming months to justify the bombing of Serbs and suffering of Serbian civilians.

The Clinton administration and NATO commanders called the death and destruction taking place in Yugoslavia "collateral damage." Already, however, it was clear that NATO was prepared to bomb all areas of Yugoslavia they considered to be military targets, no matter how close they were to civilian areas. Week after week, the main intent of the bombing was to fulfill NATO's military objectives, regardless of their consequences to civilians. During the war in Bosnia, when civilians in Sarajevo were killed or injured during fighting between Bosnian Serbs and Muslim forces, the Clinton administration accused the Serbs of "war crimes." Now, the Clinton administration took no responsibility for its own "criminal" behavior against Yugoslav civilians. NATO seemed to be sparing nothing in Yugoslavia in blurring the line between military and civilian targets. NATO warplanes pummeled Belgrade's international airport, fuel depots, and heating plants, polluting the air in Belgrade with acrid black smoke, shattering windows of apartment buildings, and killing three civilian work-

ers and injuring five others.[74] As NATO widened its attacks on military
and civilian areas throughout Serbia, two refinery workers were killed and
four wounded when NATO hit the Pancevo oil refinery, three more people were wounded when a fuel depot was hit near Kraljevo, and a 73-
year-old woman was killed and seven were wounded when NATO missiles
pounded the "Sloboda" factory making electrical appliances in the industrial town of Cacak—also destroying surrounding homes.[75]

Major U.S. newspapers and television channels were almost exclusively
flashing images of Albanian refugees and hence continually reinforcing the
Clinton administration's argument that bombing Yugoslavia was justified.
On April 5, NATO missiles hit another 27 targets in Yugoslavia, including
a row of apartment buildings in the town of Aleksinac, killing 11 people,
including men, women, children, and several elderly individuals, and injuring 30 others. At least three NATO bombs also damaged scores of
buildings, an ice cream factory, and an animal feed plant. It was the worst
single report of civilian casualties in Yugoslavia since NATO bombing
began, yet the next day, two major U.S. newspapers, the *Washington Post*
and the *New York Times*, continued to solely feature the faces of Albanian
refugees and stories of forced expulsion. The American public was shown
no photographs or television footage of dead or wounded Serbian civilians
from the attack on Aleksinac—only brief images of rubble of destroyed
buildings. It was not until two days later that a single photograph of a
wounded Serbian boy was shown on page 10 of an April 7 issue of the
New York Times. On the day of the attack on Aleksinac, CNN featured
long segments of reports from refugee camps in Albania, with footage of
elderly refugees and Albanian women crying, while a report on NATO
bombing of Aleksinac, shown without substantial commentary, was accompanied by less than 10 seconds of video showing wreckage from buildings
and covered dead corpses on a stretcher.

On April 7, NATO missiles reduced much of downtown Pristina to rubble, killing at least 10 civilians, destroying the post office, a welfare center,
at least 30 stores, dozens of houses, and government buildings, the Serbian
National Bank offices, and a Serbian Orthodox cemetery.[76] The reaction
by NATO was for its Supreme Commander, American General Wesley
Clark, to ask for even more U.S. and allied warplanes to intensify NATO's
attack on Yugoslavia. Again, only bland photographs of the debris from
houses were shown in U.S. newspapers. In the weeks to come, although
media wire services regularly reported NATO attacks and Yugoslav civilian casualties, the incidents tended to be downplayed by the mainstream
U.S. media, and few if any sympathetic photographs accompanied the reports.

Yugoslavia appealed to NATO and the United States to at least stop
the bombing on the upcoming Serbian Orthodox Easter by offering a unilateral cessation of all its military actions against the KLA. The Kosovo

Albanian leader, Ibrahim Rugova, was already participating in talks with Yugoslav President Milosevic on how Serbs and Albanians could live together in Kosovo. On Saturday, April 10, thousands of Americans of Serbian, Greek, Russian, and other ethnic backgrounds rallied in front of the White House to appeal to President Clinton to stop the bombing for the Christian Orthodox Easter holiday that Sunday. The response from the White House was cold and intransigent. NATO continued to bomb.

On April 12, NATO warplanes fired several missiles in three separate attacks hitting a passenger train crossing a bridge through southern Serbia. Three railway cars were incinerated and 27 people were killed, including a large number of children. Although foreign reporters arrived on the scene to witness workers pulling charred bodies out of the wreckage, no photographs of victims of the NATO attack made the pages of major U.S. newspapers. An April 13 *New York Times* article that described the gory details of the aftermath featured only a photograph of the wrecked train. By putting a human face on the victims of NATO bombings, the Americans public would have likely cried out against the policy. Instead, the U.S. media supported the Clinton administration policy by keeping a lid on sympathy and emotion in week after week of bombing, "dehumanizing" the enemy's victims, and waiting for the Yugoslavs to surrender. To deemphasize the train attack fiasco, the Clinton administration stepped up its propaganda. The White House immediately held a press conference in which Yugoslav President Milosevic was accused of war crimes. Although no new information or newsworthy items were presented, the press conference managed to effectively monopolize much of television air time that day. The train tragedy received no further mention.

Two days later, NATO bombed a column of Albanian refugees traveling through the town of Djakovica in Kosovo, hitting wagons and tractors and killing 64 people. NATO at first denied the attack, claiming Yugoslav jets were responsible, but later retracted the statement and said instead that NATO warplanes fired at the column under the belief that they were hitting military targets. President Clinton continued to defend his policy of bombing Yugoslavia by saying that civilian deaths were "regrettable" and "inevitable" in warfare.[77] Clinton was not willing to concede, however, that civilian deaths were also "regrettable" and "inevitable" in warfare between the Yugoslav army and KLA guerrillas, and did not occur as a policy of "genocide" or "ethnic cleansing" as the Clinton administration claimed. One standard of warfare was applied to the United States and another to Yugoslavia. When NATO bombs fell on Belgrade on April 18, killing a 3-year-old girl, Milica Rakic, as she slept in her crib, the Associated Press reported the incident, but neither the *New York Times* nor the *Washington Post* mentioned the attack. In comparison, through years of war in Bosnia, both papers, as well as U.S. television channels, often featured stories of injured children in Sarajevo with poignant images of their faces.

   Although the White House and NATO military officials insisted that the killing of Yugoslav civilians was accidental, at least one civilian target was planned and executed with deliberate calculation. On April 22, NATO warplanes attacked and destroyed the Serbian Radio and Television building, killing over 30 Yugoslav reporters who were buried in the rubble and seriously wounding 18 other employees. Again, no photographs of the killed or wounded journalists made the pages of either the *New York Times* or the *Washington Post*. Secretary of State Albright, her deputy, James Rubin, and other Clinton administration officials repeatedly claimed the Serbian television was Milosevic's "propaganda machine," and for that reason considered Yugoslav journalists as a legitimate target. In explaining the reason for this and other attacks, Pentagon spokesman Ken Bacon said it was to send a message to the Serbian populace to "put pressure on their leadership to end this."[78] However, NATO was clearly crossing a moral line. Targeting journalists as a tool of military coercion was the same as accusations against alleged Bosnian Serb targeting of "civilian areas." If a foreign terrorist group decided to bomb the Voice of American building in Washington, D.C., because it allegedly served as a "propaganda machine" for the United States, Americans would be appalled. The standards applied at home, however, were not applied abroad where NATO warplanes were involved in what were becoming clearly criminal acts. If the U.N. War Crimes Tribunal was a truly objective body, it would have surely judged NATO actions against civilians to be a war crime. The Tribunal, however, made no such statement.

   As NATO stepped up its aerial assault on Yugoslavia, NATO bombs destroyed dozens of homes on April 28 in the Serbian village of Surburica, killing at least 20 civilians, including five children. The incident was again discretely reported in the *New York Times* and the *Washington Post* without any photographs of the victims. As part of an effort to destroy all bridges in Yugoslavia, on May 1, NATO missiles cut a bus in half crossing a bridge in central Kosovo, killing 47 people, including women and children. NATO planes even attacked an ambulance that was assisting people after the attack. Two days later NATO missiles destroyed a second bus near Savine Vode in Kosovo, west of Pec, killing 20 people. As civilian deaths from NATO bombing mounted, on May 6 NATO cluster bombs hit a hospital, outdoor market, and university in the city of Nis, killing 15 civilians and wounding 70, including an elderly Serbian woman who was killed as she carried her groceries home. Thirty homes were also destroyed in the attack. While Reuters and other wire services reported the incident, neither the *New York Times* nor the *Washington Post* covered the story, and it was given only a brief mention on television news channels.

Although Clinton administration officials argued that the Serbian people were being fed propaganda, the American public was itself unaware of the level of suppression of information taking place within the United States. All NATO attacks on Yugoslav civilians were downplayed both by the White House and the U.S. media, so that the American public was not aware of the level of death and destruction inflicted by U.S.-led NATO warplanes on the mostly Serbian population in Yugoslavia. The May 7 NATO attack on the Chinese embassy in Belgrade, however, could not be swept under the rug quite so easily as attacks on Serbs. The Chinese government was furious, as the attack resulted in the deaths of three Chinese journalists and brought serious injury to 20 others. Anti-U.S. and anti-NATO demonstrations erupted throughout China, and the American embassy in China was attacked by rioters. Unlike in weeks of attacks against Yugoslav civilians, where no apology was ever issued by President Clinton, the Clinton administration issued several days of apologies to the Chinese for what he called "an isolated tragic mistake" due to what U.S. officials called an intelligence failure.[79]

The Chinese embassy bombing, however, was anything but an "isolated" tragedy. On May 10, NATO missiles continued to pound civilian areas, hitting a Serbian village in Kosovo, killing five people, including an elderly married couple and a four-year-old girl. Four days later, on May 14, NATO dropped cluster bombs on yet another convoy of ethnic Albanian refugees camping at the Korisa village in Kosovo, killing 87 people, many of whose bodies were burned beyond recognition. State Department spokesman James Rubin at first denied responsibility, saying that based on what he called previous "Serbian propaganda," it was likely to have been another Serbian lie. The next day, however, the denial was retracted. Pentagon spokesman Ken Bacon justified the attack at a press briefing, arguing the village was a "legitimate military target" because it was used as a military camp for the Yugoslav army.[80] Again, unlike in the case of attacks on Serbian civilians, NATO issued a statement after the attack on Albanian refugees at Korisa that it "deeply regrets accidental civilian casualties that were caused by this attack."[81]

As in the incident when NATO bombed the train in southern Serbia, Clinton administration officials fought off possible criticism of their latest fiasco with fresh accusations against the Serbs. Immediately after the Korisa attack, Defense Secretary William S. Cohen claimed that 100,000 Albanian men had disappeared and may have been executed by Serbian troops. It was a tactic that worked very well in the war of words against Serbs—diverting attention from one failure by demonizing the Serbs. U.S. government accusations were rarely scrutinized by the press and were usually accepted at face value. Interestingly, after the war was over, the accusation that 100,000 Albanian men were missing was never heard again.

BOMBING AND PROPAGANDA INTENSIFIES: PEACE DEAL ON THE HORIZON

By mid-May, Washington's interventionists were clamoring for U.S. ground troops in Kosovo to prevent a "humanitarian disaster" for Albanian refugees in the coming winter. "NATO must be prepared to use ground troops," cried out editors of the *Washington Post* in a May 20 editorial. Recalling how a similar media hype of the alleged humanitarian catastrophe said to be imminent for Bosnia's Muslims prior to the winter of 1992 was used as a catalyst for more aggressive U.S. action, Washington's "humanitarian hawks" were pushing to extend the Kosovo conflict to include American ground forces. However, no alarm was raised by Washington's human rights–conscious activists for the ongoing Yugoslav civilian deaths and destruction by NATO. The U.S. media continued to be a conduit of one-sided images in support of White House propaganda as it put forth an unsympathetic depiction of Yugoslav civilian casualties from NATO bombs.

On May 20, NATO missiles pounded Belgrade, hitting the Dragisa Misic hospital where I was born. Four hospital patients were killed and the lives of hundreds of infants and pregnant women were endangered as doctors scrambled to move them to another location. *Associated Press Television News* had video footage available that showed two corpses in the hospital morgue, including a "woman's body caked in blood and half of her right arm missing."[82] None of the U.S. news channels decided to use the footage. In comparison, gory scenes from Bosnia, which were a staple of daily American television reports. The *Washington Post* featured only a small photograph of the destroyed hospital on the bottom of a front page article, while the *New York Times* buried a similar photograph on page 13, preceded on page 12 by a larger photograph of Albanian children and their drawings of "war crimes." Neither newspaper showed the human face of Serbs after the NATO attack.

Drawing attention away from NATO attacks on the hospital in Belgrade on May 20, the *New York Times* printed a photograph under a caption that read "Evidence of Atrocities" and "Corroboration of a Videotape of a Massacre."[83] The photograph was taken from a two-month-old video made by a Kosovo Albanian which showed dead bodies of Albanian men. The caption claimed 127 "ethnic Albanian men" were killed in the village of Izbica on March 28, and that the State Department matched the video to "aerial images of Izbica where NATO had reported sighting mass graves." The idea portrayed by the State Department and repeated by numerous media sources was one of "mass graves" recalling World War II "genocide" and "ethnic cleansing," and was the subject of widespread media speculation and sensationalism. The reality of war in Kosovo, however, was that both KLA fighters and Yugoslav solders were being killed.

On the same day that the *New York Times* printed the photograph of these Albanian men, the Associated Press reported that KLA rebels "ambushed a Yugoslav unit, killing 20 soldiers" and that the rebels "buried the soldiers."[84] The situation was clearly the same. Yet few in Washington were willing to understand the realities of war. Instead, the U.S. government and media were willing participants in sensationalizing the Kosovo crisis to support their political goals.

Amid a growing propaganda war against the Serbs, on May 21 British Foreign Secretary Robin Cook met with U.S. Secretary of State Madeleine Albright and convinced her that contingency plans needed to be made for the introduction of U.S. ground troops in Kosovo, even within a hostile environment. In an interview on PBS's *Newshour* the same day, Cook praised NATO bombing as "successful" and was positively glowing in describing the KLA when he said, "I talked with Thaci last week and he said his forces are doing better." State Department spokesman Rubin similarly reiterated in daily press conferences that NATO bombings had been successful and that the KLA guerrillas were "doing well" against Yugoslav government forces. The British government, as well as the Clinton administration, nevertheless continued to deny that NATO attacks were aimed at helping the KLA.

The NATO bombing campaign over Yugoslavia was by now clearly a U.S.- and British-led operation. The British NATO spokesman, Jamie Shea, was in charge of the "spin" in support of NATO action, while U.S. General Wesley Clark was in charge of the bombing. The Clinton-Blair policy of escalation was increasingly opposed by Europe's continental powers. As Europe grew weary of Washington's aggressive approach in dealing with the Balkans, talk of ending the bombing and getting back to negotiations grew more prevalent in many European capitals. With NATO continuing to make bombing blunders or inflicting what it called "collateral damage" against Yugoslav civilians, hospitals, embassies, and ethnic Albanian refugees, support for the bombing was quickly eroding among important NATO allies, including France, Germany, Italy, Greece, and Canada.

German Foreign Minister Joschka Fischer headed for Washington to press Albright for a diplomatic solution, fearing that NATO was losing its moral standing.[85] Italian Premier Massimo D'Alema urged an implementation of a three-day cease-fire, while Canadian Foreign Minister Lloyd Axworthy emphasized that "it is important that we accelerate and underline the important search for a resolution of the conflict."[86] Russian Special Envoy for Kosovo Viktor Chernomyrdin scolded the Clinton administration in a May 27 *Washington Post* editorial in which he stated that the "United States lost its moral right to be regarded as a leader of the free democratic world when its bombs shattered the ideals of liberty and democracy in Yugoslavia" and accused Washington of violating "international law, the Helsinki agreements, and the entire world order that took shape after World War II."[87] He appealed to NATO leaders to "show the courage to suspend the air raids" or else he threatened to "advise Russia's president to suspend Russian participation in the negotiating process, put an end to all military-technological cooperation with the United States and Western Europe, put off the ratification of START II and use Russia's veto as the United Nations debates a resolution on Yugoslavia." Closer to home, former President Jimmy Carter criticized the Clinton administration approach of "presenting an ultimatum to recalcitrant parties and then [taking] punitive action against the entire nation to force compliance."[88] "Even for the world's only superpower," Carter argued, "the ends don't always justify the means. . . . The United States' insistence on the use of cluster bombs, designed to kill or main humans is condemned almost universally and brings discredit to our nation."

As criticism grew, and less than one week after Chernomyrdin met with Yugoslav President Milosevic to discuss a plan by Russia and seven leading industrialized nations to end the Kosovo conflict, the U.N. War Crimes Tribunal indicted Slobodan Milosevic for war crimes. The indictment charged the Yugoslav president and four other senior officials of three counts of crimes against humanity and one count of violation of customs of war. The first was deportation, second and third were murder, and fourth was persecutions on political, racial, and religious grounds.[89] The indictment appeared to be yet another tool of political pressure against Milosevic, supported and encouraged by the White House. With NATO unable to "win" the war by coercing the Serbs to give up Kosovo, the Clinton administration was searching for other means to make Milosevic back down. As one diplomatic source at NATO headquarters in Brussels said, "it's another way of squeezing him."[90]

The war crimes indictment was based on unverified information from Albanian refugees, gathered with help from authorities in northern Albania—a region dominated by KLA guerrillas and their supporters with a vested interest in encouraging U.S. military actions against Yugoslavia. Furthermore, there was no credible evidence that any harassment or violence that may have been committed against Albanian civilians was approved by the Yugoslav government. On the contrary, the Yugoslav government had arrested several hundred individuals said to have been committing various types of crimes in Kosovo, including looting and violent crimes. While popular opinion on American talk shows attempted to correlate alleged war crimes with the very existence of Albanian refugees, the phenomenon of refugees in a war situation did not in and of itself indicate that crimes had been committed. Throughout human history, whenever an armed conflict has taken place, people have fled from danger. It was not unexpected that destruction caused by NATO bombing in Kosovo and intensified battles between the Yugoslav army and the KLA would cause a steady stream of primarily Albanian, but also Serbian, refugees. Yugoslavs of Albanian ethnicity, however, continued to live among Serbs and other ethnic groups in other parts of Yugoslavia, particularly in Belgrade, contradicting the claim that Serbs wanted to forcibly and permanently expel the Albanian population from Yugoslavia.

The political motivations behind the indictment against Milosevic were clear. The double standards of the War Crimes Tribunal demonstrated that the organization was an entirely politicized body, with little moral authority or credibility to pass judgment on the Yugoslav crisis. It was created by countries that were currently waging war against Yugoslavia, and its decisions were greatly influenced by the United States. Although Clinton administration officials claimed that the Tribunal's activities were independent, the United States was the main source of "evidence" to the body, the tribunal's presiding judge was American, and all indictments had U.S. approval.

The Tribunal was quick to indict Milosevic at a time when war was still going on, and at a time when it was impossible to investigate what was happening in Kosovo. When compared to the Tribunal's slow investigation of the Croatian government—considered by Washington to be an ally in U.S. operations in Bosnia—the political nature of the indictment was obvious. It took the Tribunal four years following the war in Croatia to finally recommend in March 1999 that three Croatian generals be indicted for the Croatian Army's war crimes, including summary executions of Serbs, indiscriminate shelling of Serbian civilian population, and "ethnic cleansing" during the 1995 assault on Krajina Serbs.[91] With regard to the attack, senior Canadian U.N. peacekeepers testified at the Tribunal that out of 3,000 shells fired at the Serb-populated city of Knin, less than 250 hit military targets, and that there was "no doubt in [their] mind that the Croats knew they were shelling civilian targets."[92] However, when Tribunal investigators asked for U.S. satellite photos of Knin as evidence that the Croat army was shelling civilian areas, Washington would not cooperate. Instead, an American lawyer at the tribunal, Clint Williamson, described the shelling of Knin as a "minor incident" and said the Pentagon told him Knin was a legitimate military target.[93] Although the Tribunal apparently had ample evidence of responsibility for war crimes by Croat President Tudjman, they still held off on indicting him—a stark contrast to their treatment of Milosevic.

While "international law" was the story of the week in Washington when Milosevic was indicted, the flagrant violation of international law by U.S.-led NATO forces on a daily basis was completely ignored. Washington's international lawyers seemed oblivious to the continuing war of aggression by NATO against Yugoslavia, and aggression committed by

Albania as it continued to fund and support an insurgency with weapons and men from KLA guerrilla bases in northern Albania. On June 2, NATO gave its first direct military support to a major KLA guerrilla offensive. NATO bombardment of Yugoslav military targets in Bucane and Ljumbarda enabled KLA rebel forces to capture the two Kosovo villages.[94] The White House and Pentagon continued to deny that it was helping the KLA, even though it was widely reported among the U.S. press that the KLA regularly communicated with NATO and kept NATO informed of KLA positions so that military attacks would solely be directed against the Yugoslav army. By June 8, NATO was dropping cluster bombs on Yugoslav troops that were gathered to thwart a KLA guerrilla offensive close to the Albanian border. The NATO attack resulted in a massive annihilation of Yugoslav soldiers, killing several hundred. As NATO attacked the Yugoslav army and its missiles continued to destroy Yugoslav factories, television stations, hospitals, schools, and private residences, killing and wounding thousands and leaving others without water and electricity, the television footage of the sad faces of Albanian refugees was continuously used to obscure the human suffering inflicted by NATO on Yugoslavia and justify NATO's "humanitarian war."

WASHINGTON'S POST-KOSOVO LEGACY IN THE BALKANS: VICTORY OR FAILURE?

Throughout eleven weeks of war, the majority of U.S. media analyses and reports focused not on whether the United States had a moral or legal right to bomb Yugoslavia, but instead on the political concerns of the White House, such as who was going to "blink" first, Milosevic or Clinton, and how Clinton was doing in the polls. On June 2, when the Yugoslav parliament voted to accept a peace plan that would include some form of peacekeeping forces in Kosovo, the war seemed near an end. The White House was pleased. The document accepted by the Yugoslav parliament and negotiated by Russian and Finnish envoys included a withdrawal of Yugoslav forces and a significant NATO and Russian presence as part of international security forces in Kosovo under the auspices of the United Nations.

The plan accepted by the Yugoslav parliament was described as a capitulation to NATO. Although it included NATO troops on Serbian soil, one major difference from the Rambouillet talks was that the forces were to be under U.N. auspices. Washington, however, viewed the U.N. as merely a front for what they intended to be a U.S.-led, NATO-dominated operation. A June 10 *Washington Post* headline read "NATO to Rule Kosovo." Washington's interventionists were ecstatic and immediately claimed victory for the Clinton policy on Kosovo. The victory, however, was a questionable one. With incoming NATO troops unlikely to intervene to protect Serbs from Albanian attacks, Albanians (including KLA members) returning to Kosovo would ultimately result in the expulsion of over 200,000 Serbs from the region.

The likely scenario of the looming "ethnic cleansing" of Serbs was of little concern to America's political and media establishment. By now, anti-Serb prejudice had sunk in so deep that many were unable to see the hypocrisy of their positions. *New York Times* columnist William Safire started an opinion piece on Kosovo by espousing the merits of "international moral standards," saying that instead of imposing a "burden on peacekeepers to protect minority Serbs," it would be "better to offer individual Serbs in Kosovo a relocation bonus to safety and let Kosovo victims have their independence."[95] A similar suggestion that Kosovo Albanians be given a "relocation bonus" to remain in Albania would have caused widespread indignation from one-sided moralists like Safire. In a similar fashion, addressing the likelihood that Albanians returning to Kosovo would instigate violence against Serbian residents, one reporter seemed content that the problem would be avoided, since "most Serbs, and Gypsies . . . are expected to flee the province before Kosovo Albanians return."[96] History appeared to be repeating itself. Just as anti-Serb propaganda left U.S. policymakers and the media indifferent to the ethnic cleansing of 500,000 Serbs from Krajina in 1995, and 100,000 Serbs from Sarajevo in 1996, so too was anti-Serb propaganda in the Spring and Summer of 1999 desensitizing Washington to the impending ethnic cleansing of Serbs from Kosovo.

Washington was equally indifferent to Serbian victims throughout Yugoslavia. In his June 10 speech to the nation, President Clinton said, "this is a victory for our democratic values." Although the Clinton administration praised NATO's actions over Yugoslavia, in reality the bombing campaign was NATO at its worst. The Clinton administration brought further shame on his presidency. U.S.-led NATO bombing had killed at least four times as many people as had been killed in Kosovo the year before the bombing started. By June 1999, over 1,200 Yugoslav civilians were dead, one-third of which were children. Over 5,000 people were seriously injured, and thousands of homes, office buildings, factories, schools, medical centers, and other buildings were damaged or destroyed. As many as several thousand Yugoslav soldiers and recruits were mercilessly slaughtered. The destruction of bridges, heating plants, power plants, food processing facilities, and water refineries put the country at a standstill. While many hospitals were bombed, those that were left standing were often without water and electricity and unable to provide for the basic needs of the sick and elderly. Environmental damage from thousands of tons of missiles and bombs falling on Yugoslavia brought long-term harm to the country, while pollution from depleted uranium dropped in missiles threatened to bring untold consequences to people's health in the region. The contamination of the country's food and water supplies resulted in widespread illnesses, birth defects, and miscarriages among the population.

Washington seemed unwilling to take any responsibility for its actions. By the end of 11 weeks of bombing, the Clinton administration vowed to withhold any economic assistance to rebuild Yugoslavia's bridges and infrastructure while Milosevic was still in power. War reparations to Yugoslav civilians were not even mentioned. This meant that the mostly Serbian population of Yugoslavia would be helpless against the poverty and humanitarian disaster inflicted upon them by U.S.-led NATO attacks.

The fate of Serbs in Kosovo as a result of NATO's "victory" was even worse than that of Serbs in the rest of Yugoslavia. Having won the sought-after role of becoming the policeman of Kosovo, NATO immediately failed in its stated mission to provide a secure environment and protect all ethnic groups in the province. NATO did not even consider abiding by Security Council Resolution 1244 (1999), which called for the disarming of KLA rebels, nor respecting the military agreement it signed with Yugoslavia, which called for a limited number of Yugoslav police to return to border posts and to important Serbian religious sites in Kosovo. As a result, KLA guerrillas poured through the border from Albania unabated, while the Serbian population was almost completely unprotected and vulnerable to attack.

Predictably, armed KLA members and other Albanians started a brutal process of murder and intimidation of Serbs, and set out to destroy Serbian properties, monuments, churches, and monasteries, and ethnically cleanse Serbs from the region, under NATO's watchful eye. By the end of July 1999, only two months after the arrival of NATO troops as part of KFOR (Kosovo Force), over 200 Serbs had been killed by Albanians— an average of three people per day. During this period, several hundred Serbian homes were burned, over 20 Serbian Orthodox churches and Serbian cultural monuments were damaged or destroyed, and more than 150,000 Serbs fled Kosovo in fear for their lives. When the Serbs left in columns of cars, trucks, and trailers, with oxen and horses, Albanians went house to house, taking whatever they could find, and then setting fire to the homes as NATO troops looked on or looked the other way. In the city of Pristina, the 40,000 prewar population of Serbs fell to less than 1,000 by early August 1999. Albanians took over Serbian homes as well as restaurants, gas stations, and other businesses owned by Serbs who were forced to abandon their enterprises after being threatened by Albanians.

Those Serbs who chose to remain in Kosovo faced daily threats from their Albanian neighbors, and were unable to receive medical treatment as Albanians turned them away from local hospitals. Serbs were unable to shop in local stores due to a lack of adequate security. Even worse, many Serbs lived in well-founded fear of being attacked or murdered as the number of Serbs killed by the KLA and other armed Albanians grew daily. In mid-June, a Serbian professor and two Serbian workers at the University of Pristina were found with their hands bound, shot to death in a classroom. Although the *New York Times* reported the killings, only a small picture of the three bodies, laying in pools of blood, was printed on the bottom of page A12. The *Washington Post* did not even report the incident. In one particularly heinous incident, on July 24, 1999, in the village of Staro Gradsko, 14 Serbian farmers harvesting hay were herded together by Albanian KLA members and shot at close range. The Serbian farmers had requested NATO protection seven days prior to the killings, but their pleas were ignored. Although the story was reported, no photographs of the dead Serbian farmers were ever printed in the *Washington Post* or *New York Times*. Yet again, no human face was put on the Serbian victims, hence downplaying the gravity of the murders.

One example of NATO's failed social engineering in Kosovo was an attempt to create inter-communal cooperation in rebuilding Kosovo's industrial institutions. An electric company was organized to be led by an Albanian, a Serb, and a British military officer. However, after six Serbian electrical engineers employed in the firm were brutally murdered in July 1999—one found stabbed to death while handcuffed to a chair, and the others gunned down—the Serbian company director felt compelled to leave Kosovo after receiving several death threats.[97]

In another demonstration of a failed American peacekeeping mission in Kosovo, by August 4, 1999, the once ethnically mixed village of Zitinje was completely purged of Serbs. Facing daily intimidation and attacks from ethnic Albanians, Serbian villagers packed up and left, with American NATO troops doing little more than providing them with an escort on their trip to safety to northern areas of Serbia, thereby enabling ethnic cleansing to take place.

One Serbian American told me of her family's experience with Albanian attacks in Kosovo during this period. As her cousin was walking out the front door of his home one day, he was shot and killed by an Albanian. With no Yugoslav police authority in Kosovo, there was no one to investigate the matter and find the culprit. Then, on July 9, in the town of Pristina, armed Albanians wearing KLA uniforms stormed into the house of her 72-year-old aunt. They abused her, locked her into a room, and told her that the KLA was taking over her property. When relatives in Belgrade asked KFOR for help, KFOR soldiers went to the house and ordered the Albanians to leave. However, KFOR did nothing but stand by as the Albanian men carried out a stereo, television set, washing machine, refrigerator, and all other valuables from the house, and began to destroy everything else that remained. When KFOR left, the KLA quickly took over the house again. This time, the elderly woman was able to escape and flee to Belgrade where she was taken in by her relatives. The first words she could utter upon her arrival were: "A dog's life is worth more in Kosovo today than the life of a Serb."

In the 11 weeks of NATO bombings, in an almost 24-hour-a-day coverage of events in the Balkans, Washington avidly debated the plight of Albanian refugees. During this time I appeared on 55 television programs. In stark contrast, in June and July 1999, while attacks, murders, and ethnic cleansing of Serbs were taking place in Kosovo, American television pundits fell unusually silent. At this point I was not invited to appear on a single American news network to address the plight of Serbs, nor were political debate shows devoted to debating what was happening to Serbs in Kosovo. Few reporters acknowledged that Kosovo was not the multiethnic society Washington's interventionists had envisioned when they began bombing Serbia. As one *Washington Post* reporter noted, "In the new Kosovo," being a Serb "is enough to get you killed."[98] U.S. officials expressed a cavalier attitude toward the plight of Serbs in Kosovo. As one U.S. official said, "It looks like it's over for the Serbs. We can talk about peace, love and democracy, but I don't think anyone really knows how to stop this."[99] Just weeks earlier, when hundreds of thousands of Albanian refugees were pouring across the border from Kosovo, no U.S. official ever said, "It looks like it's over for the Albanians. There is no way to stop it." To the contrary, the United States was willing to commit significant forces and resources and launch a war against a sovereign nation rather than accept the situation. Clearly, the United States could have taken a number of steps to stop the extermination and ethnic cleansing of Serbs from Kosovo: (1) disarm the KLA; (2) protect Serb-populated areas; (3) allow Yugoslav police to safeguard Serbian neighborhoods; and (4) allow Russian troops to be placed in Serb-populated towns.

Instead, the Clinton administration continued to give strong support to the KLA. Rather than condemn the KLA's criminal activities committed in front of the eyes of NATO troops and other international observers, the Clinton administration became a leading apologist for the rebel group. Clinton and his advisers strengthened ties with KLA leader Hashim Thaci. An agreement signed with Thaci in June 1999 envisioned turning the KLA into a civilian police force, and left open the possibility of creating an Albanian military force in Kosovo. It was not until the war in Kosovo was over that an article was published in the *New York Times* by Chris Hedges on June 25, 1999, exposing the criminal nature of these KLA "friends" of the Clinton administration. The article reported that in addition to terrorizing Serbs, Thaci and his henchmen were responsible for assassinations, arrests, and purges within their own ranks to thwart potential rivals, including the murder of at least six top rebel commanders.

The Clinton administration continued to pursue a policy of double standards in Kosovo, as it did elsewhere in the Balkans—a policy of lofty rhetoric supporting democracy and human rights, but which actually violated those principles at every turn. From Bosnia to Kosovo, NATO seemed to be on an unstoppable war path, determined to dominate the Balkans and to destroy the Serbs in the process. As in Bosnia, Washington was prepared to take over and run yet another region of the Balkans, with no end in sight.

From 1991 to 1999, Washington's handling of the Yugoslav conflicts in Croatia, Bosnia, and Serbia exposed a major weakness in its decision-making process—a tendency to favor solving complex foreign ethnic problems by using propaganda and force rather than sober reasoning and negotiations. With the bombing of Yugoslavia, the United States had allowed force to become a substitute for diplomacy. The use of air power to pummel a small European country into submission without suffering any U.S. casualties removed America's leaders and its public from the tragic realities of war. It obscured Washington's sense of reality and true comprehension of the depth of destruction the United States caused and the criminality of its actions. It brought warfare into the realm of video games, with Washington's political establishment and the media more concerned with "who's going to blink first" and "who's the winner and who's the loser" than the fact that the United States was committing an aggression against a sovereign nation. As in Croatia and Bosnia, any sympathy Washington may have expressed for human suffering during the Kosovo crisis was guided primarily by television images that determined the politically correct "victim" of the day. An anti-Serb frenzy was created among Washington's political and media elite that formed the basis of all past and present U.S. decisions on the Balkans.

For the better part of the post–Cold War era, the United States pursued unbridled interventionism in the Balkans without adequate public scrutiny of its government's actions. U.S. foreign policy throughout eight years of ethnic clashes in the Yugoslav region demonstrated the dangers of media-generated images and sound bites in a modern age, which is leading Washington towards the 21st century with a significant problem: a decreasing understanding of the world amid increasing abilities to communicate. Strong rhetoric by Clinton administration officials explaining U.S. policy in the Balkans through easily digestible reasoning may have appealed to the media, but has provided a weak foundation for U.S. actions abroad.

The media has done little to alleviate this problem. As some critics observed, journalism "has attracted its share of zealots who set out to prove a thesis regardless of the evidence."[100] Competition generated by the growing media industry has left little time for questioning stories and enforcing standards of good journalism. Understandably, in the fast-paced news industry of the 1990s, it was easier to write an impressive story with simplistic, good-versus-evil depictions of events that were sure to draw public attention. No doubt, these media trends will continue to influence U.S. foreign policy. The new challenge of the information age will be to go beyond sensationalism and instead provide even-handed, honest reporting that will help U.S. policy makers and the public truly understand foreign events.

As the world's last remaining superpower, the United States is watched closely by nations and groups around the world. The message Washington has been sending with its Balkans policy has not been a good one. At a time when U.S. policymakers have said they wished to build a world based on international law and universal moral principles, a Balkans policy based on double standards and anti-Serb policies continues to undermine the credibility of U.S. commitments towards that end. To remedy this impression, Washington needs to devote clear, rational, and substantive thought in reexamining its policy in Bosnia-Hercegovina, Croatia, and Serbia's southern province of Kosovo. The United States can and should assist in creating democratic institutions in all areas of former Yugoslavia—to the benefit of all ethnic groups. U.S. intervention favoring one Balkan warring party over another will only be a catalyst for widespread warfare for decades to come.

NOTES

1. "From 'Terrorists' to 'Partners': The Kosovo Liberation Army: Does Clinton Policy Support Group with Terror, Drug Ties?" United States Senate Republican Policy Committee (March 31, 1999), 3.

2. Republic of Serbia, Ministry of Information, *Serbia in the World* (Belgrade, Yugoslavia, March 1998), 23, 25.

3. Chris Hedges, "Serbs Force a Crude Burial for 51 Left Dead in Kosovo," *New York Times* (March 11, 1998): A10.

4. Chris Hedges, "Kosovo Rebels' New Tactic: Attack Serb Civilians," *New York Times* (June 24, 1998): A1.

5. Ibid.

6. Chris Hedges, "Kurds Flee Violence in Turkey," *New York Times* (July 10, 1994): 10; and "1,700 Kurds Feeling Turks Cross into Iraq," *Boston Globe* (March 27, 1995): 4.

7. "Kurds Flee as Turkey Attacks in Iraq," *New York Times* (July 8, 1995): 2.

8. Alan Cowell, "War on Kurds Hurts Turks in U.S. Eyes," *New York Times* (November 17, 1994): 3.

9. Samuel P. Huntington, *The Clash of Civilizations and the Remaking of World Order* (New York: Simon and Schuster, 1996), 276.

10. "The Explosion of Kosovo," *Washington Post* (June 17, 1998): A26.

11. Chris Hedges, "With Kosovo's Rebels: A Growing Confidence in Battle," *New York Times* (June 29, 1998): A3.

12. William Drozdiak, "Further NATO Action in Kosovo Now in Doubt," *Washington Post* (June 18, 1998): A32. See also the *Washington Post* website http://www.washingtonpost.com/wp-srv/inatl/longterm/balkans/overview/kosovo.htm, "Background: Kosovo" (June 12/98), and "The Explosion of Kosovo," *Washington Post* (June 17, 1998): A26.

13. "NATO Mulls Use of Troops or Air Power to Prevent Outbreak of Regional War," *Buffalo News* (June 9, 1998): 3A.

14. "Albania: Seeking Friends," *The Economist* (July 24, 1993): 55.

15. Huntington, *The Clash of Civilizations*, 279.

16. Chris Hedges, "Both Sides in the Kosovo Conflict Seem Determined to Ignore Reality," *New York Times* (June 22, 1998): A10.

17. Craig R. Whitney, "Rebel Success in Kosovo Worries Europe," *New York Times* (June 30, 1998): A6.

18. Hedges, "With Kosovo's Rebels," A3.

19. National Public Radio's *Fresh Air*, June 23, 1998.

20. Hedges, "With Kosovo's Rebels," A3.

21. "U.S. Signals Approval of New Sanctions on Yugoslavia," *Washington Post* (June 9, 1998): A18.

22. Stacy Sullivan, "Albanian Americans Funding Rebels' Cause," *Washington Post* (May 26, 1998): A12.

23. Hedges, "Both Sides in the Kosovo Conflict Seem Determined to Ignore Reality," A10.

24. Bob Dole and Joseph I. Lieberman, "Don't Allow Kosovo to Become Bosnia II," *Newsday* (July 6, 1998): A21.

25. Johnathan S. Landay, "Should Iran Help Fund War in Muslim Kosovo?" *Christian Science Monitor* (April 15, 1998): 9.

26. Mathew Tully, "Through the Revolving Door," *Journal of Commerce* (March 24, 1998): 4A.

27. Steven Erlanger, "First Bosnia, Now Kosovo," *New York Times* (June 10, 1998): 14.

28. Steven Lee Myers and Steven Erlanger, "U.S. Is Stepping Up Military Threats Against the Serbs," *New York Times* (October 7, 1998): A8.

29. Roger Cohen, "Yes, Blood Stains the Balkans. No, It's Not Just Fate," *New York Times*, Section 4 (October 4, 1998): 1.

30. Guy Dinmore, "Serbians Leave Sites of Civilian Slayings," *Washington Post* (October 1, 1998): A32.

31. Jim Hoagland, "Kosovo: Before the Bombs Fall," *Washington Post* (October 4, 1998): C7.

32. Bob Dole, "We Must Stop the Kosovo Terror," *Washington Post* (September 14, 1998): A19.

33. ABC's *Nightline*, June 15, 1998.

34. National Public Radio's *Fresh Air*, June 23, 1998.

35. Henry Kamm, "Macedonia Sees Its Albanians as Its 'Biggest Problem'," *New York Times* (May 5, 1994): A15.

36. Hedges, "With Kosovo's Rebels," A3.

37. Jeffrey Smith, "Belgrade Continues to Balk at U.N. Demands on Kosovo," *Washington Post* (October 7, 1998): A26.

38. Jane Perlez, "Serbs Display Death Site; Identity of Remains Not Known," *New York Times* (October 4, 1998): 12.

39. Mike O'Connor, "Yugoslavia Assures NATO of Pullout to Avoid Attack," *New York Times* (October 26, 1998): A11.

40. Steven Erlanger, "NATO May Act Against Serbs in Two Weeks," *New York Times* (October 2, 1998): A1.

41. PBS's *Newshour*, January 18, 1999.

42. CNN's *World View*, January 18, 1999.

43. "Chechnya: Yes, It's an Internal Matter," *Los Angeles Times* (December 17, 1994): B8.

44. David Filipov, "Russia, Chechnya Agree to Disagree Peacefully," *Boston Globe* (May 13, 1997): A2.

45. Daren Butler, "Turkish Fighter-Bombers Hit Kurd Camps in Iraq," *Washington Post* (May 16, 1997): A30.

46. Barry E. Carter and Phillip R. Trimble, *International Law* (Toronto, Canada: Little, Brown), 428.

47. *National Public Radio News*, February 3, 1999.

48. Ibid.

49. Patrick Buchanan, "Should We Be in Kosovo?" *Washington Times* (January 25, 1999): A17.

50. Jane Perlez, "Trickiest Divides Are Among Big Powers at Kosovo Talks," *New York Times* (February 11, 1999): A8.

51. "Clinton on Kosovo: 'We Can Make a Difference'," *New York Times* (February 14, 1999): 6.

52. Jane Perlez, "Kosovo Plan Takes Shape as Russians Prod Belgrade," *New York Times* (February 16, 1999): A3.

53. "From 'Terrorists' to 'Partners': The Kosovo Liberation Army: Does Clinton Policy Support Group with Terror, Drug Ties?" United States Senate Republican Policy Committee (March 31, 1999), 5.

54. John M. Broder, "Clinton on Kosovo: A Humane Factor," *New York Times* (February 25, 1999): A10.

55. "Why Kosovo?" *Washington Post* (February 16, 1999): A16.

56. Amos Perlmutter, "Peacekeeping or Peacemaking?" *Washington Times* (February 16, 1999): A14.

57. Benjamin C. Works, "Out of Focus Lens on Kosovo?" *Washington Times* (February 18, 1999): A17.

58. Carlotta Gall, "Monitor Chief Calls Kosovo Close to Flare-Up," *New York Times* (March 5, 1999): A6; Carlotta Gall, "Envoys Push for Talks as Kosovo Fights On," *New York Times* (March 6, 1999): A5.

59. "Clinton Voices Anger and Compassion at Serbian Intransigence on Kosovo," *New York Times* (March 20, 1999): A5.

60. Eric Schmitt, "Senators Clash over U.S. Role in a NATO Bombing Campaign," *New York Times* (March 23, 1999): A11.

61. Charles Babington and Helen Dewar, "President Pleads for Support," *Washington Post* (March 24, 1999): A1.

62. Alessandra Stanley, "Albanian Fighters Say They Aid NATO in Spotting Serbs Targets," *New York Times* (April 2, 1999): A10.

63. Peter Finn, "Albania Asks West to Arm Rebels," *Washington Post* (April 20, 1999): A20.

64. Charles Krauthammer, "Confused on Kosovo," *Washington Post* (March 26, 1999): A33.

65. "Kosovo Rebels Seek Refugee Recruits," Associated Press (March 31, 1999).

66. *Fox News*, Report by Nick Jennings (May 23, 1999).

67. Anne Swardson, "Kosovo Rebels Send Family Members Out of Province," *Washington Post* (May 5, 1999): A27.

68. Daniel Williams, "Serbs Seek Control of Key Kosovo Sites," *Washington Post* (March 31, 1999): A23.

69. For list of NATO attacks at this time see George Jahn, "Milosevic's Offer Rejected by NATO," *Washington Times* (March 31, 1999): A1.

70. Daniel Williams, "Serbs Seek Control of Key Kosovo Sites," *Washington Post* (March 31, 1999): A23; Philip Smucker, "Cause of Kosovar Exodus from Pristina Disputed," *Washington Times* (March 31, 1999): A12.

71. Ibid.

72. Ibid.

73. Steven Lee Myers, "Missiles Strike Headquarters for Serbian Police Forces," *New York Times* (April 3, 1999): A1.

74. Guy Dinmore, "Daily Life in Belgrade Teeters Under Strikes," *Washington Post* (April 5, 1999): A11.

75. Steven Erlanger, "As Raids Broaden, Yugoslavia Says 4 Die," *New York Times* (April 5, 1999): A9.

76. "10 Civilians Reported Killed as NATO Hits Kosovo's Capital," *New York Times* (April 8, 1999): A11.

77. Katharine Q. Seelye, "Civilian Deaths Inevitable in Warfare, Clinton Says," *New York Times* (April 16, 1999): A13.

78. Steven Erlanger, "Survivors of NATO Attack on Serb TV Headquarters: Luck, Pluck and Resolve," *New York Times* (April 24, 1999): A6.

79. Associated Press (May 10, 1999).

80. *CNN* (May 15, 1999).

81. Michael R. Gordon, "NATO Describing Kosovo Village as a Serbian Military Post, Admits Strike," *New York Times* (May 16, 1999): 10.

82. Katarina Kratovac, "NATO Bombs Damage Diplomat's Home," Associated Press (May 20, 1999).

83. *New York Times*, (May 20, 1999): A15.

84. Kratovac, "NATO Bombs Damage Diplomat's Home."

85. William C. Mann, "NATO Blunders May Erode Support," Associated Press (May 23, 1999).

86. Ibid.

87. Viktor Chernomyrdin, "Impossible to Talk Peace with Bombs Falling," *Washington Post* (May 27, 1999): A39.

88. Jimmy Carter, "Have We Forgotten the Path to Peace?" *New York Times* (May 27, 1999): A31.

89. "Charges vs. Milosevic and 4 Others," Associated Press (May 27, 1999).

90. William J, Kole, "War Tribunal May Indict Milosevic," Associated Press (May 26, 1999).

91. Raymond Bonner, "Crimes Panel Urges Indictments of 3 Croatian Generals in '95 Assault on Serbs," *New York Times* (March 21, 1999): 1.

92. Ibid, 10.

93. Ibid.

94. Dana Priest and Peter Finn, "NATO Gives Air Support to Kosovo Guerrillas," *Washington Post* (June 2, 1999): A1.

95. William Safire, "Lessons of Kosovo," *New York Times* (June 7, 1999): A29.

96. Ibid.

97. Peter Finn, "NATO Losing Kosovo Battle," *Washington Post* (August 4, 1999): A18.

98. Ibid., A1.

99. Ibid.

100. Richard Harwood, "How Lies See the Light of Day," *Washington Post* (July 13, 1998): A21.

Appendix 1

Population Statistics of Bosnia and Hercegovina

	Muslim	Serb	Croat	Total
1910	612,137	825,418	434,061	1,897,962
	32%	44%	22.8%	100%
1921	588,200	829,400	444,300	1,890,400
	31%	44%	24%	100%
1931	718,100	1,028,100	547,900	2,323,600
	31%	44%	24%	100%
1948	788,400	1,139,200	614,100	2,565,300
	31%	44%	24%	100%
1953	892,000	1,264,000	654,000	2,848,000
	31.3%	44.4%	23%	100%
1971	1,482,000	1,393,000	772,000	3,746,000
	39.6%	32%	20.6%	100%
1981	1,630,033	1,334,852	758,140	4,124,256
	40%	33%	18%	100%
1991	1,905,000	1,364,000	752,000	4,355,000
	43.7%	31.3%	17.5%	100%

Source: *Statistical Yearbook of Yugoslavia* (Belgrade, Yugoslavia, 1990), 436, 440; International Population Statistics Reports, *The Population of Yugoslavia*, Series P-90, No. 5 (Washington, D.C.: U.S. Government Printing Office, 1954), 126.

Appendix 2

Maps

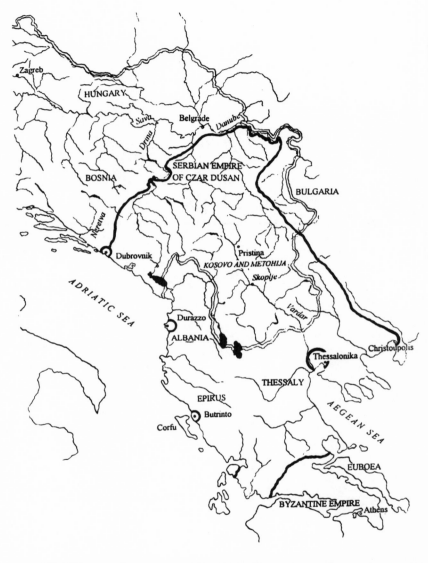

MAP 1.   Serbian empire of Czar Dusan: The expansion of the
          Serbian state at its peak during the Middle Ages.

━━━━━   Border of the Serbian empire in the mid-1300s

═════   Border of Yugoslavia from 1945 to 1992

258

MAP 2.	Ottoman Turkish conquest of southern Slavic regions during the 14th and 15th centuries.
▬▬▬	Directions of Turkish advances and year of conquest
═══	Border of Yugoslavia from 1945 to 1992

MAP 3.   Military Frontier formed by Austria and Hungary against
          Ottoman invasions, expanded from the 16th century to
          the mid-1800s (shown here).

━━━━   Border of Military Frontier

══════   Border of Yugoslavia from 1945 to 1992

MAP 4.   Yugoslavia, "Kingdom of Serbs, Croats, and Slovenes."

——   Boundaries of the provinces in 1921

═══   Border of Yugoslavia from 1945 to 1992

MAP 5.	Kingdom of Yugoslavia.
▬▬▬	Boundaries of Banovinas in 1931
═══	Border of Yugoslavia from 1945 to 1992

MAP 6.   Administrative divisions of Yugoslavia, 1945-1992.

MAP 7.   Ethnic population of Yugoslavia: location of ethnic
           majorities based on the 1981 census.

Serbs		Macedonians
Croats		Albanians
Slovenes		Hungarians
Slavic Muslim		

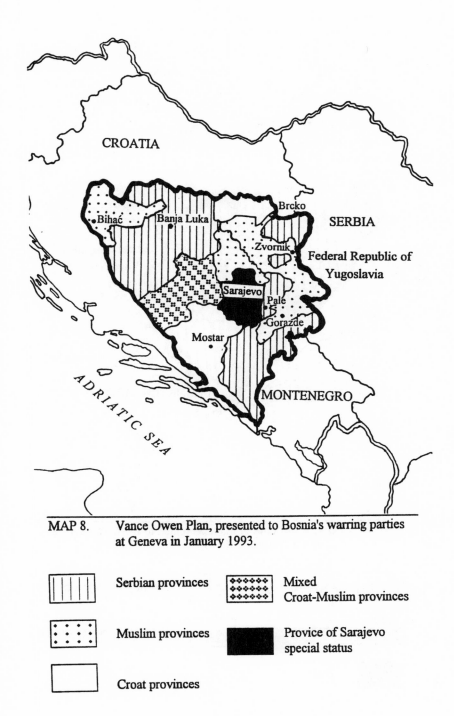

CROATIA

Bihać •   Banja Luka   Brcko

SERBIA

Zvornik

Federal Republic of
Yugoslavia

Sarajevo

Pale

Gorazde

Mostar

MONTENEGRO

ADRIATIC SEA

MAP 8.   Vance Owen Plan, presented to Bosnia's warring parties
at Geneva in January 1993.

‖‖‖	Serbian provinces	◆◆◆◆◆◆	Mixed Croat-Muslim provinces
⋰⋰⋰	Muslim provinces	■	Province of Sarajevo special status
☐	Croat provinces		

265

CROATIA

SERBIA

Brcko

Federal Republic of
Yugoslavia

Srebrenica

Sarajevo Zepa

Gorazde

Mostar

MONTENEGRO

A D R I A T I C   S E A

MAP 9.   Owen-Stoltenberg Plan, presented to Bosnia's warring
              parties in Summer of 1993.

| | | | | | Serbs   Mostar, EC supervision

◊◊◊◊◊◊
◊◊◊◊◊◊   Muslims   Sarajevo, UN supervision
◊◊◊◊◊◊

■■■■■   Croats

CROATIA

Bihac

Tesanj

Zepce

Kiseljak

Vitez

SERBIA

Federal Republic of
Yugoslavia

Srebrenica

Žepa

Sarajevo

Gorazde

MONTENEGRO

ADRIATIC SEA

MAP 10.   Bosnia and Hercegovina, areas of control by warring
parties, January 1994.

Serbs

Krajina and Slavonia
Serbs

Muslims

Croats

MAP 11.   Contact Group Plan, presented to warring parties in July
           1994.

Serbian territories

Muslim-Croat territories

Sarajevo, under UN protection

Mostar, under EC protection

CROATIA

Bihac

Brcko   SERBIA

Federal Republic of
Yugoslavia

Sarajevo

Gorazde

Mostar

MONTENEGRO

ADRIATIC SEA

MAP 12.   Dayton Agreement, November 1995.

|||||| Republika Srpska -- Bosnian Serb territories

□   Muslim-Croat Federation

Appendix 3

Time Line

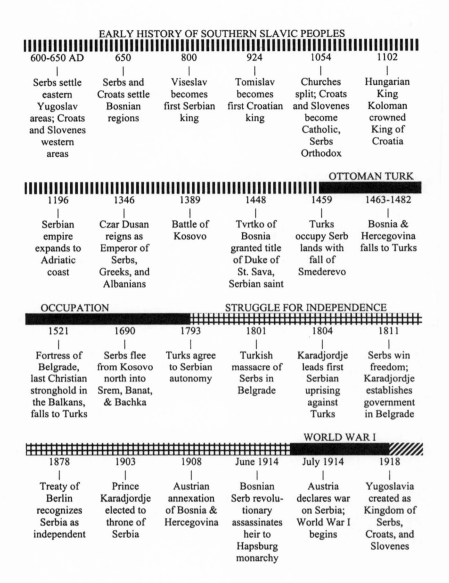

EARLY HISTORY OF SOUTHERN SLAVIC PEOPLES

600-650 AD	650	800	924	1054	1102
Serbs settle eastern Yugoslav areas; Croats and Slovenes western areas	Serbs and Croats settle Bosnian regions	Viseslav becomes first Serbian king	Tomislav becomes first Croatian king	Churches split; Croats and Slovenes become Catholic, Serbs Orthodox	Hungarian King Koloman crowned King of Croatia

OTTOMAN TURK

1196	1346	1389	1448	1459	1463-1482
Serbian empire expands to Adriatic coast	Czar Dusan reigns as Emperor of Serbs, Greeks, and Albanians	Battle of Kosovo	Tvrtko of Bosnia granted title of Duke of St. Sava, Serbian saint	Turks occupy Serb lands with fall of Smederevo	Bosnia & Hercegovina falls to Turks

OCCUPATION   STRUGGLE FOR INDEPENDENCE

1521	1690	1793	1801	1804	1811
Fortress of Belgrade, last Christian stronghold in the Balkans, falls to Turks	Serbs flee from Kosovo north into Srem, Banat, & Bachka	Turks agree to Serbian autonomy	Turkish massacre of Serbs in Belgrade	Karadjordje leads first Serbian uprising against Turks	Serbs win freedom; Karadjordje establishes government in Belgrade

WORLD WAR I

1878	1903	1908	June 1914	July 1914	1918
Treaty of Berlin recognizes Serbia as independent	Prince Karadjordje elected to throne of Serbia	Austrian annexation of Bosnia & Hercegovina	Bosnian Serb revolutionary assassinates heir to Hapsburg monarchy	Austria declares war on Serbia; World War I begins	Yugoslavia created as Kingdom of Serbs, Croats, and Slovenes

WORLD WAR II — TITO ERA

1934	April 6, 1941	April 1941	1941-1945	1945	1948
Croatian nationalist assassinates Yugoslav King Alexander in France	Hitler invades Yugoslavia; Serbian monarch flees to England	Ustashi declare Croatian state; massacre of Serbs and others begins	Ustashi kill 750,000 Serbs, 60,000 Jews, and 26,000 Gypsies; 100,000 Serbs flee Kosovo	World War II ends; Tito's Communists head new Yugoslav state	Tito breaks with Stalin, wins favor with U.S.

YUGOSLAVIA — PRE-WAR TENSIONS RISE

1974	mid-1970s	1980	June 28, 1989	1990	July 1990
Autonomy given to Kosovo & Vojvodina	Croatian nationalist movement "Maspok" begins	Tito dies; ethnic problems begin	Serbs rally in Kosovo	Elections in Yugoslav republics	Kosovo Albanians declare independence; Serbia suspends autonomy

WAR IN

August 1990	April 1, 1991	May 12, 1991	June 1991	June 25, 1991	June 27, 1991
Krajina Serbs vote on independence, clash with Croat police	Krajina Serbs declare independence	Krajina Serbs vote to unite with Serbia	Serbia agrees to make Yugoslavia a loose confederation	Croatia and Slovenia declare independence	Yugoslav army (JNA) clashes with Slovene forces

SLOVENIA — WAR IN CROATIA

July 18, 1991	July 28, 1991	Sept. 26, 1991	Oct. 15, 1991	Nov. 9, 1991	Dec. 23, 1991
JNA pulls out of Slovenia	Croat forces battle Krajina; Serbs helped by JNA	Yugoslav presidency collapses; UN arms embargo imposed	Bosnian Muslims and Croats declare independence	Bosnian Serbs vote to remain part of Yugoslavia	Germany first to recognize Croatia and Slovenia

Jan. 4, 1992	mid-Jan. 1992	Jan. 15, 1992	Feb. 1992	March 1, 1992	March 17, 1992
Serbian president signs UN plan to end war in Croatia	Serb and Croat front lines set between UN buffer zones	EC recognizes Slovenia and Croatia	Bosnian Muslim and Croat gunmen kill Serbs at wedding	Muslims and Croats vote on independence; fighting starts in Bosnia	Lisbon meeting; parties agree to three-way division of Bosnia

April 6-7, 1992	May 1992	May 27, 1992	May 30, 1992	June 1992	July 3, 1992
EC and U.S. recognize Slovenia, Croatia, Bosnia & Hercegovina as independent	Serbia and Montenegro form Federal Republic of Yugoslavia	17 people killed in Sarajevo bread line	U.N. imposes economic embargo on Yugoslavia (Serbia and Montenegro)	U.S. announces plans for airdrops in Bosnia	Bosnian Croats declare independence

Oct. 9, 1992	Oct. 21, 1992	Dec. 1992	Jan. 3, 1993	Feb. 5, 1993	April 1993
U.S. and allies agree on imposing no-fly zone over Bosnia	Fighting starts between Bosnian Croats and Muslims	U.S. plans air strikes to enforce no-fly zone	Geneva peace talks; Vance-Owen Plan	U.N. peace talks begin in New York	U.S. announces considering air strikes

U.S.

May 2, 1993	May 6, 1992	May 7, 1993	July 8, 1993	Feb. 5, 1994	Feb. 27, 1994
Karadzic signs peace plan in Athens	Bosnian Serb Assembly rejects plan	UN makes five Muslim towns "safe areas"	Bosnian Muslims reject Vance-Owen plan	Explosion at Sarajevo market	NATO downs Serbian aircraft; 1st use of force

April 10, 1994	April 29, 1994	June 22, 1994	Aug. 6, 1994	Nov. 20, 1994	May 2, 1995
Fighting in Gorazde; NATO bombs Serbs	12 Serbs killed by U.N. in worst clash so far	Muslims launch largest offensive on Serbs	NATO bombs Serb anti-tank vehicle in Sarajevo	NATO bombs Serbian airfield in Krajina	Croats attack Serbs in Western Slavonia

May 25, 1995	May 26, 1995	July 10, 1995	Aug. 1995	Aug. 28, 1995	Sept. 1995
NATO bombs Serbs in Pale	UN peace-keepers held by Serbs	NATO attacks Serb positions around Srebrenica; Serbs take over town	Croatia launches Operation Storm; 250,000 Serbs flee	NATO launches two weeks of bombing of Bosnian Serbs	Joint Croat-Muslim attacks on Bosnian Serbs

Nov. 19, 1995	Dec. 1995	March 1996	July 1996	Sept. 1996	Oct. 1996
Dayton Peace Plan signed by warring factions	IFOR in Bosnia	Sarajevo comes under Muslim control; 100,000 Serbs flee	Karadzic transfers power to Plavsic	Nationalist parties re-elected in Bosnia	Brcko arbitration begins

WAR IN KOSOVO

Dec. 1996	July 1997	Feb. 1998	Summer 1998	Oct. 1998	March 15, 1999
SFOR replaces IFOR	NATO troops kill Bosnian Serb war crimes suspect	Albanian KLA guerrillas increase attacks on Yugoslav police	War intensifies in Kosovo; KLA take over 40% of Serbian province	U.S. oversees cease-fire agreement on Kosovo	Rambouillet talks between Yugoslav government & Albanian separatists

WAR IN KOSOVO

March 1999	March 24, 1999	early April 1999	April 1999	June 1, 1999	mid-June 1999
KLA steps up attacks on Yugoslav army and Kosovo Serbs	U.S.-led NATO bombers attack Yugoslavia	Refugees flee to Macedonia, Albania, and other parts of Yugoslavia	NATO steps up attacks; hits many civilian areas, including Belgrade	Yugoslav parliament approves plan to allow U.N. peace-keeping forces in Kosovo	Yugoslav army begins withdrawal

Index

About the Author

DANIELLE S. SREMAC is a Balkans expert and Director of the Institute for Balkan Affairs in Washington, D.C. As a visible commentator on Yugoslav issues, she has appeared on hundreds of television and radio programs in the United States and internationally. She represented Serbian-Americans throughout the 1990s. Born in Belgrade, Yugoslavia, she also provides first-hand knowledge of ethnic relations and life in Yugoslavia, which had such a profound effect on the country's civil war.